Strategic
Electronic Marketing
Managing E-Business

Brad Alan Kleindl, Ph.D.

Missouri Southern State College
Joplin, Missouri

THOMSON
™
SOUTH-WESTERN

Australia · Canada · Mexico · Singapore · Spain · United Kingdom · United States

THOMSON
SOUTH-WESTERN

Strategic Electronic Marketing: Managing E-Business, 2e
Brad Alan Kleindl

Editor-in-Chief:
Jack W. Calhoun

Team Leader:
Melissa S. Acuña

Acquisitions Editor:
Steven W. Hazelwood

Developmental Editor:
Mardell Toomey

Marketing Manager:
Nicole C. Moore

Production Editor:
Amy A. Brooks

Manufacturing Coordinator:
Diane Lohman

Compositor:
Lachina Publishing Services

Printer:
Quebecor World Taunton
Taunton, MA

Design Project Manager:
Chris Miller

Internal Designer:
Chris Miller

Cover Designer:
Chris Miller

Cover Image:
Tin Box Studio

Photography Manager:
John W. Hill

Photo Researcher:
Sam Marshall

Library of Congress Cataloging-in-
Publication Data
Kleindl, Brad Alan, 1955-
Strategic electronic marketing :
managing e-business / Brad Alan
Keindl.—2nd ed.
p. cm.
Includes bibliographical references
and index.
ISBN 0-324-17893-X (hc. : alk.
paper)
1. Telemarketing. 2. Database
marketing. I. Title.

HF5415.1265 .K44 2002
658.8'4—dc21   2002028766

ISBN: 0-324-17893-X

Dedication

For Jane, Alex, Peter, Elizabeth, and John.

About the Author

Brad Alan Kleindl is the assistant dean of the School of Business and an associate professor at Missouri Southern State College in Joplin, Missouri. He has been teaching computer technology to students since 1984. In 1994, he started a virtual marketing course that focused on using multimedia applications to create CD-ROM promotions. The course evolved with the growth of the World Wide Web to become an Internet marketing course with an e-business strategic emphasis.

Professor Kleindl's research and publication interests are related to entrepreneurship, innovation, strategy, and Internet marketing. He has a Ph.D. in marketing from Oklahoma State University and an M.B.A. from Southern Illinois University. Dr. Kleindl is a Fulbright senior scholar. He served as a consultant for numerous businesses on Web page design, Web portal development, and business plans for Web business IPOs. He was the director of the Center for Entrepreneurship at Missouri Southern. Dr. Kleindl is also a potter, showing his art in studios and galleries.

Brief Table of Contents

Contents

chapter 10   E-Business Management   292

Preface

The second edition of this textbook continues to focus on the evolving e-business environment. The turn of the millennium came as the Internet was transforming into a business tool. Over the past ten years, the Internet has grown from a communication medium to a driver of the technological transformation of business processes. The current focus on e-commerce has forced managers to see technology as a business tool to restructure business models and improve business value chains. This focus has had an impact on both pure-play e-businesses and brick-and-mortar companies. The emergence of brick-and-click e-business strategies characterizes business strategy at the beginning of the current millennium.

Businesses are adapting a number of technologies to improve the marketing process, including not only the World Wide Web but also databases, extranets, customized production, customer relationship management software, intranets, and other technologies outlined in this text. Internet marketing courses have evolved from Web page design to e-commerce courses and are now moving toward courses that integrate an e-business perspective. E-business is not just about start-ups; it is also about transforming existing businesses to gain efficiencies. Students of marketing must be prepared to enter this new environment and understand the role they will play in organizations. To paraphrase Peter Drucker, the young people who understand technology will be running companies in this technology-based environment. As educators, we train marketing students to act as an interface between the customer and the company. There is not enough room in a traditional marketing curriculum to turn marketing students into network specialists, systems analysts, graphic designers, or Webmasters. The marketer's role is to be able to devise strategies that enhance relationships with customers by working with technology specialists to implement strategies.

This text is targeted toward undergraduate and graduate students who will be undertaking the process of e-business development. It seeks to close a knowledge gap by introducing marketing students to the current state of the art in e-business practice. The references in the text are fairly exhaustive and represent e-business practice as of the year 2002. The heavy reliance on trade journals is due to the rapidly evolving business environment. Information in trade journals typically precedes material found in textbooks, journals, or academic papers. The text is designed to be academically sound by linking technology and techniques currently being used to established and emerging marketing and strategy theories. The text also takes an international perspective by reporting on changes occurring in nations and markets outside of the United States.

Organization of the Text

The text is designed to allow marketing instructors and students to build from pre-existing knowledge bases. The order of the text has shifted slightly from that of the first edition. One of the major changes is to integrate legal and ethical issues throughout the text, which allows instructors to bring up these issues as they relate to chapter content. Chapter 1 starts by building an overview of the e-business system. This overview is based on the major business functions and the economic flows that allow a business to meet customers' needs in a competitive environment. The second chapter is an infrastructure primer designed to give students a fundamental understanding of the technologies used to create e-businesses. The chapter is not about computer systems design; instead, it allows the student to understand the Internet technology that underpins e-business communication. It is followed by an appendix that delves more deeply into the technology related to e-business. The communication process has been split into two chapters, one on hypermedia communication and one on e-business promotion. Chapter 3, "E-Business Communication," covers the hypermedia communication process in an e-business environment. This chapter is included early in the text because the Internet is primarily a communication medium. In addition, many of the assignments that instructors may wish to use will be focused around the creation of a Web page, and so the fundamentals of Web page development are covered early. To aid in this coverage, an appendix related to basic Web page design is included. Chapter 4 explores the changes in distribution that are impacting e-businesses. This chapter is more theoretical and covers the justifications for business change.

E-business value strategies have been split into two chapters, one on value strategies and one on e-commerce. Chapter 5, "E-Business Value Strategies," outlines the major business models being used in the creation of e-businesses. Most e-businesses use a combination of these methods to develop relationships with customers and meet their needs. Chapter 6 covers the e-commerce process, grounding students in the e-commerce process and strategies. The seventh chapter covers Internet advertising and promotion. It illustrates how hypermedia are being used strategically for advertising and promotion. Once students understand the possible e-business models, they investigate how individuals deal with the change process in Chapter 8, "The Market." This chapter gives students a perspective on who will accept these new business models, including an exploration of the diffusion process, online consumer behavior, and online communities. Chapter 9 investigates the use of information within e-businesses. It addresses not only how data are collected on customers but also how these data are turned into information to be used as a strategic tool.

One of the skill areas marketing students need to have is the ability to aid in the process of transforming businesses. This internal marketing process is covered in Chapter 10. This chapter also includes organizational considerations that must be addressed to allow businesses to structure themselves to be competitive. The appendix to this chapter outlines various e-business careers students may wish to pursue. The final chapter, Chapter 11, ties together the preceding chapters by exploring e-business strategy. It uses strategy theories and an analysis of the strategies e-businesses are currently using to give students a perspective on the competitive dynamics in the current e-business environment.

Pedagogical Features

This text follows an active learning approach to allow for a deep level of understanding. While reading a textbook is the first step in understanding a field of study, students learn by doing and by thinking about course material. The Active Learning exercises found at the end of every chapter can act as a basis for written or oral analysis and discussion, allowing instructors to use their knowledge and experience to create a rich learning environment. These exercises are designed to have students integrate the information they find in each chapter by actively working with ideas and concepts. Some of these exercises require a minimal amount of time to complete, while others require that students integrate the real world into the classroom. In addition, the Active Learning exercises can be used as competitive exercises. Each chapter starts with a Vignette designed to illustrate the major issues found in the chapter. Each of the vignettes and chapter cases is followed by a Thinking Strategically section that includes thought-provoking questions and exercises. New terms and concepts are defined within each chapter. A number of nSite features are included throughout the text to broaden students' understanding of strategic and historical issues, and E-Business Professionals boxes give them real-world insights. A list of the major Terms and Concepts is included at the end of each chapter, along with a Concepts and Questions for Review section.

Professors are faced with two new challenges. The first challenge is that students today expect to receive more than just a lecture over material they find in textbooks. They expect colleges and universities to develop their minds to allow them to better compete in a dynamic world. The second challenge is posed by distance learning. Web-based education is expected to grow rapidly over the next decade. Professors must be able to provide a rich learning environment to hold students in a classroom setting. Both the student's and the professor's time is best spent in developing a deeper understanding of issues rather than lecturing on terms and basic concepts. To meet these challenges, this text is designed to provide the groundwork understanding necessary to allow for more active learning environments. In addition, a series of Web page link suggestions appears at the end of each chapter. These were checked in 2002 to be sure that they were all operational and not linked to any sites that could be deemed offensive.

Support for the Instructor

Web Site: http://kleindl.swcollege.com
All ancillary materials, including an instructor's manual, PowerPoint® presentations, and sample syllabi, are found at the site. In addition, there are Internet exercises with additional Web listings, interactive quizzes, and hot topics. Finally, there is an example of an Internet marketing plan and also a complete product tour.

With this edition, we also offer an instructor's resource CD-ROM (ISBN 0-324-19090-5), which includes the instructor's manual, PowerPoint® presentations (over 350 slides), and a test bank.

The instructor's manual for the text is developed from ten years of experience with an Internet marketing course. It is designed to support the text and act as a springboard for instructors to develop their own course. Included are the following:

☐   suggested syllabi
☐   project guides
☐   teaching aids
☐   lecture guides
☐   teaching suggestions
☐   feedback guides for the cases and Active Learning exercises as well as additional Active Learning exercises, Web links, and reading suggestions
☐   Web page development and multimedia development guides
☐   a complete test bank with over fifty multiple choice, true/false, short answer, and essay questions for each chapter

Acknowledgements

I would like to thank a large number of individuals who were instrumental in helping to get this text into the market. First of all, I would like to thank the late William G. Zikmund of Oklahoma State University. He was my professor, a mentor, a friend, and recommended me to South-Western. Without him this book would not have been written. South-Western has been very supportive in the development of the text. I appreciate the contributions of Steven W. Hazelwood, acquisitions editor. For the first and second editions, I have been operating under the guidance of a developmental editor, Mardell Toomey. Her words of encouragement have been very helpful in keeping me focused. Amy Brooks, the production editor, has been essential in taking my raw material and turning it into a book.

The entire team was able to take a basic set of ideas and turn it into a teaching tool.

I would like to thank the reviewers who carefully scrutinized the manuscript and made numerous suggestions:

John Bennett, Stephens College

Ted Clark, State University of New York College at New Paltz

Robert Galka, DePaul University

Ceyhan Kilic, DePaul University

Karen Machleit, University of Cincinnati

Robert Moore, Mississippi State University

Albert Muniz, University of California at Berkeley

Shelley Rinehart, University of New Brunswick, New Brunswick, Canada

Don Sciglimpaglia, San Diego State University

Roberta Silverstein, San Francisco State University

Ray Sola, University of Arizona

Ken Williamson, James Madison University

Debra Zahay, North Carolina State University

I think the text is much stronger because of their questions, comments, criticisms, complaints, and suggestions. I would also like to thank my students, who for over twenty years have taught me how to teach—especially those students who have taken my virtual marketing class and had to read articles from magazines, work with crashing Web browsers, and learn how to use Macromedia's Director. I really appreciate my dean, Jim Gray, and his willingness to set up labs, purchase computers and software, and put up with me while I wrote this text. Without his support, I wouldn't have a course or textbook.

I would like to thank my parents, Jim Kleindl and Elaine Kleindl, who are both retired teachers and who have taught me to love to learn and to teach. Their early lessons have given me the self-confidence to reach for and achieve many goals. I would especially like to thank my wife, Jane Kleindl. She has put up with me through a Ph.D. program, two house remodelings, and writing both editions of this textbook. Her support has been vital in all that I do. Finally, I would like to thank my children for making me realize that we all have a duty to make the world a better place. I hope that this textbook, in some small part, helps to accomplish that goal by aiding students and faculty in learning and teaching about the new and exciting world of e-business.

chapter 1
Introduction to E-Business

*The year 2001 was a transitional year for businesses. The economic boom years of the 1990s ended with a dot-com market crash. Security concerns were heightened when terrorists attacked New York City and Washington, D.C. Some observers thought these events would end the Internet era; instead, businesses realized that adopting e-business practices to gain efficiencies and competitive advantages was more important than ever. **E-business,** or electronic business, is the process of conducting business using computer-mediated technologies. This includes the use of not only the Internet but also other technology tools that are changing marketing practice.[1]*

Marketers are at the epicenter of e-business for both online-only and traditional businesses. For example, database marketing is being used to enhance customer relationship management systems. Firms gather data on people's behavior and then use these data to individualize products, advertisements, and services to develop stronger relationships with customers.[2] This chapter gives an overview of the changes that e-business is bringing to marketing process and strategy.

Some 61 percent of all businesses in the United States and 83 percent of businesses employing more than five thousand workers use e-business tools and techniques.[3] Business students must understand this new competitive environment and know how to use and implement these techniques in current business models.

1. Explain what a business model is and how it is used.
2. List the technologies that are being used to foster e-business.
3. Describe the size of the Internet economy.
4. Recommend how a business can use e-business techniques to develop long-term marketing relationships.
5. Identify the components of a marketing system.
6. List the components of an e-business-based marketing system.
7. List the components of an e-business value chain.
8. Explain how and why businesses need to evolve and change to maintain competitiveness.
9. Explain the importance of evaluating the ethical practices of a business and outline an ethical framework for e-businesses.

General Electric

The Edison General Electric Company was formed in 1892 to develop, build, and market Thomas Edison's lightbulb and electrical generation business. Today, General Electric (GE) is the only company remaining from the Dow-Jones Industrials' original list. In the later 1990s, under the leadership of CEO Jack Welch, GE was one of the dominant corporations in the world; however, GE's marketing process was not involved heavily in e-business. Welch's wife, Jane, was an avid Internet user. She used the Internet to search for information, purchase products, and link to online communities. When Jack Welch followed his wife's lead and started using the Internet, he realized the implications for his company.

As the chief strategist, Welch realized that adopting e-business would allow his company to maintain its competitive advantages. In 1999 Welch decreed that by the end of the year every division of GE would have a fully operational Internet capability, "or else." GE began a strategic planning exercise called "Destroy Your Business." Each unit had to visualize how dot-com businesses could affect GE's competitiveness. Welch believed that if GE didn't identify its weaknesses, other companies would. During this process a new initiative called "Grow Your Business" was developed. It focused business units on how they could use e-business models to gain competitive advantages.

By 2002 GE had fully integrated the Internet and e-business into its marketing processes and operations. Customers can now order products directly online. The product is then shipped from inventory, or a production order is routed to the factory. Suppliers are forced to fight for GE's business by using e-auctions where they bid against each other, lowering the price for GE. Full-time Internet connections allow GE to remotely monitor heavy equipment, checking on operations. GE enhances customer service by placing these data into databases and then lets customers know how efficiently they are using the equipment compared to other companies around the world, and how they could work more effectively. GE sees e-business as a productivity tool as well as a selling and procurement tool. GE saved $1.6 billion in 2001 by cutting overhead costs by as much as 50 percent. The company expects to save $10 billion over just a few years.[4]

End users can also take advantage of GE's Internet initiatives. Consumers can shop at GE's Web site (http://www.GE.com) and purchase products from appliances to airplanes. Consumers can view products, obtain sales information, register appliances, order parts, schedule service, and contact service support. In addition to its business-to-business and business-to-consumer e-business applications, GE also runs consumer-based Internet companies such as NBCi (http://www.nbci.com), Snap.com, Xoom.com, CNBC.com, AllBusiness.com, MSNBC.com, and the personal finance GE Financial Capital Network (http://www.gefn.com).

A culture of information sharing was needed to speed the change in GE's **business model.** By 2001, GE did not see itself as totally transformed. The retiring Jack Welch stated: "We're at the beginning of one of the most important revolutions in business."[5]

*A **business model**, or commerce model, is the basic process flow indicating how a business operates. It shows how business functions are linked together.*

Source: <http://www.GE.com>. Courtesy of General Electric Corp.

▶ **Thinking Strategically**

Explain why Jack Welch would see e-business as important for GE. Consider where e-business could have a bigger impact for GE, in the business-to-business arena or the business-to-consumer arena. List reasons why GE has been able to implement a new e-business model so quickly. Visit the GE Web site (http://www.ge.com). Speculate on the advantages of using a Web site to develop and maintain customer relationships.

"To say the new economy is over is like somebody in London in 1830 saying the industrial revolution is over because some textile manufacturers went broke."

Alvin Toffler[6]

E-business tools and techniques have fundamentally changed the nature of marketing. Businesses collect data electronically at the point of sale and route that information from the retailer to the supplier, the manufacturer, or both. Electronically linked distribution systems speed products through the channel of distribution and help to forge strong relationships between firms. The World Wide Web allows businesses to reach customers around the world rather than just in local markets. Information on customers' shopping behavior is stored in databases to profile individuals for targeted promotions and customized products. The use of these new technologies in combination is creating a paradigm shift in how marketing is used to compete.

E-Business

GE transformed its business model to take advantage of new technologies and marketing practices by developing an e-business-based model. E-business, or electronic business, systems use a number of information technology–based business practices to enhance relationships between the business and the customer. Developing e-business models requires an understanding of changes in marketing communications, distribution systems, business models, and customer behavior. Managers must also understand the use of databases to build relationships, the development of strategies to respond to a changing environment, management techniques for new types of employees and new business practices, and emerging legal and ethical concerns.[7] E-business models allow for the development of strong customer relationships and the lowering of the cost of doing business by increasing productivity, reducing labor costs, and lowering supplier prices. Companies around the world are in the process of rethinking how they structure their business models and deliver value to customers.[8]

This text covers e-business and e-commerce practice and strategy. This applies to traditional business and online-only business models. **E-commerce** is the practice of engaging in transactions online, but this does not fully explain the changes that business systems are facing. E-business is a broader concept and includes the use of **extranets**, which are **Internet** links between business suppliers and purchasers, and **intranets**, which operate inside a business. It also takes into consideration the changes in strategy and management practice needed to be successful in today's environment. Table 1.1 defines some of the current terminology used in this emerging field.

The Impact and Future of E-Business

Researchers at the University of Texas working with Cisco Systems conducted a study and defined four layers of the Internet economy. Layer one is the **Internet infrastructure layer** including companies with products and services that help

Table 1.1   E-Business Industry Terms

Name	Description
Internet	This is a global network of computer networks that uses a common interface for communication. The **World Wide Web** uses graphically based Internet standards that have allowed easy access to information and communication around the world.
E-Business	This is the process of using information technology (IT) to support a fuller operation of a business. This could include generating leads, providing sales support, integrating partners, and linking aspects of the business operation to suppliers and distributors through extranets.
E-Commerce	E-commerce consists of using electronic information-based systems to engage in transactions or commerce online. This includes automating Web site purchases.
Extranet	An Internet-based connection between a business and its suppliers, distributors, and partners, an extranet is not open to the general public. These systems are replacing older proprietary electronic data interchange (EDI) systems.
Intranet	This is an internal private network that uses the same types of hardware, software, and connections as the Internet. It can link divisions of a business around the world into a unified communications network.

Sources: Terms compiled from TechEncyclopedia [online], available from <http://www.techweb.com/encyclopedia/>; Chuck Martin, "Defining E-Business," *NewMedia,* July 1998, 26; Gary A. Bolles, "Is E-Business Your Business?" *Sm@art Reseller,* August 3, 1998, 1–7.

create an IP-based network infrastructure. Layer two is the **Internet applications layer** that builds off layer one and includes the products and services that make it technologically feasible to perform business activities online. Layer three is the **Internet intermediary layer.** This layer allows the investments in infrastructure to turn into business transactions by facilitating the meeting of buyers and sellers over the Internet. Layer four is the **Internet commerce layer** and includes the sales of products and services to consumers or businesses over the Internet. Figures for 1999 indicated that the Internet economy generated $507 billion and 2.3 million jobs in the United States and grew 68 percent from 1998.[9]

These figures do not include traditional businesses that use layers one through three to enhance their business processes. It is projected that the United States will have up to $7 trillion in online trade by 2006. Even with the downturn of the world economy in 2001, businesses are looking to e-business technology and practice to improve relationships with customers, enhance productivity, cut costs, and generate revenue.[10] A study by the Momentum Research Group found that on average 61 percent of U.S. organizations used some Internet-based business solution. This has resulted in a cumulative cost savings from 1998 to 2001 of $155 billion and is expected to product an additional $373 billion in cost savings by 2005. Internet business practices could account for up to 40 percent of projected increases in U.S. productivity from 2001 to 2011.[11]

A number of companies are using different research methodologies to estimate the number of users and to project commerce figures.[12] Table 1.2 compiles past and projected figures for Internet use and expected future growth. It is difficult to predict the future with very little history, but these figures indicate rapid growth. To reach a level of 50 million users, Internet use grew faster than both radio and television use.

The E-Business-Based Marketing System

The areas of business practice facing the largest changes due to technology include traditional marketing practices, customer service, and sales, all of which are part of a business marketing system. **Marketing** is the process of planning and executing the conception, pricing, promotion, and distribution of ideas, goods, and services that create exchanges that satisfy individual and organizational needs.[13] Marketers must wear many hats in an organization. Marketers not only are involved in the purchasing and selling of goods and services but also are instrumental in the designing, promoting, pricing, and distributing of products. An important role for marketers is the development and maintenance of customer relationships. Customers can easily find alternative sources of supply, so marketers must use a **systems approach**, ensuring that all parts of a business system are focused on developing and maintaining long-term relationships between the marketers and the customer. A marketing strategist must understand how e-business can be used as a strategic tool to enhance customer relationships and develop and maintain competitive advantages.

A systems approach helps decision makers look at how all aspects of a strategic business unit (SBU) interact with each other. Systems are also seen as being organic in that they must change in response to their environment or face the possibility of becoming extinct.

Table 1.2 E-Business Growth and Projections

	1996	1999	2002	Projected by 2005
Internet Hosts (Domains)	12.9 million	56.2 million	125 million	Projected as high as 1 billion
Web Users	28 million	65 million (U.S.) 163 million (worldwide)	183 million (U.S. and Canada) 500 million (worldwide)	1 billion (worldwide)
Percentage of Users Who Buy Goods or Services	25 percent	39 percent	46 percent	more than 50 percent
Business-to-Consumer Web Commerce	$2.6 billion	$13 billion	$108 billion	$156 billion (U.S.)
Business-to-Business Web Commerce (Includes Transactions over Extranets)	Less than $43 billion	$109 billion	$1.3 trillion (9% of U.S. sales)	$4.3–8.5 trillion
Advertising Revenue	$236.5 million	$2 billion	$7.9 billion	$18.8 billion (U.S.)

Sources: Dick Kelsey, "Online Ads Grow Fastest," *Newsbytes,* [online] (December 19, 2001), available from <http://www.newsbytes.com/news/01/173116.html>; "IDC Research: Major Growth Forecast for B2B Revenues," NUA [online] (October 17, 2001), available from <http://www.nua.ie/surveys/index.cgi?f=VS8&art_id=905357306&rel=true>; "EMarketer: B2C Will Continue to Grow in U.S.," NUA [online] (Sept. 21, 2001), available from <http://www.nua.ie/surveys/index.cgi?f=VS&art_id=905357218&rel=true>; "IDC Research: A Billion Users Will Drive Ecommerce," NUA [online] (May 28, 2001), available from <http://www.nua.com/surveys/index.cgi?f=VS&art_id=905356808&rel=true>; "Worldwide Business-to-Business Internet Commerce to Reach $8.5 Trillion in 2005," Gartner [online] (March 13, 2001), available from <http://www.gartner.com/5_about/press_room/pr20010313a.html>. For earlier sources see Brad Kleindl, *Strategic Electronic Marketing,* 1st ed. (Cincinnati: South-Western, 2001), 9.

Relationship Development

Relationship marketing *refers to the strategies a business must undertake to hold desirable customers over a long time period.*

Changes in information technology are both threatening and enhancing the ability of a business to develop long-term relationships with its customers, requiring **relationship marketing.** The Internet allows a customer to contact a business any time of the day or night from any location to gather information, make purchases, or obtain information on the status of accounts. This information can be personalized to the needs of the individual customer. This has shifted power to the customer because the Internet allows buyers to easily find information on competitive products and services. Companies can also more easily find new customers and serve existing customers by using databases to develop personal profiles and then targeting customers with customized information that can meet specific needs. Amazon.com, for example, personalizes e-mail, customizes Web pages, and offers products based on a buyer's past purchases. Dell develops purchase portals for businesses, allowing for customized purchasing and invoicing. The Internet is bringing about a hyper-competitive environment where IT is used as a vital part of marketing strategy and relationship development.[14] Customer-centered companies focus on improving satisfaction by using a number of e-business techniques. These include gathering customer data to gain a better knowledge of customers and improve sales, personalizing content for customers, increasing the speed of product delivery and service, and allowing for interactivity between the customer and the business. Raising customer satisfaction levels is considered the number one priority of IT executives. This requires that businesses find a way to leverage their technological abilities to keep their customers happy.[15]

Information is also allowing businesses to estimate the lifetime value of customers. The **lifetime value of a customer (LVC)** is an estimate of the potential lifetime profit of a customer. If a customer's long-term value does not exceed the cost of maintaining that customer, the customer may be charged a higher price or dropped. For example, many individuals have seen an increase in their individual checking account charges or their long-distance bills because they do not provide enough value to their bank or phone company. The ability to collect and use this type of information is refocusing companies; rather than just pursuing market share, which can result in high expenses, companies are deciding which customers to maintain over a lifetime. This allows companies to increase overall profits by dropping negatively valued customers.[16]

Developing an e-business system allows businesses to leverage information technology to develop and maintain relationships. Figure 1.1 represents the components of a traditional marketing system, including the traditional 4 Ps of marketing (product, price, place, and promotion). It also takes into consideration the customer as the targeted market, as well as the payment flow and the information-gathering

Lifetime value of a customer (LVC) is the sum of expected lifetime earnings minus the lifetime costs (acquisition, operating, and customer service expenses) of a customer.

Figure 1.1 The Traditional Marketing System

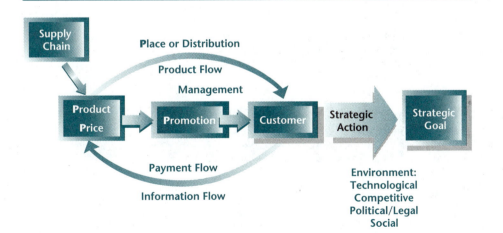

processes undertaken by a business. Managers must devise and execute a plan to reach organizational goals by considering the business's resources and the nature of the environment in which it operates. They must use the components of a marketing system to devise a business model that will operate both efficiently and competitively.

Changes Due to E-Business Systems

All the components of a business must work in unison to allow the marketing system to operate in its environment. This system must organize itself and find an advantage over its competitors to ensure long-term sustainability. E-business systems are fostering a number of changes to the marketing system, including the following:[17]

1) Customized products

2) Increased price pressure resulting in lower prices

3) Shorter channels of distribution dominated by facilitators

4) Extranet-enhanced supply chain management

5) Nonlinear promotions

6) Electronic transfer of funds

7) Database information management systems and CRM (customer relationship management)

All of this is occurring in a dramatically changing environment requiring management to reorganize and develop new strategies. Figure 1.2 illustrates the new

Figure 1.2   The E-Business-Based Marketing System

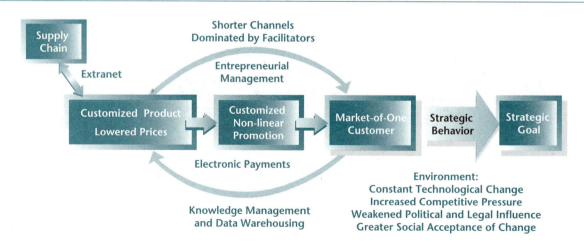

e-business system. It shows that e-business practices will encourage enhanced relationships by allowing a business to focus on its customers at an individualized, or market-of-one, level.

The e-business model is a framework for understanding how e-business impacts the marketing process and can be used as a basis for understanding how to structure and implement new e-business models and strategies for both online-only businesses and businesses that combine e-business with traditional business practice. The ultimate goal of restructuring business models is to gain competitive advantages by lowering costs, delivering greater value to customers, and developing and maintaining long-term relationships with customers. A value chain analysis is a valuable tool for evaluating the components that result in a competitive advantage.

The E-Business Value Chain

Identifying the individual activities that a business undertakes to design, produce, market, deliver, and support products or services is the first step in determining how to deliver value to customers. An e-business value chain considers the inbound logistical process (obtaining raw materials, inbound logistical procedures, and production) and the outbound logistical process (outbound logistical procedures, marketing, sales, and support). To gain a distinctive competency, a business must be able to perform some function in its value chain better than its competitors. This could mean providing a function at a lower cost or in a unique way. Businesses that compete in similar industries serving similar markets may have value chains that differ from those in other industries.[18]

With the growth of e-business tools and techniques, a new perspective has been added to the value chain. The e-business value chain views information technology as part of a business's overall value chain and adds to the competitive advantages

E-Business Professionals

Roger Asay
President
Asay Publishing
http://www.asaypub.com

Roger Asay

Roger Asay started *Locator Magazine* in 1987 in his apartment with a single computer. By 1993 Asay Publishing was recognized as one of *Inc.* magazine's 500 fastest growing private companies. *Locator Magazine* brings together buyers and sellers of used equipment for the print-on-paper market. This includes used copiers, fax machines, printers, and other related items, parts, and supplies. The publication helped to organize an office equipment market of more than $79 billion. In 1997 Asay Publishing expanded on its mission of bringing together buyers and sellers by developing an online vertical portal for the print-on-paper market. By 2002 the business had expanded to seven Web sites.

Asay Publishing's Web sites act as industry information centers by organizing online discussion forums, hosting Web sites for businesses, offering information on products for sale, providing a medium for industry advertising, facilitating the shipping of products, and much more. According to Mr. Asay, "E-business practices have made us a worldwide business. We provide 24/7 services to our industry. Our information systems have lowered prices for some customers while allowing others to raise prices because they have found multiple buyers. Our customers are able to develop very targeted business models."

Mr. Asay sees his biggest e-business challenge as getting paid for the online services. "One of our major difficulties is determining how much value our services create and how to charge for that value. Our customers are too good at using the Internet to work around payment systems that we develop."

The skills that Asay Publishing looks for in college students are deep computer skills and a strong understanding of marketing and relationship development. A good grasp of marketing is considered more important than simply being able to sell. Employees are expected to have strong verbal and writing skills, and a foreign language is a plus.

Figure 1.3   E-Business Value Chain

E-Business Technological Infrastructure (Chapter 2)
E-Business Communication Platforms (Chapter 3)

of a business.[19] This text will outline a number of techniques that an e-business can use to gain advantages throughout its value chain. Figure 1.3 illustrates how these technologies impact the components of an e-business value chain.

The chapters that follow explore different aspects of this e-business value chain. Table 1.3 shows which chapters will explore the various components of the e-business system.

International E-Business

International e-business issues are covered throughout the text. The United States is expected to account for only half of the expected global $7 trillion in e-business-facilitated transactions. Markets outside of the United States are expected to grow the fastest in areas such as wireless and HDTV delivery of Internet content. Yet there are a number of barriers to seamless global e-business, including cultural issues, language differences, currency conversions, shipping problems, a lack of global brand recognition, differing legal and ethical standards, and a lack of trust in foreign markets. A U.S.-oriented Web site will reach only 5 percent of the world's population and 25 percent of the world's buying power, and by 2004 the United States is expected to have only 29 percent of the world's Internet users. Companies are using the Internet to search out global customers and to find low-cost suppliers. An *Internet Week* study found that businesses undertook global e-business strategies to maintain competitiveness, increase sales, support current

Table 1.3 Components of an E-Business System

Component	Chapter	Description
Technological Environment	2	The next chapter is a primer on the technology behind the Internet and the World Wide Web. It gives a perspective on how the Internet works and where it is going.
High Technology	Appendix	Chapter 2 Appendix is a more in-depth primer on the technology behind e-business.
E-Business Communication	3	"E-Business Communication" looks at how communication is changing over the Internet. This includes how the Web is being structured for nonlinear communication systems.
Hypermedia Design	Appendix	Chapter 3 Appendix is a guide to the tools, techniques, and theory related to designing for hypermedia.
Distribution	4	Chapter 4 looks at the dynamics of change in distribution systems and supply chain management systems, illustrating how these add value to an organization.
Value Creation	5	This chapter explores the current practices being used by e-businesses to create value for customers.
E-Commerce	6	Chapter 6 explains the process of e-commerce and how this fits into an e-business value creation process.
Internet Advertising and Promotion	7	"E-Business Promotion" illustrates how hypermedia are being used strategically for advertising and promotion.
The Customer	8	Chapter 8 focuses on the market, including an exploration of the diffusion process, online consumer behavior, and online communities.
Information Collection and Use	9	This chapter looks at how firms are collecting and using information to gain competitive advantages, including environmental scanning, data use collecting, data warehousing, data mining, knowledge management, and marketing research. It also illustrates how firms set up and use customer relationship management systems to develop and maintain relationships with customers. In addition, the chapter examines the impact of e-business on services.
Management	10	Chapter 10 explores the process of developing the management systems required to operate in a dynamic and technical environment.
Careers	Appendix	Chapter 10 Appendix is a guide to job opportunities and career paths that students may pursue.
Strategy and Business Models	11	The highly dynamic environment in which firms find themselves requires a more innovative approach to strategy. This chapter looks at how businesses are restructuring value chains to gain competitive advantages. It also outlines the process of developing and analyzing business models and determining how e-business models create value.
Political, Legal, and Ethical Issues		Integrated throughout the text is information related to political, legal, and ethical issues. This information gives the reader an understanding of how these issues impact Internet marketing strategy development.
Case Studies		These case studies integrate text concepts and are focused on both online and brick-and-click businesses.

Case 1.1

eBay

In 1995 Pierre Omidyar designed a Web site called Web Auction to allow his girlfriend to sell Pez dispensers. Demand was so strong for the service that Omidyar began charging sellers. This initial idea turned into the online auction business eBay (http://www.ebay.com). By 1998 the founder had become a billionaire and eBay was valued at $7 billion, a valuation higher than Kmart's. By 1999 eBay accounted for the largest dollar volume of consumer sales on the Internet.

However, running an online auction is not without problems. eBay attempted to auction a jacket autographed by members of the *Today Show* for charity. The *Today Show's* Katie Couric announced that the bids had reached $200,000. Unfortunately, pranksters had escalated the bids. The highest legitimate bid was only $11,400. Sales can be subject to pranks, and scam artists can also use online auction sites to bilk bidders. One scam artist first developed a positive reputation at eBay's auction site. The scammer then offered additional products online, received payments, and never sent the products. eBay does not give rebates, and the customers lost their money. To overcome the problem of fraud, eBay has offered customer service support and educational resources including a feedback forum, third-party escrow accounts, verification of eBay users' personal information, insurance, and expert opinions for authentication and grading. Another problem occurred when eBay's server crashed and it received a number of complaints on its discussion list. When eBay attempted to control the listing of complaints, it was accused of censuring free speech.[21]

Auction fraud is the number one complaint in e-commerce. Auction sites are attempting to deal with this problem by allowing discussion lists to rate buyers and sellers. The industry is also using escrow services, digital certificates, and insurance systems.[22] The industry knows that if it does not take care of this problem, it may face federal regulations.

eBay is only one example of the creative new business models that governments would like to see develop on the information superhighway. These new sales systems are bringing efficiency to the market by increasing competition, lowering costs, and expanding customer bases.

global operations, and enter new markets. They accomplish these goals by collaborating with suppliers, customers, or other businesses around the world. A number of e-business tools are used by businesses, including automating currency conversion and language translation.[20]

Global e-business is not just about selling online. Worldwide, company intranets are currently the most widely adopted e-business initiatives, followed by the development of non-transaction-based Web sites. In addition, access to global e-business requires multiple platforms. In the United States, Internet access is primarily through PCs. Around the world, the Internet is moving to cellular-based systems.

▶ Thinking Strategically: Case 1.1

Consider whether or not society is better off because of the introduction of eBay. Discuss both sides of this economic welfare question. Consider why a government would be interested in fostering the growth of a business like eBay. Decide what types of government actions would benefit e-business like eBay, and what government actions would limit such e-businesses. Discuss whether it is proper for e-businesses to collect data on their customers' shopping behaviors and personal profiles. Determine how a customer could benefit and how a customer could be damaged if an e-business uses this data.

The Political, Legal, and Ethical Environments

Are the overall benefits of the Internet worth the costs? E-business systems are having a major impact on the way that business is conducted. Just as the television

Source: <http://www.ebay.com>. These materials have been reproduced with permission of eBay Inc. COPYRIGHT © EBAY INC. ALL RIGHTS RESERVED.

and telephone changed society, the e-business age is changing how individuals interact with businesses, governments, and each other. Governments around the world are fostering the growth of Internet services to obtain the benefits outlined in this text. To receive these benefits, a new level of responsibility needs to be pursued by both businesses and individuals. Businesses must learn to gain customers' trust, governments must ensure a safe Internet environment, and individuals must become Net savvy for the Internet to remain a truly free and dynamic system of communication, commerce, and efficiency.

The development of an e-business-based competitive arena has given rise to a number of unique political, legal, and ethical considerations, and the rules of the game of business are being reshaped to fit these new realities. As a truly global medium, the Internet allows businesses to operate across borders. The rules that govern business practice in one location or state may not pertain in other areas. Governments around the world are seeing their business constituencies facing competition from global competitors. These governments are working to set regulations that foster the growth of their own e-business systems. Individuals and businesses can benefit from using e-business systems, but only if they have access to the Internet and the information, goods, and services offered there. Without access, individuals may not benefit. This may leave a portion of society relatively worse off. In addition, the global nature of the Internet makes it hard to regulate. This has allowed some unscrupulous individuals to take advantage of others by running scams, offering access to pornography, or otherwise exploiting Internet users. Every chapter in this text will investigate the emerging political, legal, and ethical issues facing e-businesses and the public.

The political and legal environment represents the rules by which businesses and society operate. Although the imposed rules may attempt to increase the overall **economic welfare** of a society, not everyone plays by the rules. Another social concern is that not everyone in society will benefit from the e-business revolution. Some individuals and businesses may be left out of the connected world.

Economic welfare *is the net benefit an economic system provides to a society.*

Ethics is the study of how individuals or businesses make decisions given the consequences of those decisions. It helps to answer the questions, *What should I do?* and *What should my business do?* When contemplating ethical considerations, an individual or business must ask, *What will be the consequences of my actions?* Often an **ethical dilemma** arises. This is when conflicting concerns surface; for example, a certain action undertaken may increase the overall returns to a business but hurt some other constituency in the process.

An **ethical dilemma** *exists when a proposed action benefits certain individuals, businesses, or societies but at the same time has negative consequences for others.*

Many businesses realize the benefits of being ethical. Employees and customers prefer companies that uphold ethical standards. Chief ethics officers for Sears must develop policies that balance the needs of three main **constituencies:** customers, employees, and shareholders. To achieve this, Sears developed a fifteen-page code of conduct guide. It also has a telephone hotline employees can use to call and receive help when faced with ethical dilemmas. Other companies, such as Columbia/HCA and United Technologies, put similar programs in place.[23]

Constituencies *are those people involved with or served by an organization. Internet constituencies include governments, businesses, customers, ISPs, and schools.*

Business decisions typically impact a number of ethical concerns across a spectrum of constituencies. Ethical and legal concerns can intermix in areas such as property rights, honesty and deception, and privacy. Ethical and political issues can also be intertwined in areas such as economic welfare, technology use (e.g., spamming and Netiquette), and access equity. It is important that e-business decision makers understand each of these areas of concern and are able to articulate the pros and cons of individual and business actions as well as understand the possible outcomes of those actions. This process can aid in the development of corporate policies.[24]

Knowledge Integration

Terms and Concepts

Business model *4*
Constituencies *16*
E-business *2*
E-commerce *6*
Economic welfare *16*
Ethical dilemma *16*
Extranet *6*
Internet *6*

Internet applications
  layer *7*
Internet commerce
  layer *7*
Internet infrastructure
  layer *6*
Internet intermediary
  layer *7*

Intranet *6*
Lifetime value of a
  customer (LVC) *9*
Marketing *7*
Relationship
  marketing *8*
Systems approach *7*

Concepts and Questions for Review

1. Describe the layers of the Internet economy.
2. Define the term *business model*.
3. Describe the components of a business system and their changes.
4. Explain why a systems approach is important.
5. Define the term *e-business*.
6. Discuss how relationships are enhanced in an e-business environment.
7. Explain the lifetime value of a customer.
8. Determine how an e-business system is different from current business systems.
9. Describe the importance of using an e-business value chain analysis.
10. Explain which businesses are likely to be early adopters of change and which ones will adopt late. Justify your answers.
11. Discuss why both students and managers need to know about the topics covered in this text.

Active Learning

Exercise 1.1 Imagining the Future

Imagine that the telephone and television were invented within the past ten years. Decide how companies would need to change to use these new tools. Determine if they would be able to use the same techniques to promote and sell their products. Decide if they would use the same outlets to distribute goods and services. Speculate on whether the relationships between suppliers and producers would be handled in the same way. Decide if companies could be managed in the same manner.

Exercise 1.2 Checking Buyer Behavior

This exercise is designed to determine whether buyers will change their buying behavior and how e-business will impact established businesses. Most customers from developed countries have a great deal of shopping experience and have already developed purchasing patterns. Decide if you are likely to change your shopping behavior. Place in the first column five of the shopping activities that you engage in most often (examples are given, but feel free to change them). Then rank-order your preferences for each of the shopping activities. Finally, indicate the number of local outlets for each shopping activity.

Shopping Activity (*Examples*)	1: Like This the Most 5: Like This the Least	Number of Local Outlets
Shopping for specialty clothing		
Shopping for groceries		
Shopping for specialty items and gifts		
Shopping for computers and software		
Shopping for cars		

Explain how the e-business techniques outlined in this chapter would affect these shopping activities. Indicate how e-commerce would affect the way you make your purchases. Determine if a smaller number of local outlets make it more likely that you would shop online. Decide which of these businesses are likely to have links to their suppliers. Explain which of these industries will face the greatest amount of change.

Exercise 1.3 Ethical Analysis

Use the following table to evaluate the ethical implications of e-business practices. List both advantages and disadvantages in each cell. Identify the ethical dilemmas that can surface when the advantages in some cells conflict with the disadvantages in others.[25]

Constituencies (Who Is Affected)	Privacy	Equity and Access	Social Welfare
Customers			
Employees			
Stakeholders (Owners)			
Communities			

Competitive Exercise 1.4 Business Model

Assume you are going to present a business proposal to a venture capitalist. Your team should outline a system for an existing business. Indicate how it currently meets the needs of its customers through its product development, promotion, distribution system, and so forth. Then draw a plan of how you think this business model should operate using the e-business techniques outlined in this chapter. Explain how you think the business could make the transition from the old business model to the new one. Determine if there are any environmental drivers leading this business model to change. Decide what could hinder the move to e-business. Outline any ethical concerns that could be raised by this e-business system.

Web Search—Looking Online

Search Term:	E-Business	First 5 out of 3,200,000

IBM E-Business Site. Offers general e-business information from a leader in the industry of business commerce and networking technology.
http://www-3.ibm.com/e-business/index.jsp

EBay. Allows individuals to sell and buy just about anything through online auctions.
http://www.ebay.com

Line56. Provides a portal to e-business news.
http://www.line56.com

Ebusiness Forum. Offers access to e-business news.
http://www.ebusinessforum.com

E-Commerce Times. Presents links to e-commerce news.
http://www.ecommercetimes.com

Search Term:	Size of the Net	First 4 out of 3,190,000

Netsizer. Displays the number of Internet hosts.
http://www.netsizer.com

Georgia Tech. Collects data on Internet use and has good links to other Internet statistics Web sites.
http://www.gvu.gatech.edu/user_surveys

Matrix. Offers services to monitor the Internet.
http://www.mids.org

NUA. Provides information of Internet statistics from an Irish-based Internet strategy, research, and development agency.
http://www.nua.com

References

[1] For more information on defining e-business, see "e-business," in whatis?com [online], available from <http://whatis.com/>; "What Is E-Business," in IBM [online] (August 23, 1999), available from <http://www.ibm.com/e-business/whatis.html>.

[2] John W. Verity and Russell Mitchell, "A Trillion-Byte Weapon," *BusinessWeek,* July 31, 1995, 80–81.

[3] Hal Varian, Robert E. Litan, Andrew Elder, Jay Shutter, "The Net Impact Study: Preliminary Report," *The Momentum Research Group* (December 2001).

[4] Lisa Vaas, "GE Keeps E-Business Turned On," *Eweek,* November 12, 2001, 49.

[5] Meridith Levinson, "GE: Destruction Pays Off," *CIO Magazine,* October 15, 2001, available from <http://www.cio.com/archive/101501/tl_ebus.html>; David Joachim, "GE's E-Biz Turnaround Proves That Big Is Back," *Internet Week,* June 12, 2000; John Ellis, "Change Partners," *Fast Company,* October 1999, 351–54.

[6] Jerry Useem, "And Then, Just When You Thought the `New Economy' Was Dead . . . ," *Business 2.0,* August/September 2001, 68–76.

[7] Bruce Caldwell and John Foley, "IBM Means E-Business," *InformationWeek,* February 8, 1998, 18–20, 124–25.

[8] Stephen Baker and William Echikson, "Europe's Internet Bash," *BusinessWeek E.Biz,* February 7, 2000, 40–44; Laura Cohn, Diane Brady, and David Welch, "B2B: The Hottest Net Bet Yet?" *BusinessWeek,* January 17, 2000, 36–37; John Wenninger, "Business-to-Business Electronic Commerce," *Current Issues in Economics and Finance 5,* no. 10 (June 1999).

[9] For more on Internet economy indicators, see "What Are the Internet Economy Indicators?" in Internet Indicators [online] (January 7, 2002) available from <http://www.internet indicators.com/indicators.html>.

10 Kevin Fogarty, "Counting the Dispossessed," *Computerworld,* December 17, 2001, 40; Tim Wilson, "Basic Instincts," *InternetWeek,* December 17, 2001, 15–20; Jeff Moad, "Beating the E-Biz Odds," *Eweek,* November 12, 2001, 45; David Rocks, "The Net as a Lifeline," *BusinessWeek E.biz,* October 29, 2001, 16–23.

11 Hal Varian, Robert E. Litan, Andrew Elder, Jay Shutter, "The Net Impact Study: Preliminary Report," *The Momentum Research Group* (December 2001); Demir Barlas, "Forrester: E-Business = Productivity," Line56 [online] (November 13, 2001), available from <http://www.line56.com/articles/default.asp?NewsID=3137>.

12 For an assessment of the major Internet research company methodologies, see Jennifer Greenstein, "How Many? How Much? Who Knows?" *Brill's Content,* November 1998, 54–58; Sari Kalin, "Reading Between the Lines," *CIO Web Business—Section 2* (April 1, 1998): 43–48; Daniel Roth, "My What Big Internet Numbers You Have!" *Fortune,* March 15, 1999, 114–20.

13 American Marketing Association definition, *Marketing News,* March 1, 1985, 1.

14 Don Tapscott, David Ticoll, and Alex Lowy, "Relationships Rule," *Business 2.0,* May 2000, 300–319; Pamela Houghtaling, "How the Internet Is Changing Marketing," *Beyond Computing,* May 2000, 26–28; Bill Blundon and Allen Bonde, "Beyond the Transaction," *InformationWeek,* November 16, 1998, 5SS–6SS.

15 Jenny C. McCune, "Customer Driven Company," *Beyond Computing,* May 2000, 18–24; Jeff Sweat, "Customer Centricity," *InformationWeek,* May 17, 1999, 46–62.

16 Adina Levin, "Relationship Management Critical to Web Success," *DM Review,* March 1999, 20–24, 92.

17 Frederick E. Webster Jr., "The Changing Role of Marketing in the Corporation," *Journal of Marketing* (October 1992): 1–7.

18 For more on value chains, see Michael E. Porter, *Competitive Advantage* (New York: Free Press, 1980).

19 Jeffrey F. Rayport and John J. Sviokla, "Exploiting the Virtual Value Chain," *Harvard Business Review* (November–December 1995): 75–85.

20 Bob Violino, "E-Business Lurches Abroad," *InternetWeek,* March 19, 2001, 1, 52–54; Tom Davenport, "E-Commerce Goes Global," *CIO,* August 1, 2000, 52–54.

21 Jennifer Tanaka and Beth Kwon, "Risky Business," *Newsweek,* December 21, 1998, 72–74.

22 Whit Andrews, "Auction Sites Seek Ways to Build Trust Between Buyers, Sellers," *Internet World,* October 5, 1998, 24.

23 Jennifer Bresnahan, "For Goodness Sake," *CIO Enterprise—Section 2* (June 15, 1999): 54–62.

24 For more on teaching ethics and ethical frameworks, see James Linderman, "Top Management's Role in Business Ethics," *Beyond Computing,* May 1999, 16–17; Chuck Huff and C. Dianne Martin, "Computing Consequences: A Framework for Teaching Ethical Computing," *Communications of the ACM* 38, no. 12 (December 1995): 75–84.

25 For a more in-depth look at ethical analysis, see Huff and Martin, "Computing Consequences: A Framework for Teaching Ethical Computing."

chapter 2
Understanding E-Business Technology

Making decisions about how to compete in an e-business world requires an understanding of the technology that underpins e-business. This includes looking at not only how the Internet works today but also how it evolved and where it is going. Business decision makers must understand this technology because they will be working with technical specialists to develop strategies using e-business for communication, the facilitation of commerce, and the creation of competitive advantages.

The World Wide Web is a major component of the Internet, and it is governed by a set of protocols. It is the interface that most people use to access and transfer data at this time. New applications are being added to browsers as the Internet and the World Wide Web evolve. Wireless applications have been growing around the world, and digital convergence is linking the Internet to various end-user tools, from television and wireless phones to appliances and automobiles. This chapter is designed to introduce the basic technological underpinning of e-business, the Internet, and the World Wide Web. The ideas, terms, and concepts presented here are the technical but necessary language of the Net. (More in-depth technical considerations are included in the Chapter 2 Appendix.)

learning objectives

Developing Infrastructure

vignette

Numerous infrastructures have been developed by both private and government enterprises. These include railroad systems, telegraph systems, and telephone systems. During the Cold War, the U.S. government aided in the development of an **infrastructure** designed to improve traffic flow and cut transportation costs. This new infrastructure bypassed established systems, forcing businesses dependent on older infrastructures to change or die. The public found this new infrastructure highly beneficial. It allowed individuals to move from city centers, to shop at locations far from their homes, and to visit family and friends much more easily than before. Businesses used this system to aid in the shipment of goods across the country, allowing for more timely delivery. This new infrastructure transformed American society.[1]

The infrastructure just described is the U.S. interstate highway system. Started in the 1950s and still under construction today, this road system helped to make the modern United States. A transportation infrastructure allows an individual to travel from one location to another and includes the small streets leading from the driveways of homes and the wider boulevards

Increasing Bandwidth on the Transportation Superhighway.

Infrastructure *is the basic structure that allows a system to operate. For the Internet, this includes lines, browsers, computers, servers, and so forth.*

leading to highways. Ground transportation infrastructure includes the intersections, the stoplights, the traffic control systems, and even the pavement on which vehicles travel. If travelers are in a hurry, they may use the air transport infrastructure to move rapidly from one point to another.

Today a new infrastructure is developing that promises to have much the same impact. (See Figure 2.1, which shows global Internet traffic.) This new infrastructure allows for the movement of electronic rather than physical products—and this digital content may prove more important in the long term.

The Internet has been compared to another great technological innovation that started the industrial revolution: the steam engine. Peter Drucker believes that the current information revolution is at a state of development comparable to the industrial revolution in the early 1820s, only forty years after James Watt improved the steam engine. The railroad system that resulted from this innovation closed distances between suppliers and customers, allowed individuals and information to travel, and forced businesses to rethink their business models and strategic analysis.[2] Much like the Internet and its recent dot-com crash, the railroad system in the United States also went through a speculative bubble resulting in an economic crash in the late 1800s.

▶ Thinking Strategically

Consider your national highway infrastructure. Speculate on how a consumer's life would be different if there were no national highway system. How would a business have to operate differently if there were no national highway infrastructure? Determine what other infrastructures are important to a consumer's life and to business efficiency.

The digital age is allowing the rapid movement of information around the globe on a digital superhighway, or I-way. Digital information flows through a complicated and rapidly growing infrastructure. This telecommunications infrastructure consists of telephone lines and exchanges, cable TV lines and broadcasters, satellite and cellular systems, and an Internet backbone. The Internet backbone includes data lines, routers, switches, servers, and the local system used to send or view information at a user's site, such as a PC with a Web browser.

In the United States, no single entity owns the telecommunications infrastructure. The existing infrastructure has developed in response to the type of information it was designed to carry. The telephone industry constructed a voice-switching infrastructure. The television cable industry developed a send-only video infrastructure. Companies such as MCI and UUNET specialize in the development and maintenance of high-bandwidth data lines, routers, and switches for digital information. Many smaller companies are providing access for the **last mile** of the telecommunications infrastructure by specializing in consumer-premises equipment, such as the television-set-top box or the PC modem connected to the

*The **last mile** is not literally a mile long. It represents the link from an exchange to an individual's home or business, which is usually the narrowest access to the Internet.*

Figure 2.1 Global Internet Traffic Map

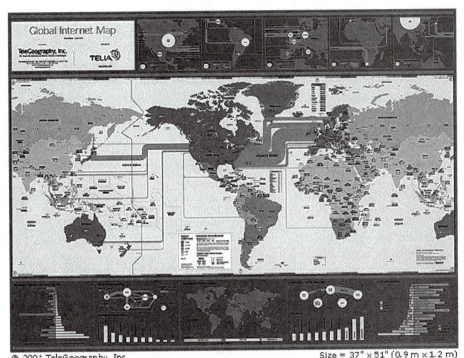

© 2001 TeleGeography, Inc.   Size = 37" x 51" (0.9 m x 1.2 m)

Map Courtesy of: TeleGeography, Inc., © TeleGeography, Inc., 2002,
<http://www.telegeography.com>.

Internet. Direct satellite and cellular systems bypass these landline-connected infrastructures. This allows electronic information to be delivered to remote areas around the world without the large expense of placing landlines.

The Internet is perhaps the best known of the digital telecommunications infrastructures. Originally just one of the many subsystems of the larger I-way, the Internet has set the standards that have allowed for the rapid growth of **e-mail** and the World Wide Web. By the year 2002, there were half a billion Web users. By the end of the year 2000, there were 891 million e-mail boxes. Of those mailboxes, 31.8 million were wireless—increasing from 3.7 million in 1999. The United States accounted for only 7 percent of wireless mailboxes.[3]

The digital electronic signals that travel over the Internet can represent words, images, sounds, instructions, or anything else a computer can produce or use. The more information to be sent, the higher the bandwidth needed to transport the information. High **bandwidth** is currently being delivered by a number of different systems, promising to bring further change to individuals and societies worldwide.

E-mail. *or electronic mail, allows for the transfer of text-based content over the Internet. Current e-mail protocols allow for the sending of HTML code and attachments (additional files).*

Bandwidth *indicates the amount of digital information that can be carried over a line. The basic rule in developing multimedia (combined text, images, and sound) is that the richer the media, the larger the file, and therefore the higher the bandwidth needed to deliver the content in a given amount of time.*

The Internet

"Sure we could build such a thing, but I don't see why anybody would want it."

Severo Ornstein

One of the early developers of the Internet, when asked if it was possible to build an interconnected computer network.[4]

The **Internet** (**Inter**connected **Net**work), or **Net**, started as a U.S.-government-sponsored project to link computing systems. The ability to send packets of information between widely dispersed computer networks was seen as a means of lowering the cost of computing. The original 1969 project was called the ARPANET.[5] By the late 1980s, the National Science Foundation incorporated the ARPANET into its own network, the NSFNET. The Internet allowed individual **computer networks** to interconnect with each other across common backbones. The NSF maintained the NSFNET backbone to which other local access systems connected. Each section of the backbone was rented from telecommunications companies. Universities using the Internet also developed and fostered **open standards**, or standardized means of sending and receiving electronic data. Around the world, countries have relied upon state-owned or private companies to develop telecommunications superhighways to support the Internet and e-business.

The National Science Foundation withdrew from the governance of the Internet to speed the development of a private-sector Internet. Currently, the Internet's open standards are controlled by a number of not-for-profit groups, some of which are described in Table 2.1.

*A **computer network** consists of a number of computers linked through a network server. The server controls the flow of information between the users.*

*Open standards **are** basic sets of instructions, such as programs or programming methods, that are not owned by a single company and are free for others to use.*

The Internet Backbone

Internet users must have some means of going online or linking to the Internet backbone. For many home users this is accomplished through the use of an **Internet service provider (ISP)** such as AOL (http://www.aol.com), EarthLink (http://www.earthlink.com), or a smaller organization. To speed consumer acceptance of the Internet and to lock in customers, ISPs in Great Britain and Denmark are providing free ISP services.[6] Smaller ISPs could use a larger ISP called an Internet access provider (such as UUNET [http://www.worldcom.com/uunet]) to link to the Internet backbone. ISPs can lease a certain amount of bandwidth access, allowing the setting of a fixed rate. The ISP is then able to charge its users either a fixed rate or a variable rate for bandwidth and time used. Business users also need an on-ramp to the Internet. They can use an ISP or, depending on their size and capabilities, link to a network access provider.

If a business or an individual wants to access a Web site outside of a local network, it must be hosted on an Internet server with access to the Internet back-

Table 2.1 Internet Governing Organizations

Abbreviation	Organization	Purpose
ICANN	Internet Corporation for Assigned Names and Numbers (http://www.icann.org)	Oversees the domain name registration system under the auspices of the Internet Assigned Numbers Authority (IANA) (http://www.iana.org)
ANSI	American National Standards Institute (http://www.ansi.org)	Represents U.S. interests related to the Internet; is the U.S. member of the International Organization for Standardization (IOS) (http://www.iso.ch)
ISOC	Internet Society (http://www.isoc.org)	Nonprofit professional membership organization that aids in developing Internet standards, public policy, education, and training.
IETF	Internet Engineering Task Force (http://www.ietf.org)	Open group that influences the standards set for the Internet.
W3C	World Wide Web Consortium (http://www.w3c.org)	Governs the set of World Wide Web protocols.

bone. Each server that is hooked up to the Internet is a **host.** When an individual logs on to the Internet from a home computer through an ISP, he or she is not a host because other users do not have access to content on the individual's computer. The number of host sites on the Internet has increased from roughly 4 million worldwide in 1995 to more than 125 million in 2002.

Table 2.2 shows the symbols used throughout the text to represent parts of the Internet superhighway and how these interconnect to make management information systems operate. Figure 2.2, on page 30, illustrates the connected infrastructure of the Internet.

Bandwidth

Bandwidth indicates the size of pipe through which electronic information must move. Phone lines were originally designed to carry **analog signals** for voice. The thin copper, or twisted pair, wires that hook up to telephones were made to carry this low-bandwidth signal. Computers use **digital signals**, or a series of ons (1) and offs (0). The more 1s and 0s being sent over a given period of time, the higher the bandwidth needed. Different types of data lines and methods of sending data allow for increased bandwidth and therefore greater information flow. Bandwidth is measured in **bits per second**, or **bps**, which are counted in thousands (kilobits

Analog signals *are waves:*

Digital signals *are a series of ons and offs:*
110101001000101101010

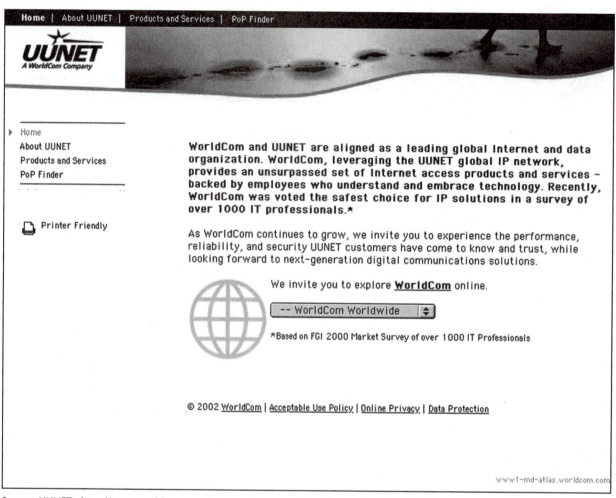

Source: UUNET <http://www.worldcom.com/uunet>. Courtesy of WorldCom, Inc.

per second, Kbps), millions (megabits per second, Mbps), and billions (gigabits per second, Gbps).

The ability to deliver **broadband,** or high-speed Internet access, is dependent on two factors: how quickly the information can be sent around on the Internet backbone, and how quickly it can move through the last-mile connection and be processed on the browsing device. Across the globe, the Internet backbone has seen tremendous growth in carrying capacity. The battle has been in providing access through the last mile. In the United States, most Internet access is through PCs. The last-mile battle has been between cable modems and phone-line-based

Table 2.2   Internet Infrastructure Symbols

Symbol	Meaning	Purpose
	Server	Computer that holds content and serves it to the Internet as requested.
	ISP	Organization that uses server farms (multiple networked servers [hosts]) or very large servers to handle a large number of users or extensive content.
	Data Line	The line (e.g., twisted pair, coaxial, fiber) that carries the electronic Internet signal. The wider the line, the more data carried.
	Web Content	The files that are sent to the individual's browser.
Web	Web Browser	The access device (e.g., PC, iTV, wireless phone) that displays Web content.
	Internet Backbone	The broadband, high-speed network of telecommunication lines that make up the Internet.
	Data Packet	A Packet, or set, of data that is usually part of a larger file. These are routed around the Internet and reassembled at the user's access device.
	Router	A device that transfers, or switches, each packet of data around a network. Internet routers route packets of information over the Internet.

DSL (digital subscriber line) systems. Projections are that cable modems will overtake DSL connections as the dominant broadband last-mile Internet connection.

Backbone Speeds

In the early 1990s, a small ISP would be linked to the Internet backbone over T-1 lines at around 1.54 Mbps. Currently, companies are deploying new Internet backbones that can carry up to 2.5 Gbps. This is enough bandwidth to send the equivalent of fourteen hundred 300-page books in seven seconds. The Internet2 (http://www.Internet2.org) is a new IP-based network designed to allow the transport of very high bandwidths of information. A consortium of more than 180 universities, businesses, and federal agencies are once again spearheading this infrastructure. This new network is being designed to send up to 9.6 Gbps across the Internet backbone. This will allow researchers at universities to share information from supercomputers. In addition, the new Internet is testing technology that will eventually move to the current Internet backbone.[7] The Internet2 is expected

Figure 2.2 How the I-Way Works

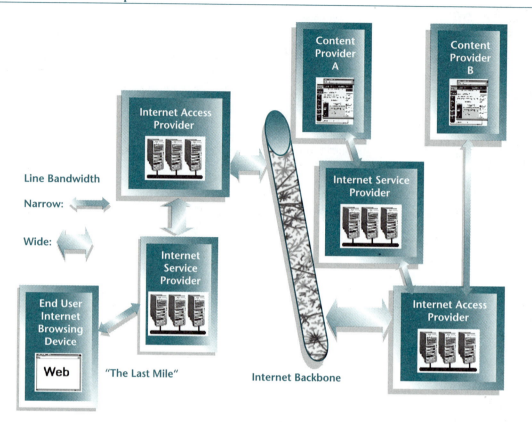

to allow for video and voice to travel over the Internet. Although these high-bandwidth lines allow for the delivery of large amounts of content, they still must be squeezed through the last mile to the individual's access device.

The Last-Mile Lines

Information must move through some type of pipeline to reach the end user. Business users are more likely to have high-bandwidth access to their local area networks and to the Internet backbone. Even though more than three-quarters of the homes in the United States have access to broadband connections, most home users use low-bandwidth connections. This is expected to change, as shown in Figure 2.3. Both cable and DSL are expected to gain dominance in broadband connections.[8]

The following sections outline the types of lines used to carry digital information the last mile.

Figure 2.3   U.S. Broadband Access (Homes in Thousands)

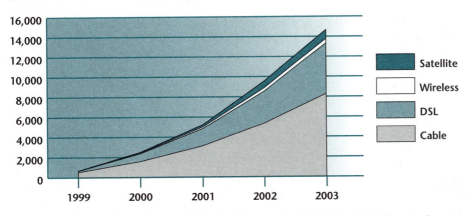

Source: Roger O. Crockett and Andy Reinhardt, "Where to Find Warp Speed," *BusinessWeek*,
         October 18, 1999.

Twisted Pair

Thin copper wires twisted together are used for analog telephones. An analog
signal is turned into a digital signal for a computer by using a modem. In most
cases, the low-bandwidth capability of the twisted pair wire has limited the speed
of phone modems to 56 Kbps. Currently, new technology is allowing twisted pair
lines to carry broadband signals. A DSL allows high-bandwidth connections but
may require the upgrading of older twisted pair wires in a home or business.

The advantage for phone companies is that they have twisted pair lines
running into most homes in the United States and have the ability to switch users
around their network. Phone companies also have the ability to operate both
upstream from the user to someone else and **downstream** to the user. The main
limitation on DSL is the short distance that broadband information can be sent
over the twisted pair lines (between 10,000 and 18,000 feet from a sending
source). Some providers increase DSL reach by using fiber-optic lines to carry data
to DSL access equipment, which then reconnects to existing copper lines.[9]

Upstream traffic *is communication from the browser to the
provider. This usually requires
small amounts of data to be
sent back to the provider,
which may then send large files*
downstream *to the browser.*

Coaxial

Cable television systems most often use **coaxial cables**, which are designed to
carry a high-bandwidth analog signal to home users. Coaxial lines can also be
made to operate with digital signals but require a cable modem for analog televisions. Cable companies can broadcast signals downstream to homes, but all homes
must share the same line. Coaxial-based Internet connections are expected to
increase. This means that many homes will be using a common line for Internet
access. As more packets of digital information are sent over a common line, access
rates may slow.

Fiber-Optic

Fiber-optic lines use light to carry digital signals. These pure digital lines provide very high bandwidths. Computers can use the digital signals they carry, but analog phones or analog televisions cannot use the digital signal. Fiber-optic systems are used throughout the telecommunications backbone but have not been widely installed in individual homes. Around the world this is starting to change. Builders in the United States, Sweden, and Japan are installing fiber-optic lines in new homes and apartments. These 10-Mbps connections allow for a number of phone lines, digital TV channels, and Internet access. This has become a selling point for these homes.[10]

Wireless

Wireless Internet access for home users can be provided through fixed **wireless** systems (broadcast between the user and a land-based receiving station), satellite broadcast systems, radio broadcast systems, and cellular telephone systems. Direct digital broadcast uses the same technology as personal satellite digital television for Internet content. This allows users in remote locations to receive high-bandwidth Internet access. In the past, satellite users were required to use phones for upstream signals. Hughes Network Systems' Direcway (http://www.hns.com) allows Internet users to bypass wire connections and communicate directly with geostationary satellites.

Some Internet service providers bypass Internet access providers by using satellite linkups that can be cheaper and easier to use than landlines. Companies such as Clearwire (http://www.clearwire.com) use an IP network to link to local radio broadcast towers that allow wireless Internet access from an end user's browser.[11] These ventures may or may not replace landlines, but wireless telecommunications are growing in countries where landlines do not exist or are too expensive to build.

Local wireless connections are promising to link small appliances and devices to the Internet. Systems such as Bluetooth (http://www.bluetooth.com) allow an electronic chip to act as a wireless sending and receiving system. This would connect products to the Internet at speeds up to 1 Mbps. Such systems could replace cables between devices in a network and allow gas meters, televisions, lights, and even toasters to connect to the Internet.[12]

Cellular wireless systems are developing rapidly around the world. Pagers, telephones, and handheld devices are linking to the Internet through wireless application protocols (WAPs), giving access to e-mail and Web pages. Over 1 billion people worldwide have access to cellular phones, and one-quarter of those are expected to have Internet access.[13] The United States is expected to lag behind Western Europe and Asia in mobile commerce revenue. In Japan, NTT's DoCoMo i-mode users (http://www.nttdocomo.com) have an always-on Internet connection and use cellular systems to spend an average of $21.60 a month on downloading music and purchasing CDs and other services such as banking, weather, and ticketing.[14] Figure 2.4 shows that wireless Internet commerce is expected to grow

Figure 2.4   Mobile Commerce Revenues (U.S. Dollars in Billions)

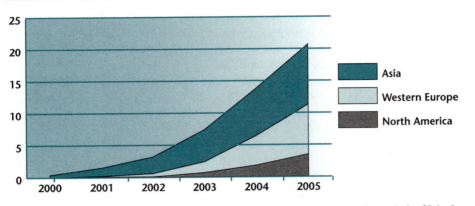

Source: Rajat Paharia, Laura Pfeifer, and Thomas J. Kosnik, "Should You Be Thinking Wireless?" *1to1 Magazine,* May/June 2001, 34–37.

faster outside of the United States. While wireless access allows a worldwide reach for the Internet, small screens, low bandwidth, and security concerns can limit the types of content delivered to a wireless device.

I Want My iTV

Media and telecommunications companies have been promising broadband Internet access linked to set-top boxes or digital televisions. This would allow interactive gaming, full-color videophone calls, home video shopping, and movies on demand. Digital HDTV (high-definition television), however, has not grown at a rate high enough to replace analog TV's dominance in American homes. By 2006, only 9 percent of U.S. homes are expected to have HDTV, far from the expected 85 percent.[15]

This does not mean that iTV is dead. Interactive TV is a reality in some countries in Europe, especially in Scandinavia and Great Britain. In Denmark a children's television game show called *ROFL* allows for audience participation. In the United States many broadcasters have been pioneering Web site simulcast to support programming. A *Drew Carey Show* simulcast required viewers to watch TV and use the Internet at the same time. This show captured 1.7 million viewers and 2 million hits on the associated Web site, with 650,000

case 2.1

Streaming Video

High-bandwidth information highways are fostering the use of Webcast video. Webcast video allows for the streaming of video signals to an individual's Web-accessing device. This technology is being used to deliver conference and entertainment video content where individuals have high-bandwidth Internet connections. Over half of U.S. workers use broadband at their jobs to access streaming video to facilitate meetings between business locations and gain access to live video broadcasts of concerts, sporting events, and news coverage.[16]

There are problems in delivering streaming video. Plug-in players must be added to the Web browser. In addition, each time an individual requests a video, a great deal of data must move over the Internet.[17]

downloads of video streams. Viewers participated even though they had to switch between a television and a PC.[18]

The growth of iTV is expected to offer many benefits. It allows for instant ordering of products or information related to a product. The number of software layers needed to access the Internet would be reduced. Younger viewers are used to and demand Internet access from multiple devices, and broadband-rich content can be delivered. There are also a number of problems. Television is a device that broadcasts to many individuals at one time, and a single individual often uses the Internet. Broadcasters must develop new advertising strategies to reach their markets and hold viewers on their channel. This will require individuals to interact with their televisions in a new way. La-Z-Boy is ready. The company has designed a new e-cliner that comes with a Microsoft WebTV receiver and an infrared keyboard on a foldout tray.[19]

▶ **Thinking Strategically: Case 2.1**

Consider the importance of streaming media. Determine how this will change the nature of communication over the Internet. Decide which types of devices will need to be used to maximize the use of streaming video. Explain how this will affect business and marketing practices.

Digital Convergence

Digital convergence implies that multiple technologies will be used to access the Internet. For example, telephones will use IP standards to send and receive e-mail and Web page data, televisions will be able to access the Net, and computers will be accessible from other independent IP devices. The Internet superhighway consists of fiber-optic wires, coaxial cables, satellites, and cellular and radio broadcast systems allowing for always-on-and-everywhere Internet access. Over the next few years the question will not be, Is it possible to access the Internet? but rather, How much bandwidth, and therefore content, can be delivered? America Online has attempted to place its Internet access everywhere. AOLAnywhere is a strategy designed to capture individuals at all points of Internet access from a PC, telephone, cellular phone, or other Internet appliance.

Security

Security of Web sites is an important consideration for the company with an online presence, for the hosting service, and for the individual user of a Web site. **Firewalls** are security measures designed to prevent hackers from gaining access through a server to a Web site. For promotion-only sites, the most that may happen is that the page design could be changed, but when the Web site is the access point to an intranet, extranet, or e-commerce application, the implications are much more grave. Web sites can be hacked, or broken into. This can result in information being changed or stolen. Firewall software is designed to limit entry into a network to authorized users and content. Entry is controlled through registrations and passwords. Firewalls by themselves are not enough to prevent attacks, however, because employees represent the greatest threat to networks. Employees have access to security procedures and computer terminals, and they know what important types of data are stored.[20]

Another method of increasing security is the use of a **virtual private network (VPN).** A VPN can connect two businesses, such as a franchise and its headquarters, by using dedicated lines (lines not open to outside users) connected to ISPs. The ISPs then use the Internet for long-distance communication, encrypting all data packets. This allows for higher levels of security between the local business and the ISP, making it less likely that outsiders can access corporate information. Establishing a VPN is cheaper than using dedicated lines for long-distance communication.[21]

Source: <http://www.aol.com/anywhere/index.html>. AOL screenshot © 2002 America Online, Inc. Used with permission.

Cybercrime

For e-business to grow, consumers and businesses need to feel safe to engage in business activity online. The ease of engaging in Web transactions, the low cost of entry, and the ability to do business across borders make the Internet a prime venue for **cybercrime,** or criminal activity on the Internet. This includes direct attacks on the Internet infrastructure, such as hacking and viruses.

The Political, Legal, and Ethical Environment

Access and Equity

Computers are currently the main interface to the Internet, and without a home PC and an ISP, access is limited. Those who have higher incomes are much more likely to be able to afford computers and line connection fees. This inequity can result in an ethical dilemma, with disparity between the information rich and the information poor. This is called the **digital divide**. In the United States the digital divide has been narrowing, but families earning less than twenty thousand dollars per year still have only one-quarter of the computers owned by families earning more than seventy-five thousand dollars per year. The U.S. government has attempted to address this problem by implementing the E-rate program. This program, part of the 1996 Telecommunications Act, was designed to provide funding for universal Internet service for schools and libraries. The E-rate program provides a lower educational rate and is funded by an additional charge to telephone long-distance services.[22]

There is also disparity of access between countries. Countries are concerned about Internet access for their populations, but for different reasons. Some countries do not wish to expand Internet access because they want to limit their population's access to information. Some countries are too poor to have an Internet infrastructure. Worldwide, 88 percent of Internet users live in industrialized countries that represent only 2 percent of the world's population. There are more Internet accounts in London than in all of Africa. This can be seen in the global Internet traffic map shown in Figure 2.1. Other countries want to open up access to prepare future workforces. Puerto Rico, for example, has given families who live in public housing free Internet access to expand employment and educational opportunities.[23]

Hacking

Hacking includes at least two types of offenses: infrastructure attack and economic espionage. **Infrastructure attack** occurs when an individual interferes with the operations of a computer system. This could involve something as prankish as changing the CIA's or the *New York Times*'s home page or much more serious violations such as rerouting Web traffic or denial-of-service attacks. In 1997, a domain name registration service, AlterNIC, rerouted Web users who were trying to reach the InterNIC domain name registration service. This attack disrupted service for thousands of Web users and resulted in the arrest of the AlterNIC founder. **Distributed denial-of-service (DDoS) attacks** have been launched at Amazon.com, Buy.com, CNN.com, eBay, and others. Such attacks flood a Web site with so much traffic that legitimate users cannot access the site. This can occur when single or multiple servers are set up to stream connection requests.[24]

Economic espionage occurs when individuals steal intellectual property. The most likely sources of this type of theft are disgruntled employees, employees who want to start their own businesses, employees about to be laid off, and recently fired employees. It is estimated that Fortune 1000 companies lost more than $45 billion from thefts of proprietary information in 1999.[25]

Hackers *are individuals who attempt to break through online firewalls for pleasure or profit. They hack their way into computer networks.*

Companies defend against hacking by using firewalls and ethical hackers—individuals hired to find ways around a company's firewall to identify security problems. The U.S. government takes the threat of hacker attacks so seriously that it has developed a cyberdefense structure with a national coordinator for security, infrastructure protection, and counterterrorism. This coordinator works with the FBI and other agencies to protect against attacks to the information infrastructure from other countries, terrorists, and cyberpunks.[26] The United States government has set up the National Infrastructure Protection Center (NIPC) (http://www.nipc.gov) to detect, deter, assess, warn against, respond to, and investigate unlawful acts that threaten or target critical technology infrastructures.[27]

Historical nSite

The CIA's Web site was hacked and its Web page name changed from Central Intelligence Agency to Central Stupidity Agency.

Viruses

The Internet can also be used to transfer viruses. The Melissa virus was the first virus to spread through e-mail. This virus hijacked Microsoft's Outlook software to send itself to others in the system's e-mail address book. In the year 2000, the Love Bug worm, a specialized virus, was the fastest spreading worm in history, causing an estimated $2 to $15 billion in damage. This worm not only replicated but also damaged computer files and stole passwords. The developer of the virus was a college student in Manila in the Philippines.[28]

> ### ▶ Thinking Strategically: Case 2.2

Describe some of the damage that could result from the creation of the Melissa virus. Explain why an individual would want to create a virus and release it on the Internet. What damage resulted from the threatening e-mail message sent to the high school? Discuss why someone would want to send such an e-mail message. How will the publicity on the rapid capture of these individuals affect future attacks over the Internet?

case 2.2

Fingered on the Net

The Melissa virus would show up as an e-mail with an attachment. If the recipient opened the attached file, it displayed a list of pornography sites. The virus then replicated itself by hijacking the individual's address book and sending a copy of itself to the top fifty names. Some business Internet servers crashed because of the amount of e-mail generated. As each new recipient opened the file, the virus spread. David L. Smith, the virus creator, spent less than three minutes modifying an earlier virus to create Melissa. Smith's actions were tracked by a number of virus hunters, and in one week he was caught. Smith faced a penalty of forty years in prison and a $480,000 fine.[29] The Love Bug worm operated much like the Melissa virus but was more destructive. The developer was located in the Philippines, but that country did not have laws to prosecute hackers.

In 2000, a high school student received an e-mail message threatening his school. The student showed the message to school administrators, and the threatened school went on winter break early. The sender of the e-mail was tracked and arrested. The message sender, another high school student in a different part of the country, faced a possibility of five years in prison and a $250,000 fine.

The Role of an Internet Service Provider

As shown in Figure 2.2 on page 30, both individual users and content providers need an Internet service provider (ISP) to access the Internet backbone. While total ISP revenue has been growing, the number of ISPs in the United States and Europe has been shrinking. In the year 2001, there were more than 6,000 ISPs offering business access services in the United States, but the top ten had more than 65 percent of all access revenues in 2000. In Europe, the total number of ISPs decreased from 4,000 to 70 between the years 2000 and 2001, with the large telecommunications companies holding about 50 percent of the total European market.[30] These trends will continue as ISPs are forced to offer broadband and wireless access to customers. These new investments may be too large for small ISPs. Figure 2.5 illustrates that the majority of online access is with ISPs holding less than 2 percent of the market, while the largest six ISPs hold close to 50 percent.

For businesses the current trends are toward outsourcing part or all of the technology support needed for e-businesses. This allows a firm to focus on core competencies and lets the service provider worry about the technological aspects of Internet connection, software, hardware, and all the other infrastructure components.[31] Studies have found that more than 73 percent of companies outsource some or all Web hosting and applications.[32] ISPs become **ASPs (application service providers)** when they perform specific applications for businesses. These applications include e-commerce transactions, server co-locating, intranet and extranet access, groupware and e-mail, and others. ASPs can minimize costs for firms, allow competition across global markets, let businesses focus on core competencies, and limit demands on a firm's IT staff.[33]

ISPs with international reach allow global businesses to have Web servers on numerous continents. In this way, corporations can target information to each location and avoid sending content over ocean cables, which can bottleneck information flows. In addition, companies that specialize in Web access can meet demand during peak periods. Barnes & Noble (http://www.bn.com) co-locates servers to support its Web site and outsources content for its GameStop site (http://www.gamestop.com) with a company that **mirrors** content on servers in thirty-five countries. Barnes & Noble's traffic volume is steady at its core site, where data for 1 million current titles and 20 million out-of-print titles is supported. The GameStop site has demand peaks when new game titles are released. Outsourced servers can move high-demand content close to the visitor.[34]

Around the world, **cybercafes** are filling the gap in Internet access for individuals. The Himalayan kingdom of Bhutan received television broadcasts for the first time in 1999, but by 2000 there were two cybercafes in the capital city. In 2001 China had an estimated 75,000 cybercafes. Many countries have been closing cybercafes. For some countries, this has been an attempt to control individual access to censured information such as pornography or political thought. For others, the Internet is seen as a competitor to state-owned telecommunications systems.[35]

ISPs provide Internet access. An **application service provider (ASP)** *uses the Internet to provide, on a subscription basis, applications and services a business would normally provide for itself.*

A **mirrored site** *is a Web site placed on more than one ISP, allowing less congestion and faster delivery of content.*

A **cybercafe** *is a small business that offers Internet access. This may be for a fee or as a draw to a business that offers coffee or food.*

Figure 2.5   U.S. Home Market ISP Share

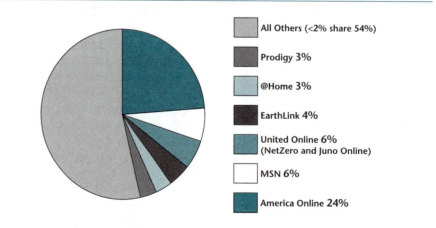

Source: Patricia Fusco, "Top U.S. ISPs by Subscriber: Q3 2001," Compaq ISP Planet [online] (November 2, 2001), available from <http://isp-planet.com/research/rankings/usa.html>.

Courtesy of Nii Abrahams.

The Political Environment

The U.S. government helped create the Internet by sponsoring and providing funding for early versions of the ARPANET, NSFNET, and Internet. Once the Internet had grown to a sustainable level, the government turned it over to the private sector. This same process is being followed around the world as governments deregulate the telecommunications industry. One of the roles that governments take is the fostering of business opportunities. The U.S. government is currently funding the development of a next-generation Internet (NGI); it has invested more than $300 million to fund pure research on increasing the speed of

E-Business Professionals

Rodney Blaukat
President
Intruos
http://www.intruos.com

Rodney Blaukat

Intruos got its start when Rodney Blaukat and his partner Robert Madole opened an ISP called Net Advantage. This ISP served both business and home users. The home users provided little of the ISP's income but took up a lot of management time, so Intruos was built from the business client base of Net Advantage. Intruos is now a small ISP specializing in developing and hosting business sites.

Smaller ISPs can gain competitive advantages through strong customer service. Intruos prides itself on working with businesses to evaluate their entire business model and determine how to leverage the Internet to meet business goals. Mr. Blaukat says, "Businesses today realize that they need to move beyond brochure sites to developing more interactive sites. We specialize in face-to-face contact with clients, helping them develop e-business strategies."

Intruos helps businesses by getting product information online, listing inventory, setting up document centers, and offering e-commerce opportunities. Businesses use ISPs like Intruos because it is less expensive than attempting to develop and host content on their own.

The challenges that Intruos faces include the movement toward broadband and wireless applications. In addition, the Internet is a global medium, and Intruos must be able to offer 24/7 services for its clients.

To work in this high-growth entrepreneurial business, college students must have strong personal-relationship skills. Students must be able to conduct competitive analyses, work with clients, and understand e-business well enough to help integrate technology into business functions.

the Internet by up to one thousand times.[36] Governments around the world are also facing a dilemma in imposing order to the current Internet. They do not want to hinder the growth of the Internet, but they often protect a number of constituencies. To avoid regulation, the Internet industry is in favor of self-regulation and software solutions rather than government intervention.

In 1996, the Clinton administration attempted to control the Internet with the Communications Decency Act. This act authorized criminal fines of $250,000 and a two-year jail sentence for those who intentionally transmitted indecent material or made it available online. The Internet community vehemently opposed this action. ISPs did not want to be responsible for what their customers posted on ISP sites. The federal courts ruled that ISPs are like bookstores in that they hold material but are not responsible for what is made available for others to view. This view of ISPs is not necessarily similar to that in other countries. An ISP in France was held liable for allowing a subscriber to place nude and seminude pictures of a model on a Web page. The French judge ruled that the ISP must monitor the content of its Web pages to ensure that no third party would be hurt.[37]

Global e-business requires an infrastructure that is reliable and secure. Intensified competition is forcing new infrastructures, lower prices, and more Internet services. In response, governments around the world are deregulating their telecommunications systems.[38] The World Bank has taken an active role in helping to wire developing countries to the Internet as a means of fostering business growth.[39]

The federal government believes that Internet commerce will have a major impact on the U.S. and world economies and has developed a National Telecommunications and Information Administration (NTIA) (http://www.ntia.doc.gov) to work with other countries to make the Internet a tariff-free zone and keep government regulations out of Internet commerce. The NTIA has set three principles for global electronic commerce: provide greater access for all Americans, champion greater foreign market access, and create new opportunities with technology. Table 2.3 outlines laws passed by the U.S. Congress in 1998 to help set the rules for e-businesses in the United States.

The World Wide Web

Source: <http://www.intruos.com>

"If I didn't give it away, it wouldn't have happened."

Tim Berners-Lee[40]

The **World Wide Web**, or **Web**, uses the Internet backbone to send information from servers, or repositories of file information, to browsers, or software designed to present the files. The Web facilitates the transfer of hypermedia-based files, allowing links to other pages, places, or applications. By following a hyperlink on a Web page, the user can transfer to anyplace in the world through the Internet backbone.

Table 2.3   U.S. Laws Governing the Internet

Law	Description
The Internet Tax Freedom Law	This law sets a national policy against interfering with interstate commerce over the Internet and imposes a moratorium on taxes for commerce over the Internet.
The Child Online Protection Act	Online distributors of material harmful to minors must restrict access to minors, according to this law. Web site operators must check visitors' IDs or face $50,000 in fines and six months in prison for each access by a minor.
The Child Protection and Sexual Predator Punishment Act	This act imposes penalties for using the Internet to send obscene material to a person under age sixteen or to sexually solicit minors. ISPs must report child pornography as soon as they are made aware of it.
The Children's Online Privacy Protection Act of 1998	Another child protection act that establishes a framework for regulating the unfair collection of personal information from children over the Internet.
The Government Paperwork Elimination Act	This legislation makes it possible to use electronic signatures for forms submitted to federal agencies.
The Digital Millennium Copyright Act	An act that sets rules for copyrighted material online. It helps limit ISPs' liability for copyright infringements by their customers and outlaws technology that can crack copyright protection devices.

Case 2.3

The Race to Wire the World

In 1998, North America accounted for close to 55 percent of the 149 million wordwide Web users. By 2002, the distribution of Web users had changed. Figure 2.6 shows that North America had only 35 percent of the projected 513 million worldwide Web users, Western Europe had 30 percent, and the Asia/Pacific region had 28 percent.[42] Growth within these regions is not evenly distributed. In 1999, Northern Europe had Internet access at near equivalency to the United States, while Southern Europe had little access. For example, only 2.9 percent of Greek citizens had access to the Internet.[43]

Tim Berners-Lee developed the World Wide Web in 1990 at the Particle Physics Laboratory in Geneva, Switzerland, as a means for helping particle physicists communicate worldwide. The Web architecture was designed to emulate the human brain by allowing the linkage of random associations.[41] The development of Web graphical browsers and the use of HyperText Transfer Protocols (HTTP) have allowed easy access to data at remote locations. Just as the Internet has protocols to govern the use and transport of data, the Web has its own set of standards (see Chapter 2 Appendix).

▶ Thinking Strategically: Case 2.3

Consider the growth of the Internet around the world. Determine how this will affect the content available online. If customers around the world are able to access the Internet, how important it is for a business to have an Internet presence? Consider what the language of the Web will be. Will a company need to have Web sites designed for multiple languages? Speculate on the social impact of the Internet when the world is connected.

Figure 2.6   World Share of Internet Users

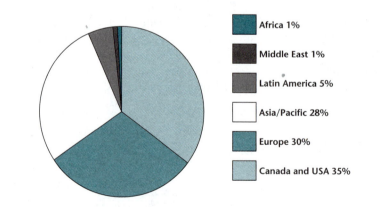

- Africa 1%
- Middle East 1%
- Latin America 5%
- Asia/Pacific 28%
- Europe 30%
- Canada and USA 35%

The Browser

The growth of the Web is due to GUI (graphical user interface) browsers that allow the user to access Web data without using UNIX- or DOS-based procedures. Mosaic, the first Web browser, could be downloaded free from the National Supercomputer Center. A number of companies licensed the technology of the browser. Netscape allowed users to download its browser for free. This strategy allowed Netscape to grow rapidly and become a standard for the industry.

Netscape used this leverage to help sell its server software to ISPs and content providers.[44] Netscape initially was able to capture 85 percent of the browser market. As competitors (such as Spry's Air Mosaic, Netcom's Netcruiser, and others) fell by the wayside, Microsoft introduced its Internet Explorer. By 1997, Netscape had only 50.5 percent of the browser market, with Internet Explorer at 22.8 percent, AOL at 16.1 percent, and all others accounting for 10.6 percent.[45] In 1998, AOL purchased Netscape and took control of its browser division. By 2002, Internet Explorer had close to 87.7 percent of the market, while AOL/Netscape's share was close to 12 percent. All others had less than a 0.3 percent share.[46]

The **browser** is the interface between the Web content and the user. The browser takes information and codes and then displays the requested design on the screen. For example, HTML code indicates color, location, size, hyperlinks, and so forth. When a hyperlink is clicked, the browser pulls up the associated file to present. New versions of code are continually being developed for the Web. This requires new versions of browsers to read the latest codes, such as JavaScript, DHTML, XML, and the most popular plug-ins. **Plug-ins** allow rich content files, such as video, radio, and other multimedia content, to play through browsers. Some plug-ins allow the streaming of content. **Streaming** brings in a number of smaller packets of information to load and play. One packet can play while others are loading, which allows seamless media presentations (see Chapter 2 Appendix). Figure 2.7 illustrates how a browser works.

The Browser as an Operating System

Because a browser can display documents, play multimedia, and run programs, it acts as a de facto **operating system.** If a single browser was to become the industry standard for systems other than PCs, it could replace Windows as the dominant operating system.[47] For this reason, Microsoft has taken an active role in setting new browser standards. It has developed operating systems for handheld, wireless, and iTV Internet systems. Windows XP is designed to integrate

An operating system is the program that controls a computer. Windows XP is an operating system, as are Linux, Mac OS, Windows NT, and DOS.

Figure 2.7   Server Browser Interactions

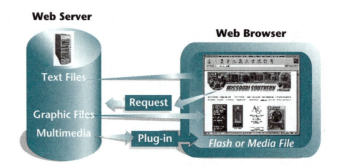

Internet features into the PC operating system. It is optimized to run Microsoft's Internet Explorer and link to the Microsoft Network (an ISP).[48] Microsoft has been accused of designing Internet Explorer so that it will play files and programs using Microsoft's standards better than those using the open standards available on the Internet.[49] Microsoft's .NET strategy is an attempt to bring Internet standards such as XML into Microsoft applications. Internet Explorer 6, however, was developed to not be compatible with Sun's Java language (an industry standard). The new browser required a plug-in to play Java-enhanced Web content.

The Web Site

Top-level domains (TLDs) are the letters to the right of the dot in a domain name. There are two types: generic (such as .com, .edu, .net) and country (such as .ie [Ireland], .de [Germany]).

For someone to visit a site, Internet addressing systems must be able to locate the IP address and domain name. The current IP address structure consists of four numbers separated by dots (e.g., 111.222.333.444). Internet name servers use these addresses like telephone numbers. An individual user does not need to know the IP address to access a site; instead, the site uses a unique domain name such as www.mssc.edu. **Domain names** are issued by accredited registrars. Originally, the U.S. government gave control of domain name registration to one company: Network Solutions (now VeriSign (http://www.verisign.com). Currently, the Internet Corporation for Assigned Names and Numbers (ICANN) acts as a coordination body for the Internet. ICANN was created in October 1998 as a not-for-profit organization to assume responsibility for the technical functions previously performed by the U.S. government. It coordinates the assignment of Internet domain names, IP address numbers, and protocol parameters. ICANN also authorizes domain name registrar companies and **top-level domains (TLDs)**. By the beginning of 2002, there were more than 33 million domains registered, of which 23 million were .com domains. This has motivated the Internet community to add TLDs.

Strategic nSite

Why Not Have Multiple TLDs?

When a company such as Amazon.com owns a domain name with a single TLD, it worries that new TLDs could allow other companies to cybersquat, or highjack, its brand name. To prevent this, firms buy all the new TLDs, such as Amazon.biz and Amazon.info.

Table 2.4   Web Top-Level Domains

Old Top-Level Domains	Meaning	New Top-Level Domains	Meaning
.com	Commercial Enterprise	.aero	Air-Transport Company
.edu	Educational Organization	.biz	Business
.gov	Government Agency	.coop	Cooperative
.org	Nonprofit Organization	.info	Information Service
.net	Network Company	.museum	Museum
.mil	U.S. Department of Defense	.name	Individual
.int	International Organization	.pro (proposed)	Professional, such as accountant, lawyer, physician, etc.
National Domain	**Country**	**National Domain**	**Country**
.ca	Canada	.au	Australia
.gb	United Kingdom	.se	Sweden
.de	Germany	.tv	Tuvalu
.fr	France	.us	United States

The domain name registration system allows registrars such as Network Solutions to maintain the dissemination of .com, .org, and .gov group names and allows other companies to handle new domain group names. National governments control the registration for their respective countries, such as .fr or .uk. To obtain a domain name, a site must have a server linked to the Internet backbone. Table 2.4 outlines the old and new TLDs.

Figure 2.8 shows a **URL (universal resource locator)** address for a Web page at Missouri Southern State College. The college's domain name (http://www.mssc.edu) is part of the URL.

Choosing a Domain Name

Like many companies, Computer Literacy wanted to change its name. The company hired the brand research company Interbrand (http://www.interbrand.com) to aid in

Figure 2.8   Universal Resource Locator

http://www.mssc.edu/pages/mssc.htm.

Hypertext Protocol	WWW Page	Host	Group	File Path	File Name	Hypertext Markup File Type

DOMAIN NAME

this process. Interbrand started with a list of twenty-five thousand names. This list had to be checked for legal clearances and to be sure there were no existing URLs. After these checks, none of the remaining names seemed to fit the company. Computer Literacy's editorial director, Deborah Bohn, came up with the name Fatbrain and the domain name http://www.Fatbrain.com. After testing, the company decided to change its name, even though some employees threatened to quit if the new name was used. When the company changed its name, its stock price rose and the number of site visits increased 200 percent.[50]

Cybersquatting *is the practice of registering domain names, even trademarked names, with the intent to sell them at a later date.*

Domain names are important for businesses. Businesses need to find domain names that match the image they want to project, and they need to protect those names against **cybersquatters.** Domain names have sold for very high prices. The domain name http://www.Business.com sold for $7.5 million. With the new top-level domain name structure, companies are forced to purchase not only the .com but also the .biz domains. The Anticybersquatting Consumer Protection Act (ACPA) makes cybersquatting on a trademarked name illegal. To have names protected, firms can file complaints through a Uniform Domain Name Dispute Resolution Policy with the domain name registry companies. This act does not protect companies worldwide. Gateway owns three Web addresses, but since each country has its own TLD, there are thirty-nine other Gateway registrations around the world with country TLDs. The company About.com spent close to a half million dollars to purchase four thousand domain names to control http://www.about.com and all possible combinations.[51]

Historical nSite

Symbolics at http://www.symbolics.com was the first dot-com company to go live on March 15, 1985. The company is now out of business.

The Future of the Web

Infrastructures can become entrenched in a society. In the United States, electrical power for homes started with 110-volt systems.

These systems are less efficient than the 220-volt systems found throughout much of the rest of the world. The U.S.-based broadcast television system developed first and therefore has fewer lines per screen (resulting in a poorer quality picture) than broadcasts in many other countries. U.S.-based cellular systems started as an analog infrastructure, and they have had to convert to digital. Plans for converting analog television broadcasts to digital HDTV broadband in

the United States have slowed to a crawl. Once an infrastructure has developed, consumers purchase equipment to use the technology. The likelihood that U.S. consumers will convert to 220-volt systems or purchase new digital televisions is about as high as the likelihood of the United States converting to the metric system. Consumers accept new technologies only when they see a clear advantage in doing so.

Infrastructure changes thus involve an interplay between the consumer, the technology company, and the content providers. For the Internet, manufacturers will mass-produce equipment to pull in rich media content when they see consumers demand such equipment, but content providers do not want to invest in rich content when there is no market for their product. Even though PCs are being sold "Internet ready," current computers are not designed to take full advantage of the type of information that can be sent digitally over the Internet. The PC is first a computer, then a multimedia player. Most consumers have a television, which is a multimedia player that can be turned into an Internet device at one-tenth the cost of a PC. In the United States, however, television screen quality does not match PC monitor quality.

Three major changes are affecting Internet technology. The first is the movement toward high-bandwidth delivery. This is already underway with the use of coaxial cable, DSL, satellite, and fiber-optic systems. The second is the movement of the Internet to devices other than the PC. Worldwide, iTV households using on-demand services are expected to jump from 1.3 million in 2001 to more than 33 million in 2005. This is currently being driven by video-on-demand. North American video-on-demand revenues are forecasted to grow from $86 million in 2001 to more than $1.75 billion by 2005.[52] The third change is the growth of wireless technologies. A study by the Intermarket Group (http://www.intermarket group.com) projects that the number of wireless Internet users in the world will grow to about 729 million by 2005, an eighteen-fold increase from 2000. Europe is expected to have the highest concentration of wireless Internet users at 194 million, followed by North America with 89 million, Asia with 79 million, and Latin America with 52 million.[53]

Regardless of the delivery system for the Internet, the growth of the Internet has remained stable since the early 1990s. A study by Dr. Lawrence Roberts (who led the team that developed the ARPANET) of Internet backbone use found that

Internet traffic has been growing annually by a factor of three from April 2000 through the beginning of 2002.[54] The growth of the Internet is due to both business and end-user acceptance of the technologies that underpin e-business. New tools are being developed all the time, and businesses must know how to integrate these into their e-business system.

Knowledge Integration

Terms and Concepts

Analog signals 27
Application service
     provider (ASP) 38
Bandwidth 25
Berners-Lee, Tim 42
Bits per second (bps) 27
Broadband 28
Browser 43
Coaxial cables 31
Computer network 26
Cybercafe 38
Cybercrime 35
Cybersquatting 46
Digital convergence 34
Digital divide 36
Digital signals 27

Distributed denial-of-
     service attacks 36
Domain name 44
Downstream traffic 31
Economic espionage 36
E-mail 25
Fiber-optic line 32
Firewalls 34
Hacking 36
Host 27
Infrastructure 23
Internet 26
Internet service
     provider (ISP) 26
Last mile 24
Mirrored site 38

Open standards 26
Operating system 43
Plug-ins 43
Streaming 43
Top-level
     domain (TLD) 44
Twisted pair 31
Upstream traffic 31
URL (universal resource
     locator) 45
Virtual private
     network 35
Wireless 32
World Wide
     Web (Web) 41

Concepts and Questions for Review

1. Define the term *infrastructure*.
2. Discuss the major players developing the telecommunications infrastructure.
3. What is the Internet and how did it come to be?
4. Describe how the Internet works.
5. Discuss the role of an ISP for an individual and a business.
6. Evaluate the alternatives that a home user has to go online.
7. Recommend a strategy that could be used to bridge the digital divide.
8. What is the World Wide Web?
9. Discuss the importance of a domain name.
10. Differentiate the parts of a URL.
11. Speculate on the future of the World Wide Web.

Active Learning

Exercise 2.1 Chasing the Net Connection

Web users must have access to the Internet. Track a single Web connection starting with an Internet device such as a PC or WebTV. What is used to connect to the last mile: a modem, coaxial cable, or fiber-optic wire? Describe how the speed of the connection influences how the Web is used. Determine how the last mile is connected to the backbone. Is it running through an ISP? Use the ISP's Web page or call the ISP to investigate how it is linked online.

Exercise 2.2 Web Devices

Explore your home and determine what benefits there could be in connecting different appliances to the Net. Explain how an individual's life could be better if remote access to appliances was possible. Speculate on which companies, such as utility companies, could benefit by accessing information from a home or a business. Determine how these connections would be made.

Competitive Exercise 2.3 Which Line to Invest In?

Assume your company has asked your team to evaluate an investment in companies that provide Internet backbone last-mile lines. Your firm will be investing considerable amounts of money in these companies. Evaluate the alternative last-mile connections. Indicate if your company should invest in technologies that are dominant now or ones that may be dominant in the future. Keep in mind that if all teams recommend investing in the same technologies, then there may be too much capacity and therefore lower prices and returns. Develop your arguments based on the issues surfaced in this chapter. Consider both global access questions and digital divide questions.

Web Search—Looking Online

Search Term:	Internet Infrastructure	First 4 out of 105,000,000

NetSizer. Provides Internet and Web growth statistics.
http://www.netsizer.com

HowStuffWorks. Shows how stuff works, including graphics on the Internet.
http://www.howstuffworks.com/category.htm?cat=Intrnt

CoolWapSiteOfTheDay.com. Describes multiple Internet sites related to wireless cellular phones.
http://www.coolwapsiteoftheday.com

DomainStats.com. Tracks the number of registered domain names.
http://www.domainstats.com/

| Search Term: | Internet Maps | First 4 out of 1,950,000 |

Atlas of Cyberspaces. Offers a wide variety of maps showing Internet traffic flows and use.
http://www.geog.ucl.ac.uk/casa/martin/atlas/atlas.html

TeleGeography. Provides maps on telecommunications flows worldwide.
http://www.telegeography.com

Internet Mapping Project. Maps the network associations of the entire Internet.
http://www.cs.bell-labs.com/who/ches/map/index.html

CAIDA (Cooperative Association for Internet Data Analysis). Displays a map of the Internet infrastructure.
http://www.caida.org

| Search Term: | Internet Service Providers | First 6 out of 2,270,000 |

ISP Planet. Provides a portal to ISP information.
http://www.isp-planet.com

HostCompare.com. Allows for the comparison of ISPs.
http://www.hostcompare.com

The Neighborhood. Gives access to MCI, a global business telecommunications company providing local, long-distance, international, and Internet services.
http://www.mci.com

UUNET. Offers Internet service for MCI.
http://www.worldcom.com/uunet

AOLAnywhere. Provides Internet service; the largest of the ISPs for the home market.
http://www.aol.com

Microsoft Network. Sells Internet access; the second largest ISP.
http://www.msn.com

| Search Term: | Internet Regulation | First 9 out of 1,490,000 |

American National Standards Institute. Represents U.S. interests related to the Internet.
http://www.ansi.org

International Organization for Standards. Offers information on standards developed by this international governing body located in Geneva, Switzerland.
http://www.iso.ch

Internet Engineering Task Force. Influences the standards set for the Internet.
http://www.ietf.org

Internet Service Providers' Consortium. Provides support services to other ISPs across the nation.
http://www.ispc.org

Internet2. Brings focus, energy, and resources to the development of new standards of teaching, research, and learning on the Internet.
http://www.internet2.edu

InterNIC. Provides information on domain name registration.
http://www.internic.net

Internet Software Consortium. Advocates maintaining the open source, or standard Internet interface protocols.
http://www.isc.org

World Wide Web Consortium. Governs the set of World Wide Web protocols.
http://www.w3.org

Internet Society. Includes good links to Internet-oriented Web sites for Internet professionals.
http://www.isoc.org

Search Term:	Alternative Net Connections	First 3 out of 2,170,000

Cybercafe Search Engine. Hosts information on how to start and run cybercafes and has a cybercafe search engine.
http://www.cybercaptive.com

DirecPC. Uses a satellite system to allow quick Internet access nationwide.
http://www.direcpc.com

Teledesic. Enables low-orbit satellites to transmit information from person to person.
http://www.teledesic.com

Search Term:	History of the Internet	First 4 out of 3,100,000

Internet Society. Provides a source page on the history of the Internet.
http://www.isoc.org/internet/history/index.shtml

Timeline of Hypertext History. Offers a short history of the "Internet's most visible component."
http://www.govtech.net/magazine/gt/1998/oct/untangling/history.phtml

Internet History Metalist. Lists links to Web sites on Internet history.
http://www.isoc.org/internet/history

Wayback Machine. Offers an archive of old Web sites.
http://www.archive.org

Search Term:	Government and Legal	First 5 out of 2,890,000

GigaLaw.com. Provides legal information for Internet and technology professionals.
http://www.GigaLaw.com

National Infrastructure Protection Center (NIPC). Detects, deters, assesses, warns, responds to, and investigates unlawful acts involving computer and information technologies.
http://www.nipc.gov

FindLaw. Offers articles and a searchable database on legal topics, including citations for legal cases.
http://news.findlaw.com/legalnews/scitech/cyber

LegalEthics.com. Helps legal professionals understand the unique ethical issues related to the Internet and Internet technology.
http://www.legalethics.com

Cybercrime.gov. Provides information from the U.S. Department of Justice on cybercrimes related to computer crimes and intellectual property.
http://www.usdoj.gov/criminal/cybercrime/index.html#nifpa

Search Term:	Digital Divide	First 2 out of 555,000

Bridges.org. Offers information on this international nonprofit organization helping to span the global digital divide.
http://www.bridges.org

Americans in the Information Age Falling Through the Net. Accesses a U.S. Department of Commerce report on the digital divide.
http://www.ntia.doc.gov/ntiahome/digitaldivide

References

1   Paul W. Timberlake, "Infrastructure Superhighway," *Intelligent Enterprise,* April 28, 2000, 55–59.
2   John Steele Gordon, "The Golden Spike," *Forbes ASAP,* February 21, 2000, 118–22; Peter Drucker, "Beyond the Information Revolution," *Atlantic,* October 1999, 47–57.
3   "Europemedia: US No Longer Dominates Email," in NUA [online] (July 12, 2001), available from <http://www.nua.com/surveys/index.cgi?f=VS&art_id=905356969&rel=true>.
4   Gary H. Anthes, "The History of the Future," *Computerworld,* October 3, 1994, 101.
5   Ibid., 101–5.

6 Mary Lisbeth D'Amico, "Danish Providers Lure Users with Free Internet Access," *InfoWorld,* May 17, 1999, 48H; Stephen Baker, Jack Ewing, and Kerry Capell, "The Race to Wire Europe," *BusinessWeek,* June 7, 1999, 48–50; Paula Musich, "Bandwidth Boon for Europe?" *PC Week,* July 12, 1999, 86.

7 Apryl Lundsten and Eileen Flick, "Internet2: Making the Connection," *Syllubus,* March 2001, 10–14; "About Internet2," in Internet2 [online] (December 5, 2001), available from <http://www.internet2.edu/html/about.html>; Barbara Grady, "New Super-Fast Net Being Built," *Internet World,* April 20, 1998, 1, 57; Brian Riggs, "Building a Better Net," *LANTIMES,* February 17, 1997, 39–44.

8 Michael Pastore, "35 Million Broadband Users Predicted by 2006," in CyberAtlas [online] (October 17, 2001), available from <http://cyberatlas.internet.com/markets/broad-band/article/0,,10099_905351,00.html>.

9 Denise Culver, "Broadband Seeds Rural Routes," *Interactive Week,* January 17, 2000, 54.

10 Rob Kirby, "Fiber—Can't Find Its Way Home?" *Network Magazine,* September 2001, 62–67; Bill Scanlon, "Getting the Home Fibers Burning," *Interactive Week,* December 4, 2000, 86.

11 Sarah L. Roberts-Witt, "Clearwire Technologies," *Internet World,* January 15, 2000, 44–45.

12 Stephen Baker, "A Revolution Called Bluetooth," *BusinessWeek,* September 18, 2000, 62–64; Andy Dornan, "Can Bluetooth Sink Its Teeth into Networking?" *Network Maga-zine,* 54–60.

13 "One Billion Mobile Users and Still Counting," in Mobile E-Commerce World [online] (November 22, 2001), available from <http://www.mobilecommerceworld.com/Tmpl/article.asp?CID=1&AID=10156&TCode=NW&T1=3/12/2001>; Brad Stone, "A Portable Web," *Newsweek,* January 17, 2000, 54–56.

14 "Japan's I-Mode Users Spend US $21.60 a Month," in Mobile E-Commerce World [online] (November 21, 2001), available from <http://www.mobilecommerceworld.com/Tmpl/article.asp?CID=1&AID=10165&TCode=NW&T1=26/11/2001>; Irene M. Kunii and Stephen Baker, "Japan's Mobile Marvel," *BusinessWeek,* January 17, 2000.

15 Thomas W. Hazlett, "The Vision Thing," *Forbes,* February 21, 2000, 36.

16 "Nielsen NetRatings: Streaming Media Use Up in US Offices," in NUA [online] (October 15, 2001), available from <http://www.nua.com/surveys/index.cgi?f=VS&art_id=905357297&rel=true>.

17 Neil Gross and Steven V. Brull, "The Net's Next Battle Royal," *BusinessWeek,* June 28, 1999, 108–12; Steven Vonder Haar, "High-Speed Net Access Has Got Game," *Interactive Week,* June 7, 1999, 36; Eric Brown, "Pipe Dreams," *New Media,* April 1999, 34–43.

18 Karen Epper Hoffman, "The Tube Gets Smart," *Internet World,* July 15, 2001, 23–24; Paul Tate, "Euro Vision," *Interactive Week,* April 9, 2001, 59–60; James Karney, "TV or Not TV," *Internet World,* April 1, 2000, 49–54.

19 Steve Jarvis, "iTV Finally Comes Home," *Marketing News,* August 27, 2001, 1, 19; Richard Williamson, "Changing Channels," *Interactive Week,* April 2, 2001, 18–22; Jonathan Blum, "The Battle for the Living Room," *Technology Investor,* April 2000, 36–41

20 Michael Bertin, "The New Security Threats," *Smart Business,* February 2001, 78–86; Jason Levitt and Gregory Smith, "Are You Vulnerable?" *InformationWeek,* February 21, 2000, 79–88; Ira Sager, Steve Hamm, Neil Gross, John Carey, and Robert D. Hof, "Cyber Crime," *BusinessWeek,* February 21, 2000, 36–42.

21 Terr Sweeney, "VPN Extranets: Proceed with Caution," *InternetWeek,* August 2001, 26–27; Ed Bott, "Virtual Private Networks," *Smart Business,* August 2000, 134–41; Kristina B. Sullivan, "VPN Market Tide Rises High," *PC Week,* March 22, 1999, 128; Derek Slater, "What Is a VPN?" *CIO Enterprise,* July 15, 1999, 74.

[22] For more information on this topic, see "Welcome to LearnNet," Federal Communications Commission [online] (November 19, 1998) available from <http://www.fcc.gov/learnet/>; "Welcome to the E-Rate Hotline," E-Rate Hotline [online] (January 13, 1999) available from <http://www.eratehotline.org/>.

[23] Mary E. Thyfault, "Global Opportunities," *InformationWeek,* March 26 2001, 65–72; Dibya Sarkar, "Puerto Rico Plugs in Populace," *Civic.com,* October 2000, 18–19; Beatrice Hogan, "Digital Despot," *Business 2.0,* October 24, 2000, 66–71;

[24] Randy Barrett, "Dot Combat: How to Fend Off an Attack," *Interactive Week,* February 14, 2000, 6–7; Matthew G. Nelson and Beth Bacheldor, "Attacks on E-Businesses Trigger Security Concerns," *InformationWeek,* February 14, 2000, 28–30.

[25] Dan Verton, "The Threat from Within," *Business 2.0,* April 2000, 329–30; Richard Power and Rik Farrow, "Crime and Punishment in Cyberspace," *Network Magazine,* November 1998, 84–85.

[26] Will Rodger, "Cyberwar: Proper Vigilance or Paranoia?" *Interactive Week,* October 5, 1998, 54–56; Tom Field, "Sweat about the Threat," *CIO Enterprise,* December 1, 1998, 34–43.

[27] National Infrastructure Protection Center, [online] (January 3, 2002), available from <http://www.nipc.gov>.

[28] Brad Stone, "Bitten by Love," *Newsweek,* May 15, 2000, 42–44.

[29] Steven Levy, "Biting Back at the Wily Melissa," *Newsweek,* April 12, 1999, 62–64.

[30] "Business ISP Market Faces Consolidation in Face of Weak Economy," Cahners In-Stat Group [online] (October 29, 2001) available from <http://www.instat.com/pr/2001/tx0109sp_pr.htm>; "Major Consolidation In Euro ISP Market" in NUA Internet Surveys [online] (July 5, 2001), available from <http://www.nua.com/surveys/index.cgi?f=VS&art_id=905356946&rel=true>.

[31] Peter Borrows, "Technology on Tap," *BusinessWeek,* June 19, 2000, 74–84; Kate Gerwig, "Easy Street?" *InternetWeek,* June 8, 1998, 67–71.

[32] Michael Pastore, "More Companies Outsourcing Web Hosting," in CyberAtlas [online] (July 27, 1999), available from <http://cyberatlas.internet.com/big_picture/hardware/article/0,,5921_169461,00.html>.

[33] Jim Martin, "Is the ASP Model Defining the Future of IT?" *Midrange Systems,* April 10, 2000, 1, 24.

[34] Ted Kemp, "Barnes & Noble Builds Dual Web Platforms," *InternetWeek,* September 3, 2001, 1, 38.

[35] Juliana Gruenwald, "Cybercafe Crackdown," *Interactive Week,* August 13, 2001, 43–46; Donna Booher, "Remote Access," *Interactive Week,* November 27, 2000, 94.

[36] Scott Berinato, "The Net's Next Frontiers," *PC Week,* March 2, 1998, 21.

[37] Jeffrey D. Neuburger and Jill Westmoreland, "Legal Link," *Silicon Alley Report,* September 1998, 76–78.

[38] Tim Wilson, "Spotty Infrastructure Impairs World View," *InternetWeek,* March 26, 2001, 1, 64–65.

[39] Christopher Kock, "It's a Wired Wired World," *Webmaster,* March 1997, 50–55.

[40] Spencer Reiss, "St. Tim of the Web," *Forbes,* November 15, 1999, 314–16.

[41] Process Software Corporation, "Understanding the Internet and the World Wide Web," supplement to *Internet World,* 1995.

[42] Elizabeth Gardner, "Net Is Advancing Quickly Toward Mass-Media Status in United States," *Internet World,* April 19, 1999, 13–14.

[43] Elizabeth de Bony, "Internet Use Doubles, But Still Low in Europe," *Infoworld,* August 23, 1999, 50B; Baker, Ewing, and Capell, "The Race to Wire Europe."

[44] Robert D. Hof, "From the Man Who Brought You Silicon Graphic . . . ," *BusinessWeek,* October 24, 1994, 90.

[45] James C. Luh, "Is the Browser War Irrelevant?" *Internet World,* June 29, 1998, 5.

[46] "Explorer Dominates Brower Market, Netscape Dwindles," in Internet.com [online] (February 23, 2001), available from <http://siliconvalley.internet.com/news/article/0,2198,3531_597681,00.html>.

[47] J. William Gurley, "The Browser Is the Operating System," *Fortune,* February 16, 1998, 128–30.

[48] Bill Roberts, "Windows 98 Hits the Web—But Who's Buying?" *Internet World,* June 29, 1998, 26.

[49] David Fiedler, "Casting a Developer's Eye on Internet Explorer 5.0," *Internet World,* June 29, 1998, 26, 28.

[50] Cheryl J. Willson, "The Name Game," *Red Herring,* January 2000, 196–200; *Newsweek,* "More Room for Internet Names," July 9, 2001, 12.

[51] Joe Ashbrook Nickell, "What's in a Name?" *Business 2.0,* May 2000, 140–45; Andrew G. McCormick and Laura N. Mankin, "The Death of Cybersquatting?" *CIO,* April, 15, 2000, 60–65.

[52] "'On-Demand' Services Poised to Revive Interest in Interactive TV," Cahner's In-Stat Group [online] (January 16, 2002), available from <http://www.instat.com/press.asp?sku=MB0114MI&Segment=Multimedia%20Broadband%20Services%20%26%20Infrastructure>.

[53] "Intermarket Group: Wireless Web Population to Soar," in NUA [online] (January 16, 2002), available from <http://www.nua.com/surveys/index.cgi?f=VS&art_id=905357560&rel=true>.

[54] "Continued Internet Traffic Growth Portends Upswing in Carrier Spending, Says Internet Founder," in Caspian Networks [online] (January 16, 2002), available from <http://www.caspiannetworks.com/pressroom/press/01.16.02.shtml>.

chapter 2 appendix
Internet Technology

In a modern corporation there is less separation between the technologist and the business strategist. This appendix is designed to give a more in-depth look at the technology that underpins e-business, including information on the Internet backbone, security, the role of standards, and choosing an ISP. With this information, an e-business strategist should be able to participate more fully in the strategic process.

1. Understand how information is routed through the Internet.
2. Be able to explain current and evolving Internet backbones.
3. Specify how businesses and home users can implement security measures.
4. Outline the importance of open standards for the Internet and specify those standards.
5. Understand site hosting and ISP choice.

"The @ sign seemed to make sense."

Ray Tomlinson
The first person to send e-mail and the individual who placed the @ between the user name and computer location.[1]

Information Routing

Data are sent around the Internet backbone in **packets.** E-mail files, HTML files, sound files, and so forth are split into small sections and then routed to different locations based on the packet's address. Separate packets for the same file may take different routes to their end location. The packets are reassembled at the receiving end to reconstruct the entire file. This strategy allows digital backbones to maximize the amount of data that flows through their networks. Broadband applications stream in, or receive, large numbers of packets of information that are assembled at the user's end. How many packets move through the Internet at a given time depends on carrier and router speeds.

These concepts are important because they relate to three areas: choosing an ISP, addressing problems with lost packets, and creating large (multimedia) files. ISPs and Internet backbones can be evaluated for effectiveness in terms of packet loss. Performance and packet loss data for the Internet backbone can be viewed at the Internet Traffic Report site (http://www.internettrafficreport.com). A user may notice packet loss at his or her browser when an entire Web page does not load, streamed video or sound files stop playing, or when a link is clicked but nothing happens. For marketers, a more important consideration is the fact that large files (e.g., multimedia video files) are split into small packets and routed to the user, eliminating the need to send the entire file at one time. The more efficient a backbone is at routing packets, the more content can be delivered. For example, wireless Internet systems tend to lose packets, so they currently deliver text messages only because the total number of packets for such messages is small. Wireless Internet will be able to deliver broadband content when it can effectively stream in the large number of data packets needed to construct a media file. Figure A2.1 illustrates the packet routing process.

Figure A2.1   Packet Routing

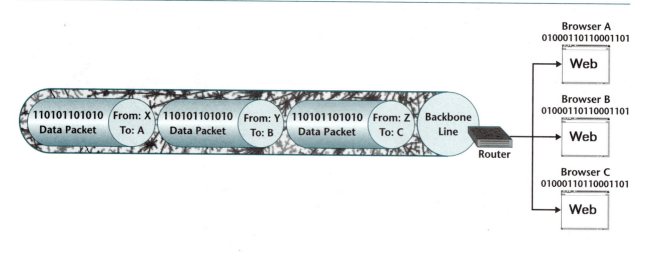

Figure A2.2 shows that the total number of packets sent around the world is increasing tremendously. This increase includes packets sent from computer network to computer network and packets sent between digital wireless networks.

Speed Considerations

Increasing the bandwidth at the last mile will not necessarily speed up slow access through the Internet. Every point of connection along the Internet can result in slowdowns. Congestion between various providers slows traffic; content providers

Figure A2.2   Data Packets Sent around the World (in Billions)

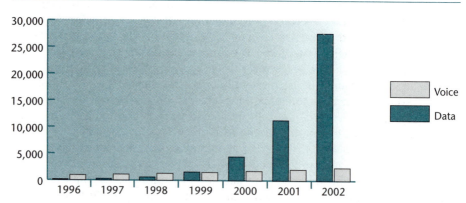

Source: Michael C. Hulfactor and Bob Klessig, "The Problem of the Bandwidth Bottleneck," *ISPWorld,* August 2000, 44–48.

can be overwhelmed by high demands for access. A large number of **hops** (places where two networks meet) slows data. Congestion at **peering points** (points of Internet backbone connection) slows the routing of packets. Each Web address is stored in a name server, and congested name servers can slow access to addressed information, and thus to the addressed data.[2] These speed considerations affect the type of content that should be developed for the market served.

Current trends are toward broader bandwidth. Depending on the location, data could be delivered to the last mile through DSL, cable lines, wireless, or some other method. Table A2.1 outlines current last-mile means of access for home users. The speed in Seconds column refers to sending ten megabits of data (roughly one megabyte of data, or one full screen of graphics). Business users may utilize high-bandwidth options such as T1 or T3 lines.

Table A2.1 Home-User Internet Delivery Options

Term	Explanation	Speed in Seconds
Modem (56 Kbps)	A modem is a modulating/demodulating device that changes analog signals to digital and back. It is used to connect a computer to a twisted pair phone line.	@ 56 Kbps: 179 seconds
T1 or T3 (up to 44.7 Mbps)	A T1 carrier line allows digital information to be sent. A T3 line can have speeds of 44.7 Mbps:.	T1 @ 1.5 Mbps: 6.6 seconds
DSL (1.54 Mbps)	Digital subscriber lines allow digital signals on existing twisted pair phone lines. A DSL modem connects a PC and telephone.	@ 1.5 Mbps: 6.6 seconds
Cable Modems (800 Kbps to 3 Mbps)	Cable modems are used with coaxial television cables.	@ 800 Kbps: 12.5 seconds @ 3 Mbps: 3.3 seconds
Direct Broadcast Satellite (200–400 Kbps)	With a direct broadcast satellite system, data are moved from the Internet backbone to a satellite gateway and then bounced off the satellite to a small dish at the user's location. It sometimes requires a return line through a phone line.	@ 200 Kbps: 50 seconds @ 400 Kbps: 25 seconds
Fiber Optic (10 Gbps)	Few homes have direct fiber-optic connections.	@ 10 Gbps: Less than .01 seconds
G3 Cellular Phones (Projected 2 Mbps Maximum)	The cellular phone format allows information to be sent digitally, which allows a broadband connection to any device that can access the cellular network.	@ 2 Mbps: 5 seconds

Sources: Raj Srikanth and Alex Barros, "Adding Fiber to Your Diet," *Upside,* July 2000, 198–204; Charles Waltner, "Bartering for Bandwidth," *Communication Week,* May 7, 1997, S16–S18; Roger O Crockett, "Warp Speed Ahead," *BusinessWeek,* February 16, 1998, 80–83.

New Data Lines

Digital information can be carried by pure digital lines, such as fiber-optic line-of-site lasers, or by analog waves that must be modulated and demodulated, such as in electrical lines or radio waves. Perhaps the strangest backbones under development are high-voltage electrical power grids, line-of-site lasers, and Internet microwave relay systems. High-voltage electrical lines can be modulated and demodulated to carry digital information, allowing electrical utilities to become broadband providers. In addition, home networking systems are being developed that link computers through a home's electrical system. Line-of-site microwave and laser light relays can carry digital signals from point to point without wires.[3] This allows businesses to link networks without physical landlines. These systems are at the edge of technological development, but as they mature they will increase the total amount of bandwidth available to transport Internet data. For the e-business strategist, the implications are that broadband will be widely available and inexpensive.

Security

Computer networks and home users linked to the Internet face security concerns. Home users have always been susceptible to cybercrimes such as viruses, but they are now becoming the target of hackers. Windows XP was shown to have a major flaw in that it allowed remote users to gain control of a home user's operating system. Security concerns have limited the use of the Internet for some markets. This includes national markets such as China, which has filtered content to limit political speech, as well as home markets where families do not allow children to access the Internet because the parents fear undesired content.

Firewall software and protocols typically evaluate information requests to be sure the requests are from valid users. Other protection software packages include virus checkers, which evaluate files to be sure they don't include viruses, worms, or other destructive programs. Filtering software monitors incoming data or Web pages and blocks data that match some type of restriction (such as keywords or prohibited Web sites). Firewalls, virus protectors, and filters offer a certain level of protection for both network and home users. Figure A2.3 illustrates how viruses, worms, and censured content can be kept from computers by being filtered through firewalls and other protection software.

Strategic nSite

Your Electrical Lines Are Bleeding

Twisted pair lines lose power because of the relationship between electricity and magnetism. Electricity "bleeds" through lines by radiating a magnetic field. Coaxial lines are sheathed in a metal mesh to limit this loss of power. Fiber-optic lines do not radiate power; however, the light signal is weakened as it travels through the glass fiber, requiring light reamplification. New types of glass fiber and faster reamplification systems are improving the data capacity of fiber-optic lines. By breaking up white light into spectrums, current fiber-optic cables could carry data at speeds as high as 1.6 terabits (trillion bits) per second, or 400 million one-page e-mails per second.

Figure A2.3   Firewall Protection

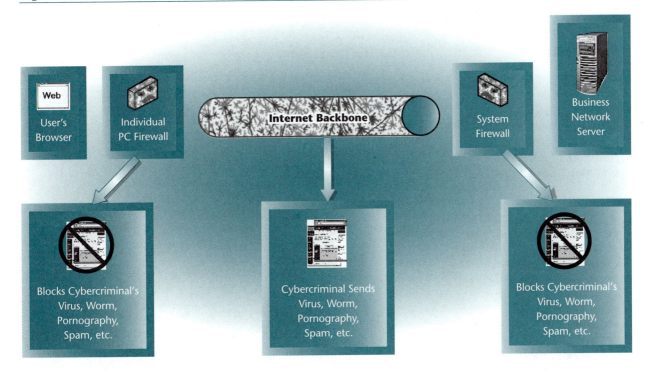

Firewalls and protection software can typically protect computers from known content, such as identifiable viruses and worms, certain keywords, or censured URLs. This may not be enough to block hackers or unauthorized users. Additional methods of security are listed in Table A2.2.

Telecommunications Standards

Proprietary computer networks have existed for a long time on the information highway. Businesses have used a variety of programming languages to run networks and communication systems. The Internet was based on a set of **open standards** (protocols of operation not owned by a single company) because it was developed and used primarily by academics. These open standards have allowed different computer systems (Windows, UNIX, Mac OS, and so forth) to develop and read the same content. In essence, it is as if all systems were using the same language to communicate. Open standards such as **Transmission Control Protocol** and **Internet Protocol** (combined as **TCP/IP**) keep individuals, entrepreneurs, and businesses from being locked into a single company's communication

Table A2.2 Internet Security Recommendations

Technique	Action
Access Controls	Authenticate users and authorize the type of action taken.
Firewalls	Permit and deny traffic flows for networks.
Management and Administration Tools	Centrally manage and report usage of site.
Auditing, Monitoring, and Alert Technologies	Monitor and record events to determine if actions occur outside of set perimeters.
Antivirus Products	Prevent, detect, and correct virus codes.
Cryptography Technologies	Provide information confidentiality.
Certification and Key Management Technologies	Support encryption and digital signatures to authenticate users.
User Authentication Measures	Use token or smart cards to enhance password protection.
Biometric Systems	Confirm user identities using a personal measure, such as fingerprints, iris scans, voiceprints, etc.
Intrusion Detectors	Scan networks to detect incidents of intrusion.
Physical Security Measures	Control physical access to hardware and software.
Consultants	Can provide an important outside perspective.

Source: Adapted from "Internet Security Task Force Releases eBusiness Security Recommendations," in Computer Associates [online] (March 14, 2000), available from <http://www3.ca.com/Press/PressRelease.asp?id5375>; Bob Violino and Amy K. Larson, "Security: An E-Biz Asset," *Information Week,* February 15, 1999, 44–56; Barbara DePompa, "Firewalls Deter Outside Attacks," Network Security Supplement to Internet Week, September 1, 1997, 3–16.

system. The wide adoption of TCP/IP standards has fostered innovation, and its ease of use is leading businesses to adopt these standards for internal and external communication. E-businesses can thus develop strategies on a single technology platform. Table A2.3 outlines the major standards used on the Internet. The Web has a set of its own standards, which are shown in Table A2.4.

Table A2.3 Internet Protocols

Term	Meaning	Description
TCP/IP	Transmission Control Protocol/Internet Protocol	A set of standards used on the Internet.
E-Mail	Electronic mail	A system that allows for the transport of text between users over the Internet.

The following protocols are now transparent, or unseen by the user, and are often integrated in other Internet applications.

Term	Meaning	Description
FTP	File Transfer Protocol	A protocol used to transfer computer files or software online. Most often used as an attachment with e-mail.
Telnet	Terminal emulation program that uses TCP/IP to exchange packets of data between computers	A program that lets a computer connect into another computer for sharing commands and data between computer systems; in essence, the remote computer becomes a terminal.
USENET	Bulletin board system for sites to share and forward discussion information	A system that creates a place for online discussions of areas of interest.
Archie Veronica WAIS	Archie and Veronica are comic book characters; WAIS stands for Wide Area Information Server	Search protocols that allow for locating content on the Internet and file content searches. Most of these are now transparent to the user through a unified Web interface, such as a search engine.

Web Languages

An **HTML tag**, or code, is a command to a computer's browser for setting the fonts, format, size, or other features of a Web page. A Web page developer must program the code or use a software program to create the code. For example, to set up a hot spot, or hyperlink, to allow a user to link to another site, a locator code must be included to direct the browser to access information at the desired Web site. To access information at the local site, such as a different location on the current page or a file on a disk drive, a hyperlink must direct the browser to that targeted location. To access information elsewhere on the Web, the URL address must be included.

Table A2.4   World Wide Web Protocols

Term	Meaning	Description
WWW	World Wide Web	A set of standards that allows hyperlinks and graphics to move through the Internet.
HTTP	HyperText Transfer Protocol	The underlying protocol to the Web enables linking to other sites and retrieving of information.
HTML	HyperText Markup Language	A text-based markup language, or set of codes, that gives a design (fonts, position, colors, and so on) to a Web page.
CGI	Common Gateway Interface	An interface that provides links to other programs from Web servers, such as when a Web form is used to collect information.
URL	Uniform Resource Locator	An address used to find a site at a server on the Web.
SET	Secure Electronic Transaction	The protocols that allow secure purchases on the Internet.
Java	Programming language	An open source language developed by Sun Microsystems that allows Web developers to add applets to Web pages.

The World Wide Web Consortium (W3C) is responsible for controlling upgrades to HTML. HTML 4 is the newest version of the code and allows greater flexibility in Web page design. Dynamic HTML (DHTML) allows movement and layering of text and images on a page and can add multimedia effects. XML is designed to add intelligence to Web pages. With XML, a Web page can act like a stand-alone program; for example, it could collect data and automatically send and verify the data without additional action by the user. This can result in more efficient searches, higher degrees of personalization, more powerful Web applications, and links to databases.[4]

Text editors (word processors) use codes to indicate how content should be displayed or manipulated. One of the earliest text editors was WordStar. Early versions of WordStar were released in 1976 and were adapted for use on the Apple IIe and the TRS-80 (ancient personal computers) and, by 1981, for the IBM PC. WordStar code used commands such as ^ PB to begin and end boldface type. These commands were manually entered into the text.[5] The word processor WordPerfect allowed for a more logical indication of code by splitting the computer screen into a text-entering section and a reveal-code section showing commands such as [Bold] for bold on and [bold] for bold off. Both of these packages showed codes because the operating systems they were designed for did not have graphical user interfaces or did not display in true fonts on the PC screen. Current word processors such as MS Word do not reveal code; instead, they have WYSIWYG (what you see is what you get) displays. Coding for these word processing packages is complex. Users rely on the software to write and edit code. Web page coding can also be complex, as shown in the following HTML examples:

☐ To locate a URL: <A HREF=

☐ To call a file on a local disk drive: <A HREF= file:///c|home/example.htm

☐ To call a Web site: <AHREF=http://www.mssc .edu/home/example.htm/

☐ To call a Web site and display it in a separate window: <AHREF=http://www.mssc.edu/ home/example.htm/" target="_blank">

Given the complexity involved in coding Web pages in Java, XML, CGI scripts, and so forth, most individuals use Web page editors. Linking Web pages into databases, creating banner displays, and other complex tasks have taken Web page creation out of the hands of most business-people. This does not mean that e-business strategists do not need to understand the process of Web page creation. They must understand the possibilities and limits of the technology.

To read or create the newest code, browsers and editors must be updated. In addition, as Web pages become more sophisticated, the level of technical expertise of Web page designers must also increase. Table A2.5 lists the major browser languages and plug-ins. These are constantly evolving as new companies enter the market, as the W3C adds flexibility to Web pages, and as the Internet backbone grows, allowing the transport of richer content. Fortunately for most Web developers, software exists to automatically insert these codes when Web pages are designed.

case A2.1

He Who Controls the Standard Controls the World

A dominant company in the computing business was under U.S. antitrust action for locking customers into a proprietary system and locking competitors out. The company signed a consent decree, but this did not keep this near-monopoly from dominating the computing industry. While this may sound like Microsoft's story, it was in fact IBM in 1956. IBM was the dominant company in the computing industry into the 1980s. IBM fostered the development of the PC, the MS-DOS operating system, and the executives behind Compaq computer. IBM's arrogant belief in its own dominance and its narrow vision, however, allowed an entirely new personal computing industry to slip through its grasp.

By 2001, IBM was advocating open computing standards for such technologies as Linux, Apache's Web server software (http://www.apache .org), Java, and XML. These packages allow IBM to sell hardware and applications that run on open source operating systems. In addition, such systems are a direct attack on Microsoft. In 2001, IBM spent $1 billion in development funds for Microsoft's number one enemy, Linux, and will spend $300 million on Linux education and training.[6]

Microsoft is currently the company under federal antitrust scrutiny. The goal of antitrust regulation can be seen as enhancing allocative and productive efficiency.[7] While Microsoft has established considerable market power, market power by itself is not a ground for antitrust action; in fact, overall consumer welfare may be increased by a firm that organizes an industry. Under this framework, consumer welfare can be enhanced when a firm has enough market power to standardize products or processes. Just as IBM helped develop the computer industry by standardizing systems, Microsoft has gained market power by performing the same function for the PC software industry.

The greater the standardization in the computer industry, the greater the amount of hardware and software sales and thus industry profitability.[8] This creates a network effect; once a standard is developed, other firms jump on the bandwagon. In industry networks, dominant firms want to make it expensive for customers to convert to rivals or compatible alternatives.[9]

With the movement toward open computing standards, there is no organizing firm. Instead, an informal body or individual programs must organize the industry. Microsoft sees its future under threat unless it can control Internet and other Web delivery standards such as wireless and iTV. In an attempt to make the Windows CE interface dominant in the iTV industry, Microsoft purchased WebTV (http://www.webtv.com) for $425 million and made a $1 billion investment in the cable company Comcast (http://www.comcast.com). Other cable companies rejected Microsoft's offers because they wanted to maintain open standards so competitive forces would deliver low-cost systems.[10] In 2002, Microsoft's Internet Explorer 6 was designed not to be compatible with industry standards such as Java. Microsoft would rather have companies use languages such as its own ActiveX.[11]

▶ Thinking Strategically: Case A2.1

Specify why standards are important to the future of the Internet. Outline how Internet standards are a threat to Microsoft. Should a company such as Microsoft be allowed to use its dominance to develop standards? Consider overall consumer welfare and argue for or against the open standards being fostered by the Internet.

Table A2.5   Web Browser Languages and Plug-Ins

Language	Meaning	Description
HTML	HyperText Markup Language	A text-based markup language, or set of codes, that gives design (fonts, position, colors, etc.) to a Web page.
DHTML	Dynamic HTML	A markup language that allows for movement and layering of text and images on a Web page, adding multimedia effects.
XML	Extensible Markup Language	A flexible language that structures data in HTML to allow access to other applications such as databases.
VRML	Virtual Reality Modeling Language	A language that allows 3-D models to be displayed and rotated on a Web page.
Java	Programming language	An open source language developed by Sun Microsystems that allows Web developers to add applets to Web pages.
Plug-Ins Type	**Example**	**Description**
Video	Apple Computer's QuickTime	A player that downloads and plays video.
Video and Audio	RealNetworks' RealPlayer	A program used to stream in video and audio.
Multimedia	Macromedia's Shockwave and Flash	An application that allows for the streaming of multimedia and interactive games.
Chat	IChat's Rooms	A software package providing real-time text conversations.
Telephony	Dialpad's PC phone	A system used to place phone calls over the Internet.

Site Hosting

Hosting the technology for an e-business can be expensive. Costs include hardware, software, personnel, programming, and content creation. Businesses must decide if they are going to host their own site, use an ISP, or outsource applications. Some questions to ask when deciding whether to outsource or develop applications in-house are listed in Table A2.6.

In most cases, businesses find that it makes sense to outsource some or all of their e-business applications. When choosing an ISP, businesses must consider a number of important issues, including the following:

- ☐ **Network reliability.** What percentage of time is the network up?
- ☐ **Value for price.** Which services are offered for the price charged?
- ☐ **Network performance.** Number of delays and packet losses.
- ☐ **Customer service responsiveness.** Does the ISP provide quick attention to problems and answers to questions?
- ☐ **Technical support.** How responsive is technical support?
- ☐ **Start-up time.** How quickly can services be readied?
- ☐ **Service-level agreements.** What types of services and training does the ISP offer?
- ☐ **Disk space.** What is the cost, and how much disk space does the business get?
- ☐ **Programming support.** What capabilities does the ISP have to provide database access, programming help, or special design skills?
- ☐ **E-commerce support.** Does the site allow for shopping carts, online transactions, and individualized marketing programs?
- ☐ **E-mail services.** How many accounts can be provided, and how can they be accessed?
- ☐ **Security.** Does the ISP ensure security for data transfer and for transactions conducted online?[12]

Table A2.6 Internet Delivery

Question	Outsource	In-House
Does the business have the technology staff to develop and maintain a Web site?	No	Yes
Is the business willing to pay the cost of continually upgrading the software and hardware necessary to maintain adequate resources?	No	Yes
Will the business have a large number of hits in a short time?	Yes	No
Does the business need high levels of security?	Yes	No
Will the business's technology needs change rapidly?	Yes	No
Do the business's customers require round-the-clock access or support?	Yes	No

Knowledge Integration

Terms and Concepts

Firewalls *60*

Hops *59*

HTML tag *63*

Open standards *61*

Packets *57*

Peering points *59*

Transmission Control
Protocol/Internet
Protocol (TCP/IP) *61*

Concepts and Questions for Review

1. What Internet advantages are gained by using packets to route information?
2. Specify the implications for an e-business strategist of the movement toward broadband delivery to end users.
3. What strategies should home users implement to prevent their computer systems from being attacked by cybercriminals?
4. Outline additional steps a business should take to ensure security.
5. How do open systems benefit the Internet?
6. Why do most individuals construct Web pages through intermediary programs such as Web page editors?
7. Outline the questions to ask when deciding whether to outsource or to develop e-business applications in-house.
8. List the criteria a business should use to evaluate an ISP.

Active Learning

Exercise A2.1 HTML Code

Open a browser and go to http://www.msn.com on the Web. Take a look at the HTML code for this page. (In Internet Explorer and Netscape, you can go to View on the command bar and then click on Source to view the HTML code.) Scroll through this code. Don't try to understand it. After viewing, close the window. Notice that unless you are trained in this code, you likely have no idea what it means. Now highlight about a third of the Web page. Copy this and paste it into your word processor. The word processor should show you a table-based structure. Many Web pages use tables to control the look and feel of content on a page.

Exercise A2.2 ISP Evaluation Exercise

Choosing an ISP for a business requires careful analysis. Investigate several ISPs based on the criteria in the following table. Discuss your findings with your classmates and determine which ISP is the best. Explore both large and small ISPs.

Criteria	Explanation	Site Evaluation
Connection Availability	How many users can access the site at one time?	
Network Considerations	How well does the ISP's network perform, based on speed, lack of downtime, and capacity?	
Reputation for Speed of Repair	If a component breaks down, how quickly can it be repaired?	
Price	What are the prices for services, and are there fixed prices or pay-as-you-go flexibility?	
Service Level Agreements	What types of services and training does the ISP offer?	
Disk Space	What is the cost, and how much disk space does the business get?	
Programming Support	What capabilities does the ISP have to provide database access, programming help, or special design skills?	
E-Commerce Support	Does the site allow for shopping carts, online transactions, and individualized marketing programs?	
Available E-Mail Services	How many accounts can be provided, and how can they be accessed?	
Security	Does the ISP ensure security for data transfer and for transactions conducted online?	

Web Search—Looking Online

Search Term: Internet Technology   First 3 out of 105,000,000

Internet Traffic Report. Gives information on how well the Internet is operating around the world, including average response times and packet losses. This information helps IT personnel diagnose network problems.
(http://www.internettrafficreport.com

The List: Web Hosts. Provides information on choosing an ISP.
http://webhost.thelist.com

ComputerUser.com. Offers help in choosing an ISP.
http://www.computeruser.com/resources/isp/intquest.html

References

[1] Russell Kay, "A History Lesson," *ComputerWorld,* November 12, 2001, 16.

[2] David Strom, "Tech ABC: What's Blocking the Fast Lane," *Internet World,* October 1, 1999, 68.

[3] Doug Allen, "The Second Coming of Free Space Optics," *Network Magazine,* March 2001, 55–63; Steven van Yoder, "A Bright Idea," *ISPWorld,* August 2000, 90–98; Dan Sweeney, "Ethernet in the Sky," *CIO,* July 1, 1999, 62–68.

[4] Joe Paone, "XML to Power Smart Web Pages," *LANTIMES,* January 19, 1998, 1, 26.

[5] Michael Petrie, "A Potted History of WordStar," [online] (2001), available from <http://www.petrie.u-net.com/wordstar/history/history.htm>.

[6] William J. Holstein, "Big Blue Wages Open Warfare," *Business 2.0,* April 17, 2001, 62–65.

[7] Robert Bork, *The Antitrust Paradox* (New York: Basic Books, 1979).

[8] Jeffrey Church and Neil Gandal, "Network Effects, Software Provision, and Standardization," *Journal of Industrial Economics* 40 (March 1992): 85–101.

[9] Richard Gilbert, "Symposium of Compatibility: Incentives and Market Structure," *Journal of Industrial Economics* 40 (March 1992): 1–8.

[10] Edward W. Desmond, "Malone Again," *Fortune,* February 16, 1998, 66–69; Andrew Kupfer, "How Hot Is Cable, Really?" *Fortune,* February 16, 1998, 70–76.

[11] Based on Brad Kleindl, "Microsoft—Devil or Saint: Balancing Market Power and Consumer Welfare," *Southern Business & Economic Review* (Summer 1998).

[12] Rebecca Wetzel, "Getting What You Pay For," *Interactive Week,* September 10, 2001, 34–37; Kate Gerwig, "Easy Street?" *InternetWeek,* June 8, 1998, 67–71; Nelson King, "Weighing Web Hosting Options for Electronic Commerce Sites," *Internet World,* March 16, 1998, 34–35.

chapter 3
E-Business Communication

This chapter explores the use of e-business communication platforms. The Internet, through the World Wide Web and e-mail, has become a dominant means of linking individuals and allowing businesses to communicate with both internal and external audiences. While Web sites act as the public face of companies by providing information to customers, employees, and the general public, digital convergence is bringing instant communication across multiple platforms and locations. Chat rooms, discussion groups, and instant messaging allow friends, coworkers, and customers to be one click away. It is important for e-business students to know how these multiple e-business communication platforms facilitate the dissemination of information, the creation of communities, and the development of relationships.

BMW in the Web Driver's Seat

Sixty-two percent of all new vehicle buyers use the Internet to obtain information to support their buying decision before they visit a dealer. For BMW customers, this number is more than 85 percent. Online automotive information is used not only to attract potential car buyers, but also to develop and maintain relationships with customers.[1] Hypermedia are ideal for developing and maintaining relationships between an e-business and its customers. The Web allows for relationship development through its ability to almost instantaneously transfer information between parties. As early as 1997, BMW of North America hosted more than 150,000 hits a day at its Web site. BMW's site (http://www.bmwusa.com) allows current or prospective customers to use virtual reality technology to take a drive behind the wheel of a BMW. Images of BMWs are morphed to show new models. Feedback links allow car designers to gather information about new features and accessories that potential customers may desire. Public relations specialists respond to inquiries through e-mail and answer questions without time-consuming phone calls. BMWUSA.com also maintains relationships between customers by hosting chat rooms.[2]

Potential customers can use rich media to build their ideal BMWs on the Web site and save their preferences or send them to a dealer. The Web site offers variations on financing, leasing, and pricing. The marketing staff at BMW uses the saved car models to identify customer needs and trends and then sets manufacturing specifications to match those needs. Individuals who save a model receive an e-mail from the company to start a communication process that could lead to a sale.[3]

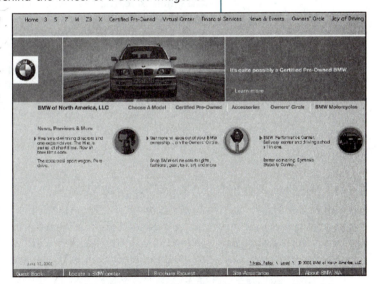

Source: <http://www.bmwusa.com/welcome.cfm?page=&bottom=0>.
© 2002 BMW of North America. Used with permission. The BMW name and logo are registered trademarks.

vignette

BMW has continued to evolve its Web site. BMW used Hollywood directors such as Ang Lee *(Crouching Tiger, Hidden Dragon),* John Frankenheimer *(Reindeer Games)* and Guy Ritchie *(Snatch)* to create short films for the Internet with stars such as Clive Owen, Mickey Rourke, and Madonna. These rich media files are downloadable and are also offered as streaming video to viewers over the Internet (http://www.bmwfilms.com). The goal is to showcase the BMW brand. The films were first posted in April 2001; by December 2001, there were more than 12 million films viewed.[4]

▶ Thinking Strategically

Visit the BMW Web site. Determine if the site is designed just for current BMW owners or if it is targeting potential owners as well. List the types of e-business communication platforms used by BMW. How does BMW develop and maintain relationships using these platforms? Decide if this site appeals to individuals with high or low levels of automotive involvement. Visit a Web site for another automobile manufacturer. Determine if that site is designed to appeal to the same individuals as the BMW site. Specify why a potential customer or owner would return to this site.

The Internet is used as a platform to communicate to constituencies, or audiences, both external and internal to an e-business. **External audiences** include customers, stockholders, the general public, and other specifically targeted groups. **Internal audiences** can include both employees and suppliers. Employees, such as field salespeople, staff members, and others, use intranets to access internal information and training. Suppliers communicate with e-businesses through extranets to check on inventory shipments, parts availability, service bulletins, or other information. The Internet is a platform for Web pages, chat or discussion boards, instant messaging, e-mail, and other computer-facilitated communication systems. An e-business strategist must understand how these interfaces are used as tools to reach specific communication goals.

Businesses use a combination of platforms to support an **integrated communication system** to facilitate communication between various constituencies. E-mail, for example, has widely replaced the telephone and interoffice memo for internal business communication. E-businesses are building on Internet-supported platforms to develop **integrated marketing communication** strategies using various media outlets. These strategies usually include **linear media**, such as broadcast (television and radio), print (newspapers, magazines, and newsletters), direct marketing (direct mail and telephone sales), and other specialized outlets. In addition, the Internet and the World Wide Web are fostering a **hypermedia environment** that allows companies to deliver targeted messages to specific audiences. A

Integrated marketing communication *uses a variety of communication technologies to reach organizational goals.*

hypermedia environment is a distributed network of **nonlinear communication** using hyperlinks and search-and-retrieval processes to deliver information.[5] The best current example of this environment is the PC-based World Wide Web, but it is expanding rapidly into interactive television, Web-based cellular telephones, and other portable devices.

Traditional communication through media often follows a **one-to-many communication model** in which a single message, such as a print ad, television commercial, or internal newsletter, is sent by one source and seen by many without the opportunity for immediate feedback. This lack of interactivity forces messages to be highly structured. For example, when a television ad is being developed, the concept is often storyboarded to create a sequence of scenes designed to reach narrow and specific goals by taking the targeted audience through a linear sequence of words, images, or events. Hypermedia allow for a type of two-way communication between the e-business and its audience; the communication process acts more like a salesperson than a **linear communication.** A salesperson is able to follow a nonlinear path to process and provide relevant information for any query a customer may have. Just as a salesperson can close a sale, current hypermedia provide direct links to e-commerce resources to close a sale with a customer.

The nonlinearity of a hypermedia site allows the message designer to tailor the message to multiple audiences. A Web page can be designed to allow a visitor to find specific areas of interest. Figure 3.1, for example, shows how visitors to a home page can move to commercial content, end-user content, commercial content by type, and end-user content by interest. Each page of the Web site meets individual needs.

*Linear communication follows a scripted flow. **Nonlinear communication** allows a free flow and an exchange of information. Most conversations are **nonlinear,** or able to branch to new areas of information at will. Good sales presentations are free-flowing nonlinear communication.*

What Is E-Business Communication?

At its broadest conceptualization, communication is the sharing of ideas and concepts with others. This process is typically illustrated in the communication flow model shown in Figure 3.2.

The **sender**, a person or a business, wishes to communicate to the target segment. The **message**, the specific information the sender wishes to get across, is carried by a media source such as print, broadcast, direct marketing, or hypermedia. When a message is sent, the receiver may not always understand the intended message. The sender must **encode** the message, or design the message in a way that will be **decoded** as desired by the targeted receiver. Each receiver interprets a message, such as an advertisement, based on his or her own perceptions about the product, spokesperson, theme, or other factors unique to the individual. The message must overcome any background noise that keeps the message from being understood.

Figure 3.1   Hypermedia Connections to Multiple Pages

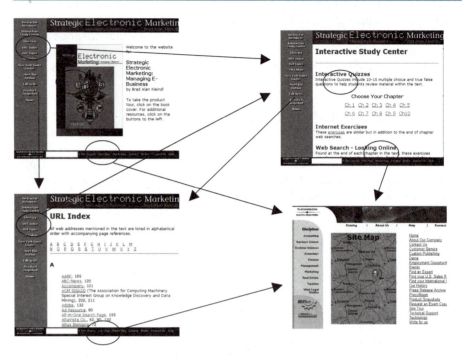

Figure 3.2   The Communication System

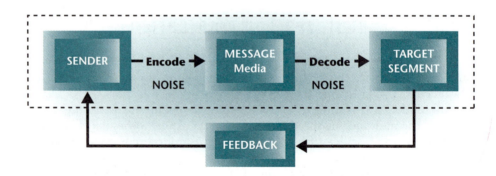

Person-to-person communication (e.g., face-to-face or over the telephone) is both time dependent and two-way. Traditional media vehicles, however, such as print and broadcast, flow one-way from the sender to the receiver (within the dotted box shown in Figure 3.2). In most traditional advertising, the message is carried by the media without face-to-face communication and with no means of immediate feedback. This follows a one-to-many model, while hypermedia allow a many-to-many model.

The Many-to-Many Communication Model

The **many-to-many communication model** places hypermedia in the center of the communication process; the hypermedia outlet becomes a meeting place where anyone can communicate with anyone else. Figure 3.3 illustrates the many-to-many model in which customers (C), businesses (B), and employees (E) can all obtain and deliver content. This allows for a typology of interactions:

- ☐ Consumer-to-consumer (C-to-C), Internet based
- ☐ Business-to-consumer (B-to-C), Internet based
- ☐ Consumer-to-business (C-to-B), Internet based
- ☐ Business-to-employee (B-to-E), intranet based
- ☐ Employee-to-employee (E-to-E), intranet based
- ☐ Business-to-business (B-to-B), extranet based.

The many-to-many model allows feedback from others involved in the communication channel. All customers can communicate with each other as well as with the business. This communication does not need to be time dependent like face-to-face communication; a customer can create a Web page or post a message and leave it for others to see. The BMW vignette at the beginning of the chapter illustrates how this model allows customers to communicate with many others. Individual consumers can leave comments on their cars and engage in online conversations with service representatives and others who share similar interests. The many-to-many model is also evident in the use of chat or threaded discussion lists at Web sites. These give individuals the ability to directly engage others with a shared interest. The individuals could be customers who discuss a product or company, members of an online course or training session, or coworkers who use an intranet to discuss strategy, sales techniques, new products, or any other topics. Many firms are using a combination of these e-business communication platforms to facilitate communication and interaction.

Figure 3.3 Many-to-Many Model

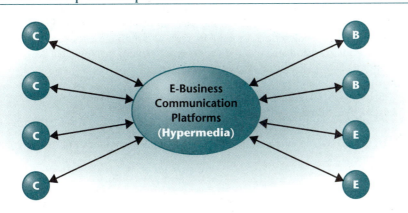

E-Business Communication Platforms

Internet-based hypermedia have evolved a number of communication platforms that support a wide variety of messaging systems. They include Web pages, e-mail, chat, discussion forums, and instant messaging. These platforms can be time dependent or time independent. Hypermedia allow for a change in the inter-activity between the sender and the receiver. Messages are sent to a repository, such as a server, where the receiver must go to obtain the message. This requires active participation on the part of the receiver. This is in contrast to the passive receiving of messages that most individuals encounter in a one-to-many model when individuals see or hear advertisements from print or broadcast media. With instant messaging, messages can be passed through to the receiver in real time. Table 3.1 outlines the types of e-business communication platforms that individuals can access.

Table 3.1   E-Business Communication Platforms

Platform	Icon	Description
Web Page		An HTML-based information document.
Text E-Mail		A text-based computer-to-computer messaging system.
HTML E-Mail		An HTML-based computer-to-computer messaging system designed to look and work like a Web page. HTML-based e-mail is allowing for the growth of rich media e-mail, or the inclusion of multimedia in e-mail messages.
Chat		A chat online involves a number of individuals who leave messages for others to see. These can be placed in a respository, or chat room, for viewing at a later time, or they can be live, with individuals writing to others in real time.
Discussion Group		Threaded discussion lists allow individuals to add to an initial message with successive messages. A discussion group user can add to a thread, or single conversation, by indicating a response to a previous message. Messages are available for others to read and are indented under topic headings such as Initial Post, First Response, Second Response, and so forth.
Instant Message		Instant messages are sent in real time from individual to individual through landline-based or wireless devices.
Rich Media		Rich media refers to Internet technology that includes more than just text, graphics, or sound alone.

Hypermedia Communication Goals

A Web site can provide a little or a lot of information for a site visitor. A single site can be designed for goal-directed buyers as well as for those who are merely surfing the Net. For **high-involvement** visitors, the Web site can provide links to other individuals who share the same interests. Customers can also interact directly with authors, artists, sports figures, chefs, and many others who are normally unreachable through traditional media. Involvement levels can be high for site visitors when they are goal directed, such as when attempting to gather information to make a purchase. Such individuals can also have high-enduring involvement with products or product categories and engage in Net surfing to obtain high levels of interactivity with sites.[6] As Internet bandwidth increases to match other multimedia delivery systems like CD-ROMs and interactive kiosks, Web-based platforms will allow even richer visitor experiences.

Individuals with high involvement are likely to see a topic as interesting or important. These individuals attend to information more, are more likely to comprehend complex messages, and may be willing to spend more time at a Web site.

Hypermedia also allow for the development and maintenance of relationships by providing in-depth information for customers. Rich information sites can help consumers engage in ongoing searches or prepurchase searches. These sites can be designed with differing levels of complexity. The simplest sites are **brochure sites** that engage in advertising or public relations. Brochure sites may contain the same information as a business's print advertising material. These sites are designed to make visitors aware of a business's image or products. This can be seen as a simple extension of traditional media campaigns. Brochure sites should be designed to enhance the overall promotional campaign.

Web sites are often the public face of a business. For non-brick-and-mortar Internet businesses, a Web site may be the only chance a customer has to interact with the business. The site must project and protect the image of the company. Protecting a company's image is a concern on the Internet. This concern is addressed by eWatch (http://www.ewatch.com), which searches the Internet for any comments related to corporate clients. To protect their public image, some companies are registering domain names that could be seen as negative to prevent others from using them.[7]

Relationship sites target individuals who may have higher levels of information involvement. Such sites often contain games, chat groups, or other interactive components to maintain relationships with customers. Web sites can be designed to take their customers from an initial stage with little information to a final stage of engaging in online transactions.[8] This process will be explained more in Chapter 4.

Strategic nSite

Web Sites and Company Image

Some individuals have set up Web sites that attack a company's image. To prevent this, a number of companies have registered domain names that could be seen as offensive to the company so others cannot use them. Charles Schwab, for example, has registered #%*schwab.com and schwab#%*.com (#%* represents an offensive word). Other companies that have registered domain names to prevent attack include the following:

- ▶ Bell Atlantic: bigyellow#%*.com
- ▶ Chase Manhattan Bank: chase#%*.com
- ▶ Cox Communications: cox#%*.com
- ▶ Vail Resorts: vailresorts#%*.com
- ▶ Volvo Cars of North America: volvo#%*.com
- ▶ Playboy Enterprises: Playboy#%*.com

case 3.1

Extranets and Intranets

Banking on a Relationship

Wells Fargo (http://www.wellsfargo.com) was an early mover into e-business communication. In 1994, the firm developed a brochure site, but by 1995 a survey indicated that its customers wanted to engage in financial transactions online. Wells Fargo was the first bank to offer online account balance information, and by 2002 it had more than 3 million online customers.[9] Wells Fargo has moved from a brochure site to a relationship site. Its site acts as a portal to financial data. Individuals can obtain information on their banking and brokerage accounts as well as on financial planning, retirement, taxes, or business finance. The portal offers a link to an interactive financial-planning tutorial site targeting kids, teens, and adults (http://www.bankingonourfuture.org/hope/default.htm).

Wells Fargo uses a number of e-business communication platforms to serve its customers. More than eight hundred ATMs in California and Arizona are being designed for a multimedia-banking channel that would feature live news feeds, movie trailers, and interactive ads. Customers who use the ATMs will receive personalized greetings and be able to access drop-down screen menus with multicolor graphics and full-motion video.[10]

E-business communication platforms are enhancing the communication process within and between firms. Extranets and intranets use the common IP interface and involve the same communication considerations as Internet-based Web communication. For example, it is important to address issues such as ease of use and content delivery for all extranet users. Like the Internet, intranets use browsers, servers, and Internet protocols but are not open to unauthorized users. Companies use intranets to disseminate information, such as policies and procedures, and to share documents, offer phone directories, provide human resources information, give online training, and conduct information searches. The relative ease of development, low costs, and high levels of user experience have caused tremendous growth in organizational intranets. Intranets encourage and speed communication, helping to facilitate change inside organizations.

Often the bandwidth available inside an organization is higher than that available to access the Internet; this gives the potential for high-bandwidth applications such as voice, video, and conferencing online. Businesses are also using intranets for a variety of strategic purposes. Some are using intranets as the hub of their communication and collaboration; others are offering narrower information services. By linking extranets, intranets, and the Internet, businesses are developing a dynamic information hub, changing organizational cultures and allowing rapid response to environmental change.[11]

▶ Thinking Strategically: Case 3.1

Describe how Wells Fargo develops and maintains relationships with customers. Justify the use of ATMs for broadband Internet delivery. Could this system help make a transition to other broadband devices for individuals?

Source: <http://www.wellsfargo.com>. Wells Fargo Internet screen captures are used with permission from Wells Fargo Bank, N.A.

E-Mail Marketing

E-mail is the most common e-business communication platform. **E-mail marketing** allows an e-business to direct messages to specific market segments or to customize messages for individuals, much the same way as direct mail. **Targeted e-mail** is one of the most effective hypermedia communication platforms. E-business marketers set a number of goals for targeted e-mail, including click-throughs to link to a Web site and direct purchase from an e-mail offer. The number of click-throughs for e-mail is higher than that for banner ads, and the

Historical nSite

cost can be considerably less. In addition, response rates are much faster than with traditional direct mail campaigns. The bulk of e-mail responses can be received in forty-eight hours, while postal responses can take as long as six weeks.[13]

E-mail is delivered in a number of different formats. By the end of 2001, the most-used form of opt-in e-mail advertising in the United States was HTML-based e-mail (it is used by 54.2 percent of companies), followed by e-mail newsletters and text-only e-mail.[14] Click-throughs to Web sites are up to four times higher for HTML e-mail than for text-based e-mail. New rich media formats such as Macromedia's Flash and video are also being embedded in e-mail. Video e-mail can be linked to a Web site to receive streamed video, or the video can be delivered with the e-mail, avoiding downloading issues. Rich e-mail providers can use a **sniffer** to determine the e-mail client (e-mail software package) of the recipient to detect plug-ins and send the proper rich media content. Rich media will become more popular when users have greater access to high-bandwidth Internet connections.

Targeted e-mail works best with individuals who have given their permission to receive messages. **Permission-based marketing** allows firms to target only those individuals who have expressed an interest and helps to avoid spamming and privacy concerns. **Virtual prospecting** using bulk lists is not permission based. While this technique can be very cheap, the e-mail can be seen as spam. Bulk e-mail lists are also poor in quality compared to traditional postal lists. Opt-in, or permission-based, e-mail allows for the capturing and creation of data that can be used for personalizing the targeted e-mail. Adding names to e-mail can double the response rates over nontargeted e-mail.[15] Personalized e-mail requires a linkage to a database. Information can be used to identify individual profiles and behavior or clusters of individuals (the process of data mining is covered in Chapter 9). This data can then be linked to create dynamic content for e-mail. Individuals can also self-select into e-mail groups to receive newsletters or other postings. Many companies, such as CNN, Yahoo!, MSN, and AOL, develop and maintain multiple e-mail lists to target individuals by interest. Table 3.2 outlines the types of opt-in used to create e-mail lists.

Permission-based e-mail marketing has been shown to be an effective and efficient tool. Response rates for e-mail are higher than those for banner ads, direct mail, and rich media. In addition, direct marketing costs for permission-based e-mail can be as low as $0.25 per address compared to direct mail costs of $0.75 to $2.00. Spam, or bulk e-mail, has a lower cost at $0.01 per address, but it is not as effective in obtaining click-throughs and purchases.[16] The effectiveness of direct marketing alternatives is illustrated in Table 3.3.

E-business strategists can put in place e-mail marketing systems to reach communication goals. Barnes & Noble sends e-mail-based promotional content to all customers and also targets geographic locations and individuals by past purchasing behavior. For example, if an author is signing a book at a specific

Table 3.2 Types of Opt-Ins

Alternative	Description	Example
Single Opt-In	Customers supply an e-mail address or check on a box to allow e-mail to be sent. This gives permission for the company to send e-mail or to allow other third-party companies to send e-mail to the individual. Customers are notified as to the terms of the permission.	Do you wish to subscribe to our weekly e-mail newsletter? ○ Yes ○ No
Double Opt-In	As with the single opt-in, customers supply an e-mail address or check a box to allow e-mail to be sent. Customers are expected to reconfirm by replying to a confirmation e-mail. This maximizes the chances of not being seen as sending spam.	Thank you for registering for our e-mail letter. So that we may serve you better, please log in and update your e-mail preferences. You can log in at this Web address: http://www.account.companyX.com/login.html. Thank you!
Opt-Out	A subscription is asssumed, and the customer must click to remove the subscription if he or she wishes to opt out of receiving e-mail for the company or other third-party companies.	Occasionally, we send our subscribers e-mail special offers from relevant businesses or organizations. If you do not want to receive such offers, please check here. ☐

Source: Eileen Colkin, "Marketing Capitalizes on E-Mail," *InformationWeek,* July 23, 2001, 55–56.

location, an e-mail can be sent to everyone in the postal Zip Code area.[17] Here are some recommendations for developing an e-mail marketing strategy:

1) Capture e-mail addresses at a point of customer contact.
   - ☐ Collect information that can be used to personalize the e-mail.

2) Don't send unsolicited bulk e-mail. It has a higher cost per sale and risks being seen as spam.

3) Clearly state the confidentiality policy.
   - ☐ Indicate that customer information will be used in-house only, if that is the case.
   - ☐ Ask permission before sending information to a third party.

4) Acknowledge the registration with a return e-mail.
   - ☐ Send a thank you and restatement of subscription to decrease the likelihood of opting out.
   - ☐ Respond quickly with targeted e-mail.

5) Maintain records of registration.
   - ☐ Use these records to handle complaints from targeted individuals.

6) Include clear instructions on how to unsubscribe.
   - ☐ Attempt to maintain low unsubscribe rates.

Table 3.3   Cost-Effectiveness of Direct Marketing Alternatives

	Customer Acquisition			Customer Retention	
	Direct Mail to Rented List	**Banner Advertising**	**E-Mail to Rented List**	**Direct Mail to In-House List**	**E-Mail to In-House List**
Cost per 1,000 (CPM)	$850	$13	$200	$686	$5
Click-Through	NA	0.8%	3.5%	NA	100%
Purchase Rate	1.2%	2.0%	2.0%	3.9%	2.5%
Cost per Sale	$71	$100	$286	$18	$2

Source: Reprinted from *1to1 Magazine,* © Peppers and Rogers Group 2001.

7) Prepare content carefully:
   ☐ Personalize content.
      • Avoid untargeted messages.
   ☐ Create content for both text and HTML formats.
   ☐ Keep content short for small file sizes and quick reads.
      • Use hyperlinks to provide access to larger amounts of content at a Web site, but be sure they link to content-relevant pages.
   ☐ Change e-mail content over time to limit individuals opting out.
   ☐ Test messages and analyze results.

8) Assign an e-mail manager or team.
   ☐ Have a contact person handle responses and problems.
   ☐ As an option, hire an ASP for e-mail services.

9) Keep e-mail lists secure.
   ☐ Do not allow e-mail receivers to obtain lists so a Reply to All command does not create spam.
   ☐ Do not sell or forward lists to third parties without permission.[18]

E-mail contact between individuals gives marketers an opportunity to expand on a customer base. E-mail contact can act as a word-of-mouth marketing system that spreads rapidly from individual to individual like a virus. **Viral marketing** is the process of encouraging individuals to pass on messages that individuals receive in a hypermedia environment, such as e-mail or other messaging systems. For example, Hotmail used viral marketing to entice new users into its free e-mail service. During the 2000 U.S. elections, viral marketing was used by political parties to motivate voters to get to the polls. Viral marketing has a strong advantage in that individuals are likely to know others who share similar interests and therefore may be interested in the message. On the other hand, this process can put current customers in the position of feeling they are spamming others.

Figure 3.4 illustrates a targeted e-mail marketing model. In this model, an individual gives permission to be placed in either an in-house or commercial e-mail database. These customer databases can provide not only e-mail addresses but also dynamic data, or data that can be used as needed to create targeted e-mail. An e-mail server manages the sending of the e-mail to the target. The e-mail client, or reader type, is evaluated by a sniffer to determine text or HTML e-mail formats. The e-mail allows for links to Web sites for richer content and can include suggestions for forwarding the e-mail to others to engage in viral marketing.

Case 3.2

E-Mail Flower Power

Proflowers developed a highly successful e-mail marketing campaign linking customer behavior to psychographic and demographic information. Proflowers used an outside research company to place its five-hundred-thousand-name database into twenty-seven different psychographic and demographic segments. This information was combined with purchase data to identify those segments that were most profitable. Proflowers was then able to identify five segments that could respond positively to a one-to-one e-mail marketing campaign. Customer segments were targeted to become repeat buyers by customizing subject lines, headers, language, and salutations. Understanding the individual segments also allowed for cooperative advertising for other products. The result of the e-mail campaign was an increase in conversion rates and response rates as well as higher-than-average order sizes.[19]

▶ Thinking Strategically: Case 3.2

Use Figure 3.4 to illustrate how Proflowers modeled its targeted e-mail campaign. Explain why this campaign was effective for Proflowers' customers and products. Evaluate the outcome measures for this campaign. Could outcomes be improved by the use of other measurements?

Figure 3.4 Targeted E-Mail Marketing Model

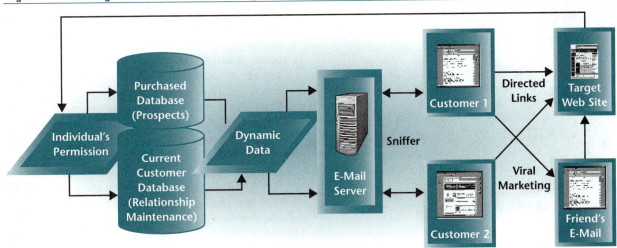

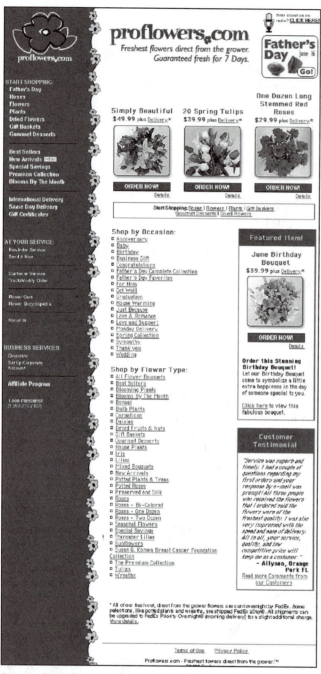

Source: <http://www.proflowers.com>. Courtesy of Proflowers.com.

Spam

The effectiveness of e-mail marketing can be hampered by the increasing amount of unsolicited e-mail, or spam, sent by unethical marketers. **Spamming** is the practice of sending unwanted e-mail to a large number of individuals.[20] Spam is usually a direct solicitation, but it can include other types of e-mail. Unlike marketers who send junk mail through the postal system, e-mail spammers do not need to purchase postage for every message sent and therefore can greatly increase the number of people they can reach. Spammers believe that the more e-mail sent, the better their chances—unlike legitimate marketers who target messages and worry about hurting their image if their messages reach unintended audiences.

Eighteen U.S. states, along with many countries around the world, have enacted antispam statutes allowing individuals who receive spam to sue for monetary damages. Spam is not easy to stop, however. The Internet community has developed a number of software tools to control the receipt of spam. These tools filter incoming e-mail by domain names and by content such as "XXX" or "earn money fast." In 1999, 25 percent of spam e-mail was adult-oriented, and 37 percent contained get-rich-quick proposals.[21] Several organizations are attempting to control spammers by setting up reporting agencies. The Mail Abuse Prevention System (MAPS) (http://mail-abuse.org) allows complaints to be registered. MAPS volunteers evaluate and contact the questionable sender; if the sender does not agree to stop spamming, its IP address is placed into a Realtime Blackhole List (RBL). When a spam sender on the RBL attempts to send e-mail to a receiver who refers to the list, the spam is blocked.[22]

Spammers are very adept at getting around these blockages. Some spammers set up temporary ISP accounts and then broadcast their spam before they are caught. They then move to the next ISP. Spammers do not even need to purchase a name list. **Dictionary attack** spammers attack large e-mail services such as Hotmail by generating random e-mail addresses such as jones@hotmail.com, a-jones@hotmail.com, b-jones@hotmail.com, and so forth. They then send the same junk e-mails to all addresses.[23] Some spammers forge the online identity of the sender. The spammer's e-mail is routed through a third-party server, changinig the sending address. This can cause recipients to **flame** the victimized sender.

Spam is a problem for the Internet. It shifts the cost of e-mail from the sender to the intermediaries and the receiver. The worldwide cost of spam has been estimated at $8 billion per year. When spam is sent to a business, the cost can be more than $100 per employee per year in wasted time. Although this may not seem high, with five thousand employees this could cost a business a half million dollars per year.[24] Marketers are very concerned that their e-mail efforts not be seen as spam. With the total amount of commercial e-mail expected to reach more than 425 billion messages by 2005, however, it is likely that individuals will be inundated with e-mail solicitations. A double opt-in can help limit the likelihood that an e-business will be considered a spammer.[25]

Flaming *is the process of sending angry e-mail messages, often characterized BY USING ALL CAPITAL LETTERS.*

Mailing Lists and Discussion Groups

A number of platforms are used to facilitate non-time-dependent communication between groups of individuals. **Mailing lists** allow for the sending of information through e-mail. This platform is used to post newsletters for members of a group, to release news or information, or to disseminate any other type of communication. Individuals can subscribe by sending in their e-mail addresses to a LISTSERV or Majordomo program on a server. Mailing lists can be **moderated**; an individual, or moderator, checks the messages before they are sent to the list of people. **Unmoderated** e-mail is automatically redistributed to the names on the mailing list. **Discussion groups** (also called **newsgroups** or **forums**) use Usenet protocols to place user-submitted messages on a server. These groups can be unmoderated, or open to all comments by members, or they can be moderated, where an individual checks the messages before they are posted.

These messaging systems are use by informal groups through a number of different hosts. Most large Internet portals such as AOL, Yahoo!, MSN, Google, and others offer discussion groups and specialized mailing lists. Such systems can be used to support communities of shared interest or as commercial communication vehicles that offer information and advertising much like magazines. Companies use forums for high-involvement contact between customers and company representatives for product support and training.

These communication platforms are also used in intranets to support internal communication. IBM had more than fifty thousand of its worldwide employees participate in a seventy-two-hour marathon chat session called the World Jam. The program used ten moderated discussion forums on day-to-day life at IBM. The discussion forums allowed employees to share ideas that could be put into practice.[26]

Instant Messaging and Chat

Individuals do not need to wait until they check their e-mail to receive messages from others; Internet protocols allow for time-dependent instantaneous connections between users. Such connections allow multiple individuals to meet in a chat room or send messages instantaneously from individual to individual through **instant messaging (IM).** Buddy lists allow individuals to know when someone else is online. This could be a friend or someone who has been identified as having shared interests.[27]

Chat allows multiple individuals to send instant messages through a common interface. Talk City (http://www.talkcity.com) has fostered thousands of chat groups at its Web site. In March 1999, Talk City had approximately 2.6 million unique visitors and generated more than 6.6 million hours of conversations. In the early evening hours, Talk City had as many as eighteen thousand users simultaneously chatting or engaging in other interactive activities.[28] Talk City is just one of thousands of Web sites that offer online chat or threaded discussion lists. Chat is used for more than just social contact. Some companies are using chat features to support online service. This approach can lower service support costs, because servicepeople can chat with multiple customers at one time.[29] One method that can be used for online support is **co-browsing.** This technology allows a sales or service representative to browse the same page at the same time as a customer, with both controlling the browsers. Co-browsing enables instant text or voice messages between the representative and customer and on-the-fly customization of content for the customer.[30]

Instant messaging has also moved beyond simple chat between buddies. The international financial firm UBS Warburg (http://www.ubswarburg.com) uses instant messaging to facilitate communication and trades between its traders and clients. The clothes company Lands' End (http://www.landsend.com) allows its customers to use IM to ask questions of service reps; these customers spend 8 percent more than non-IM customers. IM technology is also being tied into automated bots, or agents that answer individual questions and post advertisements based on IM behavior.[31]

Rich Media

The term **rich media** refers to the use of Internet technology that adds more than just text, graphics, or sound alone. Rich media include a wide variety and growing number of new tools, such as multimedia, 3-D virtual environments, streaming video, and other digital techniques. These media can be delivered through any of the e-business communication platforms. The major limiting factor is the amount of bandwidth deliverable to the access device. Studies show that consumers are willing to pay for broadband technology to receive rich media access to simulation games, kids' activity sites, entertainment on demand (TV shows and movies), videoconferencing, language resources, music, continuing education, and multimedia encyclopedias.[32]

Rich media often take advantage of streaming technology, which allows large files to be broken into packets that are sent over the Internet backbone to the browsing device. This process is illustrated in Figure 3.5. The various components of rich media are developed separately and then coordinated through an authoring software or Web page interface. Authoring software such as Macromedia's Flash controls how the various media components interact. Content can be animated and controlled through independent programming. Media players can play rich content, such as video, and allow for hyperlinks. A Web-based interface is more static.

Companies that look to use rich media must carefully consider bandwidth restrictions, the access devices used by their target market, and the market's propensity to view or interact with online content. As bandwidth expands, rich media content will be deliverable to a broader base of users, bringing down the cost per contact. Multimedia Message Service (MMS) standards are under development

Figure 3.5 Rich Media Process

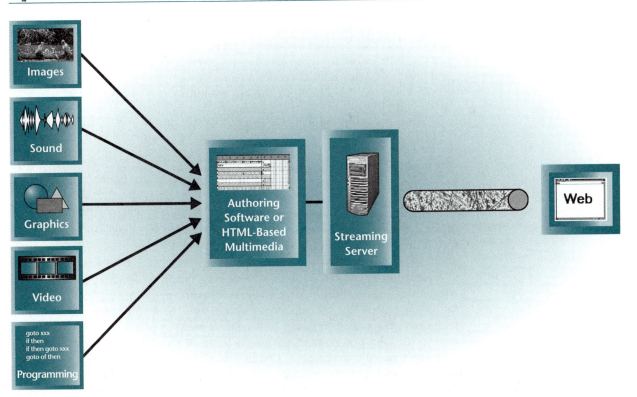

for wireless devices, and this rich media alternative is expected to grow as hand-held systems increase in power.

Wireless Communication

Wireless devices allow for instant communication anywhere a connection can be made. As discussed in Chapter 2, the total number of data packets sent through wireless devices is expected soon to be larger than the number sent via voice lines; however, the small size of wireless devices limits the type of information that can be sent. Text-based wireless e-mail and wireless instant messaging are being used by individuals to maintain contact, play games, receive news, make purchases, and view advertisements. In Southeast Asia, 60 percent of individuals between the ages of sixteen and fifty-four prefer to use **short message services (SMS)** to maintain contact.[33] Wireless messaging services are so popular in some countries that individuals spend more time watching their cellular phones than speaking through them. In December of 2001, more than 1.3 billion SMS messages were sent in the United Kingdom alone.[34]

Wireless has strong business applications. A survey of executives found that wireless access to business information will soon be essential for sales personnel, executives and senior management.[35] Advertisers are currently developing promotional models for wireless. These models will be covered in Chapter 7.

Free Speech

Is society better off when there is no place to hide from an interconnected world? The ubiquity of e-business communication platforms makes it possible for individuals to communicate from virtually anywhere to anywhere. While this has both personal and business advantages, perhaps the greatest social benefit is the Internet's ability to act as a free speech venue. A fundamental shift in power has occurred due to the use of the Internet. Companies no longer control widely broadcast public speech through media outlets. Individuals can and do develop Web sites and engage in discussion boards, chats, or other many-to-many communication systems to discuss companies, products, and other topics related to businesses.

Companies are snooping through discussion boards and chat rooms looking for defamatory comments. EWatch searches the Internet to find defamatory or incorrect speech and to track down the individuals who engage in such speech (even discovering the persons behind made-up screen names), and then provides the information to a company to have its public relations or legal staff take action. In some cases, companies sue individuals for **cybersmearing**, or defaming online.[36] ITEX (http://www.itex.com), an online trading company, filed suit against one hundred John Does who made defamatory statements about ITEX on one of Yahoo!'s message boards. The John Doe names were used because ITEX could not identify the individuals who made the comments.[37] **Rogue sites** allow individuals to express their feelings about companies, products, or organizations. Rogue sites have targeted

Wal-Mart, America Online, Kmart, Chase, and others.[38] When these sites are considered parodies, they have First Amendment protection in the United States.[39]

In the United States, the First Amendment to the Constitution guarantees freedom of speech. The free speech right is seen as fundamental and protects most forms of expression. This can lead to ethical dilemmas. Regulations against pornography are sometimes seen as encroaching on free speech rights. For example, libraries often provide Internet access. A Virginia library attempted to limit its patrons' access to certain sites. A U.S. district court ruled that libraries do not need to provide Internet access, but if they do, they must not censure what adults view.[40]

Pornography can flow across borders and violate laws in other countries. China attempted to control the flow of information to its citizens by having all Internet access travel through one gateway. The Chinese system was designed to operate like America Online, with the power to control access to content, both pornographic and political.[41]

For some individuals, the Web is a free speech forum for political information. Political elections around the world have demonstrated that candidates are able to use the Internet to spread information at a fairly low cost. Political thoughts can also travel across borders, allowing dissidents, human rights advocates, and alternative political parties to provide information to those who gain access to the Web. For more information on limitations to online free speech, visit the Reporters without Borders' Enemies of the Internet site (http://www.rsf.org/ennemis.php3).

E-Business Professionals

Sarah Greenstreet
Webmaster
TAMKO Roofing Products
http://www.tamko.com

Sarah Greenstreet

"I graduated in May of 1997 with a double major in marketing and management. Throughout my college program I participated in independent studies that focused on Web site development. Upon graduation I became a marketing director for a company where I did advertising layout and promotional pieces. I also supported the online new publications that this company produced, which gave me experience in graphics.

"I currently work at TAMKO Roofing Products, a leading manufacturer of commercial and residential roofing products. I work in the Web Development Department. I do feel like I'm drowning at times, but I like the challenge. I maintain and develop all corporate Web sites—http://www.tamko.com, http://www.roofreclaim.com, http://www.epochwood.com—plus many intranet sites. I spend most of the day in front of the computer writing code or doing graphical work. Another very important part of my job is visiting my internal customers to make sure their sites are performing the functions needed to complete their job. I work along with the Marketing Department, going over layouts and the next additions to http://www.tamko.com. It is very important to know the products your company produces.

"My day-to-day duties include development and making sure servers are up and running. I field calls concerning browsers, e-mail, or anything connected to the Internet or intranet sites. I participate in a lot of teamwork projects. Not only do I work with marketing, but also with database departments, managers, directors, and new and old customers.

"The skills that are required to do my job include an understanding of database, HTML, JavaScripting, and editing software, as well as communication skills. Graphical ability helps. You need to be detail orientated and have marketing and advertising knowledge. I love the fact that things change so fast in this industry. My workload and training can be a real balancing act at times. I see a long future in Web development; the growth in this area is unbelievable."

Rumors and Net Literacy

The ease of posting information over the Internet allows the dissemination of rumors. In the beginning of 1995, an e-mail message reported to be from the Associated Press was sent around the Internet; it stated that Microsoft had purchased the Vatican. This fraudulent AP news release should have been seen as an obvious hoax, but Microsoft received a number of complaints.[42] The news release might have been the result of careless reporting, or it might have been deliberate misinformation. It is vital for Internet users to cast a critical eye on information sent over the Internet. Consumers of Internet information must learn **Net literacy**, or how to evaluate information they find online.[43] A number of sites evaluate online rumors. Hoax-busters (http://hoaxbusters.ciac.org/HoaxBustersHome.html) aids in this process by describing hoaxes, suggesting what can be done about them, and offering a history of hoaxes on the Internet.

Netiquette

Netiquette is proper etiquette over networks, and it includes the rules for common courtesy online and in cyberspace. Virginia Shea has written a book called *Netiquette* outlining these rules. An online version is available on the Web at the Netiquette site: http://www.albion.com/netiquette.[44] The following are some basic considerations when going online with e-mail:[45]

- ☐ Be respectful of others online. Behave as if you were having a conversation with someone in person.
- ☐ Remember that the Internet is a global medium; others online may have a culture, language, or humor different from yours. Jokes and sarcasm may not travel well.
- ☐ Respect the copyright on reproduced material.
- ☐ Don't send chain letters through e-mail. Chain letters are forbidden on the Internet.
- ☐ When in a chat group, observe the discussion to get a feel for the group culture before making comments.
- ☐ Use mixed case. UPPER CASE LOOKS AS IF YOU'RE SHOUTING.
- ☐ Keep file sizes small.
- ☐ Don't send large amounts of unsolicited information to people.

Knowledge Integration

Terms and Concepts

Concepts and Questions for Review

1. Explain the role promotion plays in the marketing system.
2. Define the term *hypermedia*.
3. Describe how the communication process works.
4. Contrast a many-to-many model with a one-to-many model.
5. Define *nonlinear communication* and how it differs from linear communication.
6. How is relationship development achieved in a hypermedia environment?
7. Explain the different types of e-business communication platforms.
8. How can e-business communication platforms be used to target consumer markets?
9. Devise a strategy for using e-business communication platforms to facilitate internal business communication.
10. What impact have e-business communication platforms had on free speech?

Active Learning

Exercise 3.1 Evaluate Web Sites

Read the following short case. Evaluate the e-mail marketing campaign used by the company. Use the Targeted E-Mail Marketing Model (Figure 3.4) on page 85 to illustrate how this campaign was designed. List the measurement criteria used to determine if the campaign was successful.

E-Mailing to the Shower

Moen produces a variety of kitchen and bath products. A new product the company wanted to promote was called the Revolution Massaging Showerhead. The showerhead models cost between fifty and sixty-six dollars and were aimed at renters and homeowners. Moen identified its target market as the female decision maker in homes close to its main retail outlets.

The company decided to use an e-mail marketing campaign. It started with a list of 16,000 Moen Web site registrants and 40,000 individuals who provided e-mail addresses with warranty cards. These addresses were combined with 164,000 names rented from an outside list.

The goal of the campaign was to aid in branding, add names to the Moen database, and generate leads. Ideally, individuals would gain an interest in the product and then purchase it at a retail outlet. The e-mail contained a link to a Flash presentation that promoted three $5,000 online shopping sprees.

The campaign resulted in a 15 percent click-through to the Web site, 17,000 viral forwards, and more than 16,000 new registrants for the Moen database at a cost ($3.61 per address) that was one-tenth the cost of traditional direct marketing.[46]

Exercise 3.2 Developing E-Mail Marketing Campaigns

Develop a strategy using e-mail marketing techniques to market a product or service. Use the Targeted E-Mail Marketing Model (Figure 3.4) on page 85 as a guide. Include information on the profile of the market you plan to target. List the measurement criteria used to determine if this was a successful campaign.

Exercise 3.3 Devising a Strategy for Intrafirm Communication

Assume that you have been placed in charge of developing an integrated e-business communication system to facilitate employee-to-employee and business-to-employee communication. Determine the types of communication needed within the firm. Which platforms would best serve those communication needs? Speculate on new platforms the employees may be using in the future and decide how your business will respond to these new technologies.

Competitive Exercise 3.4 Devising a Strategy for Business-to-Customer Communication

Assume that you are asked to develop an integrated e-business communication system to serve your customers. What types of communication would your customers like to have with your business? Identify the platforms that would best serve those communication needs. What new platforms will your customer base be using in the future? How will your business use these new technologies? Justify why your plan should be adopted by your company.

Web Search—Looking Online

Search Term:	Digital Direct Marketing	First 5 out of 630,000

Target Marketing. Supports direct marketing efforts.
http://www.targetonline.com

TMX. Provides one-to-one digital broadcasting solutions to businesses around the world.
http://www.tmxinteractive.com/

Radical Communications. Offers digital direct marketing.
http://www.mindarrow.com/

MindArrow. Helps companies manage e-mail marketing campaigns and one-to-one sales communications through integrated applications.
http://www.mindarrow.com

Mobile Commerce World. Organizes a portal for mobile commerce and communication information.
http://www.mobilecommerceworld.com

Search Term:	Spam	First 4 out of 3,830,000

Responsible Electronic Communications Alliance (RECA). Promotes best practices for companies involved in online marketing.
http://www.responsibleemail.org

Mail Abuse Prevention System (MAPS). Defends the Internet's e-mail system from abuse by spammers.
http://www.mailabuse.org

The Spamhaus Project. Tracks known spam gangs and spam support services and works with ISPs to identify and remove spammers from the Internet.
http://www.spamhaus.org

Coalition Against Unsolicited Commercial E-mail (CAUCE). Advocates for a legislative solution to the problem of spam.
http://www.cauce.org

Search Term:	E-Mail ASP	First 1 out of 4,670,000

Boldfish. Provides global outgoing e-mail.
http://www.boldfish.com

Search Term:	Instant Messaging	First 2 out of 639,000

ActiveBuddy. Creates software for developing and hosting interactive agents.
http://www.activebuddy.com

FaceTime. Offers solutions for instant messaging networks for businesses.
http://www.facetime.com

Search Term:	Rich Media	First 3 out of 2,090,000

Macromedia. Produces software to bring multimedia to the Internet.
http://www.macromedia.com

EyeWonder. Allows for the delivery of streaming video and audio through a browser.
http://www.eyewonder.com

ExpandMail. Develops and delivers video e-mail.
http://www.expandmail.com

TurboAds. Offers information on rich media.
http://www.turboads.com

References

1. "Car Shoppers Increase Use of Internet," in CyberAtlas [online] (November 27, 2001), available from <http://cyberatlas.internet.com/markets/retailing/article/0,,6061_929231,00.html>.
2. Ruth Greenberg, "The Road to Interactivity," *CIO Web Business,* November 1, 1997, 70.
3. Dan Carmel, "BMW Drives New Web Strategy," *EC World,* October 2000, 66–68.
4. John Gaffney, "Forget the New M3. BMW's Hottest Product Is Streaming Online," in *Business 2.0* [online] (August 2001), available from <http://www.business2.com/articles/mag/0,1640,16730,FF.html>.
5. Donna L. Hoffman and Thomas Novak, "Marketing in Hypermedia Computer-Mediated Environments: Conceptual Foundations," *Journal of Marketing* 60 (July 1996): 50–68.
6. Ibid., 62–63.
7. Andrew Marlatt, "Who's Owner of Chasesucks.com and Chasestinks? Three Guesses," *Internet World,* June 15, 1998, 52.
8. Tracy Emerick, "Media and Marketing Strategies for the Internet," in *Cybermarketing,* ed. Gegina Brady, Edward Forrest, and Richard Mizerski (Lincolnwood, Ill.: NTC Business Books, 1997), 93–110.
9. Michael Nolan, "Building Corporate Identities Is Tricky on Net, But Payoff Can Be Great," *Web Week,* April 28, 1997, 31.
10. Brian O'Connell, "Bank on It," *Telephony,* January 28, 2002, 60; Russell Redman, "Wells Fargo to Web-Enable 6,300 Machines," *Bank Systems & Technology,* July 2000, 18.
11. Lew McCreary, "The Birth of the Do's," *CIO Web Business,* July 1, 1998, 45–47.
12. "E-Mealstrom: Snail vs. E-mail," *Business 2.0,* April 1999, 11.
13. Roberta Furger, "E-Mail's Second Shot," *Upside,* April 2000, 160–68.
14. "Functioning E-Mail Formats for Marketers," in eMarketer [online] (28 January 2002), available from <http://www.emarketer.com/estatnews/estats/email_marketing/20020128_opt.html>.
15. Eileen Colkin, "Marketing Capitalizes on E-Mail," *InformationWeek,* July 23, 2001, 55–56.
16. Cathleen Santosus, "Email Everywhere," June 27, 2000, *Business 2.0,* 308–11.
17. Jane E. Zarem, "Predicting the Next E-mail Business Model," *1to1 Magazine,* May/June 2001, 24.
18. Jason Compton, "Launch an E-Mail Ad Campaign," *Smart Business Magazine,* May 2001, 112–14; Evantheia Schibsted, "Email Takes Center Stage," *Business 2.0,* December 26, 2000, 64–71; Roberta Furger, "E-Mail's Second Shot," *Upside,* April 2000, 160–68.
19. Melissa Campanelli, "Proflowers Goes Beyond RFM to Lift Conversion Rates," *iMarketing News,* December 4, 2000, 19.
20. "Spam Spam Spam . . ." *Newsweek,* March 30, 1998, 10.
21. "How Much Spam Can You Stand?" *Newsweek,* June 21, 1999, 16; Lee Chae, "Tools That Help You Can Spam," *Network Magazine,* November 1998, 68–71.
22. Todd Spangler, "Anti-Spam Crew Carries Big Stick," *Interactive Week,* November 16, 1998, 40.
23. David P. Hamilton, "You've Got Mail (You Don't Want)," *Wall Street Journal,* April 23, 2001, R21.

24 Kimberly Patch and Eric Smalley, "Email Overload," *Network World,* October 26, 1998, 1, 45–48.

25 Matt Hicks, "What, Me SPAM?" *Eweek,* September 10, 2001, 51–57.

26 Paul McDougall, "IBM Intranet Unites Workers, Boosts Morale," in InformationWeek.com [online] (September 17, 2001), available from <http://www.informationweek.com/story/IWK20010913S0047>.

27 Julia Angwin, "Money Talks," *Wall Street Journal,* February 12, 2001, R23.

28 "Our Story," in Talk City Corporate Site [online] (September 14, 1999), available from <http://www.talkcity.com/corp/story.htmpl>.

29 Zhenya Gene Senyak, "Talk Shops," *Business 2.0,* June 13, 2000, 187–89.

30 Michelle Delio, "Show and Tell," *Customer Relationship Management,* March 2001, 42–48.

31 Marc Weingarten, "The Medium Is the Instant Message," *Business 2.0,* February 2002, 98–99; Tischelle George and Sandra Swanson, "Not Just Kid Stuff," *InformationWeek,* September 3, 2001, 37–39.

32 Michael Pastore, "Certain Applications Could Lead Consumers to Broadband," in Cyber-Atlas [online] (February 13, 2002), available from <http://cyberatlas.internet.com/markets/broadband/article/0,,10099_974301,00.html>.

33 Prudencia R. Orani, "SE Asians Prefer Mobile Phones, SMS to Keep in Touch," in Metropolitan Computer Times through Newsbytes.com [online] (February 6, 2002), available from <http://www.newsbytes.com/news/02/174267.html>.

34 Mobile Commerce World, "British SMS Records Smashed in December," in Mobile Commerce World [online] (January 24, 2002), available from <http://www.mobilecommerceworld.com/Tmpl/article.asp?CID=1&AID=11525&TCode=NW&T1=13/2/2002>.

35 Anne Chen, "Driving Wireless," *Eweek,* October 29, 2001, 53–59; Michael Cohn, "Message in a Mobile," *Internet World,* January 2002, 50–52.

36 Scott Kirsner, "Your Good Name," *Darwin,* December 2000/January 2001, 56–58; Read Stepanek, "'You Called Our Widget a What?'" *BusinessWeek,* September 25, 2000, 188; Jennifer Tanaka, "Beware What You Post," *Newsweek,* October 30, 2000, 90H.

37 Robert Hertzberg, "The Limits of Free Speech," *Internet World,* September 21, 1998, 10.

38 Mike France and Joann Muller, "A Site for Soreheads," *BusinessWeek,* April 12, 1999, 86–90; Charles Bermant, "Pest Control," *Business 2.0,* January 1999, 24–25.

39 Matt Gallaway, "Parody Sites Prevail in Court," in eCompany Now [online] (February 13, 2001), available from <http://www.ecompany.com/articles/web/0,1653,9452,00.html>.

40 Todd Spangler, "Court Rules against Library Filters," *Interactive Week,* December 7, 1998, 58.

41 Amy Cortese, John Carey, and David Woodruff, "Alt.Sex.Bondage Is Closed. Should We Be Scared?" *BusinessWeek,* January 15, 1996, 39; Kathleen Murphy and Ellis Booker, "China Builds an Internet, But Limits the Access," *Web Week,* February 3, 1997, 40–43.

42 "Stop the Presses! Microsoft Has NOT Bought the Vatican," *Open Systems Today,* January 9, 1995, 54.

43 For more on this topic, see Esther Dyson, "The End of the Official Story," *Brill's Content,* July/August 1998, 50–51.

44 In Netiquette Home Page [online] (December 8, 1998) available from <http://www.albion.com/netiquette/index.html>.

45 Adapted from Sally Hambridge, "RFC 1855: Netiquette Guidelines," in Delaware Tech Computer Services [online] (October 24, 1995), available from <www.dtcc.edu/cs/rfc1855.html>; Netiquette Home Page [online].

46 Based on Mickey Alam Khan, "New Names Pour in from Showerhead E-Mail," *iMarketing News,* February 18, 2002, 1, 18.

chapter 3 appendix
Web Page Design

Designing effective Web pages is beyond the ability of most individual developers. Many tasks are involved: determining strategic goals, writing copy, producing images, designing the layout, choosing fonts, coordinating colors, and writing programs to link to databases or enhance page content. Rarely do all these skills exist in a single individual; instead, teams of individuals work together to create sites. Marketers must be able to work with specialists to be sure that a Web site's goals are reached.

1. Understand how Web pages are structured.
2. Be able to explain the differences between word-processed files and Web pages.
3. Understand how hyperlinks work and what types of file locations they can go to.
4. Explain how content is sent to and called from a host.
5. Outline the elements of Web page design.
6. Identify locations for help on Web page design.

Web Page Structure

A page of Web content consists of text, images, and other associated elements such as sound files, programs, and so forth. Pages can be created in word processors, Web page editors, or other software packages that manipulate and display content. What differentiates Web pages from word-processed pages is the underlying code that tells a computer how to display and print the page content. For example, here is some formatted **ASCII** text: special. This text appears in bold-faced, italic, underlined, blue Arial type. The computer needs codes, or tags, to know how to display or print this text. A word processor would use tags such as these to turn formatting on and off: [Bold][Italics][Underline][Color: blue][Font: Arial]special[bold][italics][underline][color: red][Font: Time New Roman]. Each word processor has its own coding system; this is why word-processed documents need to be converted when they are moved from one word processor to another. HTML uses a set of open codes. The HTML tags for the example text are as follows: <p class=MsoNormal><b><i><u><spanstyle='color:blue'>special</span></u></i></b></p>.

> **ASCII** (American Standard Code for Information Interchange) is the built-in code used by most computers to represent the basic characters. For example, a computer stores a letter A in ASCII code as 1000001.

Word-processed pages are different from Web pages in that they hold all content in one file. For example, a Microsoft Word file can contain text, images, links, embedded sound files, and other content. A Web page contains only text and instructions, such as codes for where text, images, tables, and so forth are to be located and where hyperlinks should go. When a word-processed file is saved as HTML, all the tags are converted and all the associated content is split into separate files. Figure A3.1 illustrates how a Web page associates links and text.

Figure A3.1 shows that there is a considerable amount of code underlying even a small Web page. For this reason, most designers use Web page editing software to create their content the same way they use word processors. Specialized software, however, is not a requirement. Most word processors will save their documents as HTML. The advantages of using a word

Historical nSite

WordStar, an early word processor, asked its users to place formatting codes manually before and after text. Different codes were required for different printers. Another word processor, WordPerfect, used a split screen to reveal its codes. This was necessary because, at the time, computers did not display pages graphically. With the Windows graphical user interface Microsoft Word dispensed with editable codes. Now, all codes are hidden, and the computer displays the manipulated text.

Figure A3.1   Web Page Content

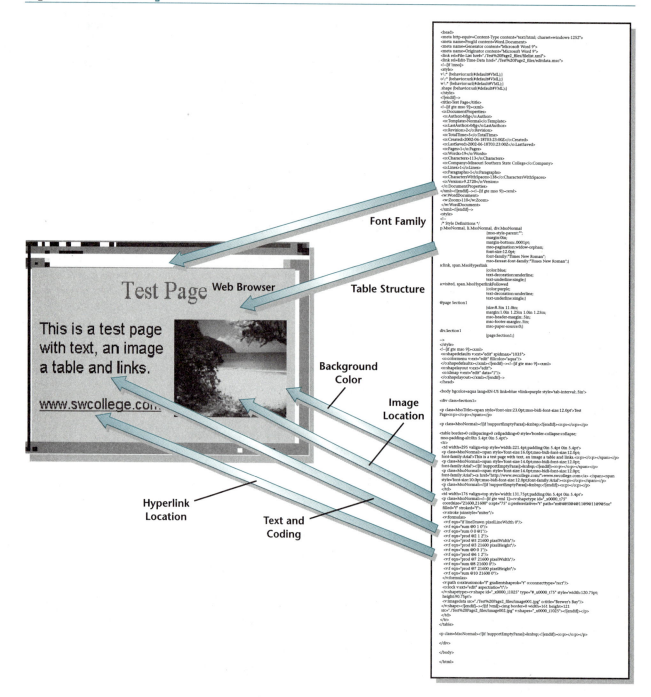

processor are that it can automatically check spelling and grammar, and most people are familiar with how to work these tools. Web page editors allow for more sophisticated page design.

Hyperlinks

Hyperlinks are the linchpin of the World Wide Web. A hyperlink acts as a command to deliver content to a browser. Hyperlinks can call files from URLs, from local disk drives, or from within the same file. A Web page editor allows a highlighted object (e.g., a word, an image, or a table cell) to be designated as a hyperlink. The link information is applied through a menu in the underlying code, which allows for precision targeting of links by listing Web pages, files, or bookmarked locations. Figure A3.2 illustrates the hyperlink process.

Hosting Options

Once a Web page is set up with page design, tables, links, and graphic images, it needs to be placed (with all associated files) on a host server linked to the Internet. A hosting ISP allocates server space and allows for an initial page to become the default, or starting, page shown when the Web site's URL is called. The ISP server delivers all requested content across the Internet to an individual's browser, as shown in Figure A3.3.

Figure A3.2   Setting Hyperlinks

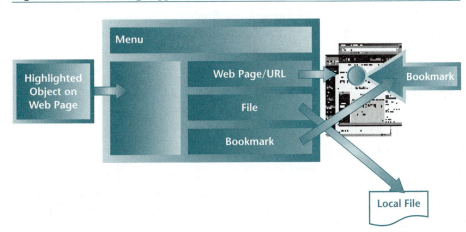

Figure A3.3   Sending Content from a Hosting ISP

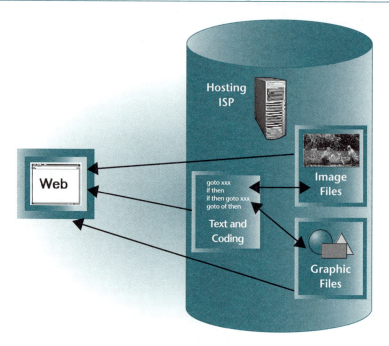

The Elements of Design

Web pages, like all promotional materials, are designed to communicate some specific messages to a targeted audience (see Chapter 7 on promotion). The first step in Web page design is to set some specific communication goals. To do this, designers of Web pages should consider the target market for the page, including the market's level of involvement with the product. They should then determine how to position the message to create competitive advantages and how to include all content of interest to the market. Once goals are set, the page can be designed. A number of design considerations have been identified in trade and academic journals, and these are outlined in Table A3.1. The application of these design considerations depends on a Web page's communication objectives and targeted audience.

Resource Sites

The Web itself is a great place to learn how to develop effective Web pages. A number of sites related to Web page design (on the non-HTML level) are listed in Table A3.2.

Table A3.1   Web Page Design Considerations

Design Consideration	Explanation
Accessibility	Access should be easy for users with all types of physical and computer capabilities.
Advertising	The type and number of ads on a Web page should fit the market's needs.
Content	The organization and type of information on the site should be based on the target market.
Customization	Delivering personalized content is best.
Feedback	Contact information should be visible, and responses should be timely.
Graphics	The background color, font size, graphics, and load time of the page impact the user's attitude toward the site.
Links	The alignment and number of links should meet the market's needs.
Navigation	The site should be consistent from page to page.
Ordering	Purchasing online should be simple and convenient.
Privacy	There should be an effective privacy policy.
Searches	Search tools should be accurate and easy to use.
Speed	Fast loading of graphics and text is important.
Updates	The site's content and format should be updated frequently.

Sources: Lisa Still and Thomasina Hutchison, "Web Site Design" (unpublished study of forty-seven trade journal articles on design); David M. Szymanski and Richard T. Hise, "E-Satisfaction: An Initial Examination," Journal of Retailing (Fall 2000); Qimei and William D. Wells, "Attitude Toward the Site," *Journal of Advertising Research 39* (September/October 1999).

Knowledge Integration

Terms and Concepts

Table A3.2   Web Site Design Resources

Site	Address	Comments
Communication Arts	http://www.commarts.com/index.html	Identifies design trends and teaches what does and does not work on the Internet.
CoolHomePages	http://www.CoolHomePages.com	Includes links to some of the best-designed sites on the Web, laid out by category.
Designing More Usable Web Sites	http://www.trace.wisc.edu/world/web/index.html	Facilitates cooperative efforts to build more usable Web sites.
Web Work: Tips for Writers and Designers	http://www.dsiegel.com/tips/	Offers a wide variety of tips on design for writers and designers.
Page Resources	http://www.pageresource.com	Provides a Web development tutorial and other information.
Usable Web	http://www.usableweb.com	Offers a collection of links about information architecture, human factors, user interface issues, and usable design related to the Web.
Web Design Group	http://www.htmlhelp.com	Promotes the creation on non-browser-specific Web pages.
Web Page Design for Designers	http://www.wpdfd.com/wpdres.htm	Provides a list of Web design resources developed from links submitted and recommended by readers.
Web Pages That Suck	http://www.webpagesthatsuck.com	Gives examples of good and poor Web page design.
Web Style Guide	http://info.med.yale.edu/caim/manual/contents.html	Offers numerous suggestions related to graphic and information design, page layout, site organization, navigation, and multimedia content.

Concepts and Questions for Review

1. Explain how word processors instruct the computer how to display and print page content.
2. How can word processors be differentiated from Web pages in relation to file structure?

3. Identify the linchpin that differentiates word processors from World Wide Web pages.

4. What are the key elements of Web page design?

Active Learning

Exercise A3.1: Page Evaluation

Find a Web site that you consider to be well designed. Evaluate this site against the design elements outlined in this appendix. How are these elements used in this Web site to create good design?

Exercise A3.2.: Page Design

Develop a Web site that takes into consideration the design elements outlined in this appendix. Justify the design choices you make.

Web Search—Looking Online

Search Term:	Internet Technology	First 1 out of 105,000,000

Internet Traffic Report. Gives information on how well the Internet is operating around the world, including average response times and packet losses. This information helps IT personnel diagnose network problems.
http://www.internettrafficreport.com

chapter 4

E-Business Distribution Systems and Supply Chain Management

Channels of distribution evolve over time in response to changes in the environment. The new technology-based information environment is transforming supply chains, channel structure, and relationships between intermediaries and those who facilitate the transport of goods. Channel functions are being taken over by cybermediaries. Power is shifting from manufacturers and retailers to customers. Conflicts are arising between channel members, as traditional middlemen face disintermediation, or the loss of their intermediary function. Individuals working for businesses operating in today's electronic environment will be involved in transforming enterprises. It is vital to understand the reasons that channels are evolving in order to understand how to construct e-business-based distribution systems.

1. Explain why distribution systems change.
2. Describe the nature of distribution systems.
3. Compare and contrast traditional distribution systems and e-business-based distribution systems.
4. Describe how each distribution function is handled in an e-business-based distribution system.
5. Outline how channel relationships are changing.
6. Discuss how power is shifting in distribution channels.
7. Explain how middlemen's roles are changing in the distribution channel.

The Car-Buying Game

"The customer is going to grab control of the process, and we're all going to salute smartly and do exactly what the customer tells us if we want to stay in business."

Robert Eaton
Retired Chrysler Corporation Chair[1]

A new manufacturing and distribution model radically transformed the automobile industry. Revolutionary manufacturing processes and a total reorganization of the industry's supply chain and distribution model characterized this transformation. These changes occurred in the early 1900s with the introduction of Henry Ford's assembly line manufacturing and development of car dealer distribution systems across the United States. The automotive supply chain system and purchasing process have not fundamentally changed since the early part of the twentieth century. Back then, car manufacturers relied on independent companies to supply parts and to establish sales and service dealerships. The manufacturers distributed cars to these dealers who, in turn, provided service and sold to the customer. Once the dealer network established itself, sales techniques were slow to change. Car salespeople worked on commissions and thus had an incentive to close the sale. When the prospective buyer entered the dealership, the salesperson's goal was to keep the prospect there and close the sale. The salesperson acted as a gatekeeper of information on the product and attempted to control the sales price.[2] Almost one hundred years later, the automotive industry is going through another revolution, this time brought about by the e-business environment.

There is a strong incentive for customers and manufacturers to drive distribution to an online environment. Customers gain bargaining power by having access to greater amounts of information and dealer choices. Manufacturers could save up to one-third of the sticker price of a car by avoiding the dealer network. The growth of the World

Wide Web is a driving force behind this change; in 1998, 44 percent of potential car buyers had Internet access, and one-third of that group used the Web for car-buying information. By 2001, 62 percent of U.S. consumers who purchased a car or truck used the Internet to aid in the shopping process.[3]

Consumers gain power by using information intermediaries such as Kelley Blue Book (http://www.kbb.com) and Edmunds.com (http://www.edmunds.com) to obtain information on auto comparisons, pricing, auto financing, and many other topics. CarPrices.com (http://www.carprices.com) provides information on dealer list prices for a car and all chosen options. Autobytel.com (http://www.autobytel.com) has a network of dealers that will supply a car at a predetermined price. Auto dealers bid against each other to make the sale. Customer-dealer intermediaries such as Autobytel and Microsoft Network's Carpoint (http://www.carpoint.msn.com) benefit both the auto dealers and the consumer. The dealer's commissions are lower, but this is offset by increased sales, lower marketing costs, and access to trade-ins.[4]

Under an e-business model, car manufacturers are using the Internet to retail cars, offer service, link suppliers, and provide other types of support. Table 4.1 illustrates the e-business strategies undertaken to restructure the automotive distribution system.

Auto manufacturers and dealerships have been forced to respond to the changes in how consumers use Internet information. Manufacturer's Web sites promote their brands, offer links to dealers, and provide other relationship-development tools. Many of the sites allow the buyer to shop from home and obtain detailed information on a car model and on competitive autos. The sites also help to determine which dealers have the car the customer desires. Prospective buyers can see the dealer's price for the car, arrange for a test drive, and order the car over the Web. GM found that implementing its strategy has some roadblocks. The Texas Department of Transportation denied GM a license to sell used cars in Texas because the manufacturer would compete with local car dealers.[5]

Manufacturers also use the Internet to link to their supply chain through extranets. DaimlerChrysler, Ford, General Motors, Nissan, and Renault joined forces and established the global automotive exchange Covisint (http://www.covisint.com) in December 2000. They were joined in May 2001 by Peugeot Citroen. This exchange has had problems because a number of channel conflicts have occurred within the partner firms and between their suppliers.[6]

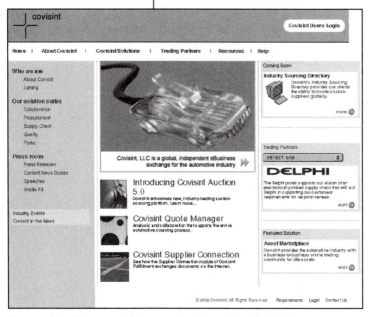

Source: <http://www.covisint.com>. Courtesy of Covisint, L.L.C.

Table 4.1   Restructuring the Automotive Distribution System

Area	Strategy	Goal
Retailing	Allow customers to customize their car purchases online, and track their orders.	Reduce working capital by lowering inventory.
Suppliers	Develop an auto manufacturing marketplace for all parts and supply purchasing.	Reduce transaction costs, speed data exchange, and lower prices through quantity discounts.
Financing	Allow for online financing and payments.	Cut costs, speed payment flows.
Marketing	Use online communication systems to inform, persuade, and develop leads.	Improve efficiency by gaining insight into customers' needs and design preferences.
Customer Service	Allow customers to use online systems to check financing, warranties, and service updates.	Improve service with instant access and collect data on customer problems.

Source: Kathleen Kerwin, Marcia Stepanek, and David Welch, "At Ford, E-Commerce Is Job 1," *BusinessWeek,* February 28, 2000, 74-78.

▶ Thinking Strategically

Decide how important a test drive is before choosing a car model to purchase. There is a belief among car salespeople that when customers come into a dealership, they have to be "sold to" before they leave or the sale is lost. Investigate the way people make decisions to purchase a car. When do they start thinking about the model to purchase? What type of information do they gather before they buy? Speculate on how the Web could help in their decision-making process. Contrast the traditional automobile business model and the new e-business-age business model. Speculate on the future of Covisint. What are the advantages and disadvantages of having a global automotive exchange for both the manufacturers and the suppliers?

The automotive industry is facing two areas of change. The first is in its **channel of distribution,** or the nature and structure of the firms and intermediaries that carry products from suppliers to customers. The second is in its **supply chain,** or the flow of raw materials, information, finances, and final products through the distribution channel. All businesses strive to become more competitive by making changes in their business systems, especially in their distribution systems and supply chains. The development of extranets is allowing suppliers, manufacturers, and dealers to link together. Traditional middlemen (individuals and firms) are threatened with disintermediation and are attempting to hold on to their positions by offering greater value. Channel conflicts are brewing as firms develop multiple distribution channels, and the dynamics of marketing relationships are changing as power shifts from manufacturers to new intermediaries and customers.

The automobile industry is not the only one facing restructuring due to these changes. Industries as varied as entertainment, retail, and manufacturing are being challenged by newly emerging distribution channels. This chapter will cover the theory behind the development and structure of marketing channels and explore the emerging distribution models. In addition, it will explain how supply chains are developing and obtaining new efficiencies.

The New Distribution System

Channels of distribution provide a standard of living for customers by moving products from producers to users in the most cost-efficient manner possible. In traditional markets, this has included producers and intermediaries such as wholesalers, retailers, or both. Marketing systems are constantly trying to lower the overall cost of distribution while striving to improve relationships between channel members. This requires the distribution system to evolve in response to changes in the environment.[7]

E-business-based distribution systems differ from traditional channel systems. They are characterized by the following:

- ☐ Electronic linkages between all distribution channel members
- ☐ Greater reliance on cybermediaries and facilitators
- ☐ Reduction in the number of traditional middlemen
- ☐ Reduced inventory and shorter inventory cycles
- ☐ Tighter relationships between trade sellers and buyers
- ☐ Power shifts from producers and retailers to customers
- ☐ Lower prices and greater variety for the consumer
- ☐ Greater responsiveness to the customer

The development of e-business channels is expected to have a substantial impact on the flow of goods from suppliers to the final customer. It is projected that business-to-business (B2B or B-to-B) online transactions will account for 36 percent of all B-to-B transactions by 2006 for a total of $5.4 trillion. The major reasons for this growth are that companies view online commerce as both a competitive advantage and a means of saving money. For example, using the Internet for procurement allows firms to cut cost and time by up to 70 percent. Manual B-to-B purchase orders can cost $107, while automated purchases can cost as little as $33.[8] Table 4.2 illustrates how the best-in-class companies using technology in their supply chains outperform the industry median measures. This change process is not without its problems. There are a number of barriers slowing the process of e-business channel development. These barriers include the cost and complexity of technology integra-

Table 4.2 Supply Chain Performance

	Delivery Performance to Request Date The percentage of orders that are fulfilled on or before the customer's requested date.		Upside Production Flexibility The number of days required to achieve an unplanned sustainable 20 percent increase in production.		Total Supply Chain Costs as Percentage of Revenue The total cost as a percentage of revenue.		Cash-to-Cash Cycle Time The number of days between paying for raw materials and getting paid for product, as calculated by inventory days of supply plus days of sales outstanding minus average payment period for material.	
	Best-in-Class	Median	Best-in-Class	Median	Best-in-Class	Median	Best-in-Class	Median
Computers and Data Storage	88.4%	61%	8.6	30	3.2%	7.3%	26	58.2
Consumer Packaged Goods	98.6%	82.9%	8.3	25.5	3.1%	8.7%	48	97.1
Electronic Equipment and Medical Devices	94.8%	76%	14	48.5	4.2%	8.9%	32.7	77.3
Aerospace Defense and Industrial	97.4%	75%	19.5	43.5	3.6%	11.9%	28.5	60.7
Pharmaceuticals and Chemicals	99%	94.5%	12.2	90	5.7%	11.5%	27	91.2
Telecommunications	86.7%	53.1%	28	70	2.6%	8.2%	60.2	103.5

Source: Courtesy of the Performance Measurement Group (PMG), a subsidiary of Pitiglio Rabin Todd and McGrath (PRTM). Based on a two-year benchmarking study of more than 110 participants. For more information contact PMG at 781-434-1470 or http://www.pmgbenchmarking.com.

tion into firms, the lack of trading-partner technological sophistication, the lack of clear return on investment (ROI), and cultural resistance.[9]

The Evolution of Distribution Channels

Channels of distribution have always evolved as new infrastructures and consumer shopping patterns have developed. In the 1800s, Sears took advantage of newly developed rail systems to build a retail empire by using catalogs to offer customers products that were not available locally. Sears's purchasing power allowed a greater variety of products, increasing its negotiation power and forcing down the prices offered to its customers. In the second half of the 1900s, customers took advantage of improved highway systems to move to the suburbs; Kmart followed and built a discount empire. The growth of suburbs led to retail concentrations in malls, which, in turn, fostered a shift in consumer purchasing patterns. The growth of national franchises and malls helped lead to the decline in retail sales in central business districts. Consumer acceptance of credit cards and 1-800 phone numbers has allowed a multitude of catalog companies to offer niche products to customers and deliver directly to their homes.

The growth of large retail outlets such as Wal-Mart has shifted power from manufacturers to retailers. **Just-in-time (JIT) inventory** systems allow firms to respond to competitive pressures by forcing lower overall costs and increasing quality and efficiency. **Electronic data interchange (EDI)** systems allow channel members to transfer transaction and inventory data electronically. Currently, Internet protocols are being used for the same types of data transfer, lowering the cost of linking suppliers, producers, sales representatives, and customers.

The Internet allows retailers to go directly into the consumer's home. Customers can order online from Sears (http://www.sears.com), Wal-Mart (http://www.walmart .com), and many other stores. In addition, Sears uses an online exchange intermediary, GlobalNetXchange (https://www.gnx.com), to facilitate purchasing from suppliers.

What Is Distribution?

Intermediaries and facilitators enable a transaction to take place between producers and customers. **Intermediaries,** such as wholesalers and retailers, split large production runs into small amounts (a process called **breaking bulk**), creating an assortment of products to offer a customer. **Facilitators** help the flow of the transaction by physically moving the product, information, or funds through the distribution channel. Figure 4.1 outlines a distribution system.

Distribution systems attempt to establish a level of coordination and control in hopes of developing the most efficient system at the lowest cost.[10] Channel members will spin off functions to other intermediaries or facilitators if these others can perform the function more efficiently. For example, if a firm had its own trucking service and decided it would be less expensive to have an independent trucking company ship its product, it would most likely close down its own operation and use the independent service.

Manufacturers break their large production runs into smaller units to sell to wholesalers. Wholesalers create an **assortment** for retailers, which, in turn, break the wholesalers' bulk into smaller units. Customers visit a retailer because it has created an assortment of products for them. This overall system is efficient; it reduces the total number of transactions because the customer does not need to

Figure 4.1 A Distribution System

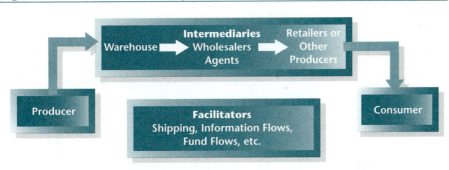

visit every manufacturer to obtain the desired products. If a channel cannot establish an efficient means of distribution to a market, the market will be left unserved. Small towns, for example, often don't have the same access to goods and services as larger communities. Figure 4.2 illustrates how intermediaries break bulk and create assortments to serve markets.

Figure 4.2 indicates that the overall number of transactions is reduced for the manufacturers, retailers, and customers. The manufacturer can produce larger production runs because it can move inventory and does not need to sell to each customer on an individual basis. The retailer and consumer, in turn, can go to a single source to purchase products. In the Figure 4.2 example, one market (customers D and E) is left unserved because it is not efficient for the channel to sell at that location.

A channel of distribution, whether it is offline or online, must perform a number of **channel functions,** described here:

- ☐ **Physical possession.** The good or service must be transferred to the customer. This includes the warehousing process and the physical movement of the product from the producer to the customer.
- ☐ **Title or ownership.** When the customer purchases or receives the product, title or ownership must be transferred.
- ☐ **Promotion.** Communication between the channel members is essential for promotion.
- ☐ **Ordering.** The channel member must also structure an ordering system. This could be through a paper-and-pencil system, or through electronically controlled data interchanges.
- ☐ **Payment.** A system for payment must be developed for goods when they are transferred. A customer may pay cash or use credit from other channel members by postponing payments (e.g., due in thirty to sixty days). The customer may also finance the purchase with a credit card or a store's charge card. This process implies risk on the part of the supplier if the customer does not pay. There is also risk on the purchaser's side in that the product may not perform as required.

The direction of flow for each of these functions is outlined in Figure 4.3.

Each of the channel functions outlined in Figure 4.3 can occur between producers (such as raw material suppliers and manufacturers) and intermediaries

Figure 4.2   Bulk Breaking and Assortment Creating

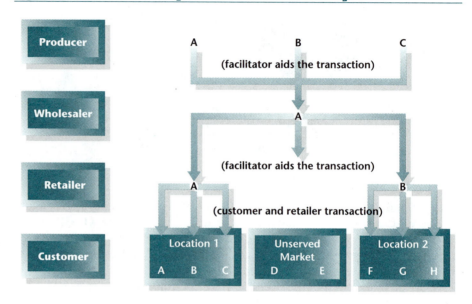

Figure 4.3   Traditional Channel Intermediary Flows

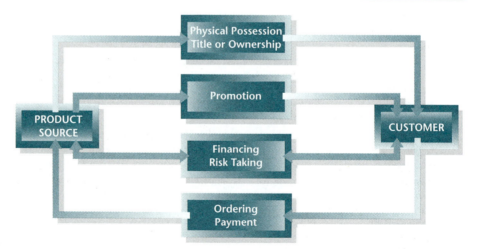

Source: Adapted from Roland S. Vaile, E. T. Gretner, and Reavis Cox, "Channels of Distribution,"
in *Marketing in the American Economy* (New York: Ronald Press, 1952); Louis W. Stern
and Adel I. El-Ansary, *Marketing Channels* (Engelwood Cliffs, N.J.: Prentice Hall, 1992).

(wholesalers, agents, and retailers) as well as between intermediaries and consumers. For example, a traditional retailer may receive products, promotion support, and financing from a distributor, which has received its products from another distributor or manufacturer. The retailer would then promote to the consumer (end user) and distribute the product. The retailer would forward its payments back through the channel to the distributor from funds received from its customers. Some of these functions may be delegated to a facilitator, such as a trucking company. Promotional flows could use advertising facilitators that provide communication services for channel members. Credit card companies also act as facilitators of payment and credit flows.

Channel systems evolve and attempt to become more efficient. The systems that grow and dominate offer a wider assortment of product choices to the customer, speed up delivery of goods and services, communicate more efficiently, lower the risk to the seller and the purchaser, ease the ordering process, and facilitate quicker payment flows. In addition, if the new distribution channel can lower costs by eliminating unneeded intermediaries and facilitators, it can gain cost advantages.

E-Business Channel Systems

E-business is changing the traditional channel structure. Electronic linkages through e-commerce and extranets are lowering the overall transaction costs associated with channel functions.[11] When customers can efficiently choose from a number of different suppliers of products or services at a low cost, they do not need to have a retailer create an assortment. In addition, the manufacturer does not need an intermediary to find customers. Inventory levels can be reduced if a manufacturer's strategy includes **mass customization,** or production to order. These strategies result in a strong incentive to sell directly to the end user and no reason to break bulk.

Mass customization *is the process of producing individualized products at mass-production speeds and efficiencies.*

Figure 4.4 illustrates how an e-business uses extranets and cybermediaries to facilitate transactions. One channel has an e-business-based retailer that uses extranets and the Internet to facilitate the transaction and to reach customers who order online. This can save on the retailer's costs because it does not need to structure a brick-and-mortar site to reach consumers. If, on the other hand, the producer finds that its overall transaction costs are lower, it is possible for the producer to sell directly to the end user by bypassing its traditional intermediary.

The **cybermediaries** shown in Figure 4.4 are organizations that operate in electronic markets to facilitate the exchange process.[12] These facilitators are taking a more commanding role and are restructuring the channel system. Facilitators support the functions required in marketing channels. Examples of facilitators that help move a physical product include trucking companies and overnight shippers. Facilitators that help payment flows include credit card companies and banking institutions. Other facilitators help the communication process, including advertising companies and host ISPs that develop promotional content.

Figure 4.4   Alternate Electronic Channels of Distribution

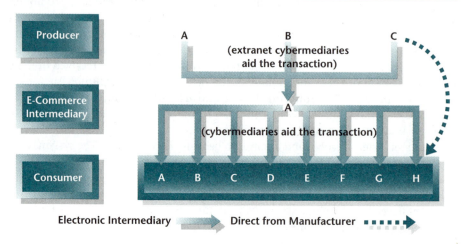

A number of e-commerce **fulfillment** companies offer complete distribution systems for businesses. These systems include electronic storefronts, warehousing, shipping, billing, and more. For companies that process a limited number of orders (this can be as low as one thousand per day), fulfillment services should be outsourced. This allows companies that specialize in the fulfillment process to meet customer needs quickly and efficiently.[13]

An e-business needs to determine the most cost-effective means of achieving coordination and control between the cybermediaries and the customer. The e-business could have its Web site communicate information about the product or service directly to the consumer. When the consumer places an order, the payment could be routed through credit card companies or banking institutions. The e-business could arrange to have the product shipped to the customer, using an overnight shipper or another shipping system. Additional inventory could be controlled online over extranets. Specialized e-businesses called **e-marketplaces** have been established for a number of industries. An e-marketplace uses e-business technology to allow trading partners to buy and sell goods and services electronically.[14] The Covisint company mentioned in the opening vignette is an e-marketplace for the automotive industry. Figure 4.5 illustrates how channel functions are performed in an e-business distribution system.

An e-business distribution system can be a large investment, but it also has the potential for a large payoff. Successful e-business supply chains allow multiple transactions to occur at one time. A single purchase order can initiate billing, inventory management, production scheduling, and distribution coordination. This process is not without problems. Implementing electronic supply chains can change traditional channel structures and relationships, requiring changes in staffing and culture. E-business facilitators, such as e-marketplaces, attempt to

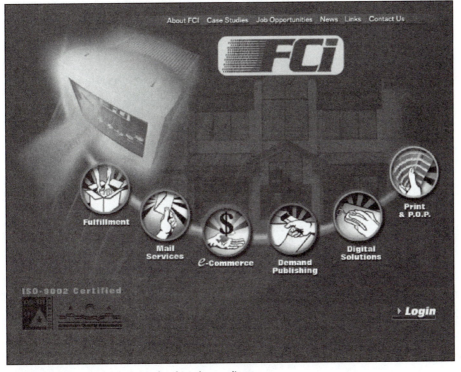

Fulfillment Concepts is an example of a cybermediary.
Source: <http://www.fulfillmentconcepts.com>. Fulfillment Concepts, Inc. Louisville, KY.

limit change within a firm by setting themselves up to act as commerce service providers that coordinate the exchange process. These commerce service providers charge a fee or take a percentage of sales (or both) for these services.[15]

Many businesses structure **private exchanges** for their supply chain. A private exchange provides the same functions as an e-marketplace but is open only to a specific firm's or industry's supply chain. Hewlett-Packard set up a private exchange for companies that produce HP logos (http://www.getsupply.com). The private exchange saved HP $7.5 million a year in logo purchases alone. Volkswagen used its private exchange to cut procurement costs by up to 50 percent and shorten contract negotiations from three months to as little as one day.[16] Private exchanges provide efficiencies to pre-existing relationships and purchasing systems. Public exchanges have not been as successful because they require the development of new or transitory relationships between suppliers and purchasers.[17]

E-Business Distribution Development

The e-marketplace shown in Figure 4.5 is positioned to become the electronic channel captain. A **channel captain** is an intermediary that organizes and controls

Figure 4.5   E-Business Distribution System

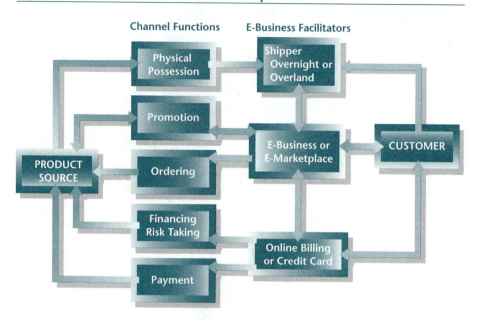

Source: Based on Brad Kleindl, "Virtual Marketing," *Southern Business and Economic Review* (Spring 1996): 10–15.

the channel. Any company that can gain this position can obtain power over other members, allowing it to take a higher percentage of the overall transaction costs. **Internet malls** were the original models for channel captains. Internet malls act as the host and coordinator for a number of individual businesses. The customer can find multiple vendors and browse the mall for products. Both the business and the mall benefit from each other's cooperation: the individual business does not have to set up and maintain Internet access and e-commerce servers, and the mall takes fees and a percentage of sales for the service. Many portals and search engines offer shopping services for established companies and individuals who wish to sell products online. One of the disadvantages of using an intermediary is that the seller must advertise the intermediary's Web address to customers to drive purchases. Once the investment has been made to make the market aware of a site's address, changing to another site means incurring additional transaction costs. To lower this dependency, the seller should consider having its own IP address and host its site on an ISP that can provide commerce functions. The downside with this approach is that the business loses the intermediary's drawing power.

The speed with which current channels move toward an e-business distribution system like the one outlined in Figure 4.5 depends on how efficient this system is over current systems. To understand this change, each of the channel functions of the e-business distribution system is discussed in the following sections.

Physical Possession

Physical possession requires physically moving products from one location to another. Shippers, such as Yellow (http://www.myyellow.com), FedEx (http://www.FedEx.com), United Parcel Service (http://www.ups.com), and others have developed logistical systems to efficiently move products from one site to another. These shippers have expanded their services to customers through technological integration. In addition to its portal Web site, Yellow allows its more than thirty-seven thousand customers to communicate using wireless media, instant messaging, and voice messages over IP networks. All of the major transportation and delivery companies offer online tracking of shipments and packages.

FedEx is expanding to include the pickup, transport, warehousing, and delivery of finished goods. FedEx handles all the logistical operations and warehousing for a number of companies, including National Semiconductor. Integration between FedEx and these companies is so tight that customers can order FedEx services directly from a product vendor, allowing the receiving customer to track a package and specify where a package should be picked up.[18]

Businesses that do not wish to be locked in to a single transportation facilitator can use information intermediaries to provide efficiency to the channel. A number of companies act as shipping information intermediaries. Freightquote.com(http://www.freightquote.com) and Transportation.com (http://www.transportation.com) allow shippers to check prices and schedule shipments.

E-Business Professionals

Matt Olson
Cerner Corporation
http://www.cerner.com

Matt Olson

Matt Olson graduated with a B.A. in marketing in 1999. He currently works for Cerner Corporation in Kansas City, Missouri, where he leads a team on Cerner's external Web property, Cerner.com. Matt is deeply involved with the day-to-day activities of the Web site, helping drive strategy on a variety of things—international sites, acquired companies, content management, and push/interactive marketing. His team of seven manages around two thousand pages of content for a $540 million company. Matt fights constant battles with gathering content, using the proper tools, developing information architecture, ensuring usability and obtaining funds.

Matt has been a member of Cerner's Marketing Leadership Team, was named to the companywide Emerging Leaders group, and was selected as a Cerner Top Gun—a Cerner-wide recognition for the top 5 percent of employees in the company. Matt is very much a jack-of-all-trades. He speaks a variety of "languages" to many different people across roles, including technical development, product development, government and industry relations, direct sales, and more.

Project management, planning, and multitasking are skills Matt uses every day. A working understanding of HTML and even fundamental Flash are important as he works with developers and technical personnel. Copyediting skills are also helpful, because his marketing department is still primarily focused on print. Transforming hard-copy content into a Web-digestible form is a constant activity that requires strong writing skills. It is also imperative to have an understanding of knowledge architecture and usability, as his team is responsible for making the Web site intuitive and easy to use for a variety of users with varying goals. Matt is critiqued in reviews on problem solving, learning on the fly, navigating the system, market awareness, knowledge sharing, defending the brand, and others.

Communication Linkages

Communication between the firm and the customer can be facilitated over the Internet through the design of Web pages, as outlined in Chapter 3. Extranets are used to link businesses together, enabling communication between companies and allowing for transactions. Wal-Mart's extranet invites buyers and suppliers to access terabytes of data on sales figures, product sales, and even individual customers' sales. The data are used to help determine customer shopping patterns. Its extranet has allowed Wal-Mart to reduce store inventories and speed up its supply chain. For example, Wal-Mart receives three to five shipments of Christmas seasonal items when it used to receive only one. This permits Wal-Mart to limit losses from excess inventory.[19]

Extranets are becoming the basis for this information flow. As these changes move more strongly toward the Web, customers, shippers, producers, and others will be able to access the status of orders, products, and processes online. This will speed communication and help limit gatekeepers' ability to control information.

Payment, Financing, and Risk Taking

One of the major considerations cited as hindering the growth of e-commerce is the consumer's perception of the risk of making payments over the Internet. There are actually four parties at risk in electronic transfers: the customer (end user), the seller (business-to-business facilitator or retailer), the producer, and the transfer agent (credit card company or banking institution). An example of the electronic flow of funds between these parties is shown in Figure 4.6.

The flow outlined in Figure 4.6 is very similar to the traditional credit payment process. In an e-commerce purchase, all the payment flows can be handled electronically. The vendor must receive approval for the purchase made by the customer. The customer's exposure to loss is much more limited than the seller's. Although a credit card holder may be liable for a limited amount, such as fifty dollars, the vendor may be the victim of fraud and liable for the entire amount of the purchase. Because these payments are made electronically, the seller must be sure that the customer is an authorized purchaser. If the vendor acts on an unauthorized payment, it may be at risk for the loss of product and funds.[20]

Some of the major concerns businesses have related to online fraud include loss of revenue, loss of staff time, and loss of consumer goodwill. The most common fraud losses are the result of physical theft of a credit card, identity theft, and credit card numbers stolen off the Internet. These numbers are often stolen from merchant and processor databases that have been hacked into.[22]

E-commerce security is a major concern for businesses conducting online transactions. As described in Chapter 2, online security is controlled through firewalls. E-payment security, however, includes some unique considerations. E-commerce sites are at the top of hackers'

The Political, Legal and Ethical Environment

Credit card theft is on the rise in Asia. Theft rings use employees at stores and restaurants to steal a card's identification by using a skimmer, a device that records card information and stores it on a chip. This information is then sold to counterfeiting rings that reproduce the cards and use them to purchase items.[21] To limit fraud, Japan has been adopting smart card technology.

Figure 4.6 Transfer of Electronic Payments (E-Payments)

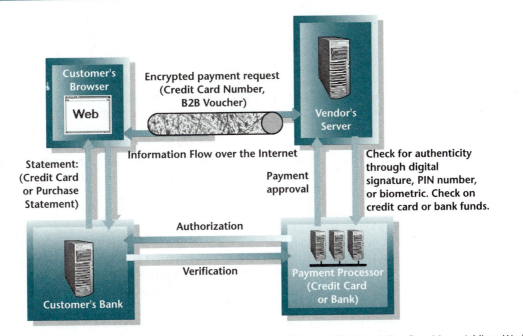

Source: Adapted from Ravi Kalakotoa and Andrew B. Whinston, *Frontiers of Electronic Commerce* (Reading, Mass.: Addison-Wesley, 1996), 319.

hit lists. Some hackers are looking only for information on how the site is maintained; others are interested in credit card theft. In 2001, online fraud losses were more than $700 million, or 1.14 percent of the total online sales of $61.8 billion. One study found that in some parts of Asia, up to 10 percent of online purchases are fraudulent. Credit card companies are attempting to lower credit card losses by implementing online security systems.[23]

To enhance the security of online payments and to make purchases easier, standards for consumer credit payments are being set for the Web. For instance, the **secure electronic transaction (SET)** system allows for the encryption of all transaction data. Merchants never see the credit card number, so it cannot be stolen from them, and they cannot fraudulently use the number. The cardholder is required to set up an account with the credit card processor to use the system. This technology has received greater acceptance in Europe and Asia than in the United States.[24] Digital and electronic signatures are also used for authentication. A **digital signature** is a unique alphanumeric number related to a document and the individual who sends the document. These numbers are encrypted and sent over the Internet. Digital signatures can be verified on purchase orders before transactions are completed. **Electronic signatures** include digital signatures and other forms of identification such as passwords and biometrics. Electronic signatures have the same legal weight as hand-signed signatures.[25]

Historical nSite

Frank McNamara developed the first credit card. He forgot to bring his wallet to pay for dinner, so his wife covered the bill. McNamara thought that there must be a better way. He developed a credit card–sized piece of cardboard that authorized the restaurant to bill him for dinner. He offered the card to two hundred friends and acquaintances, and it was honored at fourteen restaurants in Manhattan. This card turned into the Diner's Club card (http://www.dinersclub.com).[26]

The payment processor attempts to lower the overall risk involved in the purchase by limiting fraud. Criminals who attempt to use credit card numbers do not have to physically steal a credit card to use it. Some criminals use computers to randomly generate card numbers until they find one that is active. Credit card companies, in turn, attempt to block unauthorized use by accessing their databases to look for any purchasing behavior that falls out of the norm for the cardholder. For example, if it looks as if the cardholder never buys products in Hong Kong, the cardholder may receive a call from the card company to verify a Hong Kong sale.

Electronic Payments

Many merchants would like to sell products or services online that would cost pennies rather than dollars. Music companies, for instance, would like to sell individual songs online; information sources such as newspapers, magazines, dictionaries, and encyclopedias would like to sell content on a per-use basis. **Micropayments** are a means of paying for these small Web transactions. The transaction cost of making payments with credit cards or voucher checks can be high for these small purchases. Micropayment systems can be set up with digital wallets or charged to an individual's credit card. A **software wallet** requires a buyer to set up an online account that allows an amount of money to be added to a Web browser's wallet. When a microtransaction is undertaken, the wallet is debited, or has money taken out. This system works much the same way as a smart card.[27]

Smart cards, or e-cash (electronic cash), allow individuals to purchase without paper dollars. Smart cards have been in use in much of the world except the United States, where magnetic-strip cards have dominated. Many Americans currently use debit cards, which authorize payments from their bank accounts to make purchases. Smart cards use a microcontroller chip embedded in a card. The microchip makes it very difficult to steal, or copy, information from a card, as can be done with a magnetic-strip-based credit card. Around the world, devices such as parking meters, newsstands, vending machines, and pay phones can read the cards for payment. The cards can be purchased and reloaded from a bank account using an ATM-style machine. Information on individual purchases can be collected from the cards for the marketer's database. This technology is becoming predominant because it reduces the overall transaction expense for businesses and decreases chances for fraud.[28] Security can be further enhanced through smart cards that use fingerprint recognition, allowing only one authorized individual to use the card.[29] Smart cards are being adapted for use on the Web. Standards are being adopted that will allow smart cards to be read on PCs for making online micropurchases. Gemplus (http://www.gemplus.fr), the French firm that developed the smart card, allows purchases to be made over France's telecommunications network.[30]

Adoption of these cards in the United States has been slow, but the rapid growth of phone cards, which are smart cards used for phone calls, indicates that consumers will accept this type of technology. The U.S.-based retailer Target issues a smart card for use in all of its stores.[31] Table 4.3 outlines a number of electronic payment options.

Online payments can reduce the cost of processing checks. The U.S. government has mandated that businesses start to make their tax payments to the federal government through online systems. In addition, the federal government is pushing the electronic transfer of checks rather than issuing paper. The cost savings to the government are substantial. In 1996, 63 billion consumer and commercial paper checks were written. Processing costs for electronic transactions are twenty-five cents versus check-processing costs of one dollar. Electronic transfers can lower fraud, and it is estimated that costs for all parties can be reduced by $300 billion.[32]

Figure 4.3 Electronic Payment Options

Option	Description	Advantages	Disadvantages
Credit Cards	Magnetic-strip-based cards that allow for charging purchases.	Widely used and accepted around the world. Infrastructure to read cards in place.	Subject to fraud through number theft, card scanning, or card theft.
Debit Cards	Magnetic-strip-based cards that allow for debiting purchases or cash withdrawals from checking accounts.	Widely used and accepted around the world. Infrastructure to read cards in place. Uses PIN number for enhanced security.	Subject to fraud through number theft, card scanning, or card theft. (PIN numbers offer additional protection.)
Smart Cards	Enhanced credit cards that use a microchip to record information.	Allows for enhanced security, micropayments, and the storage of additional information. Can be tied to PCs for payments.	Cards can be stolen, but if linked to PIN numbers or biometrics, security can be enhanced.
Online Wallets	Software-based payment system tied to a PC.	Allows for micropayments online.	Technology not widely available or accepted by all retailers.
Wireless Purchases	Wireless device system that allows purchases to be made and charged to a phone bill.	Allows for micropayments and security.	Technology not widely available.

Case 4.1

Britney Powers Chips

Smart cards have not received wide acceptance in the United States. To change this, two companies are targeting the seven-to-fifteen-year-old "tween" market. One company is targeting boys with a video game site, while Britney Spears is targeting girls with her Web site. To use the smart cards, the tweens must have a card reader for their PC.

StatCard Entertainment (http://www.statcard.com) has developed the smart card targeted at boys. This card builds off the young male tween's interests in gaming and card trading. Tweens can play each other online and win points from other tweens' cards, and they can gain points by doing tricks on the game Web site. They can trade cards and use an $8.99 card reader to show how much value is on a card. Each card is tied to a well-known skateboarder and costs $7.99.[33]

The Britney Spears site (http://www.britneyspears.com/smartflashcard/index.php) offers girls an inside view of Britney's world tour. To view the Britney site, the tween must purchase a Britney card and reader for $29.99. Purchasing new cards allows access to different parts of the Web site.

Electronic Billing

Electronic billing, or sending bills and making payments over the Internet, would greatly reduce transaction costs for companies. Paper bills need to be printed and envelopes stuffed and posted, and there also must be a person available to record when payments are made by check. This can result in a cost to the company of up to $1.75 per bill. Online billing can cut that cost to around 15 to 40 cents per bill. Online bill-consolidation companies such as CheckFree (http://www.checkfree.com) will consolidate individuals' bills, allowing them to make one payment online. These consolidators also get the public to visit their sites many times in one month, facilitating advertising.[34] Online billing from business-to-consumer has not taken off as quickly as expected. Online bill paying is expected to increase to include 14 percent of all U.S. households by 2004.[35] Business-to-business online payments, in contrast, are widespread; electronic payments are used for making small transactions, such as travel reimbursement and parts and supplies payments, as well as large transactions between firms.[36]

▶ Thinking Strategically: Case 4.1

Speculate on the future success of smart card technology in the United States. Indicate the advantages these systems have over credit cards. Outline the business model for the boys' smart cards. Where else could this type of application be used? How close are these payment systems to replacing cash?

Relationship Development

The search for channel members is a time-consuming and expensive undertaking for a business. Once these relationships are established, firms have an incentive to maintain the best possible relationship. Each channel member, however, must balance its needs with those of its fellow channel members. To make this balancing act work, a firm must take into consideration the behavioral aspects of channel **relationship development**, including dependence, cooperation, conflict, power and power bases, satisfaction, and relational issues. The electronic marketplace is changing how marketing relationships develop. New business models are increasing the power of some facilitators while removing other intermediaries. The following sections will investigate some of the behavioral dimensions of channel relationships.

Source: <http://www.britneyspears.com/smartflashcard/index.php>. NVU Productions/Britney Brands, Inc.

Power

Part of the total power of a channel member is due to the dependency of one channel member on another; a channel member is dependent if it does not have alternatives to provide the same channel functions. In e-business channel relationships, the dependency of one member on another can be lessened when partnerships are no longer limited to geographic convenience. **Transaction cost analysis** typically governs how much effort is used to keep channel members as partners. If the cost of finding alternative sources is too high, then alternatives are not pursued. The Internet allows businesses to find intermediaries and facilitators easily and offers the possibility of bypassing some channel members, causing a reduction in the **power dependency** of some members.

Transaction cost analysis *is the process of assessing the overall cost of a transaction. If the total cost of maintaining the current relationship is higher than developing a new relationship, a firm will change partners.*

Consumers' Power

The consumer, or end user, is perhaps the biggest winner in the e-business distribution channel. Many consumers have limited alternative sources of supply because they are not geographically centered in large market areas. The Internet's ability to provide information increases the customer's power because the customer can become aware of a wider variety of providers. In addition, customers are able to voice their opinions on businesses and products at discussion sites and business sites. At Amazon.com, for example, customers can make comments on a book so others can see an average reader's opinion.

A consumer in a local market area may wish to purchase a specific brand of automobile. That individual has traditionally been locked in to using the local dealer or dealers within a limited driving area. Now, with Web-based searching and online sales systems, the customer can shop the entire country (or world) for the automobile. There may be additional costs in having the auto shipped from one location to another, but lower prices (due to increases in the customer's negotiation

Fighting for the Middle Position

Ingram Micro (http://www.ingrammicro.com) is the world's largest warehouser and distributor of software and computer products. It has positioned itself as the back warehouse for some 175,000 corporate resellers in more than one hundred countries. Ingram acts as a company's warehouse, facilitating frictionless inventory delivery. Information moves online from a buyer through the reseller's site to Ingram for assembly or delivery. Information then flows back to the material suppliers over the firm's extranet system, indicating delivery times and conditions.

Ingram remains in the channel because it manages a number of distribution functions in an effective way. This includes providing a large assortment of different products from different vendors. Ingram will undertake credit checks and extend credit. It will **drop-ship** a product directly to the buyer. These services increase the power of Ingram in the distribution channel, but they also allow niche businesses to start with little capital or without a brick-and-mortar physical location by using Ingram's system.

Ingram does not see itself as becoming the channel captain. The companies it serves undertake the research and development necessary to develop new products, create pull-through promotion, and interact with the market. Ingram has extended its power by hosting or partially funding branded Web transaction sites for its customers. In this process, Ingram can ship and invoice a product so it looks as if it came from any retailer. This service allows a retailer to exist with no supply chain functions and also gives Ingram the first chance to fulfill orders and to offer a direct link to inventory.[37]

To **drop-ship** *means a manufacturer or wholesaler ships directly to the customer at the request of the seller (a retailer or broker).*

power) can more than make up for these costs. The buyer can also obtain information such as invoice costs, dealer costs, complaints, and repair notices for the brand of car to aid in the purchase decision.

▶ Thinking Strategically: Case 4.2

Consider the position of Ingram Micro. Explain why it exists in the channel by looking at the benefits it provides to the seller and the buyer. Determine the long-term viability of Ingram. Could the manufacturers of software and hardware bypass Ingram? Consider Ingram's customers. Recommend to Ingram whether or not it should start selling directly to the end user.

Channel Conflicts

A **channel conflict** exists when a company sells products to the same market through more than one distribution system. Manufacturers consider channel conflicts the strongest consideration when evaluating e-commerce opportunities. In some cases, manufacturers have refused to supply online sales businesses due to fear of channel conflicts. Companies are undertaking a number of strategies to handle channel conflicts.[38] To avoid these conflicts, some companies will not risk alienating their resellers by selling their products online; instead, they only promote their products and provide information on retail outlets. VF (http://www.vfc.com), a maker of clothing products such as Lee and Wrangler jeans, decided that the $5 to $10 million it could make with e-commerce was not worth the risk of alienating the $5 billion in business it obtains through traditional channels of distribution. VF's Web sites are designed as destination sites offering information and entertainment. When customers want to buy, they are linked to a vendor site.

Other approaches to handling channel conflicts include companies setting up e-commerce sites and then having the products delivered through traditional distributors. Companies may sell products online that are different from current offline products. Another approach is to offer products at the same price as retail outlets and then add a shipping fee. This raises the price of distribution but allows the seller to reach a wider audience than would be available through the retail outlet alone. Finally, some companies press ahead with a commerce site. Many firms are offering product lines and services that distributors do not carry.

Death of the Middleman or a New Role?

Middlemen are facing **disintermediation**, or elimination, of their role between the producer and the customer. Obviously, this is having a strong impact on the traditional middleman. Many salespersons have made their living by leveraging both their knowledge of customers' needs and their access to goods and services. For some industries, new commerce models have the potential to replace salespeople. Industries as varied as real estate, stock brokerage, insurance sales, travel agencies, automotive sales, and order-taking sales could face extinction if they do not find a way to add value to the exchange process.[39]

The middlemen most likely to be hurt are those who do not add value to the exchange but are only go-betweens, information brokers, or order takers. Middlemen concerned about their careers should offer value to the exchange process. If they are only acting as a go-between for the buyer and the seller or only providing information to the client, they are in danger of being disintermediated. VARs, or value-added resellers, must make use of new technologies to shorten lead times and create greater efficiency.[40] Without adding value, information gatekeeping is not enough for survival.

> **Disintermediation** *is the process of eliminating the middleman from the exchange process.*

Knowledge Integration

Terms and Concepts

Assortment *112*
Breaking bulk *112*
Channel captain *117*
Channel conflict *126*
Channel
    functions *113*
Channel of
    distribution *109*
Cybermediaries *115*
Digital signature *121*
Disintermediation *127*
Drop-ship *126*

Electronic data inter-
    change (EDI) *112*
Electronic signatures *121*
E-commerce security *120*
E-marketplaces *116*
Facilitators *112*
Fulfillment *116*
Intermediaries *112*
Internet malls *118*
Just-in-time (JIT)
    inventory *112*
Mass customization *115*

Micropayments *122*
Power dependency *125*
Private exchanges *117*
Relationship
    development *124*
Secure electronic
    transaction (SET) *121*
Smart cards *122*
Software wallet *122*
Supply chain *109*
Transaction cost
    analysis *125*

Concepts and Questions for Review

1. Explain what distribution channels do.
2. Why do distribution channels evolve?
3. List the distribution channel functions and explain why they must be performed.
4. How do e-business distribution functions operate?
5. Compare and contrast alternative online payment systems.
6. Why would a supply firm want to participate in a public exchange where its products could be directly compared in features and price against its competitors? Why would it not want to participate?
7. Describe how the behavioral dimensions of channel functions differ under an e-business environment.
8. Consider relationship development in an e-business channel. Who loses power, and who gains power?
9. How is e-business shifting power to customers?
10. Speculate on how a business can minimize dependency on a fulfillment company when trying to meet the needs of customers.
11. How can channel conflicts be controlled in an e-business channel?
12. Explain what disintermediation is and who will feel this effect.
13. What should middlemen do to keep their jobs?

Active Learning

Exercise 4.1 Lassoing Jeans Online

Lee Jeans (http://www.leejeans.com) and Wrangler Jeans (http://www.wrangler.com) push online purchasing to other vendors. Arizona Jeans (http://www.arizonajeans.com) allows sales online. Levi Strauss (http://www.levi.com) allowed sales online in the past, but then pulled back from this strategy. Visit each of the sites listed. Decide why these brands have adopted different strategies for using the Web in aiding distribution. Consider who owns the brands and how that may make a difference in the chosen strategy. Why do you think Levi Strauss changed its strategy?

Exercise 4.2 Outlining a Distribution System

Use the Web to find a business engaging in e-commerce. Diagram its distribution process in the figure shown here. Determine how each of its distribution functions is being performed.

1. Describe the role of the e-business in the distribution model.

2. How is each function being performed?

Example of an E-Business Distribution System

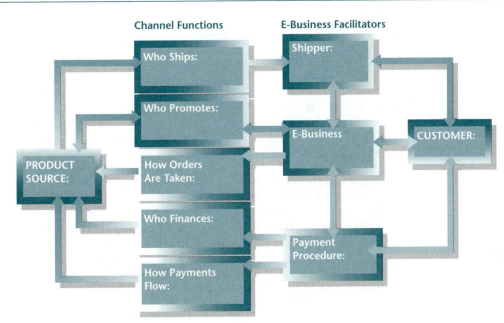

3. Determine if the cost of the product offered is different from the cost of the product available locally.

4. Do you see any channel conflicts that may occur with this system?

Competitive Exercise 4.3 Developing an E-Distribution System

Some businesses find it is more efficient to allow others to control some aspect of their distribution functions. These businesses may turn to commerce service providers or fulfillment companies for support. Assume you (or you and your team) are going to present a distribution strategy proposal to management. Evaluate fulfillment providers online and determine which would be best at providing support (use a search term such as *e-commerce fulfillment*). Consider if a cybermediary fulfillment company is best at handling services for small businesses or large businesses. What are the risks of placing your inventory in a fulfillment company? Contrast the pros and cons of developing these services in-house or outsourcing. Make a final recommendation.

Web Search—Looking Online

Search Term: Online Auto Sales   First 5 out of 1,639,213

Autobytel.com. Offers a site where dealers bid to sell cars to individuals.
http://www.autobytel.com

AutoNation.com. Links new and used car dealers with car buyers. When potential buyers go to the AutoNation site, their information is sent to the dealer. AutoNation also provides services such as insurance and financing.
http://www.autonationdirect.com

CarPrices.com. Provides pricing of options for vehicles.
http://www.carprices.com

DealerNet.com. Allows the comparison of auto prices between dealers.
http://www.dealernet.com

GM Buy Power. Gives buyers the chance to find the General Motors vehicle they want and check its availability through local dealers.
http://www.gmbuypower.com

Search Term: Shipping Companies   First 3 out of 267,342

FedEx. Offers customers the ability to track sent items via tracking numbers.
http://www.fedex.com

United Parcel Service. Also allows the tracking of sent items via tracking numbers.
http://www.ups.com

United States Postal Service. Provides special delivery items with a tracking number accessible via the Internet.
http://www.usps.com

Search Term: Electronic Payments   First 7 out of 961,342

SET Secure Electronic Transaction. Outlines the SET security protocols.
http://www.setco.org

Trivnet. Allows purchases to be charged to the user's ISP bill.
http://www.trivnet.com

VeriSign. Provides a secure server system that ensures the safety of online transactions.
http://www.verisign.com

Smart Card Alliance. Works to accelerate the acceptance of smart card technology.
http://www.smartcardalliance.org

Smart Card Industry Association. Offers information on smart card technology.
http://www.scia.org

Gemplus. Provides smart card technology.
http://www.gemplus.com

Smart Cards Online. Gives information on what smart cards do.
http://www.smartex.com

References

1. Clinton Wilder, "Online Auto Sales Pick Up, Transforming an Industry," *InformationWeek,* February 9, 1998, 73.
2. Alex Taylor III, "How to Buy a Car on the Internet," *Fortune,* March 4, 1996, 164–68.
3. "Car Shoppers Increase Use of Internet," in CyberAtlas [online] (November 27, 2001), available from <http://cyberatlas.internet.com/markets/retailing/article/0,,6061_929231,00.html>; Wilder, "Online Auto Sales Pick Up."
4. Robert McCarvey, "In the Driver's Seat," *Upside,* April 1999, 66–72.
5. Brian S. Akre, "Carmakers Profit Selling Off-Lease On-Line," *Marketing News,* March 15, 1999, 11; Bob Wallace, "GM Hits Bump in Used Car Sales," *Computerworld,* July 12, 1999, 1, 16.
6. David Joachim and Chuck Moozakis, "Can Covisint Find Its Way?" *InternetWeek,* September 17, 2001, 1, 35–37.
7. For a further discussion of channel evolution and development, see Oliver E. Williamson, "The Economics of Organizations: The Transactional Cost Approach," *American Journal of Sociology* 87, no. 3 (1981) 548–77.
8. "E-Procurement Can Reduce Costs and Time by 70%," in CIO.com [online] (March 27, 2001), available from <http://www2.cio.com/metrics/2001/metric178.html>; "B2B Forecast for 2006 Trimmed to $5.4 Trillion," in CIO.com [online] (September 27, 2001), available from <http://www2.cio.com/metrics/2001/metric270.html>.
9. Steve Jarvis, "Up the Down Supply Chain," *Marketing News,* September 10, 2001, 3.
10. Wroe Alderson, "Factors Governing the Development of Marketing Channels," in *Marketing Channels for Manufactured Products,* ed. Richard M. Clewett (Homewood, Ill.: Irwin, 1954).
11. Robert Benjamin and Rolf Wigand, "Electronic Markets and Virtual Value Chains on the Information Superhighway," *Sloan Management Review* (Winter 1995): 62–72.
12. Matrabarun Sarkar, Brian Butler, and Charles Steinfield, "Cybermediaries in Electronic Marketspace: Toward Theory Building," *Journal of Business Research* 41 (1998) 215–21.
13. Elise Chow, "Should You Outsource E-Commerce Fulfillment?" in Advisor.com [online] (April 16, 2002), available from <http://www.advisor.com/Articles.nsf/aid/CHOWE01>.

[14] Lee Copland, "E-Marketplaces, Definition," in Computerworld [online] (February 12, 2001), available from <http://www.computerworld.com/industrytopics/manufacturing/story/0,10801,57523,00.html>.

[15] Christopher Koch, "The Big Payoff," in CIO Magazine [online] (October 1, 2000), available from <http://www.cio.com/archive/100100_payoff_content.html>.

[16] Steve Konicki, "Let's Keep This Private," *InformationWeek,* July 30, 2001, 22–24.

[17] Elana Varon, "What You Need to Know about Public & Private Exchanges," *CIO,* September 1, 2001, 92–98.

[18] Monua Janah and Clinton Wilder, "Special Delivery," *InformationWeek,* October 27, 1997, 42–60; Warren Karlenzig and Steve Barth, "Will FedEx Reposition as Supply Chain Manager?" *Knowledge Management,* February 1999, 10; John Evan Frook, "FedEx Extranet App Customizes Tracking," *InternetWeek,* June 29, 1998, 25–26.

[19] Clinton Wilder, "Chief of the Year," *InformationWeek,* December 22, 1997, 43–48.

[20] For more on this topic, see Gene Koprowski, "Cache and Carry," *Business 2.0,* October 1998, 24–26; Amy K. Larsen, "Virtual Cash Gets Real," *InformationWeek,* May 31, 1999, 46–58.

[21] Ken Belson, "Like Stealing Plastic from a Baby," *BusinessWeek,* December 11, 2000, 62.

[22] CyberSource Corporation, "2001 Online Fraud Report," September 2001; Anne Kandra, "Consumer Watch: The Myth of Secure E-Shopping," in PCWorld.com [online] (July 2001), available from <http://www.idg.net/crd_idgsearch_2.html?url=http://www.pcworld.com/features/article/0,aid,49929,00.asp>.

[23] Michael Pastore, "Fraud Continues to Haunt Online Retail," in CyberAtlas [online] (March 4, 2002), available from <http://cyberatlas.internet.com/markets/retailing/article/0,,6061_984441,00.html>; "South China Morning Post: Online Fraud Rampant in Asia-Pacific," in NUA [online] (January 23, 2002), available from <http://www.nua.ie/surveys/index.cgi?f=VS&art_id=905357585&rel=true>.

[24] For more information, see Lydia Lee, "Getting SET for Electronic Commerce," *NewMedia,* September 22, 1997, 22; Lincoln D. Stein, "SET—Who Needs It?" *Web Techniques,* August 1998, 10–14; Connie Guglielmo, "Set Ready to Go—Again," *Interactive Week,* May 17, 1999, 8; Ellen Messmer, "MasterCard, Visa Trade Strong Security for Ease of Use," *Network World,* March 22, 1999, 18.

[25] Tom Melling, "Digital Signature vs. Electronic Signatures," *e-Business Advisor,* April 2000, 48–51; Rutrell Yasin, "Online Signatures May Drive E-Business," *InternetWeek,* August 27, 2001, 18.

[26] "Celebrating 50 Years of Debt," *Joplin Globe,* March 12, 2000, 1E–2E.

[27] For more information, see Eric Brown, "Micropayments: No Small Change," *NewMedia,* June 23, 1997, 30–37; Russ Jones, "Small Change," *Web Techniques,* August 1998, 51–56; Whit Andrews, "Microsoft Bets $15M on Maker of Micropayment Technology," *Internet World,* March 15, 1999, 13, 15; Jim Kerstetter, "Micropayments Rebound," *PCWeek,* March 22, 1999, 22.

[28] Janet Guyon, "Smart Plastic," *Fortune,* October 13, 1997, 56.

[29] Amy Leung, "Smart Cards Seem a Sure Bet," *InfoWorld,* March 8, 1999, 37–38; Jim Kerstetter and Scott Berinato, "Smart Cards Get Hand," *PCWeek,* September 1999, 6.

[30] "About Smart Cards," in Smart Cards Online [online], available from <http://www.smartex.com/smartcards_guide.html>.

[31] Zack Martin, "Big Push for Smart Cards Finally underway in U.S.?" *Card Marketing,* July–August 2001, 1, 13.

[32] Julekha Dash, "Uncle Sam Wants You! to Stop Writing Those Checks," *Software Magazine,* October 1997, 69–71.

[33] Don Davis, "Star Power for Chips?" *Card Marketing,* April 2002, 1, 20–21.

[34] Alan S. Kay, "Pay Dirt," *CIO Web Business,* November 1, 1998, 36–45.

[35] Rachael King, "E-Billing Still in the Ether," *Net Economy,* March 19, 2001, 62–64; Lucas Mearian, "Research Points to Sharp Rise In Number of E-Billing Users," *Computerworld,* December 3, 2001.

[36] Maggie Biggs, "New Paradign for B-to-B," *Infoworld,* October 22, 2001, 51–52; Gregory Dalton, "E-Bills Arrive," *InformationWeek,* April 19, 1999, 18.

[37] Richard L. Brandt, "Ingram Micro: The Tech World's Warehouse," *Upside,* August 1998, 94–98, 142–46; John Evan Frook, "Serving Up E-Commerce," *InternetWeek,* July 13, 1998, 1, 52.

[38] Alorie Gilbert and Beth Bacheldor, "The Big Squeeze," *InformationWeek,* March 27, 2000, 46–56; Sari Kalin, "Conflict Resolution," *CIO Web Business,* February 1, 1998, 28–36.

[39] For more information, see E. B. Baatz, "Will the Web Eat Your Job?" *Webmaster,* May/June, 1996, 40–45; John Berry, "Death of a Middleman," *Internet World,* March 1997, 39–41.

[40] Howard Anderson, "http://www.you're_fired.com," *Sales & Field Force Automation,* April 1997, 38–46; Clinton Wilder, "Middlemen Beware?" *InformationWeek,* October 20, 1997, 94–95.

chapter 5

E-Business Value Strategies

All businesses must determine a means of delivering value to customers. This chapter explores seven e-business strategies that allow for the creation of value. Implementing these new strategies in e-business models requires more than simply applying technology to the business system; it also implies new ways of developing relationships with customers, employees, and suppliers.

Technology is allowing for the delivery of many types of products directly to the consumer in a manner customized to their needs. Increased competition and consumer access to information are having a major impact on the ability of businesses to maintain prices. Consumers use the Internet to gather information about products and to find alternative suppliers. To gain competitive advantages, businesses use the Internet as a means of enhancing services offered to customers. Before they can gain such advantages, businesses must analyze current business models and value creation and how these models need to change in the face of new technologies.

1. Explain the seven strategies e-businesses are using to create value for customers.
2. Be able to perform a benefit analysis of alternative sales channels.
3. Discuss how digital communication adds value to a business.
4. Analyze the impact of each of the intellectual property areas on e-business.
5. Describe how the delivery of services is changing because of new technologies.
6. Outline how relationships can be enhanced through strong customer service.
7. Explain how business process strategies are providing value.
8. Discuss how a market-of-one strategy will affect businesses.
9. Show how auctions are used to facilitate commerce.
10. Describe the impact of e-business strategies on pricing.

Online Travel—The Sky's the Limit

The airline agent's traditional role has been that of an information intermediary and ticket broker. An agent created value by providing information on flight schedules, travel opportunities, hotel reservations, and other services needed by a traveler. With the growth of the Internet, a number of pure-play (devoted to a single business) online companies have developed value offerings for the travel industry. Close to 43 percent of all Internet users in the United States visited online travel sites in early 2002. Sales in the online travel industry (for airfare, rental cars, cruise ships, and hotels) for 2001 were $24 billion. This is expected to grow to $64 billion, or 22 percent of all travel, by 2007.[1] Price is considered the single most important attribute for those making online bookings, and online customers believe they get the best price online by comparing multiple sites. Information available online also influences individual's decisions as to where to travel.[2]

The major pure-play online travel agencies are Travelocity (http://www.travelocity.com) with a 32 percent share, Microsoft's Expedia (http://www.expedia.com), and Priceline (http://www.priceline.com), a reverse-auction, name-your-price seller. These companies compete directly with brick-and-mortar travel agents. Online agencies are convenient, open 24/7, offer a wide selection, and have relatively low operating costs and expenses. The large volume of business done by Travelocity, Expedia, and Priceline has led to a network of alliances with airlines, hotels, and rental car companies, making it difficult for brick-and-mortar businesses to compete.[3] Airlines have placed additional pressure on brick-and-mortar agencies by cutting ticket discounts.

Source: <http://www.travelocity.com>.
Courtesy of Travelocity.com.

To compete, airlines are bypassing agents by offering low-cost tickets online and issuing paperless tickets at lower costs. United, American, Continental, Delta, and Northwest started Orbitz (http://www.orbitz.com). Like other online agencies, Orbitz sends out travel alerts to customers via e-mail, pagers, or Net-enabled mobile phones. Orbitz enhances customer service by using live operators on toll-free telephone lines to provide updates and predict possible flight delays. Orbitz found that customers who called spent an average of eleven minutes talking to live service personnel.[4]

Figure 5.1 illustrates the travel agent business model. Under the traditional process a customer would ask a travel agent about travel options and prices. The agent would search a travel database such as Sabre (http://www.sabre.com) and then provide feedback from the database, issue the tickets, and take a commission or charge for the service. This process left the customer out of the search process, increasing the search time and possibly resulting in higher prices to the traveler. Online-only models operate in almost exactly the same manner. The online companies act as the agent, allowing the customer to directly access flight information. This lets the customer search for travel alternatives and compare prices. Travelocity's majority owner is Sabre, and it therefore uses the Sabre database system. Orbitz designed a new database, allowing for a larger search. Most online customers will visit multiple sites to be sure they receive the lowest possible fares. They will even bypass agents and search directly on the airlines' sites.

Figure 5.1 Travel Agent Model

▶ Thinking Strategically

Consider the future of brick-and-mortar airline ticket sales. Determine how an offline agent can provide the value needed to compete against online companies. Visit Travelocity and Expedia. Determine how these companies provide value to their customers. What advantages do these companies have over their brick-and-mortar counterparts? Evaluate the agent model in Figure 5.1. What other types of agencies (real estate, insurance, etc.) could be affected the same way as the travel industry? Determine how these intermediaries can stay in the distribution channel.

"The newest innovations, which we label information technologies, have begun to alter the manner in which we do business and create value, often in ways not readily foreseeable even five years ago."

Alan Greenspan
Chairman, Federal Reserve Board, May 6, 1999[5]

Creating Value

Businesses create value for their customers by providing quality goods and services at acceptable prices.[6] A **business model** that provides more benefits to its customers, sells at a lower price, or both will take market share away from competitors. Information-technology-based e-businesses are leveraging new technologies to gain competitive advantages. Seven strategies have emerged that help e-businesses use technology to develop business models that provide value to customers:

- ☐ **Online purchasing strategy.** Allows the buying and selling of products and information on the Internet and other online services.
- ☐ **Digital communication strategy.** Organizes the delivery of digital information, products, services, or payments online.
- ☐ **Service strategy.** Reduces the cost of services, improves the quality of services, and increases the speed of services.
- ☐ **Business process strategy.** Automates business transactions and workflows.
- ☐ **Market-of-one strategy.** Develops products for a single customer with close to the same costs as mass production.
- ☐ **Auction strategy.** Offers a site to bid for products online.
- ☐ **Pricing strategy.** Allows businesses to pursue market share by selling at low prices or giving away products and services for free.[7]

A business model, or commerce model, is the basic process by which a business obtains its inventory, produces its good or service, and delivers to its customer.

Figure 5.2 illustrates how these strategies work together. The value delivered to the customer can be enhanced by seeing the market as a market of one, improving communication through digital media, and allowing for online purchases. Businesses can obtain efficiencies by restructuring business processes. Customers can increase the value they receive by increasing their ability to negotiate price through auctions and dynamic pricing strategies. All of these strategies are underpinned by a strong service system (often called a customer relationship management system).

Many businesses combine a number of these strategies in developing business models. Amazon.com's site provides value by using all seven e-business strategies.

Figure 5.2   Model of E-Business Value Creation

In the year 2000, the American Customer Satisfaction Index (http://www.bus
.umich.edu/research/nqrc/acsi.html) included e-commerce companies in its index
of satisfaction. Amazon.com ranked the highest of all businesses, online and
offline, receiving a score of 84 (out of an index of 100). These scores are updated
quarterly. Figure 5.3 illustrates how Amazon.com uses all of the value strategies at
its site.

Businesses must design models that maximize value for their customers.
E-business practices allow for the layering of technology and processes on business
models to create new ways of adding value. This layering transforms industries by
forcing a restructuring of past practices to maintain competitiveness. The Internet
is the major technological factor fostering this change. At one time, pure-play
Internet companies gained advantages in cost because they were first to market,
but brick-and-mortar businesses have moved online using their brand names and
the ability to service accounts to regain competitiveness.

Creating value requires an understanding of what customers consider important when they purchase a product. A survey of individuals purchasing online
indicated that 81 percent value convenience, while only 33 percent value price
savings. A study in Britain indicated that consumers saved almost 64 hours per
year by shopping online.[8] Personalized sites are also better at influencing individuals to buy.[9] Customers experience additional value by using the Internet to
search for product information, purchase products, and receive service.

The change in competitive business models for many industries has been
much more rapid than was expected, and the amount of sales created through the
use of these new models has exceeded expectations. For other industries, the pace
of change has been slower, allowing brick-and-mortar businesses the chance to
transform. The following sections outline each of the strategies e-businesses can
use to create value.

Figure 5.3 Amazon's Site

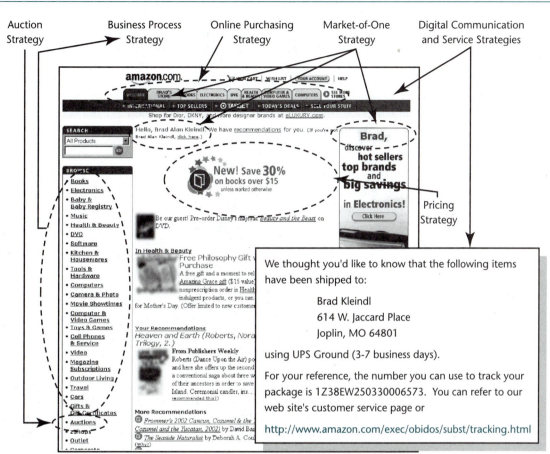

Courtesy of Amazon.com, Inc.

Online Purchasing Strategy

E-commerce is the process of allowing Web-based technologies to facilitate commerce or trade. E-commerce can be set up on the retail level, or between an e-business and an end user, or for business-to-business transactions; all of these are online purchasing strategies. An e-business could be the producer of the product, as in the case of Dell Computer, or an intermediary that coordinates the sales and distribution process, such as Amazon.com. E-commerce will be covered in more depth in Chapter 6.

Digital Communication Strategy

Individuals use the Internet to collect information about a product before making a purchase, but an e-business with an effective digital communication strategy can also deliver information-based products directly to the customer. **Digital products** such as multimedia entertainment, online information services, published documents, music, or video can be transferred over the Internet. A number of businesses are currently taking advantage of the Internet's ability to transfer digital content by setting up online versions of newspapers, magazines, or other media. These sites use one or both of the two main models: **advertising supported** and **subscription based**.

With the growth of broadband, multimedia sites are offering streaming content online. Broadcast media are using the Internet to deliver their own rich content, including news broadcasts, radio broadcasts, and special programming. An idealized business model for the movie industry would be to send digital films over the Internet directly to a viewer's home and then—importantly—be paid for the content. This model has not been implemented for the mainstream Hollywood movie industry, but small producers have found a number of alternatives online. Alwaysi (http://www.alwaysi.com) allows independent producers to deliver motion picture and television-type entertainment to Internet users around the world. Alwaysi gives these producers a place where their work can be viewed by individual viewers, entertainment talent representatives, acquisitions executives, and other industry professionals. Alwaysi permits viewers to see samples but requires a subscription to view additional content. Shockwave.com (http://www.shockwave .com) provides a variety of broadband content, including games, films, and animations. One of Shockwave.com's divisions is AtomFilms (http://www.atomfilms .com). It offers rich media clips and uses an advertising-supported business model.

Perhaps the greatest advantage of online content is the lower cost involved in transfer and delivery. Just like online advertising, electronic content allows for a publish-once, read-many-times environment. This gives existing content developers a wider audience and opens the door to smaller firms at low start-up costs. If sold, digital content is usually purchased on a per-time-period-subscription or per-use basis. Subscription-based sites generally target individuals who have a high need for information. The *Wall Street Journal* Online (http://www.wsj.com) has been able to sign paying subscribers to its services. At the *Wall Street Journal* Online site, subscribers access large amounts of information by company and industry. Online-only electronic magazines (or **e-zines**), such as *Slate* (http://www.slate.com), offer free content online. In most cases, advertising-supported business models do not provide enough revenue to online-only e-zines.

Traditional media have found that they need to include Web sites to satisfy advertisers' demands for multiplatform audience reach.[10] Not all digital communication sites require payments. Newspapers and magazines, such as the *New York Times* (http://www.nytimes.com) and *BusinessWeek* (http://www.businessweek.com), and information sites, such as CNN (http://www.CNN.com), MSNBC (http://www

.MSNBC.com), and ABCNews (http://www.ABCNews.go.com), offer digital content on an ongoing basis. These sites follow radio and broadcast television models and obtain revenue through advertising. They also play a role in supporting and enhancing the associated traditional media.[11]

Business-to-business sales of digital content also exist online. Lawyers in small offices who can't afford to purchase legal reference books or CD-ROMs can obtain the same information online from legal publisher Matthew Bender (http://www.bender.com). Lawyers pay a subscription fee or pay per view. The system also uses push technology to send summaries of requested content to the lawyer's office.[12]

Some traditionally tangible products, such as music CDs, are now available as digital content. As early as 1997, musician Todd Rundgren sold directly to his listeners over the Web. For twenty-five dollars a year, fans could download music files; for forty dollars a year, they obtained music files, news, and two CDs.[13] Sending music digitally over the Internet is currently done using an MP3 format.

Intellectual Capital

The Internet is moving from a freewheeling, lightly scrutinized communication medium to a more mainstream business system. The importance that businesses are placing on the Internet is forcing compliance to the same laws and regulations that pertain to other business systems. This is especially true of the rules governing intellectual property or a firm's intellectual capital in the digital environment. **Intellectual capital** refers to the ownership of a company's knowledge, the results of ideas and creativity, and the symbols that represent products, companies, or brands.[14] Ownership of intellectual

E-Business Professionals

Jeff Bezos
Amazon.com
http://www.amazon.com

Jeff Bezos

Like many entrepreneurs, Jeff Bezos was gifted with insight and lucky timing. Mr. Bezos graduated from Princeton in 1986 summa cum laude and Phi Beta Kappa, with a degree in electrical engineering and computer science. He worked with the investment firm Bankers Trust Company of New York evaluating computer-related businesses. He helped manage over $250 billion in assets, becoming the company's youngest vice president in February 1990. In the early 1990s, Mr. Bezos investigated a new computer-based medium and learned that the Internet was growing at a rate of 2,300 percent per year. To the budding entrepreneur, this growth was an opportunity to become a first mover in e-commerce.

Mr. Bezos chose his product carefully. He started with a list of the top twenty mail-order products and looked for one to which he could provide greater value through the Internet by offering selection, convenience, and low prices. Books were products that consumers were familiar with and could purchase without a physical examination. Bezos attended a book trade show and found that book wholesalers such as Ingram and Baker & Taylor used databases extensively. Mr. Bezos's business started in a garage with three Sun workstations and desks made from wooden doors. A beta site opened in June 1995, and the Amazon.com site went live on July 16, 1995. Amazon.com soon became one of the fastest-growing companies in the history of U.S. business.

Amazon.com looks for employees who can build personalized virtual marketplaces, help customers visualize and listen to products by working on 2-D and 3-D streaming video and audio, develop and work with systems that manage the worldwide supply chain, build models for customer lifetime value and trend analysis, and fill many other positions.

Sources: Margarett Loke, "Jeff Bezos: Amazon.com's Whiz Kid," Gist [online] (December 8, 2000), available from <http://www.gist.com/tv/article.jsp?adf=dn120800.adf>; Joshua Quittner, "Person of the Year 1999: Biography" Time.com [online] (July 21, 2002), available from<http://publishing.about.com/gi/dynamic/offsite.htm?site=http%3A%2F%2Fwww.time.com%2Ftime%2Fpoy%2Fintro.html>; "Welcome to Amazon.com," Amazon.com [online] (July 21, 2002), available from <http://www.amazon.com/exec/obidos/tg/feature/-/199138/104-3804328-0811933>. Photo: © Reuters NewMedia Inc./CORBIS.

Case 5.1

The Market Still Wants Its MP3

MP3 has become the de facto standard for music delivery over the Internet. The recording industry sees this delivery system as a threat to copyrighted sales. The Recording Industry Association of America (http://www.riaa.com) recently lost a lawsuit against Diamond Multimedia's Rio portable MP3 player (http://www.sonicblue.com). With portable devices such as the Rio, individuals can download music over the Web for later playback. This process allows unknown bands and musicians to use Web sites such as MP3.com (http://www.mp3.com) to reach audiences.

Downloading MP3 files is very popular. By 2002, more than 40 percent of home Internet users in the United States downloaded MP3 files to their home computers. The largest percentage of users (81 percent) were between the ages of eighteen and twenty-four. They downloaded and stored an average 350 clips, songs, and files. Fewer individuals between twenty-five and thirty-four download music (62 percent), but they store twice as many files as the younger users.[15] Napster (http://www.napster.com) attempted to turn its free song-sharing site into a subscription-based site but found this e-business model would not work when copyright restrictions were enforced. Sixty-two percent of college-age music consumers plan to continue accessing free MP3 music files through noncommercial channels, such as peer-to-peer file-sharing networks and e-mail.[16]

The music industry has conceded that it must deliver music online. To tap into this market, record companies have attempted to launch their own subscription music sites, such as MusicNet (http://www.musicnet.com) and Pressplay (http://www.pressplay.com). Their plans include letting individuals purchase and record information online and then limiting their ability to transfer the music to other persons or computers. Another procedure will place codes that prevent copying into the music files.[17]

capital is covered by copyrights, trademarks, legal notices, and patents. Each of these will be discussed in this section.

▶ Thinking Strategically: Case 5.1

Determine the advantages and disadvantages of MP3 for the consumer. Consider the advantages and disadvantages of this format for the music industry. Compare and contrast those advantages and disadvantages, and speculate on the future of MP3. It is projected that within the next five years, an entire movie will download in twenty minutes or less. How will this affect the movie and video rental industries?

Copyrights

A **copyright** protects original works of authorship, which include literary, dramatic, musical, artistic, and certain other intellectual works, both published and unpub-

© *is the symbol used to indicate a registered copyright.*

lished. Under current U.S. copyright laws, protection exists from the time the work is created in fixed form. The copyright immediately becomes the property of the author who created the work, and only the author or those assigned rights from the author can rightfully claim copyright. No registration with the U.S. Copyright Office is required to secure a copyright. A copyright notice is no longer required under U.S. law, but it can act as a signal to others that the author is interested in protecting the work. Older copyright laws did contain a notification requirement, so the use of notice is still relevant to the copyright status of older works.

Copyright registration with the Copyright Office establishes a public record of the copyright claim. If registration is made within three months after publication of the work or before an infringement of the work, the copyright owner can collect statutory damages and attorney's fees in court actions; otherwise, only an award of actual damages and profits is available to the copyright owner. Registration also allows the owner of the copyright to record the work with the U.S. Customs Service for protection against the importation of infringing copies.[18] The 1971 Berne Convention allows copyrights granted in one country to automatically be upheld in all other member countries.

Strategic nSite

The music industry is being directly attacked on college campuses throughout the world. The MP3 standard is being used to compress CD music files. On some college campuses, the largest use of the Internet by students is the downloading of illegally recorded and forwarded music files.

Many of the elements used to create content for the Internet, such as pictures and graphic files, sound files, text, or programs, are copyrighted by companies or individuals. The ability to copy and transfer digital information makes copyright violations relatively simple. This has alarmed a number of industries. For example, the music industry is concerned about unauthorized copying of its material. Newly released albums are being copied to unauthorized Web sites for downloading. Individuals then take this music and record it to CDs. This is a clear violation of copyright restrictions. Individuals can also violate copyright restrictions by using sound clips in a Web site. BMI (Broadcast Music, Inc.), a media licensing firm, looks for unauthorized use of copyrighted material and then forces compliance through the payment of royalties. BMI has developed a Web bot, or spider, that searches the Web looking for unauthorized use of sound clips.[19]

There are numerous sources of copyright-free material on the Internet, or such material can be purchased on CDs. Businesses that develop Web sites must be sure they are not violating copyrights when they develop content. They should ensure they do not develop links to third-party sites that engage in copyright violations.

Software theft has been a problem for a considerable time. Worldwide losses due to theft from illegal copying were close to $12 billion in 2000. It is projected that the piracy rate for software in the United States is 24 percent; in China, 94 percent; and in Japan, 37 percent.[20]

This copyright problem is hindering the ability to sell many products over the Internet. Book publishers do not want to sell digital books if they can be freely copied and dispersed. Music companies do not want to lose control of their products. Television and movie producers do not want to have their products distributed without compensation. Software protection systems are being developed for images, sound files, DVD files, and video files. A number of protection routines are outlined in Table 5.1. Laws have been passed in the United States and Europe making it illegal to develop technologies that break digital copyright protection systems.[21] Many of the companies involved in creating digital media content have advocated developing hardware-based copyright protections. This would force hardware producers to develop standards that prevent digital media from being copied. Some technology companies, however, feel that such standards hinder the advancement of innovation.[22]

Table 5.1   Technological Copyright Protections

Technology	Description
Digital Watermarks	This technology allows images to be sent over the Internet with visible watermarks over a page or with watermarks that will show up only after an image is copied.
Secure Containers	The publisher can encrypt a file, stipulate conditions for use, and then send the content to a user. The user can then send payment and receive a key to unlock the product. If the data are sent on to others, they must also have a key to unlock the file.
Information Metering	Metering provides an auditing trail, allowing the owner to determine who forwarded the protected material.
Hardware Solutions	Government-mandated hardware solutions could prevent the copying of protected digital media products.

Sources: Partick Thibodeau, "Copyright Holders Turn to IT," *Computerworld*, 1, 57; Alan Zeichick, "Digital Watermarks Explained," *Red Herring*, December 1999, 270–72; Richard Wiggins, "Corralling Your Content," *NewMedia*, October 13, 1997, 40–45; and Otis Port, "Copyrights New Digital Guardians," *BusinessWeek*, May 6, 1996, 62.

Trademarks

® *is the symbol used to indicate a registered trademark; otherwise, notice is given as follows: Dr. Brad Kleindl(TM).*

A **trademark** or service mark refers to any word, name, symbol, or device that is used to indicate the source or origin of goods or services and that distinguishes one company's goods or services from another's. Trademark rights cover such practices as preventing others from using a confusingly similar mark, dilution of the trademark, and unfair use of the trademark.

Owners of registered trademarks can challenge the ownership of domain names. This prevents an individual from using a domain name such as http://www.Pepsi.com for a privately owned Web site. The owner of a trademark must protect its use or face the possibility of losing that ownership because the trademark can become a generic reference. A trademark could be considered abandoned if its owner allows a Web site to display the trademark without permission. For example, Billy Joel® has registered his name as a trademark to prevent unauthorized use of his name.

Because a trademark represents the image of a firm, the firm may want to determine who can set up automatic links to its site. Disreputable firms could hurt another firm's positive image. When devel-

The Political, Legal, and Ethical Environment

Plagiarism

The Internet offers students vast access to all types of term papers. Cheating sites provide free papers and papers charged by the page. Students can also pull content from numerous Web sites and claim the work as their own. To counteract this cheating, a number of countermeasures are used. Plagiarism.org (http://www.plagiarism.org) uses both software algorithms and Web spiders to search for plagiarized content. A companion site, Turnitin.com (http://www.turnitin.com), allows educations, editors, and others to check for copyright violations.

oping a Web site, the designer should not use copyrighted material or trademarks without permission. When building a link to another site, it is advisable to notify that site's Webmaster.[23] Some Web site designers have attempted to increase the number of hits obtained in Web searches by using trademarked names in metatags. This is a trademark violation and could result in a cease-and-desist order or a lawsuit.[24]

Companies have filed suit against search engines for trademark violations due to the use of targeted advertising. For example, an individual who wants to run a search on AT&T may see ads paid for by rival telecommunications companies or ads that could hurt AT&T's image. The courts may find that it is unfair competition when competitors pay to have their ads displayed with the results of a search based on a company's trademarked name.[25]

Legal Notices

The following is a list of five suggestions to limit Web site problems with intellectual property laws:[26]

☐ Independent contractors should release to the business all copyrights related to the creation of a Web page. The independent contractor should also obtain copyright releases from all subcontractors.

☐ Place a copyright notice on the Web page, such as © 2003, South-Western Publishing. This serves as notice.

☐ For extra protection, register the site with the Copyright Office.

☐ The Web site should have a legal page so people see the rules for using the site. This should include notices about downloading material from the site, especially material owned by third parties.

☐ To protect from being sued for copyright infringement, obtain written permission before using any other Web site's material or when developing links to other sites.

Patents

Patents allow individuals or firms to monopolize or gain exclusive rights to the use of an invention; the term of a patent is twenty years from the date of the application. There are different types of patents. A utility patent includes machines, industrial processes, compositions of matter, and articles of manufacture. A design patent protects the appearance or shape of a product instead of the function. Plant patents are granted for biological species. Software patents have grown considerably, from 1,300 issued in 1990 to almost 12,000 by 1997. Internet-related patents grew from 433 in 1997 to more than 2,500 by the first half of 2000.[27]

In January 1999, the Supreme Court of the United States let stand a lower court's decision in *State Street Bank & Trust Co. v. Signature Financial Group,* upholding the patenting of business methods. This has allowed the Internet business community to patent a number of business processes.[28] Amazon.com patented its one-click purchasing process and then sued Barnes & Noble for patent infringement. Priceline (http://www.priceline.com) holds a number of patents on its business model in an attempt to control the process whereby consumers submit prices they are willing to pay to a business, and the business can then accept or reject the online bids. Price-line's claim for a patent was based on using a computer to facilitate payment between a buyer and a seller when the buyer inputs the conditions for the sale. Patents on business models can force firms to pay royalties for the use of technology or business models. While it is possible to fight patents in court, it is expensive to try to overturn (or defend) a patent. Instead, many businesses have opted to pay royalty fees to use a business process.[29]

Market-of-One Strategy

Many companies are using personalized Web sites to form tighter relationships with their customers, but a market-of-one strategy goes beyond this technique. Dell Computer's business model allows buyers to place custom orders directly over the telephone or the Internet. The computer is then designed to meet the specifications of the buyer. Dell's ability to customize production is due to the development of the **digital factory**, an automation process in which software and computer networks are more important than production machines. When this digital manufacturing process is combined with the human worker, the resulting soft manufacturing process brings flexibility to production and allows manufacturers to produce individualized products at mass production speeds. For example, Motorola (http://www.motorola.com) manufactures pagers using flexible production techniques. Resellers and salespeople deliver orders to the factory specifying colors, tones, and other details. These specifications are relayed to pick-and-place robots that deliver the parts and orders to the assembly line. The finished product can be shipped the same day the order came in.[30]

This build-to-order business model is also called **mass customization** and is a market-of-one process. Don Peppers and Martha Rogers's book *The One to One Future* (http://www.1to1.com) expands on how this process allows marketers to develop tight customer relationships.[31] The Internet is bringing mass customization to a wide range of products. Companies are now allowing customers to design golf clubs, bicycles, fishing rods, and CDs. Smaller firms may use mass customization to gain competitive advantages, but larger firms are using the process to lower costs. Building to order cuts down on inventory costs that can amount to 10 percent of sales per year for some companies.[32] A market-of-one approach means that the firm must develop strong relationships with its customers and understand their individualized needs. Using the Internet for communication can facilitate this relationship development process. Once the relationship is established, customers are less likely to leave as long as their needs are being met.

Technology is also used in-store to facilitate purchases. Eyewear manufacturer Paris Miki (http://www.paris-miki.com.au) takes a digital picture of an individual's face. The customer then enters self-image and lifestyle information (such as *intelligent, sexy, distinctive*) into a computer. The customer is shown a 3-D representation of his or her face with different lenses and frames on a computer screen. The custom frames can then be ordered, with no extra charge for using the computer system.[33] Once a company has acquired data on a customer's needs, there may be little incentive for the individual to switch to another provider.

Service Strategy

The service strategy has an impact on two areas. The first is in supporting individuals or businesses that specialize in providing services to a customer, including educational institutions, physicians, banks, realtors, insurance agents, and many others. The second includes enhancing the service component of a business by meeting customer service needs before, during, and after the sale. This might mean answering questions about a product and how it is used or how it fits a specific purpose. Very importantly, it also includes handling any problems that may occur after the sale. This process is being enhanced through customer relationship management systems.

Service Industries

As illustrated in this chapter's opening vignette, the use of traditional business models by service industries is being threatened by e-business models. Service businesses are typically characterized as having the following:

- ☐ **Intangibility.** It is often difficult to see or feel what a service business does. For example, the education an individual receives is intangible. After years of college or university education, a student sees only a diploma.
- ☐ **Perishability.** Services often cannot be placed in inventory or stored. If a movie theater shows a film to empty seats, it loses the chance to receive revenue from that showing.
- ☐ **Inseparability.** A service cannot be easily separated from its provider. Medical services typically require that the patient be in direct contact with the physician.
- ☐ **Variability.** Services can often vary in their quality of delivery because of the human interface required.

A number of service industries are changing business models to take advantage of e-business practices, allowing these industries to meet customers' needs more efficiently. Table 5.2 outlines the characteristics of services and how technology can be used to change service delivery.

The financial services industry has been affected by e-business. Online-only banks can obtain a national presence without the cost of brick and mortar. They are also able to reduce operating costs because they do not have large staffing requirements. Bank transaction costs that require tellers can cost one dollar; online transactions cost as little as one cent. Online-only banks such as NetBank

Table 5.2 Technology's Impact on Service

Service Characteristic	Technology Leveraging	Industry Example
Intangibility	The Internet enables buyers to directly compare products and services offered online, allowing them to search for the greatest value.	HSH Associates (http://www.hsh.com) offers information on mortgage rates. Quotesmith (http://www.quotesmith.com) and 4Insurance (http://www.4insurance.com) allow individuals to obtain quotes from multiple carriers.
Perishability	Digital information can be stored and delivered as needed. Online services do not perish; they can be created as needed by the user. Online sales systems can also fill unused capacity for transport companies, such as airlines.	National Public Radio (http://www.npr.org) stores its radio programs for individuals to download and play at their leisure. Priceline (http://www.priceline.com) sells excess capacity for airlines.
Inseparability	Real estate buyers can use the Web to view homes and take virtual walk-throughs. The medical industry is using the Web to deliver services directly to the user's home computer. Retailers are providing shopping services online.	WebMD (http://www.webmd.com) provides information on medical issues. Lands' End (http://www.landsend.com) has both a personal model and a personal shopper to suggest products for customers.
Variability	Databases and standardized procedures can remove the variability of service delivery.	Amazon.com, Dell, and many other companies use e-mail, FAQs (frequently asked questions) sites, and other technologies to standardize services.

(http://www.netbank.com) and E*Trade (http://www.etrade.com) offer many of the same services as physical banks, such as checking, money market deposits, CDs, home and business loans, and investing. Because of their reduced overhead, they attempt to provide higher returns on deposits and lower fees for services.

Many brick-and-mortar banks have embraced e-business to overcome the threats posed by online-only banks. Citigroup (http://www.citigroup.com) has set a **stretch goal** of increasing its customer base from 100 million customers in five states and fifty-seven countries to 1 billion customers by 2012. To reach this goal, it plans to use the Internet for Citibank online banking (http://www.citibank.com) and to offer e-commerce solutions for other financial services such as insurance, brokerage, and investment banking.[34] More than 20 million American households banked online in 2001, and 33 percent of all households are expected to bank online by 2005.[35]

Small- and medium-sized community banks are responding to the threat from online-only banks and large banks with vast resources by leveraging e-business technologies. By 2002, close to 50 percent of community banks allowed customers to view account balances and transfer funds online, 40 percent allowed electronic bill payments, and about 30 percent allowed the viewing and printing of online

Stretch goals *are goals that may seem impossible to reach. A stretch goal focuses a business on what it would like to achieve and motivates employees to be creative.*

statements. By 2003, 87 percent of community banks plan to offer customers Internet banking.[36]

Banks provide a number of services that are being targeted by niche businesses. Companies such as CheckFree (http://www.checkfree.com) let businesses post their bills online and have customers make transfers without writing a check. The benefits to customers include taking less time to pay their bills; businesses benefit from reduced transaction costs by not handling checks.[37] Banks are following this lead by providing their own online bill-paying services.

Figure 5.4   Traditional Brokerage System

Issuing Company → Underwriting Company → Stock Exchange → Stockbroker → Stock Investor

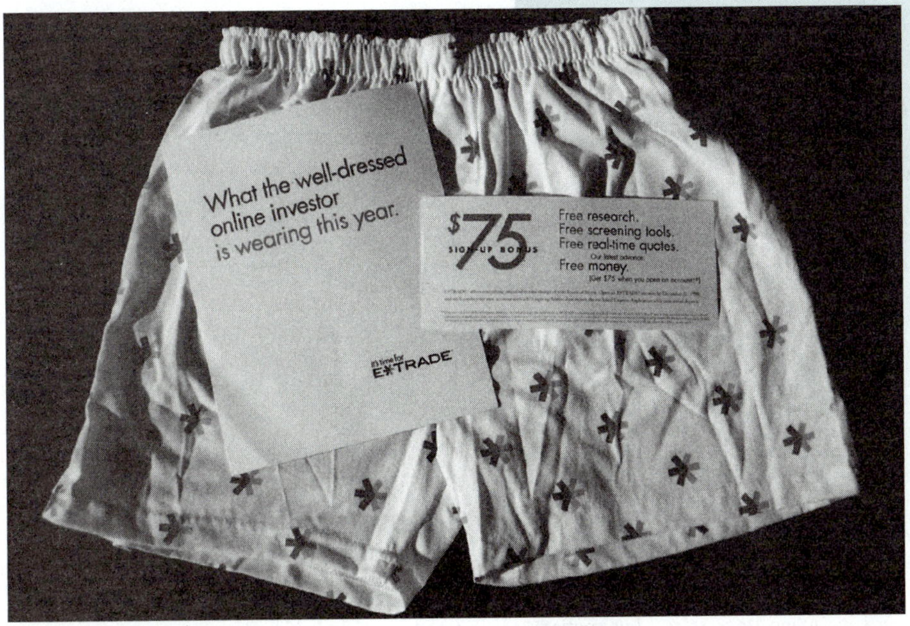

E*Trade's wearable ad.

continued on next page

---

case 5.2

How Quickly Can Business Models Change?

"It was easier for me to do it and more convenient."

John Steffens
Vice Chairman of Merrill Lynch & Company, on online trading.[39]

The stock brokerage industry has adopted a number of value strategies to develop new models of exchange. What happened in this industry may be a precursor of what other service industries could face. The brokerage industry's traditional business model has been shaken by the speed of change since 1997 because online trading offers many advantages over the traditional model of stock investing.

The traditional business model for stock sales is outlined in Figure 5.4. A firm issues stock through an underwriting company. The underwriting company offers this stock through an exchange where stockbrokers sell the stock to individual purchasers. Each of these intermediaries has traditionally received a commission because they all have had access to some part of the exchange process. Stockbrokers communicated with the investor because they could buy or sell stock and had access to information on the company issuing the stock as well as the current sales price.

The Internet brings both information and brokerage services directly to the investor. Investors can access information on stocks from the exchange; they can also obtain information through a number of businesses designed to offer information and advice without the sales pressure of traditional brokers.[40] E*Trade launched a $100 million advertising campaign in 1998 to promote its free stock-trading information site. The goal of this campaign was to add 1 million new accounts to its already 500,000 active accounts.[41] By 2002, E*Trade had over 3 million household accounts and $52.8 billion in assets and deposits. Table 5.3 outlines the advantages and disadvantages of the new brokerage business model.

The major reasons individuals choose to use online brokerages include lower commissions, the ability to research investments online, convenience, and control of the transaction process.[42] One study found that 41 percent of high-value investors (those with more than $500,000 in investment assets) would move $550 billion in assets to receive Internet-based financial services. Eighty six percent of high-net-worth individuals aged sixty and younger use the Internet for financial activities, such as gathering market information and account management.[43]

How quickly can an industry change? Figure 5.5 outlines the results of the competitive dynamics during 1997 as online trading moved from a niche business to more than 150,000 trades per day. Prices dropped over this time period; for example, the online brokerage Web Street charged nothing for trades of at least one thousand shares on the NASDAQ exchange. Brokers also make money on margins and holding investors' cash between trades. Since online investors trade more than other investors, online brokers saw increases in revenues and overall commissions paid. By 1998, Internet trades reached 340,000 per day; by 1999, average online commissions had stabilized at around $15 per

continued on next page

All types of loans—auto, student, installment, mortgage—have moved online. Online mortgage companies are already having an impact on the lending industry. In 1998, $4.2 billion in mortgage loans were transacted online, a small percentage of the $1.5 trillion mortgage market. By 2001, this grew to $45 billion and is expected to grow to $180 billion by 2005 (or more than 12 percent of total U.S. mortgages). The key drivers for online acceptance of mortgage companies include the offering of online advice and the use of automated decision-making tools. These techniques allow customers to submit loan preferences and financial profiles online where automated decision-making systems can respond with a loan approval and firm interest rate offer within minutes. Real-time status information is delivered through e-mail and secure Web pages.[38]

Table 5.3   Benefit Analysis of Traditional versus Online Brokers

Benefit	Traditional Brokers	Online Brokers
Purchaser's Cost for Transaction	Depends on broker and amount of stock.	One-third to one-tenth of traditional brokers' cost.
Information on Companies and Quotes	Requires that broker act as a gatekeeper between corporate information and customer. Broker is also required to receive quotes.	Uses online data to obtain information and stock quotes immediately.
Speed and Convenience	Requires customer-broker interface for information and trades.	Obtains immediate information at customer's convenience and places trades immediately.
Expertise of Advice	Depends on the broker.	Depends on the buyer.

Source: John Thackray, "Defining Moment: Online Stock Sales," *InformationWeek,* October 20, 1997, 115–22.

▶ Thinking Strategically:
Case 5.2

Speculate on the future of the traditional stock brokerage system. Specify the value a broker brings to the investment process. How can e-business be used by a broker or brokerage company to enhance the value delivered to the customer? What other industries could be affected in the same way as the stock market industry?

Customer Relationship Management

Customer relationship management (CRM) systems combine software and management practices to serve the customer from order through delivery and after-sales service. Enhancing customer service is rated by IT managers as the number one method to gain competitive advantage, followed by

trade.[44] This change in behavior has continued in the financial field. Charles Schwab placed about 35 percent of its trades over the Internet in 1996. In 1999, online trading accounted for 65 percent of Schwab's retail trades, and by 2001 online trades were 80 percent of Schwab's total trades.[45]

To survive this challenge, full-service brokers have been forced to find new ways of adding value to their services. Electronic trading put such pressure on traditional exchange models that the price of a seat on the Chicago stock exchange dropped 50 percent in value; the growth of electronic stock exchange had lessened its value. Old-line brokers were forced to move to online trading. In 1999, Merrill Lynch decided to offer online trading at $29.95 for one thousand shares, an 80 percent decrease from its normal $210.00 fee. Merrill Lynch's brand name put direct pressure on other online traders, although Merrill Lynch's late move had allowed online firms to capture market share. Merrill's fourteen thousand brokers did not adjust well to this change; facing lower commissions, many left for other full-service firms.[46]

Even though Merrill Lynch was a late mover, the brick-and-mortar company has embraced e-business. Merrill has developed personalized reporting systems for both institutional and individual customers. These are printed to paper and accessible online. Merrill provides online digital information for its clients and has set up Webcasts of streaming video from Wall Street analysts to support its institutional investors.[47]

The shortest brokerage channel would be sales from the stock exchange directly to the investor. NASDAQ investigated a new exchange model wherein it would sell directly to the investor and bypass the broker.[48] Other exchanges are also moving to electronic trading, forcing brokers to reconsider their role in the exchange process.[49]

In addition, the broker may be bypassed altogether for some issuing companies and stock buyers or sellers. The broker has been used as an intermediary between a company issuing stock and the investor because the broker had access to the stock purchasers and could sell the stock more efficiently than the issuing company. By selling stock online, a company can bypass the broker, keeping more of the money raised in the stock issue. This process is used for both buying and selling of

Figure 5.5 Online Brokerage Prices and Volume

Prices per Trade	Volume
Full-Service Average: $116.90	150,000 a day
Discount Average: $66.09	Growth Rate: 44%

DLJ Direct: $20
Fidelity: $28.95
Ameritrade: $8 Suretrade: $7.95
Lowest Profit Limit: $5
Web Street: $0

Jan. 1997	July	Aug.	Sept.	Oct.	Nov.	Dec. 1997
15	Number of Online Brokers					60
15	Schwab Percentage of Trades Online					40

Source: Suzanne Woolley, "Do I Hear Two Bits a Trade?" *BusinessWeek,* December 8, 1997, 112–13.

continued on next page

previously issued stock and for **IPOs (initial public offerings)**. Instinet (http://www.instinet.com) allows buyers and sellers to post their prices directly to each other. Instinet has been offering this service to large traders such as pension funds and insurance companies but will join a number of other electronic trading networks already selling to the individual customer. These electronic trading networks cut out the broker, allow 24/7 trading, and decrease transaction costs.[50]

Issuing or purchasing IPOs is a more complicated transaction, and many businesses use brokerages to help them through the process. Some firms are willing to offer their stock to the public through the Internet, either directly from the company or through online facilitators. This could mean that buyers have increased risks because they become responsible for all the evaluation of the business before they buy and may not have the same expertise in stock evaluation as a broker.[51] OpenIPO (http://www.openipo.com) uses **Dutch auctions** to bring buyers to a stock offering. When potential buyers bid enough to reach the amount of money the company plans to raise, the stock is issued, with a low commission.

A Dutch auction works by having the seller lower the price continuously until a buyer decides to purchase at the stated price.

improving internal business processes.[52] The ability of the Internet to give almost instant access to information makes it an ideal solution for offering product support services, with the advantage of reducing costs. A typical service transaction with a live representative costs five dollars, a voice-response system costs fifty cents, and a Web-based system costs only a few pennies.

Cisco (http://www.cisco.com) has estimated that it saved $550 million in its customer care division and increased customer satisfaction by leveraging the Internet. Cisco allows its customers to engage in real-time question-and-answer sessions with intelligence agents. It personalizes information for its customers, and customers can use Internet telephony systems to interact with live representatives.[53] Companies such as Michelin (http://www.michelin.com) have deployed extranets to serve the same functions as a sales support staff. Michelin's 280 dealerships are able to look up inventory, order tires, check order status, and obtain answers to questions.[54] National Semiconductor (http://www.national.com) posted detailed descriptions for over thirty thousand products, allowing its customers access to information twenty-four hours a day.[55]

Most firms rely on a combination of methods to service their customers, including live human interfaces through call centers and technology-based solutions. Technologies to serve customers include auto-response e-mail, knowledge bases on customers' service needs, personalization of automated responses, and wizards that allow individuals to ask questions. Web-based consumer service systems can also track individuals' actions online and offer help if it appears that someone is having a problem. Pure technology-based CRM systems have proven expensive to develop and may not be ideal for serving customers.

Figure 5.6 illustrates how customer relationship management systems can automate the service function. Ordering can be undertaken online or supported by a marketing service person, such as a call agent or a sales representative. A number of functions are often automated, such as order confirmation and order tracking. When there is a problem, customers can be asked to first try to find help online (at a lower cost) through Web sites, e-mail, chat systems, or co-browsing (discussed in Chapter 3). However, human contact is often desired by customers, even if they have to wait for the service. Table 5.4 outlines the best practices being used by businesses that focus on customer relationship management.

Figure 5.6 Automating the Service Function

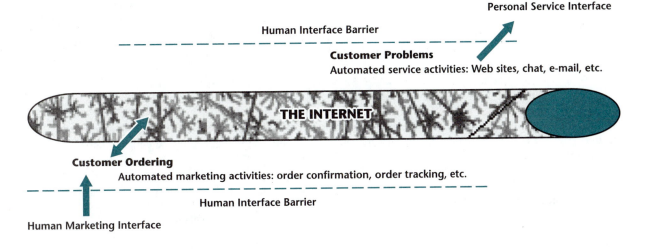

Business Process Strategy

Business process strategies include business-to-business transactions such as e-commerce (explored in-depth in Chapter 6) and supply chain management (covered in Chapter 4). In addition, numerous other business processes are being enhanced or facilitated using e-business technologies. Applications include the linking of individuals online to engage in research and development, telecommuting to work, customer and employee support, and many others to be discussed in later chapters. The following two examples give a taste of how organizations are transforming their processes to enhance value to customers.

The medical industry is using e-business to help lower costs, improve patient care, and enhance caregiver skills. Over 55 percent of physicians use the Internet to search for information, communicate with colleagues, and e-mail patients. Estimates of the savings gained by cutting waste from inefficiency and duplicated paperwork run as high as $250 billion.[56]

Governments are using e-business to lower costs and improve services offered to citizens, such as access to publications and databases. One study found that Canada had progressed the furthest in developing **e-government** initiatives, using customer relationship management tools to transform the government into a deliverer of services to citizens and to enhance administrative effectiveness.[57] Perhaps the biggest U.S. government effort to automate its processes involves the submission of federal tax forms online. More than 45 million taxpayers submitted their forms online for the 2001 filing year.

E-government *is the delivery of government information and services online through the Internet or other digital means.*

Table 5.4   Providing Service Online

Best Practice	Goal	Technology Leverage
Respond Quickly	Respond to customers within six hours if possible, but definitely within twenty-four hours.	Knowledge bases and intelligence agents provide instant feedback.
Link to Inventory	Be sure products are available for delivery.	Extranets and inventory databases can be linked to e-commerce software.
Use Automatic Order Confirmation	Send confirmations automatically through e-mail to customers, giving confirmation numbers and routing numbers.	Confirmation can be sent from databases through automated e-mail systems.
Furnish Information	Provide product, security, and shipping information.	Information delivery can be designed into a Web site. The use of FAQs (frequently asked questions) allows self-service.
Provide Alternative Means of Contact	Allow customers to place orders, inquire about orders, or receive service information.	Web-based or chat systems can be a low-cost alternative to 800-number phone systems. IP telephony can also be used if customers possess the technology.
Avoid Extra Fees	Offer online service support or gift wrapping, if offline businesses do not change for such services.	Lower costs available through the Internet should allow services to be delivered at little or no cost.
Train Customer Response Specialists	Use live individuals to support automated service transactions.	Customer response can be facilitated by chats or through the use of intelligence agents or wizards.

Source: Aileen Crowley, "Order? What Order?" PC Week, March 8, 1999, 82–86; and Justin Hibbard, "Web Service: Ready or Not," *InformationWeek,* November 16, 1998, 18–20.

Auction Strategy

Auction strategies add value by bringing together buyers and sellers who dynamically determine a market price online. Auction sites are changing the pricing structures traditionally controlled by businesses; they shift power from a business to the customer. Auction sites also allow businesses to use pricing strategies to reduce unwanted or unused inventory.[58] Table 5.5 outlines the major types of auctions.

Auctions can be business-to-consumer, business-to-business, or consumer-to-consumer. These are often hosted on auction sites such as the consumer-to-consumer industry leader eBay and the business-to-consumer leader uBid. Auctions are often facilitated through industry exchanges for the business-to-business market.

Table 5.5 Types of Auctions

Auction Type	Explanation	Example
Sales Auction (Traditional)	Sales auction sites allow individuals and businesses to sell products online and have potential customers bid on the product.	EBay, uBid, Yahoo! Auctions, and many others have set up online auction sites.
Reverse Auction	This auction system has sellers bid each other down until a lowest price is reached. Is is often used by businesses to have suppliers compete.	Procter & Gamble uses reverse auctions to help cut procurement costs by 10 to 15 percent.
Dutch Auction	A Dutch auction works by having the seller lower the price continuously until a buyer decides to purchase at the stated price.	OpenIPO uses Dutch auctions to bring buyers to a stock offering.
Buyer-Driven Commerce	These sites allow customers to specify how much they are willing to pay for a product or service and then let the provider determine if it will take the bid.	Priceline has a patent on the computer submission of buyer-driven bidding.

The consumer-to-consumer Web site at eBay (http://www.ebay.com) allows individuals to post products for sale. Sellers post information at the site, and bidders place their bids online. Once the preset time expires, the seller pays eBay a commission and consummates the deal offline. In 1998, eBay had more than 150,000 items for sale and estimated sales of over $100 million a year; by 1999, the numbers were more than 3 million items and estimated sales of over $1.3 billion.[59] In 2000, eBay transacted more than $5 billion in merchandise sales. Consumer-to-consumer auctions have been subject to buyer and seller fraud (which we will discuss in more detail in Chapter 6). Third parties are moving into auctions to help guarantee merchandise, confirm sales, and collect money.

Businesses are also using auction sites to sell new products and excess inventory. Government bodies set up **reverse auctions** to lower acquisition costs by having sellers bid for the sale. Businesses that use reverse auctions often have bidding companies check the status of the lowest bid (with the bidding company's name withheld) and then add their bid.[60]

The **buyer-driven commerce** Priceline (http://www.priceline.com) offers individuals the opportunity to name their own price for airline tickets and automobiles. It offers additional consumer services such as home mortgages, telecommunications, hotels, cruises, and new cars. Priceline receives the bid price from the purchaser and then submits the bid to companies that accept or decline the offer to purchase. The purchaser must be very flexible when purchasing airline tickets because airlines will sell excess capacity at less-than-ideal travel times.

Pricing Strategy

The e-business environment is affecting pricing strategies in a number of different ways. As stated earlier in this chapter, some businesses are becoming more efficient and are therefore able to sell with lower overall costs. Cost savings can be found in lower fixed costs because of minimized use of brick-and-mortar assets and lower variable costs due to reduced staffing requirements. EMarketer (http://www .emarketer.com) reports that businesses that sell online have an economic advantage in the lower marginal costs needed to reach and serve additional customers. Table 5.6 compares the costs of traditional transactions versus online transactions.

The Internet also allows a customer to obtain information and prices from a larger number of alternative sources of supply. This has a tendency to make the demand curve for products more elastic. Businesses are forced to bid against each other, lowering the price. Customers are using buying agents and shopping services to obtain price information. The Internet's ability to offer pricing information to all buyers and sellers at any place at any time is leading to a dynamic pricing market. **Dynamic pricing** implies that products will sell for something other than list prices. Prices are set dynamically based on market demand for that product, which can lead to higher or lower prices depending on how the market bids for the product.[61]

Product Pricing Information

Intelligent shopping agents are software-based search systems that return product and pricing information from multiple vendors. To use these systems, the customer specifies the product or other criteria, such as a price range for a product category. The agent then returns information on sales outlets, prices, and availability. When Web agents were first used, many merchant sites blocked them from receiving pricing information. Now merchants see agents as a means of delivering customers to sites. Although this forces price competition, merchants can use service, brand names, or means other than the lowest price to get the sale.[62]

Table 5.6 Transaction Cost Comparisons

Traditional Method	Average Amount	Internet	Average Amount
Telephone transaction cost plus related customer service charges	$5.00	Automated Internet transaction cost	$0.01
Bank transaction cost	$1.07	Bank transaction on the Web	$0.01
Airline ticket cost for processing	$8.00	Airline ticket transaction on the Web	$1.00

MySimon (http://www.mysimon.com) uses shopping agents to provide price and product comparisons. Shopping agents are useful for products that have multiple vendors and are easily compared. For more complicated purchases, a number of businesses are acting as **shopping services** for customers. Shopping services such as Respond (http://www.respond.com) and Imandi (http://www.imandi.com) allow individuals to submit requests for products; live agents at these sites then solicit bids for the requested products and services.[63]

Retailers have been fighting back against the consumer power gained through price searching. Some retailers have begun to use dynamic pricing software to determine customer demand given product inventory, which allows for instantaneous price adjustments to meet demand. This type of analysis has been used by the airline industry and is now moving to hotel rooms and other products sold online. Amazon.com received a number of complaints when it started selling products at different prices to different customers based on their past purchase behavior. In response to these complaints, the company dropped its dynamic pricing strategy.[64]

In the 1990s, many Web sites gave away services for free. This was part of a **penetration pricing strategy** where prices were set low in an attempt to capture market share. Free products and services included greeting cards, e-mail, site hosting, and Internet access. Low product prices and free products may mask ulterior motives. In some cases, limited services are now offered for free, and enhanced services are charged. In other cases, free products have tie-ins. RealNetworks (http://www.realnetworks.com) and Adobe (http://www.adobe.com) give away players or readers for their proprietary media formats, but software packages must be purchased to create files in these formats to send over the Internet.[65]

Two broad pricing strategies are used to set prices: skimming and penetration. Skimming pricing sets high initial prices to skim off payments from individuals. Penetration pricing sets prices lower in an attempt to capture market share for a product.

Knowledge Integration

Terms and Concepts

Advertising-supported revenue model *140*
Auction strategy *137*
Business model *137*
Business process strategy *137*
Buyer-driven commerce *155*
Copyright *142*
Customer relationship management (CRM) *151*
Digital communication strategy *137*
Digital factory *146*
Digital product *140*

Dutch auction *152*
Dynamic pricing *156*
E-commerce *139*
E-government *153*
E-zines *140*
Inseparability *147*
Intangibility *147*
Intellectual capital *141*
Intelligent shopping agent *156*
IPO (initial public offering) *152*
Market-of-one strategy *137*
Mass customization *146*

Online purchasing strategy *137*
Patent *145*
Penetration pricing *157*
Perishability *147*
Pricing strategy *137*
Reverse auction *155*
Service strategy *137*
Shopping services *157*
Skimming pricing *157*
Stretch goal *148*
Subscription-based revenue model *140*
Trademark *144*
Variability *147*

Concepts and Questions for Review

1. List the seven strategies e-businesses are adopting to provide value to customers.
2. What types of digital products are offered by e-businesses?
3. Outline the two revenue models used by digital communication businesses.
4. Define each of the major types of intellectual property.
5. How do copyright laws affect the creation of Web pages?
6. Explain how trademark laws affect the creation of Web pages.
7. What software solutions are being used to protect intellectual property?
8. Describe the impact of patent laws on e-business.
9. What impact is e-business having on service businesses?
10. Explain how customer relationship management techniques can improve the overall value offered to customers.
11. Define the market-of-one process. How does this process affect the way companies deliver products?
12. List and describe the various types of auctions being used online.
13. Justify how a business can give away products for free or at a low price.

Active Learning

Exercise 5.1 Business Model Strategies

Use the Web to evaluate different business models. Determine how many of the strategies outlined in this chapter are used at the Web sites you visit. How are those strategies used to create value for the business?

Exercise 5.2 Evaluating Business Models

Use the following table to compare e-business models against traditional business models. Determine the benefits a business provides to its customers. Are these benefits delivered more efficiently with an online model or a traditional model? Determine what the business would need to do to get you to purchase online. What would the business need to do to keep you buying at its traditional site?

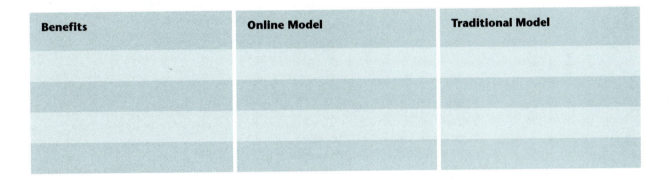

Benefits	Online Model	Traditional Model

Exercise 5.3 Evaluating Service Models

Service agent business models are perhaps the most under threat. Service agents that act only as intermediaries and information controllers can easily be replaced by e-business service systems. The following figure illustrates a real estate agent business model. What impact could e-business have on this model? Evaluate current real estate Web sites. How do they perform these functions online? Outline alternative real estate sales models, such as the seller working directly with the buyer. Explain the role of perceived risk in purchasing a home under an e-business model. What impact could perceived risk have on other agent-based models, such as insurance?

Real Estate Agent Business Model

Competitive Exercise 5.4 Business Model Building

You are going to present an e-business-based value strategy to your boss. Pick a business-to-consumer or business-to-business industry where you would be interested in working. Use the concepts in this chapter to determine the best e-business model for meeting your customers' needs. Which of the strategies outlined in this chapter would be beneficial in providing value to customers? If this business has a brick-and-mortar counterpart, determine the advantages your business model would have over the traditional model.

Web Search—Looking Online

Search Term:	Digital Communication	First 2 out of 1,534,000

E-ZineZ. Provides information on producing and publishing an Internet e-mail newsletter.
http://www.e-zinez.com

Live365. Organizes the world's largest network of independently produced audio.
http://www.live365.com

Search Term:	Intellectual Capital	First 4 out of 233,000

United States Copyright Office. Offers access to the copyright office.
http://www.loc.gov/copyright

Copyright Clearance Center. Grants permission to reproduce copyrighted content such as articles and book chapters in your journals, photocopies, coursepacks, library reserves, Web sites, e-mail, and more.
http://www.copyright.com

United States Patent and Trademark Office. Offers information on applying for patents or trademarks.
http://www.uspto.gov

Software Patent Institute. Provides information on software technology to help improve the patent process.
http://www.spi.org

Search Term:	Service Firms	First 4 out of 982,000

Investing Online Resource Center. Serves the individual consumer who invests online or is considering doing so.
http://www.Investingonline.org

CRM Forum. Gives access to an independent resource center for customer relationship management.
http://www.crm-forum.com

eMarketer. Provides reports, statistics, and consulting for businesses engaging in e-commerce.
http://www.emarketer.com

Customer Relationship Management Benchmarking Association (CRMBA). Offers association members an opportunity to identify, document, and establish best practices through benchmarking.
http://www.crmba.com

Search Term:	Auction	First 1 out of 365,000

Internet Auction List. Provides a Web portal to the auction community.
http://www.internetauctionlist.com

References

[1] Robyn Greenspan, "Online Travel Expected to Fly High," in CyberAtlas [online] (April 2, 2002), available from <http://www.cyberatlas.internet.com/markets/travel/print/0,,6071_100261,00.html>.
[2] Michael Pastore, "2001: An Online Travel Odyssey," in CyberAtlas [online] (January 16, 2002), available from <http://www.cyberatlas.internet.com/markets/travel/article/0,,6071_956051,00.html>.
[3] Eric Wahlgren, "Can Travelocity Fly Higher?" in *BusinessWeek* Online [online] (November 26, 2001), available from <http://www.businessweek.com/magazine/content/01_

48/b3759611.htm>; Scott Kessler, "The E-Commerce Winners," in *BusinessWeek* Online [online] (August 3, 2001), available from <http://www.businessweek.com/investor/content/aug2001/pi2001083_267.htm>.

4 Darnell Little, "Orbitz Leaps into the Not-So-Friendly Skies," in *BusinessWeek* Online [online] (June 19, 2001), available from <http://www.businessweek.com/technology/content/jun2001/tc20010619_391.htm>.

5 "The Emerging Digital Economy II," in U.S. Department of Commerce [online] (June 1999), available from <http://www.esa.gov/508/esa/TheEmergingDigitalEconomyII.htm>.

6 For more on the concept of perceived value, see Valerie A. Zeithaml, "Consumer Perceptions of Price, Quality, and Value: A Means-End Model and Synthesis of Evidence," *Journal of Marketing* (July 1988): 2–22.

7 Ravi Kalakota and Andrew B. Whinston, *Electronic Commerce, A Manager's Strategy* (Reading, Mass.: Addison-Wesley, 1997).

8 Michael Pastore, "Convenience Key to Successful Holiday Season," in CyberAtlas [online] (October 31, 2001), available from <http://cyberatlas.internet.com/markets/retailing/article/0,,6061_914131,00.html#table2>; Tamsin McMahon, "Britons Save Time Online," in Euromedia.net [online] (April 23, 2002), available from <http://www.europemedia.net/shownews.asp?ArticleID=10202>.

9 Paul A. Greenberg, "Nielsen Reports on Keys to Online Sales Success," in *E-Commerce Times* [online] (October 19, 1999), available from <http://www.ecommercetimes.com/news/articles/991019-2.shtml>.

10 Michael Mechanic, "Doing the Bare Minimum," *Newsweek,* March 19, 2001, 62P.

11 Anna Maria Virzi, "News Sites Are Coming of Age,"*Internet World,* September 14, 1998, 13.

12 David F. Carr, "Enabling 'By the Slice' Sales of Site Content," *Internet World,* February 9, 1998, 25–27.

13 Peter Fabris, "Funky Music," *CIO Web Business,* December 1, 1997, 68–76.

14 Derek Slater, "Storing the Mind, Minding the Store," *CIO Web Business,* February 15, 1998, 46–51.

15 "Parks Associates: Nearly Half of U.S. Users Download MP3s," in NUA [online] (March 26, 2002), available from <http://www.nua.ie/surveys/index.cgi?f=VS&art_id=905357787&rel=true>.

16 Ronald Grover and Tom Lowry, "Can't Get No . . . ," *BusinessWeek,* September 3, 2001, 78–79; Michael Pastore, "Little Has Changed on Digital Music Front," in CyberAtlas [online] (September 27, 2001), available from <http://cyberatlas.internet.com/big_picture/applications/article/0,,1301_893461,00.html>.

17 Steven V. Brull, "Are Music Companies Blinded by Fright?" *BusinessWeek,* June 28, 1999, 67–68; James C. Luh, "Going Public with MP3," *Internet World,* June 7, 1999, 46; Ann Harrison, "U.S. Music Biz Accepts MP3, Global Publishers Rebel," *Computerworld,* March 29, 1999, 43.

18 "What Is Copyright?" in United States Copyright Office [online] (May 1, 2002), available from <http://www.copyright.gov/circs/circ1.html#wci>.

19 Kathleen Murphy, "Roving Robot Will Unmask Online Music Pirates," *Web Week,* October 20, 1997, 7.

20 "Sixth Annual BSA Global Software Piracy Study," in Business Software Alliance [online] (May 22, 2001), available from <http://www.bsa.org/resources/2001-05-21.55.pdf>.

21 Juliana Gruenwald, "EU Approves Digital Copyright Law," *Interactive Week,* February 19, 2001, 18.

22 James Lardner, "Hollywood versus High-Tech," *Business 2.0,* May 2002, 40–48; Patrick Thibodeau, "Copyright Holders Turn to IT," *Computerworld,* 1, 57.

23 James Evans, "Whose Web Site Is It Anyway?" *Internet World,* September 1997, 46–50.

24 Elizabeth Gardner, "Trademark Battles Simmer behind Sites," *Web Week,* August 25, 1997, 1, 45; John Fontana, "Trademark Trickery," *Internet Week,* September 29, 1997, 1, 124.

25 Eileen Glanton, "Firms Claim Search Engines Abuse Their Names," *Marketing News,* March 15, 1999, 16.

26 This information is compiled from David Zielinski, "Stop Thief," *Presentations,* July 2001, 30–40; Maxine Lans Retsky, "On-Line Work Needs Copyright Protection, Too," *Marketing News,* December 7, 1998, 21; Sara Shay, "Stealing Beauty," *CIO Web Business,* September 1, 1998, 22–25.

27 "Idea Deluge," *Business 2.0,* October 24, 2000, 34.

28 James Heckman, "Marketers Can Say 'Mine!'" *Marketing News,* February 15, 1999, 1–2; Bradley C. Wright and Gregory J. Carlin, "Patenting Methods of Doing Business," *Knowledge Management World,* March 1999, 42–43.

29 Doug Brown, "Agency Still Struggling to Handle Flood of Tech Filings," *Interactive Week,* June 18, 2001, 65–66; Mel Duvall, "Patents Hook Start-Ups," *Interactive Week,* August 16, 1999, 72–74; Brett N. Dorny, "Stop, Pay Toll," *CIO Web Business,* November 1, 1998, 64–66; Becky Waring, "Patently Obvious," *NewMedia,* October 1998, 6.

30 Jacqueline Emigh, "Agile Manufacturing," *Computerworld,* August 30, 1999, 56; Gene Bylinsky, "The Digital Factory," *Fortune,* November 14, 1994, 92–110.

31 Don Peppers and Martha Rogers, *The One to One Future* (New York: Doubleday, 1996).

32 Candee Wilde, "Personal Business," *InformationWeek,* August 9, 1999, 76–80; Elizabeth Gardner, "'Build It Yourself' Is Motto of Sites Selling Everything from Golf Clubs to CDs to Bicycles," *Internet World,* March 2, 1998, 13, 15; Larry Marion and Emily Kay, "Customer of One, the Next Market Paradigm," *Software Magazine,* November 1997, 38–50.

33 Eric Torbenson, "As You Like It," *CIO Enterprise,* February 15, 1998, 61–64.

34 Bob Violino, "Banking on E-Business," *InformationWeek,* May 3, 1999, 44–52.

35 "Growing Number of U.S. Households Banking Online," in eMarketer [online] (April 18, 2002) available from <http://www.emarketer.com/estatnews/estats/efinancial_services/20020418_onlb.html>.

36 Independent Community Bankers of America, "2001 Community Bank Technology Survey Results," in InFinet Resources [online] (2001), available from <http://www.infinetresources.com/fpit1.htm>.

37 Jennifer Lach, "Point, Click and Pay," *Newsweek,* August 17, 1998, 66–67.

38 Michael Pastore, "Net Plays Increasing Role in Mortgage, Home-Buying Process," in CyberAtlas [online] (July 24, 2001), available from <http://cyberatlas.internet.com/markets/finance/article/0,,5961_807451,00.html>.

39 Carol Marie Cropper, "Online Trading Changes Landscape for Old-Line Brokerage Firms," in *New York Times* [online] (September 22, 1999) available from <http://www.nytimes.com/library/tech/99/09/biztech/technology/22crop.html>.

40 Amy Dunkin, "For Investors of All Stripes, a Cornucopia on the Net," *BusinessWeek,* December 22, 1997, 104–6.

41 Susan Moran, "A Plan to Spend $100M to Lure New Online Traders," *Internet World,* September 14, 1998, 6.

42 "Internet at a Glance," *Business 2.0,* February 1999, 102; Nelson Wang, "E-Brokerages in Bruising Fight," *Web Week,* January 12, 1998, 38–41; Gregory Dalton, "Nasdaq, Online Brokerages Crack under Trade Volume," *InformationWeek,* November 3, 1997, 28.

43 Robyn Greenspan, "Cashing in on Online Financial Services," in CyberAtlas [online] (April 22, 2002), available from <http://cyberatlas.internet.com/markets/finance/article/0,,5961_1014001,00.html>.

44 Leah Nathans Spiro and Edward C. Baig, "Who Needs a Broker?" *BusinessWeek,* February 22, 1999, 113–18; Maryann Jones Thompson, "Online Trading," in Industry Standard [online] (February 8, 1999), available from <http://www.thestandard.com/article/0,1902,9886,00.html>. "Special Study: On-Line Brokerage: Keeping Apace of Cyberspace," in U.S. Securities and Exchange Commission [online] (November 22, 1999), available from <http://www.sec.gov/news/studies/cyberspace.htm>.

45 David Hallerman, "Growth Falters among Online Brokers," in eMarketer [online] (April 19, 2002), available from <http://www.emarketer.com/analysis/marketing/20020419_mark.html>. Bronwyn Fryer, "Trading Push," *InformationWeek,* April 13, 1998, 97–100; Gideon Sasson, "E-Commerce Success Story: Charles Schwab.Com," in *E-Commerce Times* [online] (December 6, 1999), available from <http://www.ecommercetimes.com/success_stories/success_schwab.shtml>.

46 Megan Barnett, "Merrill Talks, Brokers Walk," in Industry Standard [online] (October 18, 1999), available from <http://www.thestandard.com/article/0,1092,6845,00.html?1447>; Leah Nathans Spiro, Timothy J. Mullaney, and Louise Lee, "Bullish on the Internet," *BusinessWeek,* June 14, 1999, 45–46; Thomas Hoffman, "Merrill Lynch Bows to Low-Cost Net Trading," *Computerworld,* June 7, 1999, 20.

47 *1to1 Magazine,* "Actionable Idea," April 2002, 14–15; Carol Pickering, "Live! From Merrill Lynch?" May 29, 2001, *Business 2.0,* 76–77; Robert Preston and Jeffrey Schwartz, "Merrill Lynch Institutionalizes E-Biz," *InternetWeek,* March 5, 2001, 1, 52.

48 Tim Wilson, "Nasdaq Puts Stock in Web," *InternetWeek,* July 6, 1998, 1, 48.

49 Paula Dwyer, Andrew Osterland, Kerry Capell, and Sharon Reier, "The 21st Century Stock Market," *BusinessWeek,* August 10, 1998, 66–72.

50 Brenon Daly, "Stock Around the Clock," *Business 2.0,* November 1999, 297–300.

51 Stephanie T. Gates, "The IPO Tease," *Red Herring,* August 1999, 140–48; Randall Smith, "So Far, 'E-Underwriting' Gets a Slow Start," *Wall Street Journal,* August 13, 1999, C1, C10; Eileen P. Gunn, "Back to the Future: From the Curb to the Web," *Fortune,* May 13, 1996, 30.

52 Kathy Chin Leong, "Customer Service Gets Royal Treatment," *InternetWeek,* September 14, 1998, 32–34.

53 Martin LaMonica, "Untangling Online Customer Service," *InfoWorld,* January 11, 1999, 75–76; Tom Stein, "Service on the Net," *InternetWeek,* December 21–28, 1998, 76–80.

54 Justin Hibbard, Gregory Dalton, and Mary E. Thyfault, "Web-Based Customer Care," *InformationWeek,* June 1, 1998, 18–20.

55 Cate T. Corcoran, "National Semiconductor Uses Web to Ease Support Services," *InfoWorld,* July 22, 1996, 62.

56 Bill Scanlon, "Vital Signs," *Interactive Week,* March 19, 2001, 26–29; Jennifer Couzin, "The Virtual Schmooze," *Industry Standard,* June 18, 2001, 42–50; Ellen Licking, "Curing an Industry's Ills," *BusinessWeek,* December 11, 2000, EB60–EB64.

57 Accenture, "Canada Wins the Gold in Moving Government Services Online, 2002 Annual Global Accenture Study Shows," in Accenture [online] (April 24, 2002), available from <http://www.accenture.com/xd/xd.asp?it=enweb&xd=_dyn/dynamicpressrelease_475 .xml>; "E-Government Makes Strides in Past Year," in CyberAtlas [online] (September 19, 2001), available from <http://cyberatlas.internet.com/markets/professional/article/ 0,,5971_887581,00.html>.

58 Amy E. Cortese and Marcia Stepanek, "Good-Bye to Fixed Pricing?" *BusinessWeek,* May 4, 1998, 70–84.

59 Phil Hood, "Seller's Market," *NewMedia,* February 10, 1998, 61.

60 Gregory Dalton, "Going, Going, Gone!" *Yahoo! Internet Life,* October 4, 1999, 44–50.

61 Robert D. Hof, Heather Green, and Paul Judge, "Going, Going, Gone," *BusinessWeek,* April 12, 1999, 30–32; Amy E. Cortees and Marcia Stepanek, "Good-Bye to Fixed Pricing?" *BusinessWeek,* May 4, 1998, 70–84.

62 Alan Majer and Mike Dover, "License to Bill," *NewMedia,* January 1999, 11; Clinton Wilder, "Call Your Agent for Online Shopping," *InformationWeek,* December 7, 1998, 126–28; Clinton Wilder, "Agents Go Price Shopping," *InternetWeek,* December 7, 1998, 23.

63 Niall McKay, "Human Touch," *Red Herring,* September 1999, 142–43; Michelle V. Rafter, "Cheap, Cheaper, Cheapest," *Industry Standard,* January 11–18, 1999, 50–51.

64 Mary Wagner, "Getting Top Dollar," *Internet Retailer,* January/February 2002, 40–44; Christopher T. Heun, "Dynamic Pricing Boosts Bottom Line," *InformationWeek,* October 29, 2001, 59–61.

65 George Anders, "Eager to Boost Traffic, More Internet Firms Give Away Services," *Wall Street Journal,* July 28, 1999, A1, A8; David Cowles, "The Best Things in Life Are Free," *Fast Company,* April–May 1998, 38–40.

chapter 6
E-Commerce

Business-to-business e-commerce is very common, while business-to-consumer e-commerce is still a small percentage of overall retail sales. Nevertheless, e-commerce is an important part of a multichannel retail approach. Pure-play e-commerce companies use the Internet to meet market needs, and traditional brick-and-mortar retailers use the Internet as a tool to reach and maintain relationships with their customers. E-commerce is also a means for smaller retailers to move into larger markets. It is important for marketers to understand the changing dynamics of retailing in this new multichannel retail environment.

1. Gain an understanding of the e-commerce process.
2. Outline why a multichannel approach is beneficial for a retailer.
3. Explain why newly formed pure-play Internet businesses may have a hard time gaining competitive advantages in the retail market.
4. Compare and contrast how e-commerce is being used as a strategic tool by e-retailers and traditional retailers.
5. Outline the major types of fraud committed online and what is being done to limit fraud.
6. Perform a benefit analysis of alternative sales channels.
7. List the limitations to international e-commerce.
8. Explain the role of an ASP in a business's e-commerce strategy.

Where Are My Groceries?

Once upon a time in the United States, small grocery stores could be found conveniently down the street from most homes. Homemakers would call the grocer, whom they often knew personally. The groceries would then be prepared for pickup. Butchers would pack meats to the buyer's specifications. If needed, a delivery boy would place the groceries in his bicycle basket and deliver them directly to a home. Most of these small grocers closed when supermarkets opened and offered greater variety at lower prices. Improved roads, multicar homes, larger refrigerators and freezers, and a growing assortment of prepackaged food enticed homemakers to shop at these supermarkets. Today, grocery shoppers have many alternatives, including hypermarkets and convenience stores. The grocery business would seem to be perfect for e-commerce. Using the Web, the shopper should be able to access more products than found in grocery stores, order from home, and then have the products delivered. Consumers have considerable experience shopping for packaged goods and should react to offers of greater convenience, lower prices, and faster service.[1]

A number of companies have attempted to service this market through different e-commerce models. Webvan developed an e-commerce model based on building the infrastructure to offer a full-service online grocery and drugstore with free delivery. Webvan attempted to lower costs of grocery delivery by building distribution centers as large as eighteen conventional grocery stores. These were to act as hubs for home delivery. Webvan's San Francisco Bay service offered more than 350 types of cheese, 700 different wines, more than 300 varieties of fresh fruits and vegetables, locally produced goods, and traditional packaged goods. Prices averaged 5 percent less than those in local grocery stores. Customers were able to create personalized lists that allowed them to complete their grocery shopping in just a few minutes. Webvan also created and delivered chef-prepared meals. Its personnel were trained to provide a high level of customer service.[2] By 2002, Webvan died. Webvan's business model was shaky from the start. Webvan needed to raise $1 billion to build an infrastructure that would be more effective than that of any other grocery business, and it needed to achieve $1 billion in sales by changing customers' shopping habits to move them online.[3] This model has been adopted successfully, however, by niche grocery delivery businesses, such as Pink Dot, (http://www.pdquick.com), serving local markets.

Other online grocers use different e-commerce models, such as a brick-and-click approach. The Dutch-owned Stop & Shop purchased Peapod (http://www.peapod.com) to offer groceries to online shoppers. Peapod allows the buyer to select groceries online, which are then pulled from local grocery stores and delivered to the buyer's home. The benefits to the customer include convenience, selection, and time savings. Safeway (http://www.safeway.com) purchased GroceryWorks to engage in the same strategy.

The grocery industry in the United States has realized that new business models are threatening current practices. A Grocery Manufacturers of America (http://www.gmabrands.com) report indicated that e-business with a business-to-business focus is the number one priority for the industry. In addition, a number of traditional brick-and-mortar grocery businesses are developing e-commerce models to sell directly to the consumer. Albertsons (http://www.albertsons.com) allows customers to order online and pick up groceries at the store or have them delivered within a ninety-minute window.

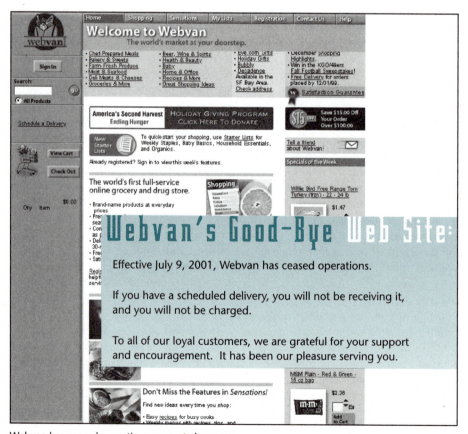

Webvan has ceased operations. www.webvan.com

Evaluate your grocery shopping habits. How often do you purchase the same products? Consider if you would trust a grocer to pick out your meats, fruits, and vegetables. On your next visit to a brick-and-mortar grocery, determine which aspects of grocery shopping could be automated. Evaluate the business model for a traditional grocery and determine where its competitive advantage lies. Estimate the expenses a business could save by moving grocery shopping online. What is the future of online grocery sales?

E-commerce is the process of allowing Web-based technologies to facilitate commerce or trade. E-commerce can be used for business-to-consumer transactions, business-to-business transactions (covered in Chapter 4), or consumer-to-consumer transactions (as with eBay, as covered in Chapter 5). An e-business could be the producer of the product, as in the case of Dell Computer, or an intermediary that coordinates the distribution process, such as Peapod. These distinctions are becoming blurred as manufacturers bypass established distributors and retailers and sell directly to end users, as outlined in Chapter 4. E-commerce is not the sole domain of online-only businesses. Traditional brick-and-mortar businesses have rapidly moved to brick-and-click models. E-commerce is becoming part of a multichannel sales approach and is seen as a vital component of selling strategies. This chapter will explore e-commerce models, processes, and strategies.

E-Retailing

As can be seen in Figure 6.1, total U.S. e-commerce sales have been increasing steadily since 1999. E-commerce has also been increasing as a percentage of total retail sales, but by the end of 2001 this percentage was only 1.2 percent. This small percentage of total retail sales is mainly due to the fact that e-commerce sales are strong in only specific industries. Figure 6.2 illustrates relative e-commerce sales by industry for October 2001.

Consumer retail purchases entail a rich and complex buying process. Consumers will often spend considerable time evaluating information, touching or sampling products, evaluating services, and asking friends and opinion leaders about what and where to purchase. The introduction of **e-retailing** will not necessarily result in an increase in overall retail sales; instead, consumers are shifting purchases by adopting a **multichannel approach** and using alternative **sales channels.** Multichannel retailers support the commerce process in a number of ways, including in-store or in-catalog marketing of the online channel, gift certificates purchased online, in-store return of online orders, catalog orders online, and

Sales channels are the models that businesses use to sell to their customers. These include brick-and-mortar outlets, catalogs, direct marketing, or e-commerce.

Figure 6.1   U.S. E-Commerce Sales

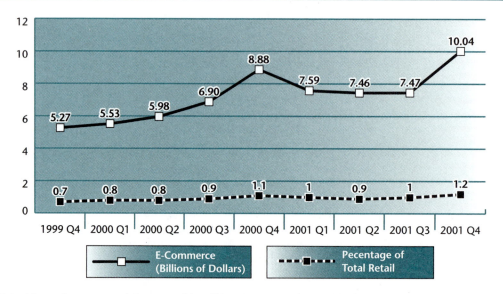

Source: "United States Department of Commerce News," in U.S. Census Bureau [online] (February 20, 2002), available from <http://www.census.gov/mrts/www/current.html>.

many others.[4] Traditional retailers as well as pure-play Internet retailers see that consumers are using the Internet to collect information, compare prices, and discuss products through e-mail or online chat and discussion groups. Developing an e-retail presence is becoming important to traditional retailers because of how much the Internet is used as a channel for information collection and purchase.[5]

Brick-and-mortar retailers are building off their brand and physical location advantages by using the Internet to enhance their present business models. The Sears Web site (http://www.sears.com) allows customers to collect information on products and make purchases for pickup in local stores. The Web site also allows vendors to check product sales and inventory levels. In 1999, the site received more than 1 million visitors a month; many customers used the site for collecting information and then visited a physical store to purchase. Supporting multiple channels has not been a smooth process for Sears. It had problems with returns; customers could not return online purchases to stores because individual store managers had those returns counted against their overall sales.[6] By 2001, Sears had more than a quarter million unique shoppers per day. In an attempt to regain multichannel dominance, Sears purchased the catalog and Internet retailer Lands' End in 2002 for $1.98 billion. Lands' End (http://www.landsend.com) has strong experience in linking its catalog sales and service system to an online sales model.

Traditional brick-and-mortar retailers such as the Gap (http://www.gap.com), Macy's (http://www.macys.com), Home Depot (http://www.homedepot.com), Office Depot (http://www.officedepot.com), Wal-Mart (http://www.walmart.com), and

Figure 6.2 Relative E-Commerce Sales by Industry

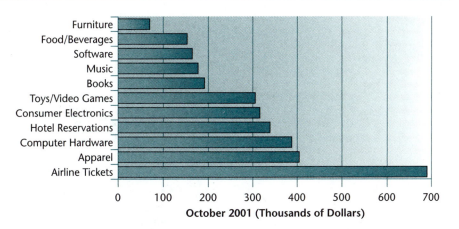
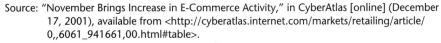

Source: "November Brings Increase in E-Commerce Activity," in CyberAtlas [online] (December 17, 2001), available from <http://cyberatlas.internet.com/markets/retailing/article/ 0,,6061_941661,00.html#table>.

many others are selling online. Catalog retailers such as L.L.Bean (http://www. llbean.com) use the Internet to increase their catalog sales. Williams-Sonoma operates both the Williams-Sonoma (http://www.williamssonoma.com) and Pottery Barn (http://www.potterybarn.com) stores. Williams-Sonoma's stores receive more than 50 million visits a year, and it has a database of over 19 million customers. These well-known brand names are leveraging their existing supply chain and purchasing power to compete online. All of these experienced retailers are placing pressure on pure-play Internet businesses.[7]

E-commerce has penetrated both large and small businesses. In 1999, 97 percent of large businesses were connected to the Internet in some way, with 33 percent conducting sales over the Internet. By 2001, this had grown to 99 percent connected and 85 percent engaging in e-commerce. In 1999, only 21 percent of smaller businesses were connected to the Internet, and 4 percent were selling online. By 2001, this had grown to 85 percent connected and 80 percent engaging in e-commerce.[8]

Not all brick-and-mortar retailers set up e-commerce sites. Those that wish to avoid channel conflicts may set up sites to support retail outlets. The goal of these sites is not just to engage in sales but also to create a **destination site**. This type of site includes interactive games, consumer surveys, contests, online chats, feature articles, and other relationship tools.[9]

The E-business model outlined in Chapter 1 (Figure 1.2) and shown in part here in Figure 6.3 gives insight into why pure-play Internet companies have had such a hard time developing successful business-to-consumer e-commerce models. This model shows that businesses must develop a payment system, supply chain system, distribution system (including a product return system), promotional system, pricing strategy, and management talent. Established businesses have

*A **destination site** is a Web site designed to entice the visitor to return over and over. This requires including extras, such as games, chats, contests, or new information, and any other content the targeted audience may desire.*

Figure 6.3 E-Business Model

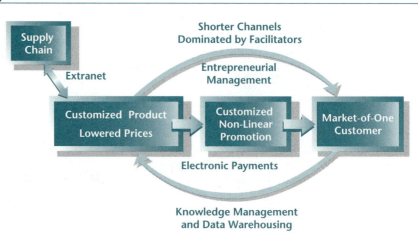

often expended considerable resources over time to develop these models. Conceptualizing the e-business model components into a value chain, as shown in Figure 6.4, gives insight into the problems encountered by newly formed online-only e-commerce companies.

Considerable investment in technology and infrastructure needs to be made to support e-commerce. Webvan attempted to match the physical infrastructure and benefits of brick-and-mortar grocers while also attempting to change the shopping patterns of its targeted market. This strategy was undertaken in an environment where the company could not block other grocers from using technology to reach out to the market. In contrast, when Sears purchased Lands' End, it purchased not only a business but also the knowledge and management expertise to sell through multiple channels. Table 6.1 illustrates that existing retailers have many advantages they can bring to the retail exchange process. Newly formed pure-play e-retailers must be able to overcome all the advantages of established retailers while building the infrastructure necessary to serve their market.

Although the auction business eBay moved the greatest amount of product of any e-retailer, eBay acts only as an agent in the sales process. Amazon.com is perhaps the best-recognized example of a pure-play Internet retailer. By the end of 2001, Amazon.com had the largest unique audience with more than 31 million visitors. From the year 2000 to 2001, Amazon.com increased its unique audience by 34 percent. Brick-and-click retailers have been moving offline shoppers online, placing pressure on pure-play Internet retailers during the same time period. Wal-Mart increased its unique audience by 133 percent, JCPenney (http://www.jcpenney.com) by 34 percent, Target (http://www.target.com) by 142 percent, and Sears by 23 percent.[10] By the end of 2001, the top e-retailers by unique audience were a combination of pure-play retailers such as Amazon.com (in the number one position), MyPoints (http://www.mypoints.com), and BizRate (http://bizrate.com), and multichannel retailers such as Columbia House (catalog and Internet),

Figure 6.4   E-Commerce Value Chain

Supply Chain	**Product and Pricing Strategies**	**Promotion**	**Distribution Channels**	**Knowledge Management**	**Management**	**Delivered Value to Customer**
Develop and deploy Inventory systems, warehousing, extranets, etc.	Create positioning strategy, image with market, etc.	Expand customer base and experience in targeting audience.	Establish locations, shipping facilitators, payment systems, and return policies and procedures.	Create database on customers and links to inventory and other business processes.	Gain experience in field and knowledge of process and industry, and develop strong relationships with employees, suppliers, and other constituencies.	

Table 6.1   Retailer Value Chain Analysis

Retailer	Value Chain Analysis
Established Online-Only Businesses	Established online-only businesses such as Amazon.com may have advantages in supply chains, image as an online-only firm, targeted audiences, shipping systems for distribution, data collection and knowledge management, and managerial expertise in e-business.
Catalog Businesses	Existing catalog businesses may have advantages in supply chains, image as a non-brick-and-mortar retailer, targeted audiences, shipping systems for distribution, knowledge management, and managerial expertise in direct marketing.
Retail Chains	Existing national retail chains may have advantages in supply chains, image, targeted audiences, prime locations for distribution, information capture and knowledge management systems, and managerial expertise in retailing.
Existing Small- to Medium-Sized Retailers	Existing small- to medium-sized retailers may not have any value chain components developed for conducting business outside of the targeted market area.
New Online-Only Businesses	New online-only businesses must develop the entire value chain system from scratch.

Toys "R" Us (brick and click), Barnes & Noble (brick and click), Best Buy (brick and click), and Wal-Mart (brick and click).[11]

Amazon.com's founder chose books as his initial product because he believed they were a product that individuals did not need to see, feel, and touch before purchasing. Amazon.com has added product lines that consumers feel comfortable

Figure 6.5 E-Commerce Personalization

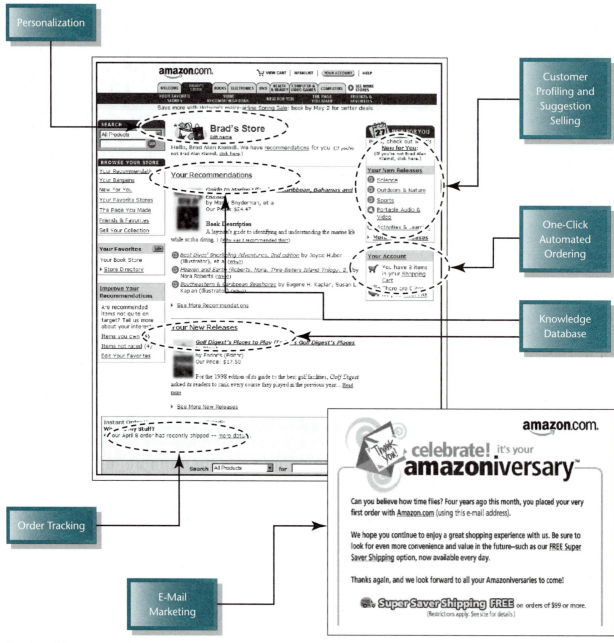

Courtesy of Amazon.com, Inc.

shopping for without physical interaction. Customer acceptance of Amazon.com's online shopping model will depend on the value that Amazon.com can deliver to its customers, as discussed in Chapter 5. Amazon.com has built off its knowledge base to develop a personalized store within its site. This site is tied to personalized e-mail that maintains relationships between the retailer and customers. Figure 6.5 illustrates how personalization can enhance customer relationships.

The competitiveness of Amazon.com's e-retail model can be analyzed by evaluating the benefits offered. Table 6.2 outlines the advantages consumers can find with online bookstores versus traditional brick-and-mortar booksellers.

Amazon.com was not designed to replace more traditional booksellers or superstores such as Barnes & Noble. A customer shopping in a brick-and-mortar store may be looking for a different type of shopping experience, but the emerging

Table 6.2 Benefit Analysis for Amazon.com

Benefit	Amazon.com	Mall Bookstore (e.g., Waldenbooks, B. Dalton)	Superstores (e.g., Barnes & Noble, Borders)
Number of Books	Millions	70,000	175,000+
Discounts on Books	Percentage off on selected titles (customer pays shipping on small orders)	Discounts on selected titles	
Ability to Browse by Topics	Online databases with links to topic areas	Books placed in topic sections	
Access to Books	Average two to three days	Immediate	
Access to Information about a Book	Immediate, online	Consumer must browse or ask for help	
Ability to Converse with an Author	Online through discussion groups or e-mail	Rare, except at a book signing	
Shipping of Gift Books	Handled online	Customer must ship	
Other Relationship Development Tools	Personalization through e-mail comments and database recommendations based on past purchases	Other stores for customers to visit	Coffee shops
Interaction with Customers	E-mail links to service personnel, chat rooms with other customers	Face-to-face sales representatives	
Returns	Must be shipped back by buyer	Can be returned to the physical location	

case 6.1

A Prescription for Success?

Pharmacy sales seemed like an ideal market for retail e-commerce. An aging baby-boomer population and a more health-conscious market-place were expected to push retail and prescription pharmaceutical sales to over $170 billion in the United States and over $406 billion world-wide by 2002. Online pharmacies promised e-mail contact with pharmacists **24/7/52.** They provided information on products and drug interactions. They delivered products overnight and provided anonymity for individuals who were embarrassed to purchase in a regular pharmacy. To generate profits, online pharmacies planned to sell prescriptions and over-the-counter drugs.

By 2000, however, only 7 percent of online shoppers used an online pharmacy. The reasons given were the desire for personal attention, concerns about privacy, and prices.[13] There are a number of other problems that pure-play Internet pharmacies must overcome. Pharmaceutical sales regulations differ among countries and states. Large offline competitors can engage in deep discounts because they have diverse product lines to maintain overall profits. Brick-and-mortar competitors such as Rite Aid (http://www.riteaid.com) and Walgreens (http://www.walgreens.com) have established brand names and existing customer databases and are now offering online e-commerce and services.[14]

online sales channel pressured a number of book retailers to follow Amazon.com's example. Barnes & Noble (http://www.bn.com) launched its own Web site offering many of the same advantages as Amazon.com. For Amazon.com, books are only one product line. The company now faces competition for all its product lines from emerging multichannel retailers such as Sears, Wal-Mart, Target, and many others.

Individuals are gaining confidence and experience with online shopping, leading to greater acceptance of e-commerce. In a lifetime of shopping, a typical shopper gains a mental model of stores, brands, products, prices, and processes related to the shopping experience. This happens online as well. Consumers use Web sites not only to purchase but also to engage in window-shopping, product comparisons, and trial purchasing. Studies have shown that consumers abandon online shopping carts because they determine prices are too high, they are just comparison shopping, they change their mind, they are saving items for later purchase, or they do not want to engage in the checkout process. Consumers will purchase online when they gain greater convenience, prices are lower, they find greater selection, they are able to track their orders, and the process is easy to use.[12]

24/7/52 or 24/7 indicates that a business is open 24 hours a day, 7 days a week, 52 weeks a year.

▶ Thinking Strategically: Case 6.1

Consider the types of products that individuals usually purchase at a pharmacy. Determine the importance of receiving that product immediately versus waiting until the next day. How important is it to talk to a pharmacist about products purchased at a pharmacy? Visit an online pharmacy. Compare the services it offers to what can be found at a brick-and-mortar store. Decide whether consumers' purchasing patterns would differ if they were buying products on a continuing basis. For example, if an individual were permanently on a heart medicine, would he or she want to order the medicine online and have it delivered to his or her home? Speculate on the future of online pharmacies.

Niche E-Retailers

Given that established retailers and brand-name e-retailers have advantages in e-commerce, is there room for smaller e-retailers? Many small e-retailers have set up shop on the Internet. These **niche e-retailers** typically target narrow market segments with clearly differentiated offerings. Table 6.3 lists four e-retailing sites, their target markets, and their product offerings. Successful niche e-retailers can offer an extensive product line and add expertise and advice that cannot be found in traditional stores. They need to develop brand names and establish credibility with their customers, however, if they are to succeed.[15]

Fraud and Scams

The National Consumers League (http://www.nclnet.org) has developed a Web site to act as a global reporting venue for Internet fraud (http://www.fraud.org/internet/2001stats10mnt.htm). The top areas for **fraud**, as reported by the Internet Fraud Watch, are shown in Table 6.4. While the ranking of these types of fraud can vary with time, online auction fraud is by far the most common, accounting for over 60 percent of all fraud.

Fraud and scams are two ways of indicatng an act of misrepresentation or deception.

Stock **scams** can be facilitated on the Internet because it is relatively easy to promote a company through a **pump-and-dump** scheme. With this type of scam, a

Table 6.3 Niche E-Retailers

Business	Target Market	Product Offerings
dELiA*s http://www.dELiAs.com	Teenage girls and young women	This Multichannel (catalog, Web site, and stores) retailer offers apparel and accessories.
Wine.com http://www.wine.com	Individuals interested in high-quality wines and gourmet foods	Wine.com, the largest online wine retailer in the United States, offers wine and advice on purchasing wine.
JustBalls http://www.justballs.com	Individuals and institutions that need unique or specialty balls and ball-related items	This site carries a narrowly focused line of products, offering expertise and information on all types of balls.
AnotherUniverse.com http://www.anotheruniverse.com	Males, average age twenty-eight, with higher-than-average income	Another Universe.com emphasizes information on television, movies, comic books, and collectibles.

Table 6.4   Top Internet Fraud Areas

Type	Description
Web Auction Scams	Items are bid for and purchased but then never delivered by the seller. Values of items are inflated. Shills are used to drive up bids.
General Merchandise Fraud	Products are advertised and sold but never delivered or are not as advertised.
Nigerian Money Offers	Individuals are contacted by e-mail and told they can help collect money from banks by paying a processing fee.
Internet Service Fraud	Individuals are charged for services that are supposedly free. Customers pay for online and Internet services that are never provided or falsely represented.
Hardware/Software Fraud	Customers purchase computer products that are never delivered or are misrepresented.
Pyramid or Multilevel Marketing Scams	Profits are made from recruiting others, not from sales of goods to end users.
Business Opportunity/ Franchise Scams	Customers are promised big profits with little or no work by investing in prepackaged businesses or franchise opportunities.
Work-at-Home Scams	Customers buy materials and equipment that are sold with false promises of payment for piecework performed at home.
Advance Fee Loan Fraud	Individuals are promised loans contingent on paying a large fee in advance. Once the fee is paid, the loans are never disbursed.
Credit Repair Fraud	Individuals are promised that accurate negative information will be removed from their credit report.
Credit Card Offer Scams	Individuals with bad credit histories are promised credit cards upon payment of up-front fees.

Sources: "2001 Internet Fraud Statistics," in Internet Fraud Watch [online] (May 20, 2002); Phillip C. McKee III, remarks to the Consumer Protection in Electronic Commerce Panel at the Public Voice in the Development of Internet Policy Conference of the Global Internet Liberty Campaign, in Internet Fraud Watch [online] (October 7, 1998 and November 25, 1998), available from <http://www.fraud.org/internet/9810stat.htm>.

stock is promoted through telemarketing or by using online chat groups, news releases, spam e-mails, or advertisements; when investors buy stock in the company, the owners sell at a high stock price or take the money and run. One individual designed a Web page to present information as if it came from the finance information company Bloomberg (http://www.bloomberg.com). The fictitious information stated that the company the individual worked for was going to be purchased.

The stock of the company rose 31 percent at the news. Bloomberg fought back by issuing subpoenas to the search engines Yahoo! and Lycos, a number of stock discussion sites, and the ISP that hosted the site, leading to the arrest of the individual for securities fraud.[16] It is vital that all online investors thoroughly investigate an investment offer before sending money.[17]

> ## ▶ Thinking Strategically: Case 6.2

Determine if Dell has an advantage over traditional computer sales businesses. Does Dell have an advantage over other online sellers? Consider what you would want if you were to purchase a computer. Would you feel it is necessary to talk to a person directly? Evaluate the Dell Web site (http://www.dell.com). Does this site provide all the information necessary for you to buy? Determine the importance of the Dell brand name. Explain if the business system that Dell has developed will work for other types of businesses. How does Dell develop and maintain relationships with its customers?

Unfortunately, fraud, scams, and theft are part of the retail environment. Strategies for limiting online credit card fraud were discussed in Chapter 4. The fear of fraud has limited some consumers' use of e-commerce. Fear of fraud varies from country to country. Eighty-eight percent of Japanese express concerns about fraud, while only 4 percent have experienced fraud or know someone who has. In the United States, 72 percent of the population have expressed concerns about fraud, while 8 percent have experienced fraud or know someone who has.[18]

The Internet also acts as a venue for fraud and scam protection. A number of Web sites are available for consumers to obtain information on legitimate as well

case 6.2

Dell Computer Company

In 1983, Michael Dell assembled customer computers in his college dorm room. Dell's business grew when he pioneered the use of telephone direct sales for computers. In 1996, Dell started selling computers over the Internet; by 1998, sales to online customers had reached more than $5 million a day. By 2001, 50 percent of Dell sales were placed online. Selling over the Internet is only part of the reason that Dell's stock price rose 29,000 percent from 1990 to 1998. Dell's business was designed to be efficient. Major competitors, such as Compaq and IBM, built distribution networks that relied on resellers to sell their products. Switching to the Internet for e-commerce would have alienated these resellers. Dell was also able to meet the needs of its customers by customizing its computers. Dell preloaded required software so its computers could be unpacked and run. By gathering customer information, Dell was able to determine trends in the marketplace.

Dell made its supply chain very efficient by demanding that its suppliers locate their inventory fifteen minutes outside of the Dell factory. Warehousing was outsourced to third parties that specialized in running supply chains, and all of the companies were linked electronically through extranets to speed information flow. Dell had no finished goods inventory and was therefore able to use the latest products and take advantage of dropping inventory costs. Rather than box and ship monitors with the computer, Dell had UPS store and deliver the specified monitor with the computer. Dell squeezed time out of every step in the business process. Dell's average sale turns into cash in less than twenty-four hours. Developing a more efficient marketing system gave Dell shareholders $1.54 in profits for every new dollar of capital investment in 1997, while Compaq returned only 59 cents and IBM, 47 cents.

Dell Computer identified areas of key competitive advantage and changed its business model to meet the customer's desire for speed of delivery, customized products, and low prices.[20] Dell is able to receive orders at 9 A.M. on one day, build the computer, and deliver it by 9 A.M. the next day. This increase in speed allowed Dell to lower inventory costs and prices to its customers. A key to this strategy was using the Internet to link Dell to both its customers and its suppliers.[21]

Dell has expanded this sales model to other markets. Corporate customers are able to order directly from Dell using the Internet. Companies such as Pillsbury and Ford have designed their own internal Web pages that link to Dell's computer system to allow for online purchasing. This customization has saved corporate customers millions of dollars. Dell moved its business model overseas to allow for rapid delivery of computers in foreign markets. By 1997, 31 percent of Dell sales came from outside the United States.

Source: <http://www.dell.com>. © 2002, Dell Computer Corp., All Rights Reserved.

as illegitimate firms. As a government watchdog, the FTC (http://www.ftc.gov) has sent notifications about deceptive practices to more than five hundred Web sites that use the words *no risk* or *get rich*.[19] Some sites provide a broad set of information, whereas others are more narrowly targeted.

Business-to-Business E-Commerce

The business-to-business commerce process needs to be considered from at least three perspectives. First, there is the supply chain system and process described in Chapter 4. This system links suppliers, distributors, and other channel members into an integrated process. Second, businesses are engaging in marketplaces where goods are bought and sold. This process will be covered in more depth in Chapter 11. Third, e-retail has had an impact on the business-to-business market. The largest category for sales in the B-to-B e-commerce arena is in the PC hardware and software industry.

Dell Computer is just one of the pioneers using information technology to change industries. Dell's business model consists of more than just selling over the

Internet. It gains efficiency by developing links to suppliers. It collects information on customers to increase its knowledge of market trends. By moving this highly efficient model around the world, Dell is forcing its competitors to change their business practices. Nations are reacting by developing the infrastructure necessary to allow their businesses to compete on the same global scale.[22]

Most computer buyers search for information before they buy. Dell's Web site allows buyers to immediately move to areas that interest them. In 1997, Dell received 1 Web visit for every phone call inquiry; by 1998, there were 3.5 Web visits for every phone inquiry. By 2001, Dell's telephone support system was greatly diminished. Potential buyers visit the Web site 5 to 10 times to obtain information, have their questions answered, and determine prices before they buy. Because a Web visit is considerably less expensive, the cost savings are given back to the buyer.[23] Dell's business model is shown in Figure 6.6.

The office supply industry has also rapidly moved to business-to-business e-commerce. Large suppliers such as Office Depot (http://www.officedepot.com), OfficeMax (http://www.officemax.com), and Staples (http://www.staples.com) have adopted a multichannel approach to serve their business clients. Staples's online sales increased from $94 million in 1999 to close to $1 billion by 2001. Office supplies are small and easy to ship, and buyers often know what they want before they buy. Businesses are expected to place more than 30 percent of their office supply purchases online because of the convenience and lower costs of ordering.[24]

Figure 6.6 Dell's Business Model

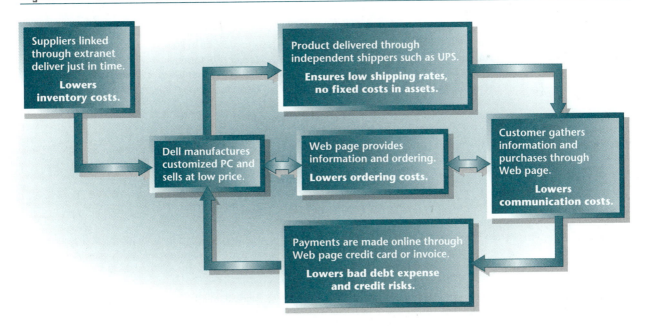

International E-Commerce

International e-commerce has lagged behind e-commerce in the United States. One study found that Europe was two years behind the United States in its e-commerce development. The reasons for this are both structural and behavioral. To develop e-commerce, four factors must be in place. First, the technical infrastructure must allow the flow of information. Second, flexibility of channel relationships is required. In countries such as Japan, where long distribution channels are maintained through personal relationships, disintermediation and restructuring will be much more difficult. Third, the political and legal structure must allow for the use of e-commerce. The ability to ship products without tariff restrictions and the free flow of capital are requirements. Fourth, although the Internet is the facilitator for this change, it is the willingness of businesses and customers to change their business and purchasing habits that allows the change to move forward. Because of these factors, many e-commerce sites are designed for a specific country. For example, in the countries where Amazon.com has set up a country-specific site, it is usually the top commerce site.[25] Table 6.5 illustrates a number of political and legal problems hindering global e-commerce.

While structural problems exist, there is considerable worldwide growth in e-commerce. Figure 6.7 shows the relative distribution of worldwide e-commerce

Table 6.5   Political and Legal Problems

Problem	Examples
Advertising and Competition	**France:** By law, all Web sites aimed at French customers must be in French. **Germany:** Some promotions, such as two-for-one deals or promotional tie-ins, may be illegal. Lands' End was forced to drop its unconditional money-back guarantee in Germany because it was seen as anticompetitive. Instead, the company's German Web site links to other Lands' End Web sites that show the guarantee. **Sweden:** Toy advertising may not be directed at children.
Payment	Credit card payments can be used, but customers may not know the exact price until the currency exchange is made. The development of the Euro should allow for smoother payments in Europe.
Delivery	The cost of shipping a product thirty miles across a border can be more than the cost of shipping it three hundred miles within the borders of a country.
Legal	Return policies may not be the same for all countries. Setting liability for faulty products may be unclear. It also may be difficult to determine how value-added taxes are assessed. Privacy laws in Europe are more stringent than those in the United States.

Source: Ann Therese Palmer, "Lands' End's End Run," BusinessWeek, October 18, 1999, 8; Martha Bennett, "The Worldwide Sell," CIO, July 15, 1998, 60–63; Henry Heilbrunn, "Interactive Marketing in Europe," *Direct Marketing,* March 1998, 56–59.

sales for selected countries. While the United States and Europe have the largest share of sales, the highest growth is in Asia.

In many countries, individuals are using the Internet to browse for products even though overall purchases are low. Browsing is the first stage in growing accustomed to purchasing online. Figure 6.8 illustrates the relative number of browsers versus shoppers in selected countries.

Figure 6.7   Distribution of Worldwide E-Commerce Sales and Growth

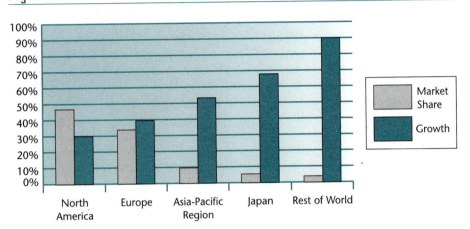

Source: Michael Pastore, "New Records Predicted for Holiday E-Commerce," in CyberAtlas [online] (October 22, 2001), available from <http://cyberatlas.internet.com/markets/retailing/article/0,,6061_908021,00.html#table2>.

Figure 6.8   Relative Number of Browsers versus Shoppers in Selected Countries

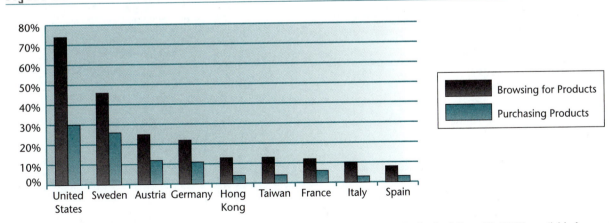

Source: Michael Pastore, "Net Users Worldwide Taking Commerce Online," in CyberAtlas [online] (June 13, 2001), available from <http://cyberatlas.internet.com/big_picture/geographics/article/0,,5911_783851,00.html#table>.

Hosting the Technology

The cost of implementing e-commerce models based on the strategies outlined in this chapter depends on the goals the company sets for itself. A number of large and small businesses would like to use the Internet as a sales channel but do not know how to start, nor can they afford setup costs. This has opened the door for a number of e-business facilitators.

Application service providers (ASPs) are companies that facilitate commerce for other businesses. Businesses can form an alliance with hosting sites such as ISPs, banks, distributors, or online malls. IBM, for example, offers a hosting service providing security, content management, and order management on a fee basis. Most ISPs offer e-commerce services. Other companies have set up malls for individual merchants to sell products. Network Commerce has a mall called InternetMall (http://www.internetmall.com); individual merchants pay a per-month fee plus a percentage of any transaction.[26] Yahoo! offers a service to host online transactions. Businesses can use Yahoo!'s merchant server system to set up their own e-commerce site, allowing buyers to use shopping carts to pick products, determine the total charges and shipping costs, and place an order with a credit card. In September 1999, Amazon.com opened its zShops site, which lets any retailer sell online. To give retailers access to its customers, Amazon.com charges a monthly fee plus a percentage of sales. Amazon.com allows these retailers access to its auction site. Customers can use an all-products search to search the Web for items they cannot find at Amazon.com's site.[27]

Table 6.6   Advantages of Selling with Stand-Alone versus ASP Sites

Issue	Benefits of Developing a Stand-Alone Online Commerce System	Benefits of Using an Application Service Provider for Online Commerce
Costs	No fees paid to the ASP, but higher costs in personnel, hardware, software, and development.	Lower costs for maintaining technology to support the site.
Control	Control over all policies related to selling.	Requirement to comply with mall's sales, credit, and return polices. If mall closes, potential to lose past customers.
Pulling Customers	Promotion must be done by business itself to get customers to site.	Retail trade concentration can pull in a larger number of shoppers.
Quality of Traffic	Higher-quality traffic more likely to buy.	Potential to attract individuals who browse and who may turn into shoppers at another time.

Sources: James R. Borck, "Building Your Site from Scratch," *InfoWorld,* October 4, 1999, 65–66; Lori Mitchell, "Using an I-Commerce Service Provider," InfoWorld, October 4, 1999, 68–70; Nick Wreden, "Retailers Seek to Capture Fly-by-'Net Traffic," *CommunicationsWeek,* November 25, 1996, 56.

The low cost associated with using an ASP is very attractive to merchants. They must still market their site as they would any other business, but they do not have brick-and-mortar costs and can reach the entire world with the e-commerce site. Table 6.6 outlines the advantages of using a stand-alone versus an ASP site.

Knowledge Integration

Terms and Concepts

Application service
    providers (ASPs) *184*
Destination site *171*
E-commerce *169*

E-retailing *169*
Fraud and Scams *177*
Multichannel
    approach *169*

Niche e-retailers *177*
Pump-and-dump *177*
Sales channels *169*
24/7/52 *176*

Concepts and Questions for Review

1. Outline the different e-commerce grocery models illustrated in the opening vignette.
2. Define the term *e-commerce.*
3. How can a retail business develop a multichannel approach?
4. List the components of an e-commerce value chain.
5. Outline the advantages that different types of retail businesses may have in their e-commerce value chains.
6. What advantages may a niche e-retailer have?
7. List the major types of fraud and how these can be prevented.
8. Outline the reasons e-commerce may be slow to develop in some countries.
9. Why would a business want to use an ASP?

Active Learning

Exercise 6.1 E-Retailer Shopping

Visit a number of pure-play e-commerce sites. Include sites that you have purchased from. Why did you purchase something from those sites? Indicate how your online shopping behavior related to your offline behavior. What were the most important criteria you used in shopping at the site?

Exercise 6.2 Multichannel Shopping

Visit a number of multichannel e-commerce sites. Include stores that you have purchased from. How does a multichannel retailer use the Internet to support its sales? Describe why you have purchased from the channel you use most often. Specify the most important criteria you use in shopping at the Web site. How is your online shopping behavior likely to change in a multichannel retail environment?

Exercise 6.3 Multichannel Shopping Analysis

Choose one of the businesses you visited in Exercise 6.1 or 6.2. Outline its e-commerce model and e-commerce value chain. Where in the value chain does the business gain competitive advantages? Undertake a benefit analysis as indicated in Table 6.2. Determine the benefit categories and compare the e-commerce site to its channel counterparts. Indicate where competitive advantages lie.

Exercise 6.4 Niche Retailers

Use the Web to find narrowly targeted niche retailers. Determine the target market for the e-retailers. How do these e-retailers target their market? Explain how they differentiate themselves from competitors.

Competitive Exercise 6.5 Developing Competitive E-Commerce Models

Management has asked you to outline an e-commerce model and e-commerce value chain that will give your business a competitive advantage. Choose an industry and identify the target market. Indicate the components that need to be included in the Web site to allow the business model to operate and the value chain to deliver value. Evaluate a number of ASPs. Should your Web site be hosted by the business or outsourced? Compare your recommendations to those of others.

Web Search—Looking Online

Search Term: E-Commerce Support   First 7 out of 3,800,001

CommerceNet. Provides research, news, promotional information, and support for developing e-commerce.
http://www.commerce.net

E-Commerce Times. Offers an online e-zine related to e-commerce issues.
http://www.ecommercetimes.com

National Retail Federation. Gives access to the world's largest retail trade association and its resources for supporting e-retailing.
http://www.nrf.com/ecommerce/ecommerce.htm

New York Times. Offers a special section on e-commerce; individuals must register to log on to this free service.
http://www.nytimes.com

Shop.org. Provides forums, research, news, and other industry support.
http://www.shop.org

U.S. Department of Commerce: Accesses the federal government's e-commerce section.
http://www.doc.gov/Electronic_Commerce/

Internetnews.com. Offers e-commerce news.
http://www.internetnews.com/ec-news

Search Term:	International Support	First 3 out of 4,949,671

AsiaBizTech. Provides a source on technology business information for Japan and Asia.
http://www.nikkeibp.asiabiztech.com

Asia Source. Accesses an online resource developed by the Asia Society to provide information on events across Asia.
http://www.asiasource.org

Information Society. Offers information from European experts on electronic commerce with the goal of ensuring that the European Union remains at the fore-front of electronic commerce.
http://europa.eu.int/information_society/index_en.htm

Search Term:	Scams and Fraud	First 3 out of 9,990,000

E-PublicEye. Provides testing, certifying, and Internet business monitoring, giving a reliability seal to participating businesses.
http://www.publiceye.com

Internet Fraud Watch. Reports on the most common fraudulent acts for online and offline commerce.
http://www.fraud.org/internet/intstat.htm

Consumers International. Offers information on this worldwide non-profit federation of consumer organizations, dedicated to the protection and promotion of consumer interests.
http://www.consumersinternational.org/

| Search Term: | ASPs | First 1 out of 32,787,323 |

C|net Internet Services. Lists Web hosts allowing for comparison of services.
http://www.cnet.com/internet/0-3761.html

References

[1] For more on changes in the grocery industry, see Barbara E. Kahn and Leigh McAlister, *Grocery Revolution* (Reading, Mass.: Addison-Wesley, 1997).

[2] Robert Lenzer, "Bagging Groceries," *Forbes,* October 18, 1999, 80; "Company Information," in Webvan [online] (October 5, 1999), no longer available.

[3] Jean Lawrence, "How Webvan Hopes to Leapfrog the Competition to the Customer's Front Porch," *Internet Retailer,* September 2000, 57–60; Connie Guglielmo, "Can Webvan Deliver?" January 31, 2000, *Interactive Week,* 26–34.

[4] Michael Pastore, "Retailers Learning from Past Web Woes," in CyberAtlas [online] (December 11, 2001), available from <http://cyberatlas.internet.com/markets/retailing/article/0,,6061_937951,00.html#table>.

[5] Blaise Zerega, "Online Shopping Gets Real," *Red Herring,* September 1999, 112–13.

[6] Clinton Wilder, "Retail Turns to Clicks and Mortar," *InformationWeek,* September 27, 1999, 257–63; Edward Cone, "Sears' Vendors Pay via the Web," *InteractiveWeek,* August 30, 1999, 22.

[7] Blaise Zerega, "Getting Virtual," *Red Herring,* September 1999, 122–26; Brian Caulfield, "Offline Retailers Size Up Net Strategies," *Internet World,* June 21, 1999, 4.

[8] "Buying Drives B2B E-Commerce Growth," *Internet Retailer,* September 2001, 48; "1998 eCommerce Report Indicates," in eMarketer [online] (October 20, 1999), available from <http://www.emarketer.com/about_us/press_room/press_releases/000099_eacommrpt.html>.

[9] Jeff Sengstack, "Foot Locker's Big Play for E-Commerce," *NewMedia,* July 1998, 66–67.

[10] Michael Pastore, "Offline Brands Bringing E-Commerce to the Masses," in CyberAtlas [online] (August 1, 2001), available from <http://cyberatlas.internet.com/markets/retailing/article/0,1323,6061_858051,00.html>.

[11] "Travel Joins the Holiday Shopping Spree," in CyberAtlas [online] (December 20, 2001), available from <http://cyberatlas.internet.com/markets/retailing/article/0,,6061_935411,00.html#table>; "Last Minute Shopping Goes Online," in CyberAtlas [online] (December 20, 2001) available from <http://cyberatlas.internet.com/markets/retailing/article/0,,6061_943821,00.html#table3>.

[12] Mary Wagner, "E-Retailers Beef Up Online Support to Corral Carts and Shoppers," *Internet Retailer,* 30–32; Michael Pastore, "E-Commerce Should Hold Its Own This Holiday Season," in CyberAtlas [online] (October 15, 2001), available from <http://cyberatlas.internet.com/markets/retailing/article/0,,6061_903401,00.html#table>; Michael Pastore, "Lump of Coal for E-Commerce Predictions," in CyberAtlas [online] (November 5, 2001), available from <http://cyberatlas.internet.com/markets/retailing/article/0,,6061_916681,00.html#table>.

[13] "Online Drugstores a Prescription for Failure, According to InsightExpress" in InsightExpress [online] (October 20, 2000), available from <http://www.insightexpress.com/news/release_102000.htm>.

14 Connie Guglielmo, "Drugstore Wars: Web Remedy," *Interactive Week,* September 13, 1999, 40; Saroja Girishankar, "Walgreen Hustles to Close Online Gap," *InternetWeek,* July 19, 1999, 1, 53; Elizabeth Gardner, "If This Were a Test, Drugstore.com Would Get a 'C'," *Internet World,* April 12, 1999, 1, 73; Evantheia Schibsted, "Prescription for Profits," *Business 2.0,* March 1999, 58–62; Brad Stone, "Nothing to Sneeze At," *Newsweek,* February 15, 1999, 60.

15 Lynda Radosevich and Dylan Tweney, "Retooling Retail," *InfoWorld,* March 22, 1999, 1, 62–63.

16 Ann Harrison, "Arrest Made in Net Stock Fraud Case," *Computerworld,* April 19, 1999, 12.

17 Geoffrey James, "Stock Scams and Spams on the Internet," *Upside,* November 1998, 77–86.

18 "Online Fraud around the World," *InternetWeek,* July 9, 2001, 13.

19 Kathleen Murphy, "Fraud Follows Buyers onto Web," *Web Week,* October 20, 1997, 15, 19; David Zgodzinski, "Buyer Beware," *Internet World,* March 1997, 42–46.

20 George Stalk Jr., "Time—The Next Source of Competitive Advantage," in *Strategy, Seeking and Securing Competitive Advantage,* ed. Cynthia A. Montgomery and Michael E. Porter (Boston: Harvard Business Review Book, 1991), 38–60; Joseph T. Vesey, "The New Competitors Think in Terms of 'Speed-to-Market,'" *SAM Advanced Management Journal* (Autumn 1991): 26–33.

21 Gary McWilliams, "Whirlwind on the Web," *BusinessWeek,* April 7, 1997, 132–36.

22 Ibid.; Saroja Girishankar, "Dell's Site Has Business in Crosshairs," *InternetWeek,* April 13, 1998, 1, 59; Andy Serwer, "Michael Dell Rocks," *Fortune,* May 11, 1998, 58–70; Lisa Dicarlo, "Dell Raises Bar on E-Commerce," *PCWeek,* June 15, 1998, 1, 16.

23 Lisa Chadderdon, "How Dell Sells on the Web," *Fast Company,* September 1998, 78–88.

24 Richard Mitchell, "Leveraging E-Business Information," *Electronic Commerce World,* January/February 2002, 23–24; Natalie Engler, "Supply in Demand," *Business 2.0,* November 1999, 56–60; Elizabeth Goodridge, "Staples of E-Commerce," *InformationWeek,* September 20, 1999, 16; Karen Epper Hoffman, "A Cyber Source for Office Supplies," *Internet World,* October 19, 1998, 15–16.

25 Michael Pastore, "Europeans Still Working the Kinks Out of E-Commerce," in CyberAtlas [online] (December 13, 2001), available from <http://cyberatlas.internet.com/markets/retailing/article/0,1323,6061_939241,00.html>; Martha Bennett, "The Worldwide Sell," *CIO* July 15, 1998, 60–63.

26 Jim Kerstetter, "Online Mall Thinks Big," *PCWeek,* September 7, 1998, 25.

27 Robert D. Hof and Steve Hamm, "Amazon.com Throws Open the Doors," *BusinessWeek,* October 11, 1999, 44; Connie Guglielmo, "Amazon.com Shopping Portal Opens for E-Biz," *Interactive Week,* October 4, 1999, 12.

10001000100101111111
11111110000000000001
00001111000 0000
11111111   1111
00000000000   01000
10101010101   1010
11100011100   0011
10101011100
01001110011

<marketing>

chapter 7

E-Business Promotion

E-business marketers must understand how promotion and advertising operate in a hypermedia environment. Marketers must not only make potential customers aware of their Web site and e-business but also use these tools to promote traditional businesses. This chapter builds on established promotional concepts and illustrates how these are used in a hypermedia environment. The specifics of hypermedia advertising are covered, including emerging agency models and evaluation systems.

1. Gain an understanding of e-business promotional goals.
2. Explain the AIDA concept and its role in promotion.
3. Describe a hypermedium's role in gaining audience attention.
4. Outline what should be done with a Web site to gain audience interest and desire.
5. Determine what is important in motivating an audience to take action.
6. Be able to explain loyalty concepts in an e-business environment.
7. Understand how e-business communication can be used in industrial markets.
8. Contrast the strengths and weaknesses of the Internet as an advertising medium.
9. Be able to design an e-business-based promotional campaign.

....

"Half the money I spend on advertising is wasted; the trouble is I don't know which half."

John Wanamaker (attributed)
Retailer and advertising pioneer

....

Amazing Amazon.com

Jeff Bezos started Amazon.com (http://www.amazon.com) in his garage in 1994. Sales have increased from $1 million in 1994 to $100 million in 1997, and by the end of 2001, sales were over $3 billion. To achieve this tremendous growth, Amazon.com developed a promotional strategy to strengthen its brand name, increase customer traffic to its Web site, build customer loyalty, and encourage repeat purchases. In 2001, Amazon.com spent over $131 million on a variety of marketing strategies to reach its goals. The company employed public relations activities along with online and traditional advertising such as radio, television, and print media. Amazon.com's Associates Program, or affiliate program, allows associates to encourage their members to purchase from Amazon.com, which then returns to them a percentage of the sales.[1] In 1998, more than 200,000 Web sites and newsletters were associates. By the end of 2001, there were more than 700,000 associates.[2] Customers can visit Amazon.com directly, or they may link to the site from numerous other Web sites. For example, when an individual requests information on a topic, a search engine may display a button that links to suggested book titles at Amazon.com's Web site. Amazon.com spends enough on banner ads to receive more than 100 million banner impressions per week.

Amazon.com uses a number of e-business communication platforms to develop interest and maintain relationships with its customers. A large number of book titles makes book buying easy, online searches provide information on titles or topics, online discussions with book authors peak interest, e-mail notification of new titles informs buyers, and customer ratings allow individuals using Amazon.com's Web site to see others' comments before they buy. Purchases are added to a customer profile database, and this information is used in e-mail messages that suggest related titles the buyer may wish to purchase. Amazon.com also customizes its home page to the individual user based on his or her past interaction with the site.

Amazon.com has moved beyond selling books and is now using this communication model to promote music CDs, merchandise, and auctions online. Customers who have an interest in a CD can often listen to clips of the music to see if they want to purchase it online. Buyers are notified by e-mail when the order is shipped and again to update order status. Amazon.com has designed its site to act as a communication interface to take the customer from interest through desire on to the action of purchasing and the maintenance of loyalty.

▶ Thinking Strategically

Make a short list of what you know about Amazon.com. Decide how much of that information comes from its paid advertising, how much from publicity seen on news programs and in the press, and how much from interacting with the Web site. Use an Internet search engine to see if there is a button linking to the Amazon.com Web site. Visit the Amazon.com Web site. Evaluate the design. What in the Web site design would encourage you to make a purchase?

Promotional campaigns are designed to reach specific goals. These can include the communication goals of informing, persuading, or reminding the external audience of a company's brand name, URL, image, new products, business locations, and so forth. Integrating e-business communication platforms into promotional campaigns allows a business to reach specific objectives such as driving visitors to a Web site, obtaining sales leads or opt-ins to e-mail lists, collecting user data, closing a sale, or enhancing loyalty. These goals should be specified by the marketing department, should be based on an analysis of the target audience, and should support the organization's marketing strategies. Adding **hypermedia**, such as Web sites and other e-business communication platforms, to the traditional promotional mix of advertising, personal selling, sales promotions, public relations, and publicity enhances a business's ability to communicate with its customers and reach specified goals.

E-business **promotion** adds new tools and strategies to a business's promotional strategy. As indicated in Chapter 3, a number of e-business communication platforms can be used to communicate with an audience. To reach promotional and other marketing goals, however, these tools are often used in combination with traditional media. Reliance on hypermedia alone may not allow a company to reach all its goals. For example, customers must be made aware of a Web site before they will go to that site. In addition, before customers take action, they must have an interest in and desire for the product or service. This chapter will illustrate how hypermedia and e-business practices are being used to enhance the promotional process for firms. It will first incorporate e-business promotional practices into the AIDA model and then turn to the process of advertising within an e-business environment.

The AIDA Model

The AIDA model will be used as a framework for understanding how hypermedia can be used to reach promotional goals. The AIDA process indicates that first the attention of the target audience must be gained, then interest created in the product or service, desire generated, and finally some action taken by the targeted audience. The AIDA process is based on attitude models in which the audience first thinks about an object (cognition), then develops feelings (affect), and finally engages in some type of behavior (conation).[3] A single message or communication vehicle will, in most cases, not move an audience through every stage of the AIDA process. An integrated marketing communication strategy brings together multiple communication vehicles to reach desired goals.[4] Incorporating hypermedia into promotional campaigns has been found to enhance the visibility of firms, create new business opportunities, offer cost and time savings, and allow businesses to reach new customers.[5] Table 7.1 outlines the attitude components of the AIDA process and relates these to the effect on e-business communication strategy.

Table 7.1 The AIDA Process

Attitude Model	AIDA Process	E-Business Communication Strategy
Cognition (Thinking)	Attention	Use traditional media to create brand attention. Make the audience aware of the Web site with offline media. Employ search engines to allow the Web site to be found in searches. Have other Web sites serve as media for advertising the Web site. Send targeted e-mail, which can be used like direct marketing to gain initial attention.
	Interest	Customize and personalize communication to meet the individual's needs. Use rich media. Send targeted, permission-based e-mail. Push information to the audience.
Affect (Feeling)	Desire	Develop a design and content that appeal to the target audience. Include relationship development components that will keep the audience at the site.
Conation (Behavior)	Action	Use promotions to entice actions. Design seamless purchasing systems.

Figure 7.1   Promotional Strategy Matrix

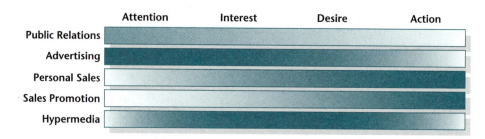

Figure 7.1 matches the components of a promotional mix, including hypermedia, with the four stages of the AIDA process. The darker the area in the figure, the stronger the influence the promotional element has on the AIDA stage. Figure 7.1 shows that each part of the promotional mix plays a different role. Public relations and advertising are effective in fueling attention, interest, and desire. Personal sales (such as two-way person-to-person communication) are not highly efficient in creating attention, due to the high costs of fielding a sales force to make cold calls. Personal sales are more effective at creating desire and closing the sale. Sales promotion (such as couponing or point-of-purchase displays) is most effective in obtaining action. Hypermedia are strongest in the areas of interest and desire but can also be used to create attention and facilitate actions such as sales. Hypermedia are a vital component of a promotional mix because they can enhance the AIDA process, but they may not be able to reach all promotional goals.

Consumer markets have traditionally been centered on advertising, whereas industrial markets have relied more on personal sales for communication. Figure 7.2 indicates the relative use of promotional elements for each of these markets.

It may not be surprising that many current Web sites and much e-commerce currently target business markets. Industrial markets are also heavy users of Internet-based communication through the use of extranets and intranets. The Web interface is becoming the standard for this interfirm and intrafirm communication. In addition, sales representatives are using **sales force automation (SFA)** tools to enhance their ability to sell to business markets. The following sections will cover the strategic use of hypermedia to reach AIDA goals in consumer and industrial markets.

Sales force automation (SFA) *uses the information power of interactive media to enhance selling efforts.*

Attention

A target audience may be unaware of a traditional business's or an e-business's existence, products, brand name, image, location, and so forth. To make the audience aware of this information, the business must first gain their attention. Traditional media gain attention by designing messages with enough impact to attract

Figure 7.2 Consumer versus Industrial Markets

and hold the audience; the messages can be repeated numerous times. Hypermedia, such as e-mail, can be used as a direct marketing vehicle to gain attention, but, as with traditional mail, viewers are more likely to view and interact with the message if they have given permission to the sender and recognize the brand name of the product or company. Other hypermedia, such as Web sites, differ from traditional media in that the receiver must use the Internet to link to content. Individuals will not be exposed to the message unless they actively view the Web site. Web sites are currently the primary vehicle to deliver large amounts of data for individuals to view and interact with. One of the goals of interactive campaigns is to drive customers to the Web site. This can be accomplished through traditional media and by using specific e-business communication strategies.

Traditional Media

The first step in getting the audience's attention is to include a site's URL or address in other media. The Web address should be included in advertising copy and layouts, business cards, banner ads located in other Web sites, direct e-mail, and other directed media. The use of URLs in print ads has increased from about 10 percent of ads in 1995 to more than 90 percent by 1998.[6] Traditional media have much wider exposure than the Internet. Using these media can help to create site preference.

Search Engines

Search engines are the primary tools that customers use to search for products online. These tools examine databases for requested information and then provide URLs that customers can use to access a company's Web site.[7] Search engines can be a cost-effective means of making people aware of a site, but they do not guarantee that a viewer will choose or remember the site. There are a number of different types of search engines. **Search directories**, such as Yahoo! (http://www.yahoo.com), require that Web sites be submitted for cataloging by persons. These sites include the most relevant and popular sites but have limited listings. **Search engines**, such as Google (http://www.google.com), use **Web spiders**, or **Web bots**, to collect information from sites. These sites will find information for narrowly targeted searches but can return a large number of hits (often

Web spiders, or bots, are software robots that "crawl" through the Internet looking at Web sites. They collect site information and send it back to the search engine database, allowing the information to be retrieved. Having key terms placed into the HTML metatags aids in the cataloging process.

Source: <http://www.askjeeves.com>. Courtesy of Ask Jeeves, Inc.

several million). **Metacrawlers,** such as Metacrawler (http://www.metacrawler
.com), use the databases of multiple major search engines. These are good for
power searches, but combining multiple results can lead to repetitive hits.

Search engines differentiate themselves by offering various search strategies for
individuals. Ask Jeeves (http://www.askjeeves.com) is a search engine designed to
use natural language queries. Some search engines are designed for paid placement of content. This allows for more targeted searches. Content is based on the
company's payments, however, the higher the amount paid, the higher the position in the search results. Many search engines, including Yahoo!, will return
sponsored sites, which are paid placements, along with nonpaid listings.[8]

Directories and search engines contain large databases of information related
to Web sites. When a Web site is posted to a server, information about that site can
be placed with the directory or search engine by filling out an electronic form at
each search engine. A new Web site could wait for a Web spider to find it, but the
new site may not have control over the search topics used in the search engine. To
ensure that Web spiders find the proper search term, a site designer should include
specific search criteria in the home page's metatags, which are located in the heading
HTML of the Web page. Some search engines ignore metatags, so they do not
guarantee proper searches, but they do help

Historical nSite

In 1999, researchers found that any Web site in the world was separated
from all others by an average of nineteen hyperlinks.[9]

Web spiders find content. A directory such as Yahoo! uses a human interface to place a site into categories. If a business tries to spam a search engine by submitting multiple listings, it may be kicked to the bottom of a list of 2 million hits and never be seen by an audience.

A business should not rely on search engines to make a potential visitor aware of the site. Search engines use rules to place URLs at the **top of the search**, or at the beginning of a search list. Those rules can include the number of key terms, the number of links to that site from other sites, how often a site is updated, the number of times it has been hit, matches of certain text, and other criteria known only to the management of the search engine.[10] Search engines may index only about 15 percent of sites and only 1 percent of the estimated 550 billion pages of Web content. Those sites that do make it to the top of searches are often from large U.S.-based businesses or paid sites.

Search engine technology is also used to speed the searching of content within a site. Search engine software can be set up on a server hosting an individual site, or a site can be indexed through a search engine such as Google to provide access to data within a site. Research has shown that 80 percent of individuals will abandon a site if they cannot find the content they are looking for. E-commerce companies such as Amazon.com, eBay, and Lands' End (http://www.landsend.com) use their search engines to allow individuals to easily find products. EBay found that every time it improved its search system, it increased the amount of bids. The Lands' End search engine has links to databases to provide product options on search terms. Amazon.com's search protocols display not only the results of the search term but also some products others have purchased based on that search term.[11]

Hypermedia Hyperlinks

It is possible to use an e-business communication platform as a means of gaining attention for online content. This can be accomplished, for example, through the use of hyperlinks embedded in Web sites or e-mail (covered in Chapter 3). Links on Web pages can be obtained through banner ads and other online ads (covered later in this chapter), sponsorships, and affiliate marketing programs.

Sponsorships integrate a company's brand to the editorial content of the Web site. For example, a firm may sponsor a news site or a community bulletin board. Sponsorship's share of advertising dollars is second to that of banner ads, accounting for 25 percent of online advertising spending in the third quarter of 2001. Over 70 percent of large companies use sponsorships to enhance their brands.[12]

Affiliate marketing strategies have content sites provide links to other, often commerce-based, sites. These are usually performance-based links, where the host site receives a percentage of sales or some other type of compensation for the click-through. Amazon.com was the first to introduce an affiliate marketing program with its Associates Program. Affiliate programs can be a low-cost way for a business to obtain new customers, but these programs require management and relationship development between the affiliate and the commerce firm.[13]

Interest

Before individuals are likely to take action, they must first have a positive predisposition to act. Companies must be able to create a positive feeling or interest in the product or service offered. Thus, hypermedia should offer a site visitor some compelling reason to stay and interact. The site designer must take into consideration the communication goal, the nature of the audience, and the level and type of technology the user will be employing. This could mean that content needs to be constantly upgraded as the Internet backbone adds bandwidth and the ability to play rich media. To maintain interest in a site, an e-business should consider both site content and design.

Web site development has been evaluated in a number of research studies. Sites can be judged on how entertaining and informative they are and on how well they are organized.[14] When the targeted audience sees a Web page, they will make a decision in the first few seconds whether or not to explore the site. The **home page**, or the first page a visitor sees at a site, becomes very important in this respect. If a visitor has specifically tried to find the Web site or has high involvement with the company or product, the visitor may wait for the page to load and spend time watching and interacting with the site. If, on the other hand, visitors are only browsing, they may zap the site and move on if it takes too long to download or is not interesting.[15] Speed of download has been found to be an important consideration. The longer the individual must wait for a site to download, the more negatively the individual rates the Web site.[16] Additional information on Web page design was found in the appendix to Chapter 4.

With so many Web sites and so little space to display information on a home page, Web sites can start to look generic. This is in part due to limited creativity in design. The use of frames, banners, animated GIF files, JavaScript, sound, and so forth, is allowing for more creativity, but these items can increase the bandwidth needed to display content. Some sites are developed with a home page that offers multiple types of elements, such as high- or low-resolution graphics, nonframed or framed pages, and Flash or Shockwave multimedia downloads. As high bandwidth becomes more dominant and download speeds increase, Web sites will need to add increased levels of rich media to interest audiences. Some businesses may have their employees' browsers disabled for plug-ins and other high-bandwidth design elements to limit traffic use on a network.[17]

A Web site should give a compelling reason for the viewer to stay and explore the page. If there is too much text, the viewer may not continue into the document.[18] Design considerations are also important. For some Net surfers, the overall look and feel of the site is as important as the content. Ease of navigation should be considered when laying out the page.

When the site designer is developing the page, he or she can control the display and also how the user interacts with the page. The viewer should not be expected to figure out how the site works. The visitor should find information easily. The site must have an easy-to-use interface that appeals to the target audience. For example, children's sites are likely to be very rich in animation and graphics.

A Web site should accomplish two goals: communicate the firm's message and foster the development of relationships. If the business is using the site as a brochure site or for public relations, the compelling reasons for the visitor to remember and return to the site should be communicated. If the firm wants the targeted audience to take some type of action, the communication should be focused around the unique selling proposition of the firm or the advantage of the product over competitive products. For high-involvement users, large amounts of information should be refreshed often, if not daily, to keep individuals returning to the site. There is little incentive for a visitor to return if the site is not updated. Figure 7.3 outlines the reasons that individuals return to favorite sites.

Historical nSite

P&G

Procter & Gamble has been a leader in new media. It was one of the first companies to move into both radio and television advertising. It was also the first to pay for advertising based on click-throughs.

Figure 7.3   Reasons for Using Favorite Sites

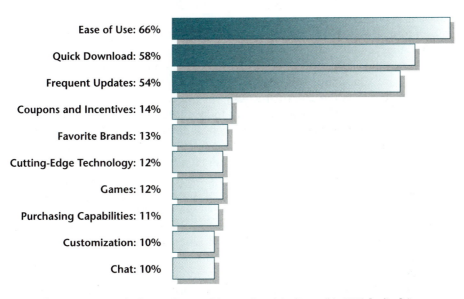

Ease of Use: 66%
Quick Download: 58%
Frequent Updates: 54%
Coupons and Incentives: 14%
Favorite Brands: 13%
Cutting-Edge Technology: 12%
Games: 12%
Purchasing Capabilities: 11%
Customization: 10%
Chat: 10%

Source: "Forrester Research: Strong Content Means a Loyal Audience," in NUA [online] (January 27, 1999), available from <http://www.nua.ie/surveys/index.cgi?f=VS&art_id=905354655&rel=true>.

Desire

An e-business communication goal may be to move the audience toward some type of behavior or action. To reach this goal, a Web site must generate desire. Strategies to generate desire are typically designed into the promotional message, enhanced through sales promotion, and acted on by a salesperson. New Internet-based techniques are beginning to create higher levels of desire. These include the use of targeted e-mail and permission marketing (both covered in Chapter 3), personalization, and push.

The cost of obtaining a new Web customer has dropped from $45 at the beginning of the year 2000 to only $12 by the end of 2001. This is considerably less than the cost of getting a new customer through print ads ($958) and radio ads ($1,457).[19] When a customer is found, a business has an incentive to keep that customer's interest and desire to return. This can be accomplished by effective message design and communication strategies.

Direct marketers practice the art of creating desire. This starts with having a narrowly defined target audience and then providing a message designed to generate interest and desire before the direct marketer asks for action. Direct marketers have often employed professional salespeople to develop sales presentations. Sales representatives will often personalize their presentation as well as shift the flow, depending on the customer's questions or objections. The better a direct marketer is able to assess the needs of the customer, the more a salesperson is able to fine-tune the presentation to help create desire in the customer.

Likewise, the interactive and nonlinear design of multimedia presentations allows a Web site to link to various parts of a message based on the customer's information needs. If visitors to the site want to know more about a topic or product, they should be only a click away from that information. A Web server can use tracking software to record where people go on the site and how long they stay at a particular point. This gives the Webmaster a map of the dead areas and most active areas on the site. Interactivity can engage the potential customer and provide feedback to the e-business on an individual's needs. General Foods developed a site (http://www.mycereal.com) were individuals could design their own ideal breakfast cereals. Procter & Gamble allows individuals to design their own Millstone coffee blend at http://www.personalblends.com. These sites hold viewers, provide product information, and help create desire for products or brands.

Direct marketing relies on computer databases to develop personalized media. This personalization allows direct marketers to send targeted messages directly to a prospective customer. Hypermedia-based promotion is following this lead by developing personalized messages and then sending them to the individual via push technology. Internet users can customize the home pages of Web portals (e.g., Microsoft Networks, Yahoo!, and others) by submitting lifestyle information, personal interests, and other segmentation information. Sites such as Amazon .com also collect past behavior data and customize their Web pages to the user. These Web sites tailor their messages and page design on the fly, or as they are sent, to match the individual user's profile, enhancing the relationship.[20]

Push allows users to have information delivered to their "doorway" without requesting or searching for it. For example, if the target individual has an interest in football, a push system will deliver football-related information to the individual's computer. Push also occurs when an individual visits a Web site. The Web server can look at the individual's **cookies** and then use a database to design and push the Web site for the individual. Web sites use software to read the behavior of the visitor by keeping track of the Web pages the visitor sees, how long they are viewed, what is passed over, what is placed in a shopping basket, and what is removed. This behavior suggests the type of information the user may be interested in.[23]

Figure 7.4 illustrates how this process works. The user first gives permission and initial profiling information to the Web site database. When there is a request from the user's browser, the Web server searches for a cookie, or identification code. If no code is found, the individual may need to register with the site to receive personalized content. Records related to the cookie are updated by tracking the individual's activity and interests. This allows for a segmentation process to identify rules for content delivery and design. Then the database creates the Web site on the fly for the user by returning dynamic data to the Web server, tailoring the site to the user's browsing interest.[24]

Two companies using personalization to target their customers are American Airlines (http://www.aa.com) and Dell Computer. American has designed a system using fifty-six interactive applications with over two hundred decision rules to personalize its site for the more than 31 million members of American's frequent-flyer program. Dell has personalized its sites by using three thousand different page designs for its clients.[25]

Case 7.1

Interest(ing) Game

Online game playing holds Internet users to Web sites. The average time users spend at the game site Pogo is forty-five minutes. With 60 percent of broadband households engaged in game playing, this is a major area of online activity. Microsoft Networks Games site had 6 million users playing more than 2 million hours of games every weekend in the year 2000. These game sites are advertising supported and offer plenty of opportunities to expose individuals to ads.[21]

Some companies have developed their own hypermedia games to maintain control over the branding process and the audience. BIC, maker of BIC pens, targeted a young market through an extreme game CD-ROM that was linked to its Web site. Secret hints were spread throughout the BIC Web site (http://www.bicworldusa.com), and the hint release was staggered over time. Nestle targets children between the ages of eight and ten by offering games at its site (http://www.verybestkids.com), such as archery, mountain climbing, and baseball. Procter & Gamble has also used interactive games. The games were designed to provide information on brands to consumers. Depending on their answers, individuals were directed to additional game questions or to brand information. P&G not only drew individuals into playing the games but also captured information on how much these individuals knew about its brands.[22]

A cookie *is a small file left on the user's computer that is used to look up information on an e-business's database. This file retrieves information such as past actions, search interests, or past purchases, which can be used to personalize the site.*

▶ Thinking Strategically: Case 7.1

Why would individuals spend time on online game sites? Consider how online games differ from televised games. List reasons why companies would develop games to hold individuals on their Web sites. Why would a company tie its branding strategy to games?

Figure 7.4   Using Push Technology

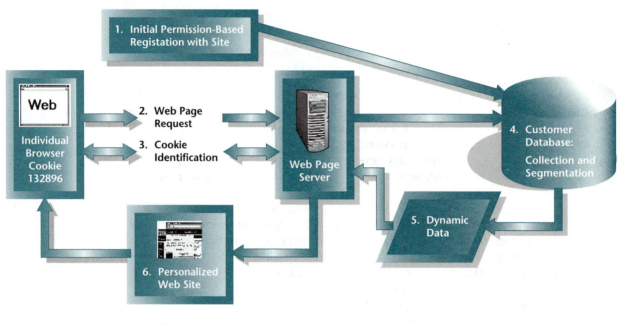

Action

The action stage of the AIDA process does not necessarily imply a purchase. The action could be to have individuals visit a Web site, provide information for databases, obtain information for future purchases, or make online purchases. Figure 7.5 indicates that to encourage an action, e-businesses can offer free shipping, use promotional incentives such as coupons, provide search engines to link a customer's desires to requested and similar products, and create a forum for product reviews.

Online coupon companies offer coupons for online and offline purchases. CoolSavings (http://www.coolsavings.com) provides personalized coupons to its 16.5 million shoppers. The coupons, rebates, and free samples offered to members are based on registration information, shopping habits, and previous clicks on the site. The coupons carry special bar codes to track use. Companies that use Cool-Savings coupons can track the effectiveness of their offers, which helps to shape one-to-one relationships with customers.[26]

Loyalty

The concept of loyalty must shift from the brick-and-mortar world to the online world. Brick-and-mortar loyalty can be measured in repeat store visits and product repurchase. Businesses have an incentive to maintain the loyalty of customers because of the high value of lifetime customers. Customers stay loyal because they believe that the cost of searching for information on new stores and products

Figure 7.5   Motivating toward Action

Free Shipping: 20%
Online Coupon: 14%
Product Search Tool: 11%
Online Product Review: 11%

outweighs the cost of new purchases from the same company. The World Wide Web has changed this equation to an extent; consumers now have access to vast amounts of information on companies, products, and consumer opinions. This requires businesses to develop an overall product value concept for consumers, as indicated in this text.

In an online environment, e-businesses are faced with the problem of maintaining viewership on Web sites and getting customers to return and repeat desired actions.[27] Companies such as MyPoints (http://www.mypoints.com) and S&H greenpoints (http://www.greenpoints.com) offer net users points for shopping, viewing ads, or reading e-mail. This may create loyalty to the incentive company, but it may not affect the brand of the e-business. More important than rewards is the overall customer experience with the e-business and its site. E-businesses can foster return visits through personalization, communication (via e-mail and chat), strong customer service, and designs that offer information, service, easy price comparisons, strong security, and search engines. These features can make the site **sticky**.[28]

Stickiness is the ability of a Web site to hold customers for a long period of time and get them to return to the site.

Campaigns

Integrated marketing communication implies that multiple media are used to target audiences. Under an AIDA framework, hypermedia can be used very efficiently in combination with other media. Often, traditional one-to-many media are used to drive individuals to more in-depth and interactive communication on Web sites. Many national brands with existing distribution chains cannot or will not sell online, so they rely on online communication to raise interest and desire and then facilitate the linkage to action.

Lee Jeans was faced with a problem. It wanted to target teenage boys but found this market was already saturated with advertisements. Lee's advertising agency, Fallon (http://www.fallon.com), recommended the adoption of a stealth campaign. Fallon ran focus groups, brainstormed ideas, and came up with Buddy Lee, a blank-eyed doll used by Lee in the 1920s and 1930s. The doll was positioned as a man-of-action deadpanning through action scenes. Two enemies were created with their own supporting Web sites. From the beginning, the campaign was designed to allow for a combination of media. To create attention, the campaign was launched with viral e-mail targeting 200,000 members of an opt-in list, designed to drive viewers to Buddy's and his enemy's sites. The e-mail contained short, unbranded film clips. A muckumentary was played on Comedy

Source: <http://www.leedungarees.com/buddylee/default.asp>. Created by Look and Feel New
    Media for Lee Jeans.

Central at 2 A.M., showing Buddy's coolness. Radio spots linked the villains to
Buddy Lee, and finally TV commercials drove viewers to the Web site, where they
could play video games that featured the villains. Codes found on the clothing
tags enhanced the online games.

The campaign's success was measured by the stickiness of the Buddy Lee site
(http://www.buddylee.com), which averaged twelve minutes. The villain sites had
one-half million viewers in two months and a 25 percent pass-along rate. The
perceptions of seventeen to twenty-two year olds changed: 64 percent more said it
was "cool" to wear Lees, and 81 percent more called Lee a "brand on its way in."
Lee jeans sales doubled in eighteen months, and Lee's junior carpenter pants
became the top-selling jeans in the stores where they were carried.[29] After the
campaign ran, the Buddy Lee site was incorporated into the Lee Jeans Web site
(http://www.leedungarees.com). It is now a rich media, Flash-based interactive
site with links to message boards so customers can communicate with members of
the Haro mountain bike team.

An e-business promotional campaign entails more than just the placement of
banner advertisements. To take the intended audience from inattention through
action and loyalty requires a combination of communication tactics. Table 7.2
outlines the strategy used by Lee Jeans in its Buddy Lee campaign and the measured
results.

Table 7.2 Anatomy of Buddy Lee's Campaign

Company	Attention	Interest	Desire	Action	Loyalty
Lee Jeans	E-mail viral marketing; Web sites; radio.	Online video clips; Web sites; TV ads.	Interactive games on Web site; TV ads.	Game codes on product; links to offline stores.	Web site hosts message boards, interactive games, rich media, and giveaways.

Measurement: Stickiness of site; number of viewers; pass along rate; attitude change; sales.

Advertising

Advertising typically implies a paid placement in some medium. For hypermedia, this has typically included ad placements delivered on and through Web pages. The Internet has promised a number of benefits to advertisers: the Web allows direct communication and interaction with customers, it tracks customers' media use, it can develop customized ads and placement, and it facilitates actions such as purchasing. Online advertising is a fast-growing medium, but it still represents only around 3 percent of overall ad spending. Some advertisers use traditional media to drive traffic to their Web site, bypassing online ads. Others do not see the Web as a good medium for building brand; individuals use the Internet for specific searches and information activities and will often go directly to a site without help from advertising. Internet advertising is not going away, however. Advertisers continue to experiment and find new ways to reach their goals online. Figure 7.6 shows the relative use of Internet-based advertising formats.

In 2001, banner ads were the most common method used to advertise on a Web page, accounting for 35 percent of all advertising dollars spent on the Web. The popularity of banner ads is dropping because they have not been highly effective in achieving click-through (the process of an individual clicking on a banner to link to other sites). **Banner ads** act like placement ads; they are usually small rectangular messages. Banners have been noted to increase overall attention to a brand name, but to catch a viewer's eye, banners are becoming more active with the inclusion of animation, Java programming, and multimedia. Banners come in many types: fat, thin, tall and narrow (skyscrapers), bulky, and with buttons.

When using a hypermedia site to obtain objectives related to attention, the site designer must consider the technology

Historical nSite

1994: The first banner ads are hosted on *Wired* magazine's HotWired Web site.

1997: Interstitial ads are first used for the You Don't Know Jack site.

2000: Flash-enabled rich media ads for Sun and Oracle are run on CNET's Web site.[30]

2001: The Internet Advertising Bureau attempts to organize online advertising by setting ad sizes and format standards.

Figure 7.6   Advertising Formats

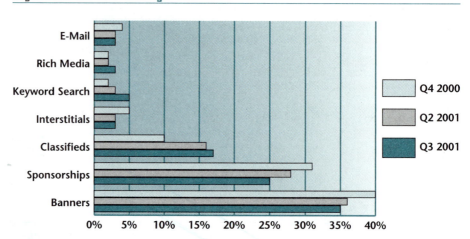

Source: Michael Pastore, "Internet Ads Still Feeling Industry Woes," in CyberAtlas [online]
(December 4, 2001), available from <http://cyberatlas.internet.com/markets/
advertising/article/0,,5941_933861,00.html#table>.

likely to be used by the audience. Interactive banners allow for a higher level of impact but may be effective only if the user has a high-bandwidth line. A study by the Interactive Advertising Bureau (IAB) indicated that banner ads were effective in creating awareness of products and in communicating information about them, but had a smaller impact on intent to purchase. The resulting increase in attention was from exposure to the ads and was not related to click-through rates. Seeing a banner ad once had a greater effect on memory than a single exposure to a television ad, but less than an exposure to a print ad.[31] The IAB has attempted to set standards for online ad sizes (http://www.iab.net/iab_banner_standards/bannersource.html). These standards would allow for comparisons across Web sites. Figure 7.7 indicates the major types of advertising found on Web sites, with example IAB standards.

Interstitials automatically load and display content as a Web site is brought up. These include pop-up and pop-behind ads that freely float to display ad content. Interstitials can slow downloads of desired content and are sometimes seen as annoying. Interstitials are much more effective in delivering rich media content than banner advertising.

The Internet has made inroads into traditional media. When asked about which activity they were likely to give up when they surfed the Web, most Internet users named television watching. The Internet is the fastest-growing medium, taking only five years to reach 50 million users, compared to radio's thirty-eight years, television's thirteen years, and cable's ten years.[32] The use of the Internet and the Web as advertising media offers some unique advantages and problems.

Figure 7.7 Major Web Advertising Types

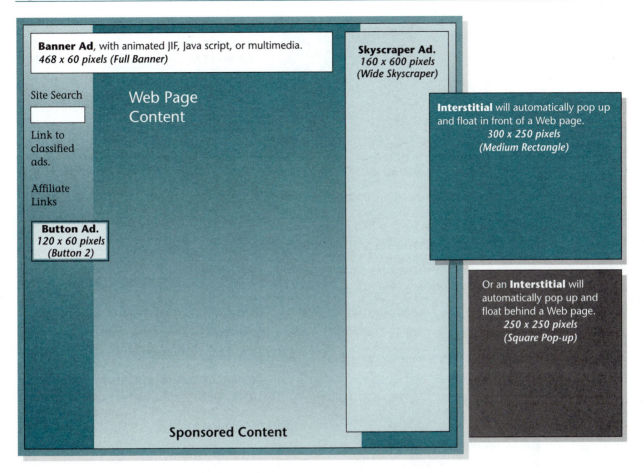

The Web allows tracking of individual behavior, including measuring the actual exposure to a message rather than just estimating exposure. In response, advertisers are demanding a change in how they pay for Web ad placement.

Relationships among the media, the advertising agency, and the business client are changing with this new promotional medium. New vendors are entering the market, offering content development, Web page hosting, media buying, and targeting services. The use of hypermedia is also affecting the timing of campaigns and payments, as well as the traditional measurements of effectiveness and reach.

E-Business Professionals

Michael Kleindl
Editor and Chief, *Tokyo Q*
http//www.tokyoq.com

Michael Kleindl

Tokyo Q is an Internet magazine and weekly guide to the city of Tokyo, Japan. *Tokyo Q* is run by an international collection of writers who have over 150 years of life experience in Tokyo. It offers a well-written, unbiased review of life in Tokyo related to food, drink, art, entertainment, clubs, baths, performances, hotels, and other aspects of city life. The site was designed to be visually interesting and act as a digital *New Yorker* for Tokyo. The site also puts out a traditional paper-printed guide. Readers are 50 percent visitors to Japan and 50 percent people living in Japan.

Mike Kleindl started as a restaurant reviewer. When the *Tokyo Q* founder, Rick Kennedy, stepped down, Mike took over as the editor and chief. Mike made the site bilingual to expand the market to all of Japan. According to Mike, "Japanese like to see the reviews by foreigners. For non-Japanese, the insight on Tokyo, the high level of writing, is a strong appeal. The site contains links to Tokyo sites, photographs of the 'real' Tokyo, and artwork."

Mike noted a few challenges: "Very few sites can exist on advertising alone." Sony first sponsored the site; Nokia currently sponsors it. "Nokia wanted to associate itself with a high-quality, 'cool' guide to Tokyo." *Tokyo Q* has a dual site. One site is for the Web, and the other is for Nokia's Imode-based phones. *Tokyo Q* allows individuals to use Nokia phones to link to content.

As editor and chief, Mike needs to find translators, writers, new content, and everything else related to the site. Mike worked to increase the number of unique viewers by using newspaper advertising to gain attention, and he used free postcards to drive interested users to the site. He also used guerrilla-advertising tactics by placing stickers around the city. *Toyko Q* pursued free promotion through magazine and radio reviews, and it put together promotional packages to sell advertising. The site is always trying to promote itself as cheaply as possible. Mike tries to answer every e-mail sent to him.

Nokia wants to be sure that the site has a certain number of viewers. Plans are to have users register for the site, allowing user data to be placed into a database for direct-marketing efforts. A database of users will help ensure continued support from advertisers and sponsors.

Mike recommends that students considering working for a Web site need to know what they can contribute to the site. Students need to gain strong writing skills. Readers want content; they want something that is interesting and enjoyable to read. Designers need to be able to design for the Web. To work in a market like Tokyo, workers need to speak Japanese. They also need to love what they do.

Agencies

In the promotional process, advertising **agencies** act as intermediaries by providing the talent to help set promotional objectives, create content, place ads in media, and provide feedback on the results of the campaign to the client. Hypermedia advertising is a multibillion-dollar business that has surpassed outdoor advertising in dollar sales, but it may never reach the size of television, newspaper, or magazine advertising. Problems include narrow target markets, privacy concerns, limited bandwidth, few effective measures of success, and hard-to-prove returns on investments. In addition, if offline media advertising and targeted e-mail are more effective in getting audiences to visit a Web site, then online advertising is not needed. Advertisers are beginning to use Web sites as centers of complex communication and use other media to drive the audience to the Web site.[33]

Traditional agencies were slow to respond to the changes brought about by hypermedia. At first, many agencies did not understand the technology or how to use hypermedia in a campaign. This left the door open for new firms to specialize in digital advertising. New York, home to Madison Avenue, gave rise to Silicon Alley, a digital advertising center with agencies, venture firms, content developers, and support businesses. In Los Angeles, another interactive services center, called the Digital Coast, has sprung up. As advertisers come to realize that Web pages should be used in conjunction with larger media campaigns, they are relying on more traditional agencies to provide interactive content.

The complexity of hypermedia advertising has led a number of businesses to specialize in the placement of ads across multiple outlets. **Advertising networks** such as DoubleClick (http://www.doubleclick.com)

and 24/7 Real Media (http://www.247media.com) put together a network of Web sites targeting multiple markets. An advertiser that wishes to reach an audience can use these advertising network agencies to place ads and develop reports on customer behavior, site activity, and other campaign-related data. This allows the advertiser to work with one company rather than a large number of different Web sites.

The Measurement of Effectiveness

Even though online advertising is the fastest-growing medium ever devised, its full potential is not being reached because advertising executives do not trust the current measurement and performance standards. Measurement of traditional media's impact is an inexact science. While an advertisement may reach the intended audience, the ad may not receive any attention. Also, just because the audience members are exposed to the ad does not mean they will remember any of the messages. Most evaluations of advertising campaigns come after the advertisements are placed. Internet advertising has the potential to allow the advertiser to collect information such as who sees which ad and for how long. Web servers can track every time an individual moves from one linked page to another. Dead pages, or pages no one visits, can be updated or deleted. These data can be collected from both the sending server and the user's PC. Data from cookies may even provide a profile of the user. A study by PricewaterhouseCoopers of eleven of the top destination sites, portals, and third-party ad networks and servers indicated that the top measurement systems included ad impressions, clicks, unique visitors, total visits, and page impressions. Of these, only ad impressions were used in revenue-generating ad contracts.[34] These and other measures are outlined in Table 7.3.

Measurements based on server data require the media hosts to do the reporting. This could be a conflict of interest; therefore, measurements should be audited. There is also a lack of standards and comparability between measurements. To overcome these weaknesses, third-party ad-serving companies such as DoubleClick place ads on multiple Web sites and provide measurement statistics. Again, there could be a conflict of interest because ad-serving companies may represent certain Web sites. These problems are not unique to the Web; other media have rating problems as well. The Internet may provide stronger measurement data as companies agree on standardized rating systems.[35]

Ad Blocking

The shift in power from businesses to consumers is also aided by **ad blocking,** which occurs when consumers filter, or block, ads from Web sites. These filters look at the HTML code and check files and file types against a filter list to block ads, interstitials, or animated banners. A stronger interest in this type of technology exists inside companies where ad blocking can improve network speed and performance. Some advertisers have retaliated by blocking users who use ad-blocking software.[36]

Table 7.3   Measures of Hypermedia Advertising

Measurement Method	Definition	Comments
Ad Impression	Measures the number of times an ad has been pulled (requested by an individual) or pushed (as with e-mail ads).	Provides no information on users.
Visit (Page View)	Tracks the number of individual pages sent to Web viewers without a period of inactivity (to ensure actions are attributed to a single browser for a single session).	Gives no indication of how many users receive or view pages and no profile data on users.
Click-Through	Gives measure of a reaction to an ad; tracks the number of times an online ad is clicked on.	Offers no information about the customers. Customers who click-through may dump a page before it loads. Click-through rates are very small.
Page Impression (Hit Counts)	Measures the number of times a page is sent to the user's browser. Pages can be requested, but the ads may not necessarily be seen by the targeted individual.	Provides information on actual hits, but there could be multiple hits counted for every click of the mouse or page refresh. Records activity regardless of the viewer's location, such as workplace, home, school, or country. Provides no information on users.
Unique Visitors	Allows tracking by the IP address of the viewer or through cookies.	Does not allow for multiple users who use the same IP address to access a site.
Reach	Measures sampled group's visits (if 25 percent of sample has visited site, reach obtained 25 percent).	Requires the use of panels or surveys. Can pair information on the individual's background with individual behavior. Panels may be narrow in scope and not account for all Web surfers, such as those at work or from other countries.

Note: Measures should be filtered to remove hits from search engines and other robots and spiders.

Source: "IAB Glossary of Interactive Advertising Terms," in Interactive Advertising Bureau [online] (March 12, 2002), available from <http://www.iab.net/index.html>; "Principles of Online Media Audience Measurement," in FastInfo [online] (September 22, 1999), available from <http://www.fastinfo.org/measurement/pages/index.cgi/audiencemeasurement>; Steven Vonder Haar, "Web Metrics: Go Figure," *Business 2.0*, June 1999, 46–47.

Ad Payment

Cost per thousand, or CPM, is the traditional payment measure used by advertisers. It is based on the number of people who see the ad. CPM can also act as a standard of comparison across media outlets. For example, if multiple outlets

Table 7.4   Advertising Payment Methods

Payment Method	Meaning	Comments
CPM	Cost per thousand	Typical method used to compare across media.
CPC	Cost per click	Charges based on viewers clicking through from a hypermedia page.
CPA	Cost per action	Cost is based on user taking some specific action, such as a purchase.
CPL	Cost per lead	Based on the number of leads that register from an ad.
CPA	Cost per acquisition	Advertiser pays only when customer makes purchase or acquisition.

Source: David Hallerman, "Online Ad Pricing: Count Heads or Count Results," in eMarketer, [online] (March 5, 2002), available from <http://www.emarketer.com/analysis/marketing/20020305_mark.html>; Jeff Frentzen, "'Flat' Web Sites Are Out; Sites That 'Pop' Are In," *PC Week,* February 3, 1997, 141.

target the same market, the advertiser can purchase a lower-cost medium if the CPM rate is lower. For traditional media, the number of thousands that each medium reports is most often based on an audited source such as ACNielsen (http://www.acnielsen.com) or Arbitron (http://www.arbitron.com). Nielsen/ NetRatings (http://www.nielsen-netratings.com/default.jsp) measures online audiences behavior by using tracking meters on more than 225,000 computers around the world. Its site also provides statistics on top advertisers, top ad banners, and global Internet usage. Web CPM rates can vary from a few dollars to seventy dollars or more depending on the outlet used and the audience reached. These rates may be higher than those for other media such as radio and TV, but the ability to reach the desired market can make the Web more cost-effective.

New methods of paying for ad placements, usually based on some type of performance, are emerging on the Web. These models shift the risk of advertising to the media; if the media cannot provide results, they do not get paid. As of the third quarter of 2001, 50 percent of campaigns used cost per thousand, 11 percent used performance-based measures, and 39 percent used a combination of measures.[37] Table 7.4 outlines the major payment systems used for Web advertising.

The Changing Advertising Business Model

E-business promotion is changing the advertising model. These changes include not only how ads are delivered but also how the audience interacts with the ads. Figure 7.8 illustrates the traditional model for magazine advertising. A magazine is obtained by the audience through subscription delivery or retail purchase. A major source of revenue comes from the magazine's advertising. Prices vary for different ad placements based on the likelihood the ad will be viewed, so back covers and inside

Figure 7.8   Traditional Magazine Advertising Model

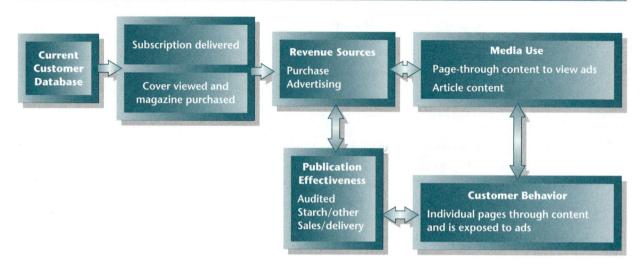

Figure 7.9   E-Business Promotional Model

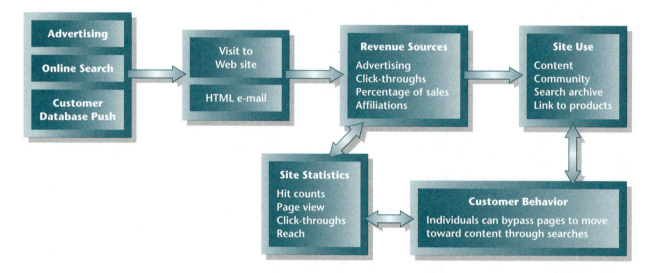

front covers demand the highest prices. Individuals are exposed to the ads as they page through the magazine. The ads must have enough interest and impact to pull the viewer to the ad content. The effectiveness of the advertisements must be determined through audits by companies such as Starch and through audited delivery.

The e-business promotional model differs. Figure 7.9 illustrates that offline and online media can be used to drive individuals to the Web site, or direct push can deliver e-mail. Revenue sources can include not only paid advertising but also a percentage of sales. Individuals are able to surf directly to content that interests them, allowing advertisements to be targeted. Statistics can be generated on a number of metrics in real time, which lets companies judge the effectiveness of their campaigns.[38]

▶ Thinking Strategically: Case 7.2

Speculate on the future of wireless advertising. Why is wireless advertising growing faster outside of the United States? Determine the limitations and advantages of using wireless ads. Develop a strategy for using wireless advertising with other e-business communication platforms.

Case 7.2

It's a Wireless World

Wireless advertising offers marketers the ability to deliver messages to customers anywhere, any time they are attached to a mobile device. Four formats are developing. The most prevalent ad format is the short text message. For broadband wireless devices, banners with click-through capability have been developed. Wireless application protocol (WAP) ads allow for text messaging and more complex messages. Finally, voice messages can be delivered to wireless phones. The effectiveness of wireless ads may be more difficult to gauge than that of online advertising; the packet-sending system used for wireless communication may not indicate if the entire ad is delivered to the customer. Also, there may be no chance for the customer to react to the ad.[39]

In the United States this market is still developing, but more rapid growth is expected in Europe and Asia. Japan has a very high adoption rate for wireless devices, and wireless advertising is growing rapidly. In Japan, minibanner click-through rates averaged 3.6 percent, and e-mail ad click-through averaged 24 percent in 2001. Ad networks such as DoubleClick are using their Japanese divisions to set up wireless media opportunities.[40]

Wireless campaigns mirror other hypermedia campaigns. Sony/Columbia TriStar put together a wireless-based campaign for the movie release of *Final Fantasy*. The campaign consisted of targeting sixty thousand 14-to-15-year-old males from an opt-in database. It was text based, announcing the film opening with the film Web site's URL. Other films that have used wireless ad broadcasts include *Lord of the Rings, Jurassic Park III*, and *X-Men*.[41]

Knowledge Integration

Terms and Concepts

Action *202*
Ad blocking *209*
Ad impressions *210*
Advertising *205*
Advertising network *208*
Affiliate marketing *197*
Agencies *208*
Attention *194*
Banner ads *205*
Bots *195*
Click-through *210*
Cookies *201*
Cost per acquisition
   (CPA) *211*

Cost per action
   (CPA) *211*
Cost per lead (CPL) *211*
Cost per thousand
   (CPM) *211*
Desire *200*
Home page *198*
Hypermedia *192*
Interest *198*
Interstitial *206*
Metacrawlers *196*
Page view *210*
Page impression *210*
Promotion *192*

Push *201*
Reach *210*
Sales force automation
   (SFA) *194*
Search directories *195*
Search engines *195*
Sponsorships *197*
Sticky *203*
Top of the search *197*
Web spiders *195*

Concepts and Questions for Review

1. Explain the role promotion plays in the marketing system.
2. List a number of e-business promotional goals.
3. Outline the AIDA process.
   a. How is attention gained using hypermedia?
   b. How is interest created?
   c. How is desire generated?
   d. How is action encouraged?
4. Describe the role of hypermedia for industrial markets.
5. How are media relationships changing?
6. What are the major types of ads used for Web sites?
7. List the major means of measuring online advertising effectiveness.
8. Describe the major standards for paying for online advertising.

Active Learning

Exercise 7.1 Evaluate Web Sites

Web sites should be designed to reach specific communication goals. Visit a Web site and determine what you believe to be its communication goals. Create a table like the one that follows and answer the questions related to the AIDA process.

Web Site Evaluation

AIDA Process	E-Business Communication Strategy
Attention	Describe how offline media make the audience aware of the Web site. Use a search engine to see which search terms allow the Web site to be found. How far is this business from the top of the list? Determine if other Web sites are used as media advertising this Web site.
Interest	Decide whether this site uses customization or personalization techniques to meet an individual's needs.
Desire	Describe how content is designed to appeal to the target audience. How does this site attempt to develop relationships with its audience?
Action	Determine which types of actions the site encourages. Does the site use promotions to entice actions?

Exercise 7.2 Determining Advertising Rates

It is relatively easy to find pricing information on advertising rates from media kits at Web sites. Go to a Web site with an advertising rate card and evaluate how it assigns its charges. Visit another site and find its advertising rates. How do these compare? Compare the target markets of the two Web sites. Which Web site is the better value?

Exercise 7.3 Devising an E-Business Promotional Campaign

Refer to Figures 7.8 and 7.9. How do other traditional media such as television, newspapers, and radio compare to e-business-based promotional media? Explain why you would prefer to use an e-business-based promotional model instead of the traditional models. Indicate the relative strengths and weaknesses of the various models.

Competitive Exercise 7.4 Devising an E-Business Promotional Campaign

Use the Buddy Lee campaign table as a model for developing an e-business-based promotional campaign. Choose a company and target market. How will you gain attention, develop interest, foster desire, and encourage action? Also include how you will maintain loyalty. Devise a number of metrics to measure the success of the campaign. Justify why your company should adopt your plan.

Anatomy of a Campaign

Company	Attention	Interest	Desire	Action	Loyalty

Measurement:

Web Search—Looking Online

Search Term: Search Engines   First 5 out of 1,111,913

AltaVista. Searches a large database of Web sites and multimedia sources.
http://www.altavista.com

Google.com. Offers searches using a large database of Web sites and images.
http://www.google.com

Yahoo! Provides a directory-based search engine.
http://www.yahoo.com

Overture. Offers a search engine site for paid sponsors.
http://www.overture.com

Search Engine Watch. Accesses a portal site for information on search engines.
http://www.searchenginewatch.com

Search Term: Online Advertising Support   First 10 out of 449,213

Ad Resource. Provides a library of advertising and marketing links.
http://www.adresource.com

AdAge. Accesses *Advertising Age* magazine's online information.
http://www.adage.com

AdWeek. Offers an online form of *Adweek* magazine.
http://www.adweek.com/adweek/index.jsp

DoubleClick. Accesses one of the world's leading Web advertising networks.
http://www.doubleclick.com

Association of National Advertisers. Organizes a trade association for the advertising industry.
http://www.ana.net

Interactive Advertising Bureau. Manages an online advertising trade group.
http://www.iab.net

Personalization Consortium. Advocates the responsible use of one-to-one marketing technology and practices on the World Wide Web.
http://www.personalization.org/

Target Marketing. Supports direct marketing efforts.
http://www.targetonline.com

SitePoint. Provides information on maintaining a Web site, including how to promote a site.
http://www.sitepoint.com

Internet Advertising History. Offers an Internet advertising timeline.
http://www.ec2.edu/dccenter/archives/ia/history.html

Search Term:	Affiliate Marketing	First 2 out of 449,213

CashPile. Organizes affiliate programs.
http://www.CashPile.com

EComWorks. Develops and manages affiliate programs.
http://www.ecomworks.com

References

1 "Amazon Form 10K," in SEC's Edgar Database [online] (September 8, 1999), available from <http://edgar.sec.gov/Archives/edgar/data/1018724/0000891020-99-000375.txt>.

2 In Amazon.com, Form 10-K [online], available from <http://www.corporate-ir.net/ireye/ir_site.zhtml?ticker=AMZN&script=10903&layout=8&item_id='http://media.corporate-ir.net/media_files/NSD/AMZN/reports/10K01.pdf'>; in Amazon.com, Historical Income Statements [online], available from <http://media.corporate-ir.net/media_files/nsd/amzn/historical_financials/HistoricalIncomeStatementsQ4.xls>.

3 The AIDA process is only one of a hierarchy of effective models in advertising. For more on this topic, see Demetrios Vakratsas and Tim Ambler, "How Advertising Works: What Do We Really Know?" *Journal of Marketing,* January 1999, 26–43.

4 Joep P. Cornelissen, "Theoretical Concept or Management Fashion? Examining the Significance of IMC," *Journal of Advertising Research,* September/October 2000, 7–16.

5 "Embracing Interactive Media," *BtoB,* October 9, 2000, 43.

[6] Steve Bennett, "Get the Message," *Small Business Computing*, September 1999, 49–50; Insane Stats, "URL Ubiquity," *Business 2.0,* February 1999, 8.

[7] Michael Pastore, "Paid Search Engines Endure Advertising Slowdown," in CyberAtlas [online] (June 30, 2001), available from <http://cyberatlas.internet.com/markets/advertising/article/0,,5941_856381,00.html>.

[8] Mindy Charski, "The Vitruous Search Engine," *Interactive Week,* June 4, 2001, 73–76.

[9] Matthew Fordahl, "The Web's 19 Degrees of Separation," in BayArea.com [online], available from <http://www.bayarea.com/mid/mercurynews>.

[10] Al Berg, "Go to the Top of the Hit List," *LANTimes,* November 10, 1997, 101; Jim Sterne, "Stacking the Deck," *CIO Web Business,* December 1, 1997, 36–37; David Haskin, "Power Search," *Internet World,* December 1997, 78–92.

[11] Robert D. Hof, "Desperately Seeking Search Technology," *BusinessWeek,* September 24, 2001, 89.

[12] Michael Pastore, "Internet Ads Still Feeling Industry Woes," in CyberAtlas [online] (December 4, 2001), available from <http://cyberatlas.internet.com/markets/advertising/article/0,,5941_933861,00.html>; "Association of National Advertisers: Most Large Firms Advertise Online," in NUA [online] (October 18 2001), available from <http://www.nua.com/surveys/index.cgi?f5VS&art_id5905357310&rel5true>; Janet Ryan and Nancy Whiteman, "Online Advertising Glossary: Sponsorships," in ClickZ Today [online] (May 15, 2000), available from <http://www.clickz.com/media/media_sell/article.php/824121>.

[13] Dan Gray, "Affiliate Marketing: New Customers, New Profit," *Web Techniques,* November 2001, 15–17; Jason Compton, "Affiliate Web Marketing," *PC Computing,* April 2000, 126–28; Paula Hendrickson, "Web Marketing Muscle," *E-Merging Business,* Fall/Winter 2000, 90–95.

[14] Goutam Chakraborty, Vishal Lala, and Warren David, "Important Factors in Business-to-Business Web Site Evaluation: A Scale Development Study," in *Proceedings of the 1998 AMA Winter Educator's Conference* (Chicago: American Marketing Association, 1998); Qimei and William D. Wells, "Attitude Toward the Site," *Journal of Advertising Research,* September/October 1999, 27.

[15] Joan O'C. Hamilton, "Do You Need A Web-Site Makeover?" *BusinessWeek E.Biz,* June 5, 2000, EB118–EB120; Carol Nelson and Rocky James, "Creative Strategy for Interactive Marketing," in *Interactive Marketing,* ed. Edward Forrest and Richard Mizerski (Lincolnwood, Ill.: NTC/Contemporary Publishing, 1996), 215–27.

[16] Jonetta Delaine Mosley-Matchett, "The Effects of Presentation Latency on Proficient and Nonproficient Users of Internet-Based Marketing Presentations," in *Proceedings of the 1998 AMA Winter Educator's Conference* (Chicago: American Marketing Association, 1998), 399–400.

[17] Elizabeth Gardner, "Analysis: What's Behind the Flurry of Redesigns," *Internet World,* June 8, 1998, 1–53.

[18] Herschell Gordon Lewis, "Copywriting for Interactive Media," in *Interactive Marketing,* ed. Edward Forrest and Richard Mizerski (Lincolnwood, Ill.: NTC/Contemporary Publishing, 1996), 229–39.

[19] "Online Retail Marketing Initiatives in 2001," in eMarketer [online] (January 9, 2002), available from <http://www.emarketer.com/estatnews/estats/ecommerce_b2c/20020109_shop.html>.

[20] Jeff Sweat and Rick Whiting, "Instant Marketing," *InformationWeek,* August 2, 1999, 18–20.

[21] Susan Kuchinskas, "Fair Gamers," June 13, 2000, *Business 2.0,* 183–85.

22 Mickey Alam Khan, "Nestle Site Sweetens Brand Appeal," *iMarketing News,* December 17, 2001, 4; Christine Blank, "P&G Tests Web Game to Tout Brand," *iMarketing News,* June 4, 2001, 4; Kenneth Hein, "Bic Makes a Game of Marketing," *iMarketing News,* July 31, 2000, 3.

23 Justin Hibbard, "Getting Personal," *Red Herring,* September 1999, 128; Rivka Tadjer, "Giving Content a Push," *Communications Week,* June 2, 1997, 73–78; Dan Richman, "Let Your Agent Handle It," *InformationWeek,* April 17, 1995, 44–56.

24 Neil McAllister, "Getting Personal," *Web Techniques,* November 2001, 35–37.

25 Julia King, "Web Success Boosts Customer Expectation," *Computerworld,* August 16, 1999, 40; John Evan Frook, "Future Trend: Getting Personal with Customers," *InternetWeek,* June 22, 1998, 11.

26 Elizabeth Gardner, "Finding a Niche as the Web's Coupon Source," *Internet World,* March 23, 1998, 13, 16; CoolSavings, "About CoolSavings," in CoolSavings [online] (September 21, 1999), available from <http://www9.coolsavings.com/scripts/frame_enter.asp?OpType=intro&SessionID=1594218253&RefURL=http//www.coolsavings.com>.

27 Don E. Schulz and Scott E. Bailey, "Customer/Brand Loyalty in an Interactive Marketplace," *Journal of Advertising Research,* May/June, 2000, 41.

28 Leslie Beyer, "The Loyalty Factor," *Internet Retailer,* July 2000, 22–28; Robert O. Crockett, "Keep 'em Coming Back," *BusinessWeek e.Biz,* May 15, 2000, EB20.

29 Kayte Vanscoy, "Can't Bust 'Em," *Smart Business,* January 2001, 3–34; Kim Cross, "Jean Therapy," *Business 2.0,* January 23, 2001, 70–75.

30 Terry Lefton, "The Great Flameout," *The Industry Standard,* March 19, 2001, 75–78; Martha L. Stone, "Online Advertising 101," *Silicon Alley Reporter,* 58–65.

31 Nelson Wang, "Researchers Find Banners Boost Product Awareness," *Web Week,* September 29, 1997, 6.

32 Tom Hyland, "Why Internet Advertising?" in AIB Advertising ABC's [online] (September 16, 1999), available from <http://www.iab.net/advertise/content/adcontent.html>.

33 Nelson Wang, "Ad Execs Predict Continued Growth, See Need for Sensitivity on Privacy," *Internet World,* June 7, 1999, 1, 16–17; "The Round Table," *Silicon Alley Reporter,* 102–121.

34 David Hallerman, "As Standards and Measurements Evolve," in eMarketer [online] (March 12, 2002), available from <http://www.emarketer.com/analysis/marketing/20020312_mark.html>.

35 Elizabeth Gardner, "But Who's Counting? Ratings under Fire," *Internet World,* July 13, 1998, 1, 10; Nelson Wang, "Ratings Firms Face Questions about Data Collection and Projections," *Internet World,* July 13, 1998, 10.

36 "Fiction Site Spurns Surfers Who Use Ad-Blocking Apps," *Computerworld,* June 12, 1999, 28; Charles Babcok, "Dollarwise, Ad Blockers Add Up," *Interactive Week,* April 5, 1999, 24; David Ball, "Online Marketing and Its Discontents," *Silicon Alley Reporter,* 94–100.

37 David Hallerman, "Online Ad Pricing: Count Heads or Count Results," in eMarketer [online] (March 5, 2002), available from <http://www.emarketer.com/analysis/marketing/20020305_mark.html>.

38 Brad Kleindl, "Leveraging the Clout of Magazines for E-Commerce Gains: A Profitable Business Model," (paper presented at the Folio Trade Show, New York City, October 30, 2000).

39 Lain Chroust Ehmann, "Wireless Advertising Tries to Fly," *Mbusiness,* March 2001, 52–60.

40 Joel Enos, "Japan Tests Wireless Ads," *Mbusiness,* May 2001, 38–39.

41 Christine Blank, "More Studios Promote Films through Wireless," *iMarketing News,* July 23, 2001, 1, 18.

chapter 8
The Market

Change is the nature of today's competitive environment. E-business managers must understand how new technologies and processes will be accepted by their targeted markets. Technological change related to the Internet and the World Wide Web is forcing businesses to take into consideration the diffusion of innovations process to design products and develop strategies. The diffusion process helps to explain what is considered to be a new product and what can be done to make the innovation more acceptable to the target audience. The adoption curve indicates that innovators will be the first to purchase new products, and these innovators will influence later adopters. Understanding this process can lead to strategies that help people adopt innovations. These same basic principles operate inside a firm. To help their employees respond to environmental change, firms must allow change agents to develop coalitions and build consensus. This chapter will examine these concepts as they relate to current e-business practice and relationship development.

1. Understand how the diffusion of innovations process works.
2. Define the term *innovation*.
3. Be able to discuss how to speed the acceptance of an innovation.
4. Outline how the individual adoption process works.
5. Explain what a product life cycle is and how this concept relates to new and older technologies.
6. Describe how online communities target individuals, and what it takes to make a successful online community.
7. List and describe the ethical considerations related to targeting a youth market.
8. Discuss why some cultures may be slow to accept technological change and the associated implications.
9. Explain how innovations diffuse in a business and what role change agents play in that process.

learning objectives

Getting the Message Across

In the late 1700s, the French developed a communication system to send messages more than eighty miles in three minutes. This was accomplished through a series of towers that displayed large wooden signs to relay codes. One of the main uses of the signaling system was to send winning national lottery numbers around France. In 1837, the U.S. Senate called for proposals for a similar system in the United States. Instead, Samuel Morse submitted a proposal for an alternative signaling process that would rely on electricity to relay messages. U.S. government support of Morse's proposal gave birth to the telecommunications industry.

After a slow start, demand for the telegraph grew to provide information on winning lottery numbers, stock prices, and other data vital for businesses. Entrepreneurs involved in this new technology grew rich, while businesspeople complained that the telegraph forced them to sell goods and set prices twenty-four hours a day.[1] In 1847, the United States had 30,000 miles of telegraph lines; by 1880, more than 32 million messages were sent over 291,000 miles of cable. Telegraph use peaked in 1945 with 236 million messages; by 1990, the telegraph system had all but vanished. The main reason for the decline of the telegraph was the introduction of the telephone and the gradual improvement of long-distance telephone lines.

After Alexander Graham Bell's 1876 invention, the growth of the telephone was rapid. Initially, the phone was used like a telegraph to send messages one way. Businesses saw the benefits and reorganized around the telephone. Salespeople reported in by phone, and manufacturing plants separated from headquarters. Although such use was at first discouraged by the phone companies, social chatting soon became common. In 1908, a company introduced a service for direct delivery of music on demand into a person's home. Homes subscribed for eighteen

Historical nSite

In the historical novel *The Count of Monte Cristo*, the title character engaged in "online" fraud by using the French signaling system to ruin one of his enemies.

dollars a year, and songs were three cents apiece.[2] The telephone began to transform society. Housewives used the telephone to place purchase orders. People interacted over the phone lines and avoided the more formal social conventions involved in a face-to-face visit. By 1980, there were over 1 billion miles of phone lines, with over 750 million calls being made every day.[3]

The country of Finland has been a leader in wireless telephone networks. In 1971, it developed a wireless network for cars. By 1982, Finland had an analog wireless network, and in 1992, Nokia introduced the first digital handheld portable phone. By 2001, 74 percent of the Finish population used cellular phones. Finland launched a third-generation (3G) wireless system in 2002.[4] The United States has lagged behind many countries in cellular telephone acceptance and use. The future of high-bandwidth digital wireless Internet access has led to a fight for standards between Finland's Nokia and the United States' Microsoft.[5] Figure 8.1 represents the relative growth, maturity, and decline of three telecommunications technologies.

▶ Thinking Strategically

Figure 8.1 illustrates the relative life cycles of three communication technologies. Why do you think the telephone was not more rapidly accepted? Explain why the telephone has grown and the telegraph has declined. Speculate on whether the landline telephone will ever decline in use as the telegraph has. Consider how the telephone has evolved, and speculate on how it may be different in ten years.

"IT [information technology] has made everything I've learned for the past thirty years irrelevant. I hate you for that!"

Maurice Saias,
Professor at the Institut d'Administration des Entreprises
in Aix-en-Provence, France[6]

Explaining how individuals react to and interact with innovations is key to understanding the growth of e-business. These innovations include the use of the Internet as a communication vehicle, as a means of engaging in commerce, and as a way of delivering services. Understanding how change is accepted is vital not only for individual buyer behaviors but also for business purchases and for implementing intrafirm change. It is the individual who adopts innovative products or processes for personal or business use by changing his or her behavior and influencing others to change. E-businesses and designers of Internet sites need to develop business models and Web sites with interfaces that are easy to understand and appealing for new users. For example, MetalSite (http://www.metalsite.com), an online e-commerce market for excess steel, spent $2 million of its $5 million in start-up costs on a study

Figure 8.1   Life Cycles of the Telegraph, Telephone, and Cell Phone

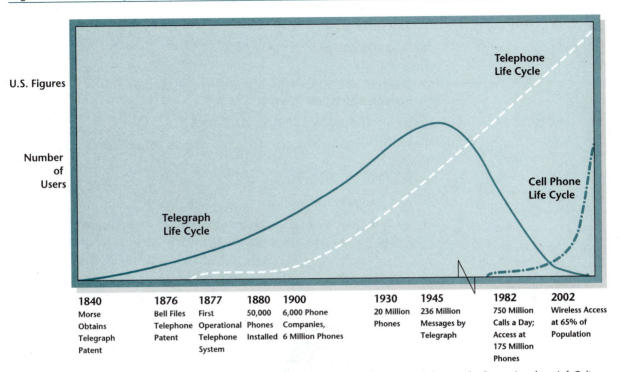

1840	1876	1877	1880	1900	1930	1945	1982	2002
Morse Obtains Telegraph Patent	Bell Files Telephone Patent	First Operational Telephone System	50,000 Phones Installed	6,000 Phone Companies, 6 Million Phones	20 Million Phones	236 Million Messages by Telegraph	750 Million Calls a Day; Access at 175 Million Phones	Wireless Access at 65% of Population

Source: Various Internet surveys, in NUA [online] (2002), available from <http://www.nua.ie/surveys/>; Steven Lumbar, *InfoCulture* (New York: Houghton Mifflin, 1993); Joseph McKendrick, "IDC Charts the World Wide Web," *Midrange Systems,* February 16, 1997, 36, 42.

exploring the exchange process between steel producers and their customers. It then spent another $1 million on a study investigating how to develop an interface for online commerce.[7] MetalSite's goal was to lower the barriers to exchange by making the online experience as familiar as the traditional process.

This chapter will explore how innovations are adopted by using the diffusion of innovations framework. The diffusion of innovations model will provide insight into how and why the Web is becoming a tool for communication and commerce and how rapidly it will grow. It will also outline how newer technologies can be designed to increase the speed of adoption and reach specific target markets to help shape new communities. Finally, it will help to explain how new ideas are introduced into firms to foster change and transform businesses.

The Diffusion of Innovations Process

The major theoretical model used to understand how new ideas and new technology spread over time is the **diffusion of innovations process.**[8] Gatignon and

Robertson[9] have outlined a model of the diffusion process that can give marketers an understanding of the following:

*An **innovation** is a new idea, product, or process.*

1) The concept of an **innovation**

2) The acceptance process for new products

3) The adoption process
  a) The personal influence process and opinion leadership
  b) The role of the innovator

4) The spread of new ideas inside organizations

5) The impact of both the social system on diffusion and diffusion on the social system

6) The role of marketers as change agents

7) The role of competitive actions

Figure 8.2 outlines a model of the diffusion process. This figure illustrates that a number of factors influence how quickly, if at all, innovations spread in a social system.

Figure 8.2 The Diffusion of Innovations Model

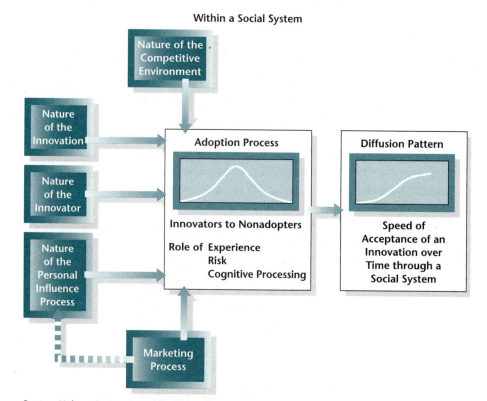

Source: Hubert Gatignon and Thomas S. Robertson, "A Propositional Inventory for New Diffusion Research," *Journal of Consumer Research* 11 (March 1985): 850.

The model in Figure 8.2 shows that five factors influence the rate of individual adoption, which in turn influences how quickly the innovation diffuses through a society. The individual adoption process influences how quickly an innovation is accepted within a society. This model can be better understood in the context of the growth of the World Wide Web. Prior to 1994, the Internet existed in relative obscurity. The ease of use of the Web's graphical interface has changed the nature of the Internet as a product, speeding acceptance of the technology. Netscape and Microsoft spurred growth by giving away their browsers and promoting the advantages of the Web as a communication medium. The press also aided in the marketing process by heavily promoting this new technology and its uses. The growth of the Web has been quite strong in the United States as well as in selected countries in Europe and Asia. The Web has migrated to two major mediums: the "traditional" Web is based on the PC, and the newly emerging Web is based on wireless devices. While Internet use in the United States has grown mostly in the PC-based format, other countries are expected to see increases in wireless access. Figure 8.3 indicates the worldwide growth of the Web from 1995 through 2002.

As with all innovations, new products and processes change behavior patterns. Figure 8.4 illustrates the projected growth of the wireless Web in selected regions of the world. As can be seen, wireless access is expected to become a major on-ramp

Figure 8.3   Growth of the Internet and World Wide Web

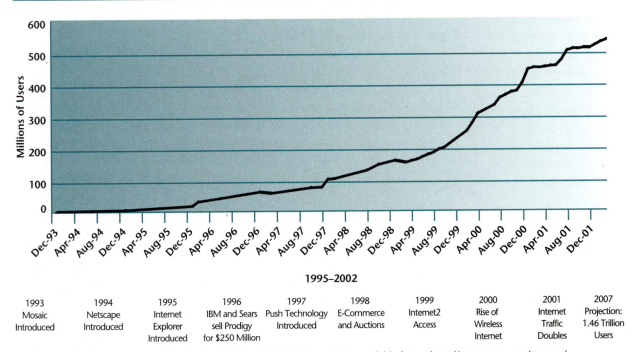

Source: "How Many Online: Worldwide," in NUA [online] (May 11, 2002), available from <http://www.nua.com/surveys/how_many_online/world.html>.

Figure 8.4   Changing Patterns of Internet Access

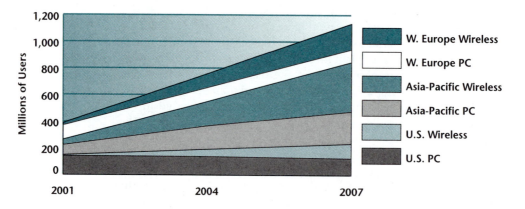

Source: "Internet Users Will Top 1 Billion in 2005. Wireless Internet Users Will Reach 48% in 2005," in Computer Industry Almanac [online] (May 11, 2002), available from <http://www.c-i-a.com/pr032102.htm>.

to the Internet. Most of the worldwide growth of both PC and wireless Internet access is expected in the Asia-Pacific region.

The Nature of the Innovation

Not all innovations are totally new to the world; most are variations of older technologies. How new an individual perceives an innovation to be is dependent on two aspects. The first is how much the user must change behavior to use the innovation. The second is how new the technology is to the user, and, therefore, how much the user has to learn or unlearn to make use of the innovation. The more the potential adopters must change their behavior and adjust to new technologies, the less likely they are to accept the innovation. Innovations can be categorized on a continuum of newness, as illustrated in Figure 8.5.

At one end of the continuum are the new-to-the-world products, classified as **discontinuous innovations**, which may arise through changes in technology or a recombination of existing technologies. Discontinuous innovations require high levels of behavioral change on the part of the user. At the other end of the spectrum are continuous innovations, which are often variations of existing products. Past experience with similar products or product categories allows **continuous innovations** to be accepted more rapidly because they do not require major behavioral change by the user. Between these two extremes are **dynamically continuous innovations.** Not all target markets will perceive the same levels of newness for a single innovation; some markets may have greater levels of experience with a product or product category and therefore may not have to change behavior as much to accept a new technology. For example, individuals who have had experience with computers and software make an easier transition to using the Web because they face a smaller behavioral change to use computer-based Web technology.

▶ Thinking Strategically: Case 8.1

Consider the World Wide Web when it was first introduced. Was it a discontinuous innovation, a dynamically continuous innovation, or a continuous innovation? Discuss whether your answer will differ for different market segments. Explain whether an individual's past experience with computers and technology would have required less behavioral change and technology learning when accepting PC-based Web browsing. Speculate whether or not wireless browsing will increase the Internet's penetration into new markets. What do new interfaces such as Web TV mean for the future growth of the Internet and for those who do not own or use PCs?

CASE 8.1

Surfing the Net—Discontinuous or Continuous Innovation?

The introduction of the Mosaic World Wide Web graphical browser in 1994 enticed many individuals to try the Internet for the first time. All that the new user had to do to surf the Net was load the browser onto a PC, configure the browser to interact with the operating system, purchase a modem, find an ISP, load and make functional the ISP's log-on software, and then learn how to interface with the browser and Web pages.

The promise of an easier-to-use World Wide Web based on Internet TVs has yet to gain dominance. Instead, the Web is expanding into new technologies such as wireless and handheld devices. The "easy" Internet remains easy for those who are technologically astute enough to understand the technology.

A key to speeding up the acceptance of discontinuous innovations is to incorporate **transparent technology** into new-to-the-world products. This decreases the level

Figure 8.5 Continuum of Perceived Product Newness

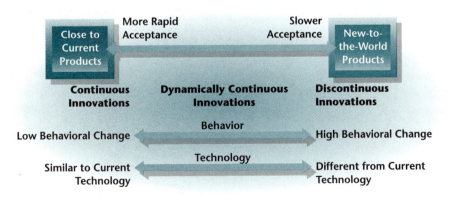

Strategic nSite

Transparent technology implies that the user does not need to be familiar with any of the technical aspects of a product to use it. Windows 95 went a long way toward achieving transparency when it provided plug-and-play technology, allowing an individual to add components to a PC without any technical skills. With Apple's iMac, users need only to plug the computer into an electrical socket and phone jack to use the computer and go online.

of behavior change needed by the market and helps to make discontinuous innovations seem like continuous innovations. Transparency is in part the reason for the growth of the Internet. At first, the Internet was used mostly in a nongraphical mode, which required that the user be familiar with nongraphical interfaces often based on mainframe computer operating systems. It is not surprising that the Web and the Internet remained mainly a tool for academics for a long time. Graphical Web browsers made the linking and searching technology more transparent, enticing more individuals to access the Internet and Web content.

Transparent technology for a browser-based Web may exist only for those who are familiar with graphically based computers. By 2002, this was slightly less than 65 percent of the U.S. population. To penetrate the remaining market, a simpler interface may be needed. At one time, Web access over a Web-based TV was believed to allow users who have less expertise with computers to use tools they are already familiar with for Web browsing. This simplified interface would use a TV remote control to access content through televisions and would require a minimum of behavioral change. Instead, many homes have purchased PCs to learn the technology. In addition, increasing populations of young people have received computer training in schools, and their expertise with PCs and the Web is considerably higher than that of their parents or older brothers and sisters.[10]

Just because an innovation requires little behavioral change does not guarantee that it will be accepted quickly. Innovations must offer significant advantages over older ideas and products to gain acceptance. Table 8.1 outlines the five factors that can speed up an innovation's acceptance.[11]

Table 8.1　Factors That Can Speed Up an Innovation's Acceptance

Factor	Description
Relative Advantage	An innovation must offer greater utility than existing products to be accepted quickly.
Compatibility	If an innovation is compatible with the market's lifestyle (social system and norms), the market will accept it more willingly.
Complexity	The less the perceived complexity of an innovation, the faster its acceptance.
Trialability	If it is easy for the market to experience an innovation, the innovation will be more readily accepted.
Observability	When the market can see others receive benefits from using an innovation, the innovation will be accepted more quickly.

Relative Advantage

The acceptance of the Internet as a communication and commerce tool will depend heavily on the advantages offered. These advantages can be viewed in terms of **economic utility** (the total level of satisfaction received from a good or service, consisting of form, time, place, and ownership utility). Table 8.2 indicates how total economic utility can be increased using the Internet as a communication tool and as a means of purchasing through e-commerce. The information in Table 8.2 is backed by research data that indicate the reasons why people use e-commerce: convenience (66 percent), avoiding crowds (44 percent), prices (42 percent), items not available locally (39 percent), selection (26 percent), and speed and delivery (19 percent).[12]

The Internet has spurred many product and process innovations, not all of which are succeeding. New technologies such as e-books, virtual reality environments, Internet telephony, and countless others have had less-than-stellar sales histories. These technologies did not have clear advantages over the products or processes they were designed to replace. This lack of utility has led to a lack of success.

Table 8.2   Relative Advantages Influencing Internet Technology Acceptance

Utility	Communication	E-Commerce
Form (The Nature of Finished Goods and Services)	The Web allows an individual to find and access vast amounts of information. Personalization technology can meet customized information needs.	E-commerce allows individuals access to many alternative vendors. A market-of-one model allows an individual to have custom-made products.
Time (When the Market Wants the Goods and Services)	Communication over the Web is close to instantaneous. E-mail allows written messages to be delivered and stored, speeding communication. Finding information or products online is aided by the use of search engines.	Online purchasing allows for time saving because of the number of venders that can be evaluated in a short time. Delivery can also be on an overnight basis. Businesses can use online supply chain management to ensure just-in-time delivery of goods.
Place (Where the Market Wants the Goods and Services)	Communication over the Web can be directed to one's business or home. As wireless access becomes more common, access may be universal across locations.	Goods can be delivered directly to an individual's home or business. Portable Web devices allow individuals to compare prices and make purchases from any location.
Ownership (The Transfer of Ownership)	Copyright laws cover ownership of information transferred over the Web.	E-commerce enhances an individual's ability to receive title by facilitating financing and payment flows.

case 8.2

The Rise of the Killer App

E-mail is considered the **killer application** on the Internet. In 1999, e-mail replaced research as the number one reason that people in the United States went online; e-mail is also a dominant reason that businesses add Internet access. The U.S. Postal Service (USPS) has projected that e-mail and e-billing will dramatically impact first-class mailing. First-class mail use is expected to peak in 2002 and decrease 2.5 percent a year until 2008.[13]

To compete with e-mail, Sweden and Finland have deregulated their postal services. Sweden's competitive postal system hosts a commerce site (http://www.torget.se). Finland Post takes e-mail messages from individuals, prints them, and then delivers them to postal addresses. The USPS has developed plans to take advantage of the Internet; it hopes to adopt services like Finland Post's.[14]

Instant messaging services allow an individual to know when a buddy goes online. Individuals can create buddy lists so they can engage in real-time communication over the Internet. This technology is of interest not only to individuals who want to communicate but also to businesses that want to know when a prospective customer goes online. This technology could allow individuals to videoconference with friends over high-bandwidth communication lines. It could also allow targeted ads to be sent to an individual's home PC or Web TV.[15]

Compatibility and Complexity

Changes in technology **interface** design are undertaken to increase the rate of adoption. It is easier for users to access information when technology uses real-life **metaphors** as an interface to computer-mediated information. For computers, this has been tried with interfaces such as Microsoft's Bob and Packard Bell's Navigator living room.[16] These products had a tendency to slow computers down and were not widely accepted or used. Microsoft's Windows environment uses the metaphors of a desktop, folders, and files. Apple's iMac was designed to make the computer and its interface very simple for home users.[17] As individuals gain experience with Web sites, they develop **mental models** of how to navigate the site. Amazon.com's Web site design has set the look and feel for millions of people whose first online shopping experience was with Amazon.com. Many other sites have copied Amazon.com's file tab interface. Amazon.com has developed a one-click payment technology that allows repeat buyers to purchase with just one button click. To maintain the ease-of-use advantage, Amazon.com filed a patent infringement suit against rival Barnes & Noble's one-button technology.

*A **killer application (killer app)** is a software product that entices a user to adopt a larger technology. Spreadsheets were the killer apps for PCs. E-mail is the killer app for the Internet.*

*An **interface** links the user to the technology. An ideal interface does not require behavioral change on the part of the user.*

*Surfing the net is a **metaphor**. It implies that one slides from place to place. Metaphors allow a person to understand a new idea by relating it to previously understood concepts.*

***Snail mail** is mail delivered through a postal service.*

▶ Thinking Strategically: Case 8.2

Consider why individuals may be shifting from postal letters to e-mail. What utility does e-mail offer over **snail mail?** If e-mail is the current killer app for the Internet, determine which other technologies an individual might adopt after growing comfortable with e-mail. Speculate on whether or not instant messaging will be the next killer application. Which technologies would be threatened by the use of instant messaging?

Two computer interface consultants recommend that technology designers change the way they develop products. Dr. Clare-Marie Karat of IBM's Thomas J. Watson Research Center feels that computer engineers must understand that the user is always right. If the system does not work, it is the technology's fault, not the user's. Donald Norman, a consultant for Apple Computer, believes that technology must become idiot-proof by hiding the technology and bringing out the benefits.[18]

Interfaces are being designed to make it easier for individuals to use the Web for communication, training, and data searching. Web pages must be designed with an interface that users can understand and operate without learning new technologies or behavioral patterns. This is true for all newly emerging hypermedia, such as handheld wireless Internet access.

Intranets must also be designed with usable interfaces. Bankers Trust uses game-based interfaces over its intranet to aid corporate training. The corporation has designed games called Sexual Harassment Solitaire and Straight Shooter for learning rules related to office conduct and derivative trading. Bankers Trust has a young workforce, and the training is designed to meet their learning styles. For individuals who do not like a game-type interface, straight question-and-answer training is available. The games are linked to a database that keeps track of the users' scores.[19]

Broadband allows for new interface designs. Web pages based on Flash and other interactive media offer a richer interface than traditional graphic- and text-based Web sites. DoCoMo's Web site (http://www.nttdocomo.com/top.html) uses Flash to provide an interactive interface. Flash is also used to build **cityscapes,** where buildings, signs, and other structures act as hyperlinks.

The process of searching for Web content is changing as well. **Hyperbolic tree** browsing allows an individual to see a topic of interest in the middle of a search area with associated branches, like the spokes of a wheel, to linked data. Xerox's Palo Alto Research Center researched computer/human interfaces to develop hyperbolic trees. Xerox started Inxight Software (http://www.inxight.com) in 1997 to market this interface. A Web site mapped with a hyperbolic tree allows individuals to see the higher-level pages with all the associated links. When a related page or topic is clicked on, it brings that topic and related branches to the center of the search. It is

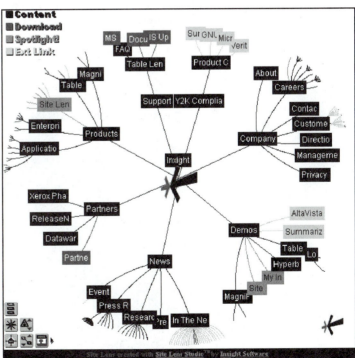

Source: <http://www.inxight.com>.

Strategic nSite

A **mental model** *is a set of relationships that a person keeps in mind to understand how the world, or a piece of it, operates.*

A **hyperbolic tree** *allows users to visually navigate hierarchies of hundreds or thousands of objects. Each level of the hierarchical structure is linked to other subcategories.*

hoped that this nonlist search system will speed a user's ability to retrieve data.[20] Similar to hyperbolic trees is the HotSauce interface. This allows a 3-D fly-through for navigating information spaces. As an individual clicks on an information node, the related information moves in from the back.[21]

Interface design is a moving target. Markets vary in their levels of experience and knowledge, and their current preferences for interfaces may be based on past experiences. Preferences change as individuals gain experience. Companies should test Web interface designs often to be sure they are acceptable to the market.[22]

Trialability and Observability

By trial and observation, individuals lower the risk of adopting a new innovation. Consumers face a number of risks in purchasing over the Internet. One study found the concerns that individuals have about using the Internet for commerce include, in order of importance, security (fear of being robbed by hackers), lack of selection, unknown quality (inability to touch the merchandise), and privacy.[23] As consumers gain greater experience with online commerce, they are increasing their amount of purchasing online. Figure 8.6 indicates how the market is shifting its purchase patterns, moving from information search and purchasing offline to greater amounts of purchasing online (the post-2001 data are projected). This figure may indicate that individuals gain trial experiences by using the Internet for information purposes first and then move to purchasing online as their comfort level grows. By 2001, 51 percent of shoppers shopped online and purchased offline, 40 percent shop online and purchase online, and 9 percent shopped offline and purchased online.[24]

Figure 8.6   Market Shifts in Purchase Patterns

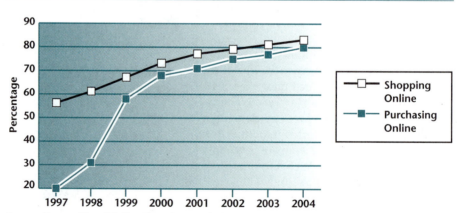

Source: Darren Allen, "Online Shopping: Pry before You Buy," in eMarketer [online] (February 6, 2001), available from <http://www.emarketer.com/analysis/ecommerce_b2c/20010206_prying.html>.

Companies are attempting to lower the perceived risks involved in using the Web for communication or purchases. Security is the primary concern, and a number of security measures are being employed to make transactions more secure (see Chapter 2). In reality, security of credit card information over the Internet may be higher than that for other forms of transactions. A security company found that it took fifty thousand CPUs working thirty-nine days to break a fifty-nine-bit encryption code. Most companies use more than fifty-nine bits, making them even more secure, but consumer perception can carry more weight than reality.[25]

The Individual Adoption Process

The individual **adoption curve** indicates how individuals react to innovations over time. The adoption process places individuals into categories and explores how the early adopters influence later adopters. Marketers can use this information to segment markets and design promotional campaigns.

The Adoption Curve

The adoption curve is used as a model to understand both who is likely to be an innovator and how interpersonal influence passes to later adopters of innovations. Figure 8.7 outlines this process by placing individuals into adopter categories based on how quickly they adopt innovations over time.

Figure 8.8 illustrates the actual penetration rate for the Internet in the United States from 1995 to the year 2002. As can be seen, the growth of Internet acceptance has slowed. This is to be expected, as the remaining markets include the later half of the late majority and the laggards. Without more compatible interfaces and

Figure 8.7   The Adoption Process

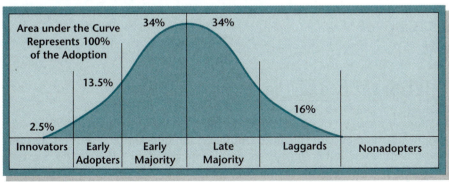

Area under the Curve Represents 100% of the Adoption

34%   34%

13.5%

16%

2.5%

Innovators | Early Adopters | Early Majority | Late Majority | Laggards | Nonadopters

Early Adoption   Late Adoption

Figure 8.8   Cumulative U.S. Internet Penetration

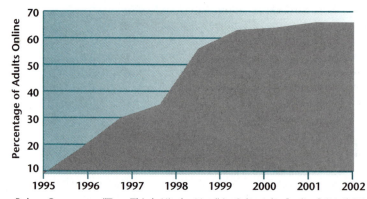

Source: Robyn Greenspan, "Two-Thirds Hit the Net," in CyberAtlas [online] (April 17, 2002), available from <http://cyberatlas.internet.com/big_picture/geographics/article/0,,5911_1011491,00.html#table>.

more transparent technology, it may be difficult to move through the last two categories of adopters.

Innovators are the first to adopt; they have personal characteristics that make them different from later adopters. Innovators are typically reported to have higher income and higher educational levels, to be younger and more socially integrated, and to have a higher risk tolerance.[26] Innovators with these characteristics are likely to have greater experience with technology and its uses. They may be able to see advantages that others do not see in using the Web for information or purchases. Using technology may be more compatible with their lifestyles and considered less complex. These knowledge advantages, along with higher incomes and more risk tolerance, may allow innovators to perceive the Web differently from later adopters. The characteristics of innovators are reflected in the profiles of early Web and e-commerce users, as illustrated in Table 8.3. This table also shows how the market is shifting. The average age of Internet users has been increasing, while the average income and educational levels have been dropping. In addition, more women than men are online. These shifts suggest that the Internet has penetrated to the "average" American.

Relationships and the Speed of Adoption

The rate of adoption of Web-based communication and e-commerce will depend on how much additional benefit the marketer can offer through this medium and how much behavioral change users need to go through. This requires a careful balance of design and content. Once a firm establishes a relationship, it has an incentive to maintain that relationship over a long time period. The catalog

Table 8.3 Web Users, Demographic Profiles

Profiling Factor	The Web as a Communication Tool 1996–97	2002
Age	**Average Age:** U.S.: 35 Europe: 21–30	**Percentage of Adults Online, U.S.:** 18 to 29 28% 30 to 39 23% 40 to 49 23% 50 to 64 24% 65+ 5%
Gender	**U.S.:** 61.3% male, 38.7% female **Europe:** 83.7% male, 16.3% female	**U.S.:** 51% female, 49% male
Income	**Average, U.S.:** $52,000	**Percentage of Adults Online, U.S.:** $25,000 or Less: 18% $25,001 to $50,000: 25%, $50,001 and over: 46%
Education	**Percentage of Adults Online, U.S.:** Some College: 80.9% At Least One Degree: 50.1%	**Percentage of Adults Online, U.S.:** High School or Less: 37% Some College: 31% At Least One Degree: 32%

Sources: Robyn Greenspan, "Two-Thirds Hit the Net," in CyberAtlas [online] (April 17, 2002), available from <http://cyberatlas. internet.com/big_picture/geographics/article/0,,5911_1011491,00.html#table>; "GVU's 9th WWW User Survey," in GVU's WWW User Surveys [online] (1996), available from <http://www.cc.gatech.edu/gvu/user_surveys/survey-1998-04/> (note that Georgia Tech updates its survey data on a regular basis); James E. Pitkow and Colleen M. Kehoe, "Emerging Trends in the WWW User Population," *Communications of the ACM 39*, no. 6 (June 1996): 106–8; David Batstone and Eric Hellweg, "Cash on the Line, Introducing the Internet Consumer," *Business 2.0,* 1998 premier issue, 28–29.

clothing store Lands' End (http://www.landsend.com) prides itself on how well it maintains relationships with its customers. Lands' End sees the Internet as a tool and wants its customers to have the same experience online as they would have over the phone or with the catalog. Its Web site mirrors the catalog by having in-depth information on products; however, the Web site can carry more in-depth and up-to-date information than the catalog. Shoppers can see how various items look together to create a coordinated outfit by placing ties over shirts and shirts with pants. Out-of-stock items are not displayed, so customers are not disappointed. On Wednesdays, the site allows individuals to purchase overstocked items. Prices are reduced every hour until they sell out. Lands' End is developing a virtual community of loyal shoppers.

The Personal Influence Process

Once individuals gain experience with a product, they may act as **opinion leaders** and communicate with others about their experience. The interaction of an **early adopter** (the second adopter category, following innovator) with an innovator lowers perceived risk. Once early adopters gain experience, they communicate to the **early majority** (the third group of adopters). This process continues down through the fourth adopting category, the **late majority**, and then onto the **laggards**. Some companies are taking advantage of this word-of-mouth system to attract new customers by engaging in viral marketing. One study found that word of mouth influence can be more important in driving traffic to a Web site than search engines or links. Ninety eight percent of satisfied users will recommend a Web site, compared to just 1 percent of dissatisfied users.[27] A Roper Starch Worldwide study found that 8 percent of the U.S. Internet population are **e-fluentials**, opinion leaders who influence the surfing habits of others. The average e-fluential influences eight other Internet users, four times the number of people influenced by a typical offline opinion leader. E-fluentials are likely to have higher levels of Internet experience; they spend more time online, visit more sites than average users, and e-mail twice as many people.[28] Tying these individuals into viral marketing campaigns (as illustrated in Chapter 3) can be very effective in disseminating information on Web sites.

    Nonadopters will never accept the innovation; this could be due to lack of access or lack of interest, or the individual could be a **Luddite** and have disdain for technology. Nonadopters of computer-based Web access may become adopters of television-based Web access. The percentage of users already accepting television as a one-way communication device is close to 100 percent in the United States.

The Product Life Cycle

The **product life cycle** is a helpful conceptualization of the cumulative adoption of an innovation by a society over time. It is generally viewed in terms of a product category, such as the use of the Internet or Web, and may not accurately represent a single product. Single products usually enter an industry at some point in the industry life cycle. The product life cycle uses a metaphor that indicates that products are developed and introduced, and then they grow, mature, and decline. The rate at which products have been moving through their life cycles has been increasing in speed over time; in many high-tech industries, life cycles for products can run from six to eighteen months. Figure 8.9 illustrates the basic product life cycle.

Historical nSite

Luddite is a name given to individuals who reject technology. The Luddites were Scottish weavers who destroyed automated weaving machines in an attempt to keep technology out of their industry. The lasting impact of their action was that their name became part of our vocabulary.

Figure 8.9   Internet Product Life Cycle

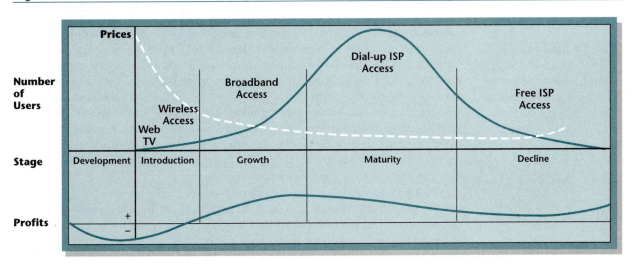

The figure shows that the number of users of a product increases over time, the growth eventually peaks, and then the number of users declines. The development of the new product results in an initial cost. As the product moves into its growth stage, profits grow. These profits can draw competition, which in turn drives down the price of the product and eventually reduces the profitability. As new technologies emerge, they replace the older product, resulting in a decline in the number of users. Eventually, competitors shift away from the product; the only purchasers who remain are those who are loyal to the product or technology, allowing prices to increase and possibly return profits to the few remaining companies. Some products, such as the telephone, saturate potential markets. These products may then evolve through continuous innovations. Dial-tone telephones have given way to Touch-Tone phones, and landline phones are giving way to cellular systems. Figure 8.1 on page 223 at the beginning of this chapter illustrates the life cycles of three products: the telegraph, telephone, and cellular phone. Figure 8.3 on page 225 shows the early life cycle stages for the World Wide Web.

Here, Figure 8.9 suggests that television-based Web access is still in the early introduction stage. Wireless access is expected to grow, but in 2002 less than 6 percent of the U.S. market accessed the Internet through wireless systems. Broadband, including DSL and cable, accounted for 15 percent of the market, and DSL was growing at more than 12.5 percent per year. The majority of market access was through dial-up ISPs, accounting for more than 78 percent of the market, but this type of access was growing at only a little over 2 percent per year. Free ISPs are in a decline stage, with less than 6 percent of the market and shrinking at a rate close to 15 percent per year.[29]

Communities

Online communities are groups of individuals who share common interests and use the Internet to foster their communities by accessing the same Web sites for information or support.

Although the Web allows the development of one-to-one marketing, it is also being used to target broader market segments through the creation of online communities. **Online communities** are created to provide mutual support or to drive Web users with shared interests, opinions, or activities to a site. Businesses develop online communities to appeal to groups of users who will use the site's products or who can be targeted by advertisers through the site. The number of participants in online communities has grown faster than the number of general Internet users, and individuals also stay longer at community sites. Online communities allow narrow targeting for advertising and e-commerce offers; these sites can also generate support for social causes.[30]

Online communities have been developed for **Netizens,** or Internet citizens, and for specialized business groups. AOL may have set the first model for Internet communities, but a number of other companies are developing and fostering communities online. Yahoo! has a club section (http://groups.yahoo.com) on its site to allow individuals to create their own communities. This includes setting up message boards, chats, e-mail addresses, online photo albums, and other community information. These can be listed publicly or kept private.

Businesses develop communities to establish and maintain relationships with constituencies. These communities could be for consumers at e-commerce sites or for employees such as salespeople or engineers. Mary Kay generates 70 percent of its business online but also maintains its person-to-person consultancy sales approach. Mary Kay's community site allows customers to gift shop, visit their consultant's Web site, learn about being a Mary Kay representative, engage in lifestyle analysis, and find information about the company. Sales consultants use an extranet (registered entry) to place orders and maintain contact with the company.[31]

Firms wishing to expand their markets online must do more than just offer products; they must develop tight relationships with their target markets. The next few sections explore a number of market segments and their use of the Web as a communication tool, a shopping source, and a means of creating community.

The Online Market Segmentation Process

Psychographics (lifestyle criteria) generally profile individuals based on their preferred activities, interests, and opinions.

It is important that e-businesses selectively target markets as the online population begins to reflect other markets in its diversity. Markets can be segmented on a number of characteristics. Many widely reported statistics of Internet use are based on demographic factors such as gender, age, and income. Businesses use additional measures such as **psychographics** to segment markets, which entails identifying lifestyle criteria and other behavioral data. Figure 8.10 illustrates the fastest-growing online markets.

Figure 8.10   Fastest-Growing Online Markets

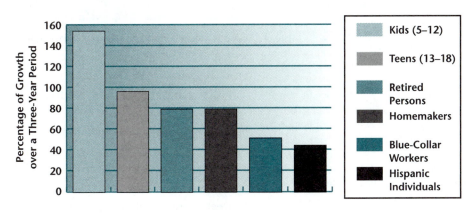

Source: "Monitoring Mothers Online in the U.S." in eMarketer [online] (May 8, 2002), available from <http://www.emarketer.com/estatnews/estats/edemographics/ 20020508_aol.html>.

Female Markets

In 1994, almost 95 percent of Web users were male; by 2002, 51 percent of Internet users were female. One study found that mothers spend on average four and one-half hours longer online than American teenagers. The most popular activities for mothers are e-mail and instant messaging, and they also enjoy getting news, current events, and local information.[32] The online market is growing to reflect the U.S. mass market, in which women account for 54 percent of the population and influence 85 percent of purchase decisions.[33] Women are responsible for more than 70 percent of traditional retail purchases and must become a vital component of e-commerce. Women did 58 percent of online shopping for the 2001 Christmas shopping season.

To target this segment, Web sites must offer benefits that women look for, including savings of time and money. In addition, Web sites must develop a sense of community. A number of sites foster Web communities specifically for women. Women's sites are adding interactive components that act as personal shoppers. Bloomingdale's gives fashion and shopping advice; shoppers can fill out a profile and receive customized advice. Bloomingdale's does not want its users to worry about technology—just to click and use the site. Clinique invites users to its Web site to build a profile of their skin type. It also provides information on skin care and how to use the Internet for saving time and money.[34]

case 8.3

It Takes an iVillage to Start a Trend

The community site iVillage is for women between the ages of twenty-five and forty and allows them to obtain information, engage in chats, and share expertise. The site provides chat rooms, news, and access to experts in different areas of interest to the women's market. IVillage started in 1995, and by 1999 it received more than 3 million unique visitors a month. Each visitor viewed an average of 25.6 pages and stayed at the site an average of 8.5 minutes. By 2001, the number of unique visitors rose to more than 6.5 million a month. The iVillage site faces heavy competition from other sites targeted to the female market, including Women.com (http://www.women.com) and Oxygen (http://www.oxygen.com), as well as specialty women's sites, such as Martha Stewart's (http://www.marthastewart.com).[35]

Source: <http://www.iVillage.com>. Courtesy of iVillage, Inc. © 2002, iVillage Inc. All rights reserved. iVillage and iVillage logo are trademarks of iVillage, Inc.

▶ Thinking Strategically: Case 8.3

Visit the iVillage site (http://www.ivillage.com). Do you think this site is too general or has too broad an appeal to entice individuals to return? Visit the competitive sites Women.com (http://www.women.com) and Oxygen (http://www.oxygen.com). How do these sites differ from iVillage? Identify some specific interests that women may have. Search the Internet for Web sites that provide support for those narrower interests. Speculate on the future of iVillage.

Children and Youth Markets

The year 2000 census data indicate that 90 percent of U.S. children had Internet access at school or home. The Internet has become the primary means of communication for young people. A study found that 81 percent of teens between twelve and seventeen used e-mail, and 70 percent used instant messaging. For older teens (eighteen to nineteen), these percentages were even higher, at 91 and 83 percent respectively. The Internet is a primary source of information about school, current events, digital music, and games. In 2000, teenagers spent $483 million online. By 2005, this number is expected to reach $10.6 billion.[36]

Both special interest and portal sites target kids and teens. Media companies such as Disney (http://www.disney.com), Fox TV (http://www.foxkids.com), and Nickelodeon (http://www.nick.com) have set up sites to entertain and promote other products and services offered by these companies. Yahoo! offers a Yahooligans (http://www.yahooligans.com) search for children to find kid-friendly sites. MaMa-Media (http://www.mamamedia.com) allows children to surf kid-friendly sites, play games, and personalize a Web page.

There are a number of safety issues related to minors. The Web can allow access to pornographic, violent, or suggestive material. Parents and advertisers are concerned about issues surrounding manipulative advertising; advertising on children's TV shows is highly regulated through governmental and industry policies. Despite these concerns, a number of firms are targeting the youth market.[37]

The Market for Pornography

Many sites on the Internet contain **pornography**. This is a concern for many individuals, families, and civil libertarians. The Communications Decency Act made it illegal to knowingly transmit electronically to a minor (a person under the age of eighteen) any comment, request, suggestion, proposal, image, or other communication that is obscene or indecent. The fines were to be $200,000, with jail terms of two years for violators. Within hours of the bill being signed, the American Civil Liberties Union and sixteen other organizations filed a lawsuit to fight the bill. A three-judge panel struck down the bill as unconstitutionally vague.

The U.S. government's attempt to censor the flow of information over the Internet through the Communications Decency Act ran head-on into the First Amendment to the U.S. Constitution. The act also had a practical problem: It would have been very difficult to enforce across national boundaries. A number of countries have shifted the burden of censoring the Internet to local ISPs. Even in the United States, two ISPs have had their news servers seized by state police because hosted news groups were sending pictures of child pornography.[38] This shifts the burden of filtering information access from the individual or family to a third party. **Filters** can be used on a PC or server to block access to sites considered pornographic. One type of filtering software uses a database of sites deemed unacceptable by a parent or business. Other software filters use rating systems to allow acceptable pages to pass through; this can be a problem because only a small percentage of all Web pages have been rated. Filters may be a poor substitute for parental control. Over half of the parents in the United States believe that they should monitor their children's Internet use.[39]

Pornography exists online when material depicts erotic behavior intended to cause sexual excitement.

A software filter blocks unwanted material, such as pornography, from being downloaded from the Internet.

Niche Markets

Niche sites are designed to target some aspect of a market's psychographic profile by focusing on narrow activities and interests. The ability to tailor information and to target these narrow markets makes the Web an ideal medium to develop niche communities.

Sports sites offer enthusiasts the ability to interact with their favorite sports leagues or teams, including not only national sports but also local sports. In 1998, ESPN's Web site (http://www.espn.com) received more than 16.9 million unique visitors. Visitors can follow major teams or link to sites that cover tennis, hockey, soccer, or other sports.[40] Companies are developing strategies around these narrow niche sports. Skateboarding.com (http://www.skateboarding.com) developed a site covering all aspects of skateboarding. This site includes photos, videos, a buyer's guide, chat, message boards, and other content.[41]

The over-fifty user market is expected to exceed 115 million people in the United States over the next twenty-five years. This Internet-user segment is one of the fastest growing, and it purchases online at rates higher than those of other segments. In 2001, more than 51 percent of U.S. adults between the ages of fifty and sixty-four had Internet access. The main uses of the Internet for this segment are e-mail, research, game playing, and investment. Of this group, 92 percent had window-shopped online, and 78 percent had made online purchases. For those sixty-five and over, 15 percent had access to and see the Internet as a means of improving their lives with the ability to connect to others online.[42] Marketers have started to see this segment as an important growth market. The AARP (http://www.aarp.org) and ThirdAge (http://www.thirdage.com) are Web sites for this mature market. They offer information, guides, support, and shopping targeted to this growing market.[43]

Many Web sites aim at very narrow communities. Web sites for TV shows such as *The Drew Carey Show,* rock groups such as the Rolling Stones, support groups for diseases, and many others offer unique benefits to their users. As these communities become more widely known, they help to expand the reach of the Internet.

The Development of Online Communities

Online communities are created not only for target markets within the general population but also for extranet communities within vertical industries and intranet communities within organizations. A study identified seven key principles that are critical for successful online community development; these are outlined in Table 8.4.[44]

The Effect of Virtual Communities on Society

Sociologist Sherry Turkle argues that the Web is redefining our sense of community. The Web is a medium that allows individuals to explore different sides of their personalities by adopting online personas. Persons can communicate globally but are forming "local" communities with individuals who share targeted interests. They are also tinkering with technology and integrating it into their

Table 8.4   Seven Principles of Success for Online Communities

Principle	Action
Focus on Design	Find activities and designs that will increase the target market's participation in the site.
Focus on the Needs of the Members	Design the site around the needs of members, such as the work they do, the hobbies they have, or the interests they share. Use individuals from the community to help in the design.
Do Not Attempt to Control	Do not attempt to control the flow of information; this may drive users away. Suggest guidelines instead, or offer open free forums along with controlled forums.
Do Not Assume the Forum Is Self-Sustaining	Designate a champion of the site to keep it up-to-date and vibrant.
Evaluate the Community's Culture	Consider how the targeted community exchanges information; a community that shares information will require a different site from one that likes to receive but not give information.
Allow Communication Growth Outside of Local Discussions	Facilitate any growth in communication or interaction directly on the site. Use tools such as e-mail, discussion lists, and buddy lists.
Use Facilitators	Find and support members who can act as facilitators to encourage others to visit, lead discussions, provoke controversy, and raise issues.

Sources: Minda Zetlin, "Creators of Online Community," *Computerworld,* October 29, 2001, 34–35; Daintry Duffy, "The Seven Principles of Community Success," *CIO Enterprise,* October 15, 1999, 38.

lives.[45] Web communities and Web use has also been criticized, however. A study funded by the National Science Foundation through Carnegie-Mellon University found that using the Internet had a weak but significant relationship to feelings of social isolation, depression, and loneliness. The results of this one study have been disputed, and further research is recommended.

Cross-Cultural Acceptance

Alexis de Tocqueville visited the United States in the 1830s and noticed that Americans were building sailing ships of much poorer quality than those built in Europe. When he inquired as to the reason, he found a logical explanation. The American builders realized that sailing technology was changing so quickly that it did not make sense to build a boat to last any longer than the technology would be current. To do so would be a waste of resources; it would also lock the owner into technology that would be out-of-date but too expensive to get rid of. What Tocqueville realized was that American society was willing to let go of past practices and accept innovations in products and processes.

Acceptance of the Internet as a communication and commerce tool is dependent on the infrastructure in place for the transport of high-bandwidth data, as outlined in Chapter 2. For Web use, individuals must have access to the Internet through computers or some other device. Businesses and the people of a country must also be willing to develop content and use Internet services. This is somewhat dependent on a culture's willingness to abandon old practices and accept new ones.

Lionel Dersot, a French national living in Japan, has noted that the Japanese do not readily accept the Web as a communication medium. This is in part due to the low level of computer penetration in Japan (only 15 percent of homes) and a cumbersome telephone system. Dersot also sees the lack of acceptance as related to the nature of Japanese culture: Japanese do not readily express their opinions to others. The Internet is, at its heart, a communication medium. The Japanese desire for consensus restricts discussion, argument, and debate, limiting the Internet's usefulness as a tool.[46]

Figure 8.11   Web Page Languages by Percentage

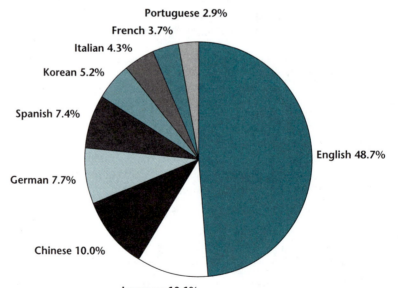

Source: "Global Reach: English Losing Dominance on the Web," in NUA [online] (January 23, 2002), available from <http://www.nua.com/surveys/index.cgi?f= VS&art_id=905357584&rel=true>.

Acceptance of the Internet varies across countries. English is still the major language of the Internet, as shown in Figure 8.11, but other languages are increasing in use as more users around the world go online.

Figure 8.12 indicates that the growth of the Internet has been concentrated in North America, Japan, urban areas in the Asia-Pacific region, and some European countries. Practices such as Internet use and e-commerce are dependent on the technological infrastructure of a country and the willingness of its people to change behaviors. In countries with few PCs and limited or expensive Internet access, citizens may not have had a chance to gain experience with technology or the Internet.

Each culture determines its acceptance of technological change. Countries that are laggards in the acceptance of Internet-based technologies will not face the disruption caused by these new communication tools. They are also less likely, however, to receive the benefits of open communication and more efficient business markets. A study by David Altig and Peter Rupert found a significant relationship between Internet use and economic growth. The relationship indicates that 100 percent Internet usage would be associated with 4 percent economic growth. The researchers concluded that the adoption of the Internet actually measures a society's willingness to adopt technological innovations. Some societies have reduced the structural barriers to adoption by deregulation and the fostering of Internet connections. A society's willingness to accept technological innovations results in higher growth rates.[47]

Figure 8.12   Use of the Internet in the Past Thirty Days

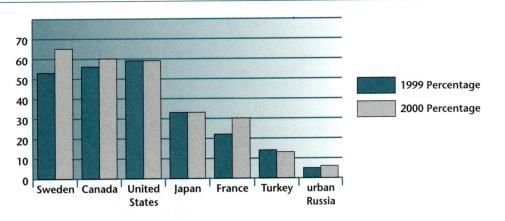

Source: Michael Pastore, "U.S. Share of Internet Users Continues to Shrink, 'Hypergrowth' Over," in CyberAtlas [online] (May 21, 2001), available from <http://cyberatlas.internet.com/big_picture/geographics/article/0,,5911_769451,00.html>.

Diffusion and the Adoption Process in a Firm

....

"I should change my title from CIO to technology personal trainer: I drag these guys kicking and screaming into the future and cause them a lot of agony along the way. But later on, when they look in the mirror, they like the results."

Ken Landis
CIO, Strong Capital Management, at an *InformationWeek*
Conference in 1998[48]

....

In 1876, the Western Union Telegraph Company refused to purchase the rights to the telephone. It could justify this by presuming that it did not make sense to replace a proven system with new technology. Western Union could not understand why telegraph operators would want to talk to each other to relay messages. Western Union did not envision placing the telephone in an individual's home. Other managers were more innovative. A vice president of AT&T envisioned sending music over phone lines into people's homes; this idea was proposed in 1890.[49]

Businesses must evolve in order to adapt to changes in the environment. New ideas must be brought into an organization. These ideas could be for new products, new business models, or new work-flows. The diffusion and adoption process outlined in this chapter is a model for the spread of new ideas and processes inside a firm. Just as individual consumers accept new products at differing rates, so do individuals inside a firm. When new business processes are introduced, they must offer substantial cost savings, time savings, or competitive advantages to justify changes to fundamental business practices. Change is disruptive. This can be frustrating for individuals who want to introduce new ideas. These individuals are the innovators, or intrapreneurs, inside an organization. The diffusion of innovations theory is very helpful in understanding how these individuals can implement change in the organization. The following sections will outline the considerations involved in the diffusion process inside a firm and discuss actions that change agents can take to implement new ideas and processes.

Historical nSite

Hindsight Is 20/20

"This 'telephone' has too many shortcomings to be seriously considered as a means of communication. The device is inherently of no value to us."
Western Union
Internal Memo, 1876

"Everything that can be invented has been invented."
Charles H. Duell
U.S. Commissioner of Patents, 1899

"The wireless music box has no imaginable commercial value. Who would pay for a message sent to nobody in particular?"
David Sarnoff's Associates
In response to his urgings for investments in the radio in the 1920s

"Who the hell wants to hear actors talk?"
H. M. Warner
Warner Brothers, 1927

Intrapreneurs

Intrapreneurs are **change agents** with entrepreneurial and leadership traits who act within existing firms by building coalitions and managing workers in innovative tasks. Intrapreneurial behavior occurs in existing companies when someone introduces new products or new ideas that allow the company as a whole to grow.[50] Intrapreneurs work well in innovative organizational cultures, are willing to change, and are often willing to operate as product or idea **champions.** This means they are willing to work with new ideas and to implement change.[51]

Intrapreneurial individuals are more likely to have outside contacts and an outward focus, and they bring outside ideas into the firm. They have personality traits such as innovativeness, a risk-taking propensity, and a proactive orientation.[52] Intrapreneurs may not attempt to act on new ideas unless there is a supportive atmosphere inside the firm. This can come both from a supportive management that stays out of the innovator's way and from an organic organizational culture that allows for the growth of new ideas. Figure 8.13 illustrates the interaction that must exist between an innovator and a firm in order for the individual to pursue a market opportunity.

*An idea or product **champion** is an individual inside an organization who acts as an advocate for an innovation.*

Communication and Coalition Building

Innovators who attempt to introduce new ideas too quickly into a firm are likely to face rejection. This has a tendency to force innovative individuals out of bureaucratic firms. To gain acceptance of new ideas, the innovator should keep in mind the adoption process discussed earlier in this chapter. As the product champion, the innovator should first communicate with the early adopters in the firm who will be supportive of a new idea. Once a coalition has developed, that core group can expand the idea and gain support throughout the organization. The

Figure 8.13 Interaction between an Innovator and a Firm

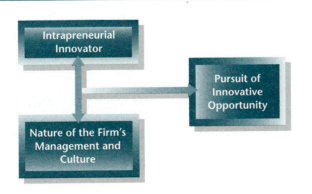

innovator acts as a change agent by developing this coalition of key participants, who could be marketing managers, R&D managers, or other management personnel. As these individuals refine and support the idea, they can then communicate to other managers and decision makers, spreading the idea throughout the organization.[53]

The rate at which the communication spreads inside an organization is dependent on the culture of the business. Businesses that are more entrepreneurial than bureaucratic will have a more rapid rate of communication. A key to implementing change is support by top management. As leaders of an organization, management sets the strategic direction for the firm. These issues of leadership and culture will be explored more in Chapter 10.

Industry Leaders and Laggards

Consumers are learning to adopt Internet technologies by starting with Web-based research and e-mail and then moving toward making purchases online. As businesses transform through the use of technology, they are also moving from information-based Internet use to business process restructuring. Companies that lead in new technology adoption are more likely to see that they can gain competitive advantages through new products and have reported financial gains from using leading-edge technologies.[54]

Knowledge Integration

Terms and Concepts

Adoption curve *233*
Champion *247*
Change agent *247*
Cityscapes *231*
Compatibility *228*
Complexity *228*
Continuous
   innovation *226*
Diffusion of innovations
   process *223*
Discontinuous
   innovation *226*

Dynamically continuous
   innovation *226*
Early adopter *236*
Early majority *236*
Economic utility *229*
E-fluentials *236*
Filter *241*
Hyperbolic tree *231*
I Generation *241*
Innovation *224*
Innovator *234*
Interface *230*

Intrapreneur *247*
Killer application
   (killer app) *230*
Laggard *236*
Late majority *236*
Luddite *236*
Mental model *230*
Metaphor *230*
Netizen *238*
Niche sites *241*
Nonadopter *236*
Observability *228*

Concepts and Questions for Review

1. Why is it important to study the diffusion of innovations process?
2. Describe how the diffusion of innovations model works.
3. Explain the major influences in the diffusion model.
4. Discuss the roles of behavioral and technical change in relation to how innovations are categorized.
5. Recommend how to increase the chances of acceptance for innovations. How do your recommendations relate to the development of Web sites?
6. Justify the use of metaphors in the development of interfaces used on Web sites.
7. Outline a strategy using the adopter categories to speed the adoption of an innovation such as handheld wireless Internet.
8. How can the product life cycle be used to understand the surge and decline of innovations?
9. Define an electronic community and discuss which segmentation techniques are used to target markets with communities.
10. List some of the markets targeted by electronic communities.
11. Recommend a strategy for developing an online community.
12. Which countries are most accepting of Internet technologies, and which are least accepting? Rank them in a list. Why are those countries at the top of the list more accepting than those at the bottom?
13. Describe how the diffusion process works within a firm.
14. Discuss the role of change agents in the diffusion process.
15. How could a change agent build a coalition within a firm?

Active Learning

Exercise 8.1 Innovation Typology

The Internet offers a number of innovations for individuals. Some of these will be discontinuous and others continuous, depending on the markets served. Develop a chart like the one that follows for a number of technologies available on the Internet. Indicate where a target market would perceive the technology to be on the chart and justify why it would be in that spot. Two examples are given. The senior market will probably have little experience with online downloads of music and would have to change behavior to use an MP3 player. The youth market will need little training or behavioral change to take advantage of buddy lists. For a list of the newest Web innovations, see Internet Product Watch at http://ipw .internet.com.

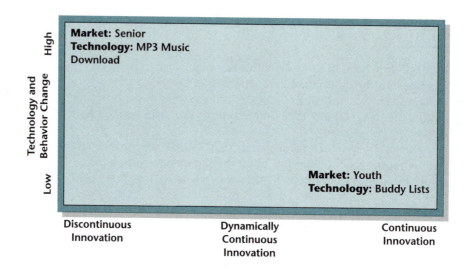

Exercise 8.2 Finding Your Community

There are a number of online communities available on the Internet. Make a list of your favorite activities, interests, and discussion topics. Choose the top two or three and place those terms into a search engine followed by the search term *community*. Explore a number of sites and see if these are designed to meet and hold your interest.

Exercise 8.3 Interface Design

Use the profile you developed in Exercise 8.2 to develop a Web page interface. Draw out the interface using a metaphor that the target market would understand. Justify your design given the experience of the target market. Why would the metaphor be beneficial to the target market?

Exercise 8.4 Intrafirm Diffusion

Consider yourself the designated change agent for introducing an e-business innovation within a firm. Using a business you work in or a group of friends or classmates you interact with, identify the key participants you would first contact. What other key players would be necessary for getting an idea accepted? Determine which e-business innovation you would first like to introduce and which innovations would follow. What arguments would you use to convince others to adopt the innovations?

Competitive Exercise 8.5 Diffusion Strategy

Assume you and your team are developing a strategy to speed the acceptance of a new e-business process or product. Identify a target market. Your team should outline a strategy using the theories in the chapter to gain acceptance. Indicate the nature of the innovation. How can the innovation can be designed to speed acceptance? Develop a process using the adoption curve to influence adoption.

Web Search—Looking Online

Search Term: Internet Diffusion Statistics   First 7 out of 49,000

CommerceNet. Works with Nielson Media Research to provide statistics.
http://www.commerce.net

CyberAtlas. Updates Web use number and profiling data on segments; also includes useful information on Web use and technology.
http://www.cyberatlas.com

GVU's WWW User Surveys. Offers extensive information collected over time on Internet use.
http://www.gvu.gatech.edu/gvu/user_surveys

IDC (International Data Corporation). Sells research reports but also provides some statistics for free.
http://www.idcresearch.com

NUA. Provides international news and information about Web use and markets.
http://www.nua.com

WorldOpinion. Offers news and information related to Web-based research; also provides a list of marketing research sites.
http://www.worldopinion.com

Nielsen/NetRatings. Collects data on international Internet use.
http://www.nielsen-netratings.com/hot_off_the_net_i.jsp

Search Term: Interface Design   First 4 out of 2,690,482

Interface Hall of Shame. Displays common interface design mistakes.
http://www.iarchitect.com/mshame.htm

Webdeveloper.com. Offers articles on Web page design.
http://www.webdeveloper.com

Yale Web Style Guide. Organizes an online style guide for Web page development.
http://info.med.yale.edu/caim/manual/contents.html

Common Front Group. Provides information on interface design.
http://cfg.cit.cornell.edu/cfg/design/contents.html

| Search Term: | Web Community Sites | First 5 out of 21,341,046 |

Microsoft Network. Offers free community development and access to a wide variety of communities.
http://communities.msn.com/people

Tripod. Keeps a well-designed site offering access to many community areas of interest and also offers free home pages and community building.
http://www.tripod.com

Yahoo! Groups. Organizes a number of clubs and community sites and allows individuals to develop their own community site.
http://clubs.yahoo.com

Community Manager. Offers information for online community management.
http://www.communitymanager.net/

Online Community Report. Provides a source of information for online communities.
http://www.onlinecommunityreport.com

References

1 Wayne Rash, "The Business Lessons of the 19th Century Internet," *InternetWeek,* February 7, 2000, 53.
2 Michael Totty, "Yesterday's Choices," *Wall Street Journal,* September 10, 2001, R4.
3 For more information on telecommunications history, see Steven Lumbar, *InfoCulture* (New York: Houghton Mifflin, 1993).
4 "It's Not Just a Phone, It's a Lifestyle," *Mbusiness,* May 2001, 52–53.
5 Mark Halper, "Steve and Jorma Make the Hard Cell," *Fortune,* April 29, 2002, 30.
6 "Quote of the Week," *InformationWeek,* March 31, 2000, 17.
7 Kevin Jones, "Buyer Behavior Is Key to Market Success," *Interactive Week,* September 7, 1998, 37.
8 David F. Midgley, "Patterns of Interpersonal Information Seeking for the Purchase of a Symbolic Product," *Journal of Marketing Research* 20 (February 1983): 74–83; Everett M. Rogers, *Diffusion of Innovations,* 3rd ed. (New York: Free Press, 1983).
9 Hubert Gatignon and Thomas S. Robertson, "A Propositional Inventory for New Diffusion Research," *Journal of Consumer Research,* 11 (March 1985): 849–67.
10 For more on this topic, see Jeff Ubois, "Mass Appeal," *Internet World,* April 1997, 62–70.
11 Rogers, *Diffusion of Innovations,* 281–84.
12 David Batstone and Eric Hellweg, "Cash on the Line, Introducing the Internet Consumer," *Business 2.0,* 1998 premiere issue, 28–29.
13 "Associated Press: End of an Era for the National Postal Service," in NUA [online] (October 21, 1999), available from <http://www.nua.ie/surveys/index.cgi?f=VS&art_id=905355356&rel=true>; "Reuters: Email Now Primary Reason People Go Online," in NUA

[online] (October 1, 1999), available from <http://www.nua.ie/surveys/index.cgi?f=VS&art_id=905355315&rel=true>.

14 Rany Barrett, "E-Mail Address Unknown," *Interactive Week,* October 11, 1999, 64; Sami Kuusela, "The Postman Always Clicks Twice," *Business 2.0,* September 1998, 32–33.

15 Steven Vonder Haar, "Gooey Copycats Get the (Instant) Message," *Interactive Week,* October 18, 1999, 19; Steven Vonder Haar, "Interface of Things to Come," *Interactive Week,* August 30, 1999, 70–72.

16 Joseph C. Panettieri, "PCs Gain Social Skills," *InformationWeek,* July 3, 1995, 32–42; Edward C. Baig, "The Trouble with Bob," *BusinessWeek,* January 30, 1995, 20.

17 Erick Schonfeld, "The Apple Touch," *Business 2.0,* April 2002, 41; Stephen H. Wildstrom, "Where Wintel Fears to Tread," *BusinessWeek,* September 14, 1998, 19.

18 Andrew Marlatt, "When Imitation Works," *Internet World,* October 15, 1999, 60–62; Connie Guglielmo, "If Amazon Ruled the World," *Interactive Week,* October 11, 1999, 45–46.

19 Nancy Dillon, "Can Games Be Training Tools?" *Computerworld,* September 28, 1998, 39–40.

20 Gary H. Anthes, "Hyperbrowsing," *Computerworld,* May 18, 1998, 74; Rich Wiggins, "Flexible XML Redefines the Web," *NewMedia,* March 24, 1998, 19–20; Whit Andrews, "Search Engines Still Chasing Goal of Simplified Interface," *Web Week,* September 15, 1997, 36–37.

21 Martin Dodge, "Fly Through the Web," in *Mappa.Mundi* [online] (May 11, 2002), available from <http://mappa.mundi.net/maps/maps_018/index.html#hotsauce>.

22 Kylen Campbell, "Use It or Lose It," *NewMedia,* July 1998, 72.

23 Information compiled from GVU's 9th WWW User Survey [online] (1996), available from <http://www.cc.gatech.edu/gvu/user_surveys/survey-1998-04/>, note that Georgia Tech updates its survey data on a regular basis; Batstone and Hellweg, "Cash on the Line."

24 Michael Pastore, "Web Influences Offline Purchases, Especially Among Teens," in CyberAtlas [online] (July 18, 2001), available from <http://cyberatlas.internet.com/markets/retailing/article/0,,6061_804141,00.html>.

25 William D. Friel, "Customer Confidence Is Key to E-Commerce," *InternetWeek,* March 23, 1998, 37.

26 David F. Midgley, "A Meta-Analysis of the Diffusion of Innovations Literature," *Advances in Consumer Research* 14 (1987): 204–7.

27 "Taylor Nelson Sofres: User Satisfaction Key to Drawing Regular Visitors," in NUA [online] (May 10 2002), available from <http://www.nua.com/surveys/?f=VS&art_id=905357937&rel=true>.

28 "Roper Starch: Online Opinion Leaders Are Highly Influential," in NUA [online] (June 19, 2000), available from <http://www.nua.com/surveys/index.cgi?f=VS&art_id=905355852&rel=true.

29 "Broadband the Bright Spot in Access Market," in CyberAtlas [online] (February 27, 2002), available from <http://cyberatlas.internet.com/markets/broadband/article/0,,10099_982021,00.html#table>.

30 Jim Cashel, "Community Is a Commodity," *NewMedia,* August 1999, 38–44.

31 Paul Roberts, "Creating E-Communities," *Exec,* October 2001, 14–18.

32 "Monitoring Mothers Online in the U.S.," in eMarketer [online] (May 8, 2002), available from <http://www.emarketer.com/estatnews/estats/edemographics/20020508_aol.html>.

33 Karen Epper Hoffman, "Women's Sites Benefit as Face of Web Changes," *Internet World,* September 28, 1998, 1, 49.

[34] James C. Luh, "How Bloomingdale's Aims to Enrich Online Shopping," *Internet World,* August 24, 1998, 27–29; Kathleen Murphy, "Undaunted by Obstacles, Cosmetics Firms Step into the Internet Fray," *Web Week,* February 1996, 20; Maricris G. Briones, "On-Line Retailers Seek Ways to Close Shopping Gender Gap," *Marketing News,* September 14, 1998, 2, 10.

[35] Richard Siklos, "Weaving Yet Another Web for Women," *BusinessWeek,* January 17, 2000, 101; Susan Karlin, "It Takes an IVillage," *Upside,* January 1999, 48–50; Lisa Hamm-Greenawalt, "Women's Sites Understand Community," *Internet World,* September 15, 1999, 56–59.

[36] Michael Pastore, "Internet Key to Communication Among Youth," in CyberAtlas [online] (January 25, 2002), available from <http://cyberatlas.internet.com/big_picture/demographics/article/0,,5901_961881,00.html>; Michael Pastore, "New Payment Options Will Open E-Commerce to Teens," in CyberAtlas [online] (September 7, 2001), available from <http://cyberatlas.internet.com/markets/retailing/article/0,,6061_880271,00.html>.

[37] "Nua Ltd: Meeting Generation Y," in NUA [online] (July 19, 1999), available from <http://www.nua.ie/surveys/index.cgi?f=VS&art_id=905355157&rel=true>; Barbara Grady, "Kid's Market Slow to Emerge as Safety Concerns Linger," *Web Week,* November 10, 1997, 4.

[38] Randy Barrett, "Porn Raid Leaves ISPs in Bind," *Interactive Week,* November 9, 1998, 38.

[39] For more information, see Kevin Reichard, "Is Your Web Site PG—or X?" *Internet World,* November 1997, 108–10; Gus Venditto, "Safe Computing," *Internet World,* September 1996, 48–58.

[40] Karen Epper Hoffman, "Sports Sites Beef Up Content to Lure Fans," *Internet World,* September 14, 1998, 8.

[41] Whit Andrews, "Sports Marketing Firm Targets Niches, Not Stadium Crowds," *Internet World,* May 4, 1998, 50; Elizabeth Gardner, "Joining Forces to Serve a Niche," *Internet World,* June 15, 1998, 17, 20; David R. Noack, "The Sporting World," *Internet World,* August 1996, 48–52.

[42] "Seniors Act Just Like Everyone Else, Online," in eMarketer [online] (September 11, 2001), available from <http://www.emarketer.com/estatnews/estats/edemographics/20010911_pew.html>.

[43] "Greenfield Online: 78 Percent of Senior Users Buy Online," in NUA [online] (September 2, 1999), available from <http://www.nua.ie/surveys/index.cgi?f=VS&art_id=905355250&rel=true>; Barb Cole-Gomolski, "Selling to Seniors," *Computerworld,* May 24, 1999, 58–59; "PR Newswire: Rising Number of Over 50s Online," in NUA [online] (October 22, 1998), available from <http://www.nua.ie/surveys/index.cgi?f=VS&art_id=905354444&rel=true>; "ActivMedia Research: Older Netizens Say WWW Improves Relationships," in NUA [online] (March 26, 1998), available from <http://www.nua.ie/surveys/index.cgi?f=VS&art_id=890934382&rel=true>; Susan Moran, "Baby Boomers Are the Target of a Different Kind of 'Adult' Site," *Web Week,* July 7, 1997, 16.

[44] Daintry Duffy, "It Takes an E-Village," *CIO Enterprise,* October 15, 1999, 32–46.

[45] Paul C. Judge, "Is the Net Redefining Our Identity?" *Business Week,* May 12, 1997, 100–102.

[46] Lionel Dersot, "Letter from Japan, Where 'Net Adoption Lags," *Computerworld,* September 28, 1998, 33.

[47] David Altig and Peter Rupert, "Growth and the Internet: Surfing to Prosperity?" *Economic Commentary: Federal Reserve Bank of Cleveland,* September 1, 1999.

[48] "Quote of the Week," *InformationWeek,* September 21, 1998, 14.

[49] Steven Lumbar, *InfoCulture* (New York: Houghton Mifflin, 1993).

[50] For more information, see Gifford Pinchott, *Intrapreneuring,* (New York: Harper & Row, 1986); Robert D. Hisrich and Michael Peters, "Establishing a New Business Venture Unit Within a Firm," *Journal of Business Venturing* 1, no. 3 (1986): 307–322.

[51] Raymond E. Miles and Charles C. Snow, *Organizational Strategy, Structure, and Process* (New York: McGraw-Hill, 1978); Michael D. Hutt, Peter H. Reingen, and John R. Ronchetto Jr., "Tracing Emergent Processes in Marketing Strategy Formation," *Journal of Marketing* 52 (January 1988): 4–19.

[52] Danny Miller, "The Correlates of Entrepreneurship in Three Types of Firms," *Management Science* 29 (July 1983): 770–91; Michael Morris and Duane Davis, "Attitudes toward Corporate Entrepreneurship: Marketers versus Non-Marketers," in *Research at the Marketing/Entrepreneurship Interface,* ed. G. E. Hills, R. W. LaForge, and B. J. Parker (Chicago: American Marketing Association, 1989): 33–45.

[53] For more on this process, see Hutt, Reingen, and Ronchetto Jr., "Tracing Emergent Processes in Marketing Strategy Formation."

[54] Rusty Weston, "The Techno-Adoption Curve," *InformationWeek,* August 23, 1999, 109; Rick Whiting and Beth Davis, "More on the Edge," *InformationWeek,* August 23, 1999, 36–48.

chapter 9
Information Collection and Use

In today's highly competitive environment, information has become a tool to gain competitive advantages. E-businesses use systematic means of collecting, storing, and analyzing data to better understand their customers, to lower the costs of running the business, and to create a base of organizational knowledge that can be used to develop strategies to enhance competitiveness. E-business marketers and managers must understand how to use electronic information to develop and maintain competitive advantages.

1. Describe how businesses are using data to gain competitive advantages.
2. Show the flow of data in a marketing information system.
3. List the sources of information for a business.
4. Explain how a business uses information to discover new knowledge.
5. Describe the role that databases play in organizational knowledge.
6. Explain how a business can incorporate organizational knowledge into its decision-making process.
7. Discuss why privacy on the Internet is an issue and what e-businesses can do to ensure privacy.

What's Old Is New Again

The financial services industry, including banks and brokerage businesses, has been the focus of much consumer outrage. Laws have been passed in some California cities making it illegal for banks to charge for ATM services. As a result, bank customers are blocked from using automatic teller machines not owned by banks where they are members. In addition, some bank customers have been subject to additional charges if they want to use live tellers at their own banks. It almost seems that banks do not want customers.

The banking industry has been mining data on customers in an attempt to learn how to increase overall profits. Banks are using databases of customer information to determine how customers will react to changes in interest rates. They can pinpoint the customers who are likely to accept new products, who are likely to default on loans, and who are most profitable. The Bank of America (http://www.bankofamerica.com) service center uses its database to develop profiles of customers to cross-sell new products. Banks mine terabyte sized customer knowledge databases to determine the profitability of households and to project the lifetime value of customers. The Royal Bank of Canada uses data modeling to segment 10 million customers according to their credit risk, future profitability, life cycle stage, likelihood of leaving, and other factors. Banks are also creating multiple terabyte databases to analyze customer data for sales and marketing. In the banking industry, different customers may receive different levels of service.[1]

In its search for profitable customers, one bank found that 10 percent of its customers incurred 90 percent of the ATM costs, and 80 percent of those customers were of low value to the bank. The bank did not drop these customers, however; the data showed that 30 percent of the low-value customers were college students who could be turned into higher-value customers if they remained loyal to the bank.[2]

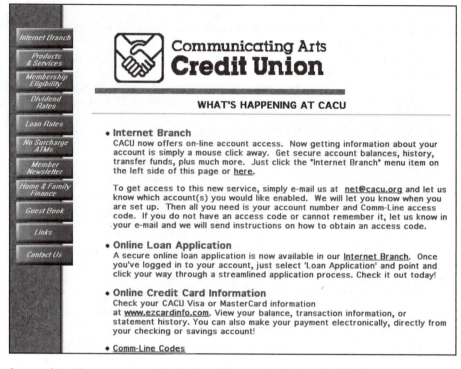

Source: <http://www.cacu.org>. Permission of Communicating Arts Credit Union.

▶ Thinking Strategically

Determine the importance of customer data in increasing the profitability of a bank. How can a bank justify charging its own customers to use live tellers? Consider whether a bank should provide free customer service as a community service. How would customers feel if they knew their bank tracked individual behaviors? Determine how customers could benefit from a bank's knowledge of their behavior.

....

"One ignorant of the plans of neighboring states cannot prepare alliances in good time; if ignorant of the conditions of mountains, forests, dangerous defiles, swamps, and marshes, he cannot conduct the march of an army; if he fails to make use of native guides, he cannot gain the advantages of the ground. A general ignorant of even one of these three matters is unfit to command the armies of a king."

Sun Tzu
The Art of War, 500 B.C., translated by Samuel B. Griffith[3]

....

"Close to 75 percent of CEOs use Internet technologies to scan business, economic, and industry news."

John Fontana,
InternetWeek[4]

Managers use information to make decisions; the higher the quality of the information, the better the decision. E-businesses are continuously collecting information from both external and internal sources. This information then becomes the collective knowledge of a company. Companies are gathering massive amounts of data. One study estimated that more data would be collected between the years 2002 and 2005 than has been collected since the dawn of civilization. The vast majority of these data are not used; more than 95 percent of the data that companies collect are never analyzed.[5] E-businesses are adapting a variety of techniques to enhance the process of knowledge creation and to use this information to gain competitive advantages.[6]

Data (raw facts that can become meaningful **information**) are collected from numerous sources such as daily transactions, Web site usage, and third-party databases. Data stored in **databases** are mined to transform the data into information for improving managerial decisions. For example, Best Buy (http://www.bestbuy.com) maintains a database of more than 1.6 terabytes from 250 different sources, including 330 million new records per day. Best Buy has transformed its business model around the use of data. It uses the information for new product launches, store design, inventory ordering, and almost all other aspects of its business.[7]

One-to-one marketing is not the only goal of database marketing. Companies are also using knowledge gained to lower costs by targeting customers who have the highest profit potential. Database marketing is still in the early stages of its life cycle, and its full potential has not yet been reached.[8] A number of businesses are successfully using new techniques in **data warehousing** and **data mining** to gain insights and improve customer relations. Companies as varied as General Motors (http://www.gm.com), Seagram (http://www.seagram.com), Philip Morris (http://www.philipmorris.com), and Harley-Davidson (http://www.harley-davidson.com) are using database marketing techniques to strengthen their relationships with customers and block competitors.[9]

Data *are raw facts.* **Information** *is constructed from facts, gives meaning to phenomena, and allows managers to make decisions.*

Data mining *is the process of using software to "drill" into a database to obtain meaningful information.*

Strategic nSite

Data warehouses are computer systems (hardware and software) designed to process large amounts of data held in databases. Many databases process tens of terabytes (trillions of bytes) of information. A terabyte of data can hold

▶ a 100-byte record for every person on earth
▶ 1 billion business letters, or
▶ 10 million MPEG images, or enough video to run for ten days and nights.

By 2007, businesses will amass petabytes (1,000 terabytes, or more than 1,000,000,000,000,000 bytes) of data. A petabyte is the equivalent of

▶ more than 250 billion pages of text, or
▶ the data contained in a 2,000-mile-high tower of 1 billion diskettes.[10]

Databases act as repositories of organizational memory, allowing firms to engage in information-based competition and possibly obtain substantial advantages over competitors. To gain these advantages, a business needs to structure a formal information-gathering system called a **marketing information system (MIS).** An MIS should be designed to collect data and provide meaningful information. There are three major categories of data that marketers collect: data related to marketing-mix elements (the effects of product, price, promotion, and place decisions), data on the behavior of individual buyers and prospects, and data from environmental scanning.[11]

Implementing an MIS requires obtaining data from internal as well as external sources. As the repository of organizational knowledge, a database becomes the hub of a business operation, providing information to managers and controlling and coordinating business operations. Figure 9.1 illustrates the major flows of data and information in a marketing information system.

Figure 9.1 shows that data for decision making come from three major sources. First, a business can get data from the firm's customers or market. These data can be gathered from customer transactions or through a marketing research process. Secondly, competitive intelligence comes from internal and external sources. A business's personnel, such as its sales force, can return information on the competitive environment. The process of environmental scanning allows managers to keep track of competitors and environmental trends to aid in strategic decision making. Environmental scanning information can come from government

Figure 9.1   Flows in a Marketing Information System

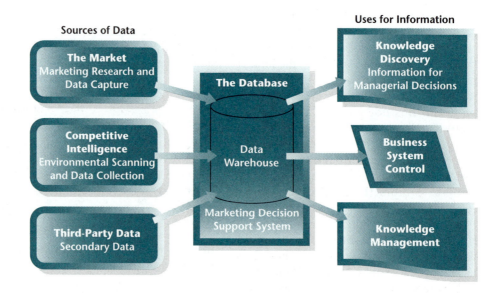

sources, industry sources, or careful observations of media articles and competitive firm behavior. Third, businesses can purchase third-party data from sources external to a business. Many companies and institutions collect information on their customers and then sell that data to firms that specialize in the collection and storage of data. These firms, in turn, sell the compiled data to interested parties.

Data mining techniques are used to extract information from data warehouses for managerial decisions. Specialized software is used to develop **marketing decision support systems (MDSS)** to provide information for developing marketing strategies. A firm's database can also be used as a hub to control the entire business by facilitating the mass customization process, aiding sales force automation, providing information for managers, and fostering knowledge organizations. The development of database warehouses is so vital that it is now considered the number one information technology priority for many businesses.[12] This chapter will cover each aspect of the marketing information system and how it affects the marketing process.

Strategic nSite

Databases

A database is a structured storage of data consisting of fields and records. A field is a column of data related to a single attribute or variable. A record is a collection of fields that represent a single case, such as the profile of an individual. The table here shows fields of information for two records.

	Field 1 (Last Name)	Field 2 (Income)	Field 4 (Gender)	Field 5 . . . (Purchase Behavior)	Field N (Psychographics)
Record 1	Jones	$50,000	Male	Product X Purchased 11/09/99	Tennis
Record 2	Smith	$54,000	Female	Product Z Purchased 09/16/98	Scuba diving

Gathering Data from the Market

The goal of data collection is to obtain the information necessary to develop and maintain relationships with customers. This goal can be achieved when marketers understand the wants and needs of their customers. There are three ways of obtaining that information from the market. The first is to collect data on a customer's behavior through the recording of transaction data, which can be done by employees, point-of-sale scanners, and electronic recording devices such as Web-tracking software. The gathered information can include transaction-based data, customer-profile data, or more complex behavioral data. A second method of collecting data is to keep track of customers' complaints or questions. These customer inquiries can be used to spot product defects or improve communication. This type of information can be recorded from a Web site or logged by telephone service operators. A third method is to collect primary data directly from the market through marketing research. We will explore each of these techniques.

Peapod uses databases to profile its customers.
Source: <http://www.peapod.com>.

Customer Behavior

Many retailers track customer activity by using **scanner data** to help determine shoppers' profiles, allowing for a market-of-one strategy. In 1998, close to 30 percent of grocery stores used card-based programs to track customers' purchases. When customers use a discount card, their identity is matched with a record of their past purchases, and the scanner records new purchases. This allows the grocer to target the needs of heavy users. For some grocery stores, the highest-spending 50 percent of shoppers can account for 90 percent of sales. These data also allow the grocery store to save on costs. For example, advertisements do not need to be sent to a mass market; they can be targeted only to the store's users. The data these grocery stores collect allow them to target products to their customers and avoid engaging in direct competition with other grocers.[13]

The British grocery chain Tesco (http://www.tesco.com) started a loyalty card system in 1994. By 2001, Tesco recorded over 200 million product purchases per day. These data are linked to customer profiles to determine who buys what, when. This information is used to improve inventory management, product selection, pricing strategies, discounting, promotion, and store layouts. Tesco has benefited from an increase in turnover of more than 50 percent and same-store sales increases from 3 to 6 percent. The company has identified more than five thousand needs segments, and it customizes individual statements, coupons, and a quarterly magazine. Tesco also uses these data to identify which products drive customers to stores, so when competitors discount products, Tesco is not forced into price competition.[14]

Web analytics are the measures used to understand Web site visitor patterns. These measures include clickstream analysis, transaction recording, and relationship tracking. **Clickstream analysis** allows Web sites to monitor individual site use, such as referral location (where the individual linked from), surfing paths, and time spent at a site. This information can be made even more valuable when behavior is matched to visitor registration information. Businesses often give incentives to obtain names, e-mail addresses, demographics, vocations, hobbies, and psychographics. Business professionals often fill out in-depth data forms for free subscriptions to trade journals.[15]

► Thinking Strategically:
Case 9.1

Describe how casinos track customers. What types of data would casinos want to collect to identify high-value customers? Speculate on the use of those data. Should casinos use gaming information to entice customers to return? Evaluate the competitive advantages that a casino would gain by having access to these behavioral data.

Customer Inquiries

Many businesses use software to track consumers' complaints. Telephone service personnel can type consumers' concerns into computers, where software looks for patterns in the text. Information on patterns of inquiries can then be provided to management for action. Whirlpool (http://www.whirlpool.com) uses customer-tracking software to notify owners of its washing machines about potential problems. It also uses the data to identify defective parts, allowing Whirlpool to repair problems. Otis Elevator (http://www.otis.com) receives over 600,000 calls per year requesting unscheduled repair service. This information is used to develop repair histories of elevators and identify possible design problems.[19]

Marketing Research

Marketing research is the systematic and objective process of generating data for making marketing decisions. Using the Internet for **online research** offers many advantages over traditional methods; data can be collected in a much shorter time and at a lower cost. JCPenney had 417 women evaluate sixty swimsuits online and paid

case 9.1

Playing for Keeps

The gaming industry is very competitive because individuals can choose from numerous options, including various cities, riverboats, and online sites. Casinos around the world are using information to gain competitive advantages. Research has shown that customers who return to a gambling resort will spend over 300 percent more than walk-in customers. To encourage return visits, casino hotels have customers fill out lengthy data forms when they check in to the hotel or sign up for gaming cards. These customers are then given magnetic cards that can be used to play at slot machines or gaming tables. Customer data are collected both electronically and by service personnel to develop customer profiles, allowing targeted marketing incentives. The more customers interact with the casino, the more incentives they receive. Customers also receive personalized newsletters sent to their homes, offering further incentives if they return to the casino.[16] Harrah's, for example, uses its database to rank customers into differing levels of profitability, provide specialized services, and engage in personalized contact.[17]

The hospitality industry also tracks user information and collects it into databases to strengthen relationships with customers. Ritz-Carlton hotels collect information from all service employees to develop databases of customers' desires. If a maid notices that a client has tennis equipment in the room, a note is made to be sure to place tennis magazines in the room when that client visits again. This allows the hotel to offer personalized service even to the point of knowing who likes the bed turned down and who does not want a mint on the pillow.[18]

Strategic nSite

Visitor Registration Information

Web developers suggest that visitors not be asked to register until they are ready to take some type of action, such as making a purchase. In addition, the more questions asked, the less likely the questions will be answered.

one-third the cost of regular survey-based research. Studies have found that using the Internet can cut research time in half and cut costs by as much as 80 percent. Errors from data collection can also be minimized. Avon found that its online research did a better job of predicting sales than did traditional research methods. Procter & Gamble found that online surveys were completed 75 percent faster over the Web at half the cost of traditional methods.[20]

There are problems with using the Internet for data collection, however. The major limitation is that Internet users do not represent a random sample of the overall population. If a research problem specifies individuals who match the profile of typical Web users, then the Web can be a very good research tool. Web users are attractive to some researchers because they represent the higher-income, heavy users of some product categories. The profile of Internet users is beginning to match the profile of the general population, making online research a more viable option for data collection.[21]

Table 9.1 outlines the research process and indicates the advantages and disadvantages of using the Internet for data collection.

Online Surveys

A number of companies have developed software that enables them to place surveys online and then aids in the analysis of results. This software allows a researcher to develop questions using categorical (e.g., choose a, b, or c) or metric (e.g., rank from 1 to 7) measures. The questionnaire can then be sent out through e-mail systems or placed on a Web site that returns CGI script. Common gateway interface (CGI) script is an Internet protocol that allows data to be sent back and forth between a user-completed Web form and a Web server. As the data are returned to the server, they are automatically analyzed, reports are generated, and charts are developed to aid in management decision making.[22]

Online Focus Groups

Traditional **focus groups** are a means of collecting a rich set of responses from a target audience. The focus group uses a moderator who works with eight to fifteen individuals discussing open-ended questions to investigate a topic of interest. The ability to have face-to-face interactions with focus group participants allows a deeper understanding of consumers' thoughts and decision-making processes.

Two types of focus groups can be established online: ongoing groups and real-time chat groups. **Ongoing focus groups** use forums or message boards to discuss the research topic. These can last for days or weeks, giving respondents time to think about their responses. The panel moderator posts questions to the focus group. The moderator or participants can post follow-up questions to obtain deeper levels of meaning.

Real-time chat groups allow several focus group members to interact online at the same time and have real-time discussions. Moderators control the focus group by using password-protected rooms where they can kick out unruly respondents.

Table 9.1 Marketing Research Steps

Step	Description	Application over the Internet
1. Problem Definition	Identify problem and develop research objectives.	Web-based research requires that the problem be related to a universe of Web users, which may represent a sample of heavy product users.
2. Research Design	Collect secondary research (previously collected data). Determine use of qualitative data (such as focus groups) or quantitative data (such as surveys, experiments, etc.).	The Web offers easy access to secondary research. Web-based research allows both qualitative and quantitative data collection, and it can include pictures, links to other Web sites, or interactive components.
3. Sample Selection	Identify sample to be used. Determine if a random or nonrandom sample should be used.	The Web allows the desired sample to find the site and answer questions at a low cost. This limits the randomness of the sample selection and may introduce a self-selection bias. Online panels can use databases to select qualified individuals for research subjects.
4. Data Collection (Primary)	Determine how the data will be collected—in person, over the phone, by mail, or via some other method. Try to control errors in data collection and data entry.	Web-based research can help limit interviewer errors. Logic checks can be built into the survey to limit contradictory or nonsensical answers. Randomizing the presentation of items can eliminate order bias.
5. Data Analysis	Determine the analysis methods to be used. Data analysis is undertaken after data is collected.	Automated software can analyze the data directly from the Web, limiting data-entry errors and providing continuous results.
6. Report Preparation	Design the presentation of information derived from data analysis.	Low cost and ease of use may lead researchers to minimize the problems of using a nonrandom sample. Charts and tables can easily be developed from software.

Sources: Dick McCullough, "Web-Based Market Research Ushers in New Age," *Marketing News,* September 14, 1998, 27–28; and Amy J. Yoffie, "The 'Sampling Dilemma' Is No Different On-Line," *Marketing News,* April 13, 1998, 16.

Product information can be delivered online by using text, graphics, or multimedia files containing audio or video.[23] Real-time chats should be limited to ninety minutes to prevent fatigue. Real-time chat groups and online focus groups may suffer from self-selection biases because they may not represent the population at large.[24]

To control sample selection, a number of companies such as Harris Interactive (http://www.harrisinteractive.com) and IntelliQuest use a database of panel members to send surveys. IntelliQuest (http://www.intelliquest.com) is a leading

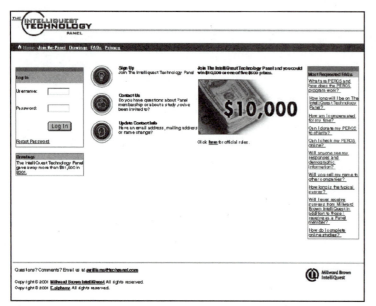

Source: <http://www.techpanel.com>. Millward Brown Intelliquest.

*A **panel** allows researchers to pull respondents from a known pool.*

online marketing research company. It uses **panels** of online respondents who answer questionnaires on technology-related products and services, providing a rapid response time. Panel members supply individual profile data and can then be selected as part of a sample pool for clients. This improves sample selection by allowing researchers to control who responds to the research.[25]

Competitive Intelligence

Competitive intelligence (CI) is a continuous process involving the legal and ethical collection of information and the monitoring of the competitive environment, giving managers the ability to make strategic decisions. The Society for Competitive Intelligence Professionals (http://www.scip.org) views competitive intelligence as a way for managers to make informed decisions about marketing, research and development, and long-term business strategies.[26]

A survey of information technology managers indicated that nearly 75 percent of CEOs used the Internet to scan business, economic, and industry news.[27] Although the Internet offers low-cost access to a wide variety of information, marketing managers can become frustrated trying to find timely, accurate, and relevant information online. Companies that use CI collect data from customers, suppliers, trade publications, company employees, industry experts, the Internet, industry conferences, and commercial databases.[28] One of the main sources of CI is the Internet. CI gatherers study company Web sites, search engine results related to a company or product, employment sites where employee projects can be found, and other sources. To protect against this type of espionage, managers and employees need to be aware of how business information can be collected and then build barriers to that collection.[29]

The Internet allows marketing decision makers to develop virtual libraries of

The Political, Legal, and Ethical Environment

Trade Secrets

There are laws to protect **trade secrets,** which are nonpublicly disclosed inventions, ideas, or information held in a firm that make it unique or give it an advantage over other firms. If trade secrets are placed on a publicly accessed Web site, they may no longer be considered trade secrets.

Firms can protect themselves by having employees sign nondisclosure and noncompete agreements, which prevent employees from giving information to or working for rival firms. Nondisclosure agreements stop employees from spreading trade secrets. Noncompete agreements prevent former employees from working at competitive firms for a stated period of time.

Internet-based sources to aid in decision making.[30] These libraries can be used by managers to monitor their environment or linked to an intranet for individuals to access inside an organization. Fuld & Company's competitive intelligence Web site is an example of a virtual library. Fuld's Internet Intelligence Index (http://www.fuld.com/i3/index.html) contains more than six hundred intelligence-related Internet sites that link on topics as varied as macroeconomic data, individual patents, and stock quote information.

Ethical Snooping

When gathering competitive intelligence, it is important to maintain both ethical and legal boundaries. The CI industry gives eight recommendations to maintain **ethical snooping,** or fairness in the collection of data.[31] These recommendations are as follows:

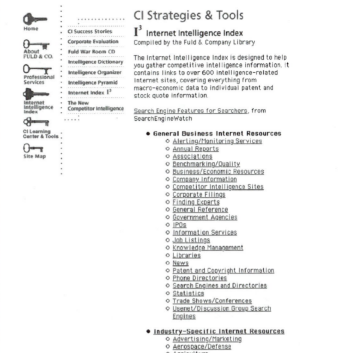

Source: <http://www.fuld/i3/index.html>. Fuld & Company Internet Intelligence Index (I³www.fuld.com).

1) **Observe legal restrictions.** It is important to know and follow the rules set up by your company and any applicable laws.

2) **Avoid misrepresentations.** Do not disguise your own or your company's identity. State the clear reason for the data collection.

3) **Do not release misinformation.** Do not try to throw competitors off by releasing false information. This could backfire and erode the credibility of your firm.

4) **Never ask for or exchange price information with competitors.** This could directly violate antitrust laws.

5) **Do not steal trade secrets.** This could be cause for legal action.

6) **Do not offer bribes.** This is illegal!

7) **Do not hack other sites.** This is illegal!

8) **Protect information sources.** Do not forward e-mail from a source. This could jeopardize reputations and jobs.

The 1996 Economic Espionage Act passed by the U.S. Congress mandated that competitive intelligence should not be collected from rival companies' customer lists or e-mails, nor should deceit be used to obtain interviews from company employees. These actions could be seen as theft of trade secrets, resulting in fines of up to $500,000 and ten years in jail.[32]

Third-Party Data Sources

Third-party data suppliers provide information for multiple uses. Almost any market-segment profile can be purchased. These data can be obtained from companies that specialize in compiling data for mailings or e-mail lists, credit ratings, geodemographic information, and so forth. Data may also be purchased from the original source of the data collection. Retailers, hospitals, and other businesses sell data on their customers to interested parties.

John Hagel and Jeffrey Rayport proposed in a *Harvard Business Review* article a new type of information intermediary, or infomediary, that would become a repository of consumer information.[33] A number of companies are positioning themselves as **infomediaries.** These infomediaries avoid privacy concerns either by engaging in permission marketing (having individuals offer their own information) or by allowing the Web user to remain anonymous. Infomediaries use their expertise in data collection, data warehousing, and database mining to provide services to their clients. Catalina Marketing (http://www.catmktg.com) has developed a data warehouse of 2 trillion bytes of information collected from more than 184 million shoppers and 15,600 supermarkets in the United States and 2,700 worldwide. Using these data, Catalina Marketing is able to selectively target customers. This has allowed coupon responses for grocery stores to increase from 0.6 percent for magazines and newspapers to over 8.9 percent.[34]

NDCHealth (http://www.ndchealth.com) purchases transaction data from 75 percent of U.S. pharmacies and produces monthly electronic data for its clients. This information includes a list of drugs doctors are prescribing for illnesses. Company-specific information is stored in data marts so a sales force can monitor how a doctor's prescription behavior changes after a sales call or a sales campaign.[35]

Knowledge Discovery

Database marketing techniques use computer data to aid in the process of making managerial decisions to reach marketing goals. Using databases for **knowledge discovery** is typically done in one of two ways. The first approach implements an **online analytical processing (OLAP)** method that allows queries, or searches, of known variables, such as asking how much of product A is sold in district 1. The second approach implements a data mining technique. Properly used, database queries allow managers to determine the profitability of product lines and customers.

The Strategic Value of Customers

A 1999 survey of one hundred leading e-commerce companies indicated that 44 percent were determining the strategic value of customers. Determining the strategic value of customer data can increase the overall profits for a company by indicating which customers should receive specialized services and which customers should be dropped or prodded to increase their purchasing.[36] Database marketing allows businesses to limit nonproductive reach by decreasing efforts to individuals who are not likely to react to a marketing strategy.

The **Pareto principle**, or 80/20 rule, dictates that 80 percent of profits come from 20 percent of a business's customers. Although the percentages may not be exact, the idea that not all customers are profitable to a business is valid. Databases are used to help determine the strategic value of all customers by running queries on their past behavior and projecting their future behavior.[37] Data miners in the financial services industry have found that only 20 to 30 percent of customers are profitable. The First National Bank of North Dakota in Grand Forks, now called Alerus Financial (http://www.fnbnd.com/alerus/index.html), conducted a profitability analysis and found that only 10 percent of its customers were profitable. Once a bank identifies profitable and nonprofitable customers, it can develop strategies to turn potentially profitable customers into higher-level users. For those customers who are not profitable, fees can be increased.[38]

The value of a customer can be based on a number of measures. The **lifetime value (LTV) of a customer** can be determined by using future-value formulas such as this one:

> LTV = initial value (revenue − costs)
>   + net present value (future revenue − costs)
>   + net present value of influence (value of influence of customer on new
>   customers)[39]

Other techniques include **recency, frequency, and monetary (RFM) measures.** A customer with a 1-1-1 would be the best customer because he or she would have made a number of purchases in the recent past for a high dollar value. Table 9.2 outlines how a business can determine the RFM measures for its customers. Relevant time periods are divided into five categories. The latest time period has the highest value and is given a rating of 1. The earliest period is of lowest value and is rated a 5. This procedure is repeated for frequency and monetary measures.[40]

Customer profiles can then be generated as shown in Table 9.3. Customer A is the highest-value customer. Customer C is of low value. Customer B, with a score of 2-3-1, may have potential as a valuable customer if frequency and recency can be increased. The **majority fallacy** in marketing occurs when a business, focusing on just an RFM measure, serves only the heavy users and avoids the lower or nonuser segments.[41] This results in missing customers who could become profitable in the future.

The strategic value of customers can also be determined through data mining, which searches for unknown relationships. An example of a data mining query

Table 9.2   Determining a Customer's Strategic Value

Recency (Time Periods)	Rating	Frequency (How Often during All Time Periods)	Rating	Monetary (Average Amount per Order or Purchase)	Rating
1/2000–6/2000	1	Over 10 times	1	$500 and over	1
7/1999–12/1999	2	8–9 times	2	$400–$499	2
1/1999–6/1999	3	6–7 times	3	$300–$399	3
1/1998–12/1998	4	3–5 times	4	$150–$299	4
1/1996–12/1997	5	1–2 times	5	Less than $150	5

Table 9.3   Generating Customer Profiles

Customer	Last Purchase	Score	Frequency	Score	Average Purchase	Score	RFM Score
A	5/2000	1	12 times	1	$650	1	1-1-1
B	9/1999	2	6 times	3	$625	1	2-3-1
C	8/1997	5	2 times	5	$100	5	5-5-5

would be to ask the database an open-ended question such as, What indicators are likely to lead our customers to purchase product A? The goal of data mining is to bypass the **normal science** method of data analysis wherein a hypothesis is developed and then tested. Instead, data mining allows the software to generate a hypothesis by telling the marketer what patterns may exist. Used in combination, the two database knowledge-discovery techniques (OLAP and data mining) can locate patterns, suggest models, and then help to confirm relationships.[42] Figure 9.2 illustrates a possible model that could be developed from mined data. This model indicates that past behaviors and individual profiles may be related to future purchases. Data mining could detect which of those behaviors or profile characteristics are good predictors of future behavior. For example, REI hired a research firm to model customer behavior. The research company used a list of 1.8 million customers and two

Strategic nSite

Data Mining

For more on data mining techniques, go to http://www.spss .com/spssbi/ and http://www.statsoft.com/textbook/stathome.html.

years of transaction data, along with demographic and lifestyle data, to identify markets for narrowly targeted marketing efforts.[43]

The ability to mine data lets companies identify and predict customer behaviors, allowing customized marketing. Table 9.4 outlines some of the major data mining applications undertaken by Fortune 1,000 companies.

▶ Thinking Strategically: Case 9.2

Determine how Capital One has gained a competitive advantage over other credit card companies. List the factors that should be included in determining the value of a credit card customer. What is the source of the data that Capital One uses to choose its credit card customers? Why is it important that Capital One's employees be able to use and share information? Speculate on the importance of the collective organizational knowledge held by Capital One employees.

case 9.2

Giving Databases the Credit

Capital One (http://www.capitalone.com) uses its terabyte database to identify how individuals use credit cards. The firm uses this information to help customers choose from more than seven thousand variations of credit cards on Capital One's Web site. Capital One offers credit cards to college and high school students; its database has indicated that college students are high-potential users. Capital One has been able to use database information to avoid higher-risk credit card users and to focus on more profitable segments. For example, Capital One offers a superprime credit card with a low fixed interest rate and frequent-flyer miles, but these superprime cards go only to those identified as heavy chargers.

To compete against other credit card companies, Capital One has linked its credit card approval system directly to credit bureaus. Applicants can get credit approval in as little as sixty seconds. Capital One also hires employees based on how well they are able to use information. By fostering a sharing culture, Capital One has attained lower-than-industry-average employee turnover.[44]

Figure 9.2   Behavioral Model

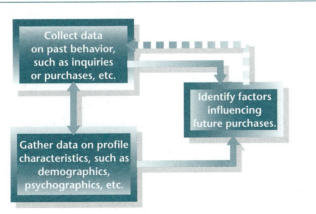

Table 9.4 Data Mining Applications Used by Fortune 1,000 Companies

Application	Description
Market Segmentation	Aids in identifying common characteristics of customers who are likely to react to similar marketing strategies. Allows for one-to-one marketing practices and identification of customer profitability.
Decision Support	Provides data to guide and support management decisions.
Customer Churn	Aids in the prediction of which customers are likely to switch to a competitor.
Fraud Detection	Rates the likelihood that a transaction is fraudulent.
Customer Service	Allows businesses to provide service to customers based on the customer's past experience. Detects patterns of customer problems.
Direct Marketing	Identifies the prospects most likely to respond to direct-marketing efforts.
Interactive Marketing	Predicts what each visitor to a Web site is most interested in seeing (and then delivers that content).
Market-Basket Analysis	Groups products or services that are most likely to be purchased together.
Trend Analysis	Aids in short-, medium-, and long-term decisions by identifying differences and trends among groups of customers over a given period of time.
Loyalty Card Profiling	Links customer profiles to purchases.

Sources: Bob Angell, "Solution-Based Data Mining," *DB2 Magazine,* Quarter 3, 2001, 12–14; "Effectively Guide Your Organization's Future with Data Mining," in SPSS [online] (January 14, 2000), available from <http://www.spss.com/datamine/applications.htm>; "Data Mining," in Synes [online] (January 14, 2000), available from <http://www.synes.com/p217.html>; Susan Osterfelt, "Searching for the Welcome Stranger," *DM Review,* July/August 1999, 59–63; Martin Marshall, "Data Mining: Rich Vein for Marketers," *CommunicationsWeek,* January 13, 1997, 1, 69.

Database Development

The process of developing a database marketing system starts with the collection of large amounts of data on an individual. These data are stored in a digital form in a data warehouse. The data in the warehouse are transformed into meaningful information through specialized software that mines the data, looking for patterns of behavior that enable the marketer to meet individualized needs.[45] Figure 9.3 illustrates the process of developing and using a data warehouse for database marketing.

Figure 9.3 The Database Marketing Process

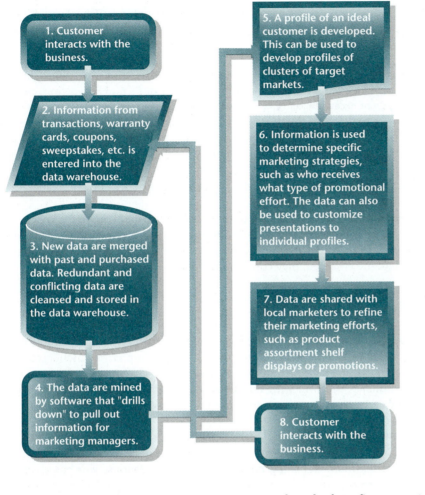

Database marketing technology is expensive, but the benefits can outweigh the costs. A study by International Data indicated that the average cost for a data warehouse was $2.2 million. Evaluating sixty-two organizations with successful data warehouses, International Data discovered that the average return on investment was close to 400 percent. The average payback on the investment was 2.3 years.[46] The benefits of data warehouses are not limited to large corporations. Small businesses are using desktop PC databases to collect data in order to develop and maintain relationships.[47]

The ideal outcome of database marketing is to tighten relationships with customers and to limit wasted marketing efforts, such as junk mail, by targeting only customers who are interested in the offering. Data mining allows the marketer to identify those profiling characteristics related to an individual's actions, and it can result in personalized marketing and customer retention.

Strategic nSite

Caveat: Correlation Is Not Causation

Beer and diaper sales are correlated between 5 and 7 P.M. This bit of data-mined gold came from an analysis for Osco Drug in 1992. Once this type of data is found, what should the company do with it? What was the reason for this correlation? Do men buy beer and diapers on the way home from work? Should the store be redesigned to place beer next to diapers? Data mined from databases do not necessarily convey information; the marketing decision maker must understand the reasons behind the data. As a result of this finding, Osco did not rearrange its stores to place beer next to diapers.

Data Warehouses

Data can be collected from a variety of sources, as outlined earlier in this chapter. In addition, customers may send in warranty cards, sweepstakes applications, coupons, and so forth. These data can be combined with data purchased from third-party sources. For example, credit card companies store virtually every customer transaction. This allows them to look at patterns and flag behavior that falls outside an individual's normal purchases. The credit card company can then contact the individual or the store to verify the purchase.

Data must first be scrubbed, or cleansed. Data cleansing combines data from multiple sources, eliminates redundant data, and resolves conflicting data. This process can take as much as 75 percent of an information technologist's time. Once the data are cleansed, they can be mined for meaning.

Data Mining

Sophisticated data mining software can be used to turn the raw data into information for managerial decisions. Data mining reaches into data warehouses and extracts relationships using sophisticated statistical techniques. Computers use massive parallel processing with hundreds of microprocessors to analyze huge amounts of data. Neural-network software builds models by finding patterns of customer behavior.

MCI, now part of WorldCom (http://www.wcom.com), used data mining to analyze 140 million households on as many as ten thousand attributes such as income, lifestyle, and past calling habits. MCI's data warehouse was based on an IBM SP/2 supercomputer. It developed a set of twenty-two statistical profiles of customers. These highly secret profiles allowed MCI to make promotional offers to clients before they engaged in switching behavior. The profiles also allowed MCI to cut the cost of obtaining leads for new customers from about 65 cents down to about 4.5 cents per lead.[48]

Data mining should not be used as a substitute for managerial decisions; rather, managers should assess the information gleaned from databases.[49] Just because patterns emerge from data does not mean that those generalizations hold for a larger population. Four pitfalls that can occur using data mining techniques are as follows:[50]

☐ **Using ad hoc theories.** When odd relationships are found, the researcher may develop a theory to fit the data.

- ☐ **Not taking no for an answer.** If a researcher has a preconception, it may be tempting to let the computer search to find it.
- ☐ **Storytelling.** It may be tempting to develop a story to fit the data.
- ☐ **Using too many variables.** The more variables, the more likely the computer is to find relationships, regardless of what true relationships exist.

Researchers must learn to use data mining techniques as a tool in model building.

The development, maintenance, and analysis required to successfully run a data warehouse and data mining process can be very complex. Although large firms, such as banks, phone companies, and credit card companies, have seen great benefits from data mining, small- and medium-sized enterprises can benefit as well. The Association for Computing Machinery's Special Interest Group on Knowledge Discovery and Data Mining (SIGKDD) (http://www.acm.org/sigkdd) offers information and support. Additional information and lists of hardware and software vendors can be found at the KDnuggets Web site (http://www.kdnuggets.com).

Business System Control

Enterprise-wide information technologies are being used to automate business systems and control process flows, allowing companies to cut costs and speed operations. Databases become the hubs of this control process, allowing customer support, sales force automation, links to inventory, and control over business processes. Figure 9.4 indicates the major business systems that can be enhanced through a database's ability to store, share, and control information.

Databases that control business systems are not always based on one large data **metawarehouse**; instead, many businesses use **data marts**, which are designed to control a single business operation but may be linked to other databases through a computer network. Customer relationship management and sales force automation have been covered in more depth in Chapters 3 and 5. The following sections will summarize those processes and illustrate how database systems are being used to enhance the control of business processes.

Data marts are small databases that serve a specific purpose in a firm. Metawarehouses are very large databases that centralize all data. Data marts can be linked together in a network to share information.

Customer Relationship Management Systems

The Web is becoming the medium of choice for customers seeking sales support. The Web can cut the cost of service calls by allowing customers to use Web pages to obtain general information on a company and its products or to make queries about order status. Integrated database systems allow companies to develop close relationships with customers by customizing information. Digital Equipment Corporation, now part of Hewlett-Packard (http://www.hp.com/), had its extranet hooked into its database collection system. Customers could go in the system and look up parts, prices, and marketing material. This information was added to the

Figure 9.4   Database System Business Control

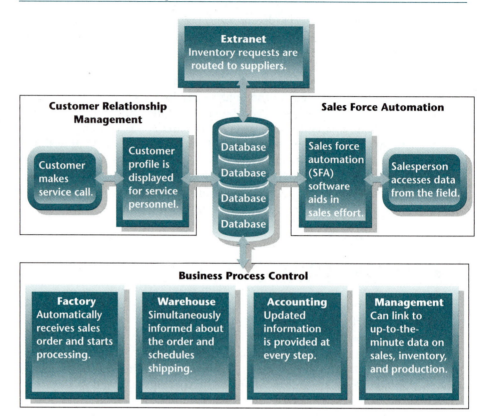

database to design personalized Web pages for the customer.[51] Table 9.5 outlines five ways a business can provide customer support over the Web.

Sales Force Automation

Sales force automation (SFA) systems are designed to be information support tools, with software to support the sales process. These tools can provide a salesperson with information on business contacts, corporate relationships, sales influencers, order fulfillment status, and sales opportunities. Structured selling methods can be retrieved to design sales approaches. SFA software can also act as a gateway to the business database, providing sales presentation information, contract fulfillment data, and links to service and shipping.[52]

Table 9.5   Web-Based Customer Support Systems

Type of Web Site	Function	Technology Used
Content Site	Offers product or company information.	Web authoring software.
FAQ Site	Organizes list of frequently asked questions with timely, accurate answers.	Web authoring software.
Knowledge Base Site	Uses database to allow users to interact and ask questions.	Web authoring software with scripting, search engine, and relational database software.
Trouble Ticket Site	Allows the customer to enter a trouble ticket, using a Web form or e-mail report. Good sites give customers case numbers, acknowledge the customer immediately, and track customer's progress.	Same as above with additional e-mail, response management, and knowledge management software.
Interactive Site	Will do almost everything a customer service representative would do. In addition to the above functions, customers can interact online.	Same as above with personalization, push, and security software.

Source: Adapted from Sari Kalin, "Tales of a Web Customer," *CIO Web Business,* September 1, 1998, 50.

Control of Business Processes

The integration of database systems into organizational processes is cutting the costs and time needed to complete tasks. Databases are being linked together to allow information to flow between functional areas and divisions. For example, warehouses have long used databases to control inventory; grocery stores are now linking together information on inventory with customer profile data to develop category management information, allowing the fine-tuning of inventory.

Database systems are becoming the hub for controlling the reengineering process for organizations. **Enterprise software** systems, often called **ERP (enterprise resource planning)** software, from companies such as PeopleSoft (http://www.peoplesoft.com) and Germany's SAP (http://www.sap.com) are linking together the diverse aspects of a business through central database servers. Enterprise software supports a number of clients, such as customers, the sales force, suppliers, and those involved in the business process (e.g., the factory floor, shipping, accounting, and management). The ability to have all the various parts of a business linked together is allowing firms to service customers better.[53] Figure 9.5 illustrates how enterprise software systems control process flows. The illustration shows that when a sales order is entered into the enterprise system, the software checks inventory, schedules production, orders raw materials, notifies personnel to

Figure 9.5 Enterprise Software and Database Business System Control

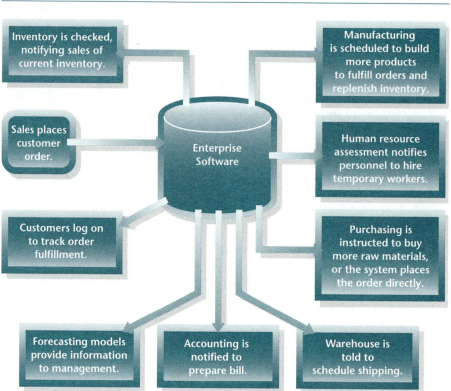

hire temporary employees, prepares the bill, schedules shipping, allows the buyer to track the purchase, and prepares reports for management on trends.

3M (http://www.3m.com) is developing an enterprise system for its 500,000 variations of products sold around the world. Its enterprise system will be open to employees and business partners, allowing over 76,000 individuals to gain access to information. Eventually, customers will be able to go online to obtain brochures, pictures, presentations, and more.[54]

The development of centralized enterprise software systems can be very expensive and time-consuming. The average total cost of implementing an ERP system (including hardware, software, services, staffing, and postimplementation costs) has been estimated at $15 million.[55] Many businesses are using databases to support individual processes, such as customer support, sales force automation, or inventories, without implementing a full ERP system. The advantage of having these diverse systems linked together is that management can access information in real time.

Knowledge Management

Knowledge management is the process of collecting corporate knowledge and developing a system to disseminate that knowledge throughout an organization. Managing knowledge is important for organizations. An *InformationWeek* survey indicated that 94 percent of companies considered knowledge management to be strategically important to their business. Knowledge management allows businesses to undertake day-to-day operations as well as become more innovative. In today's business environment, workers can be far from the center of the organization and the shared organizational knowledge. What one employee knows may be important to others, but without the ability to share that knowledge, the business is not working efficiently. In addition, when workers retire, quit, or otherwise leave an organization, the knowledge they possess can be lost.

Knowledge can reside in databases, on paper, and in workers' heads. This knowledge should be available to workers when they need it. A survey of U.S. and European companies indicated that more than 94 percent felt they could better leverage their organizational knowledge. It is only in the past few years, with the introduction of the Internet, intranets, and data warehousing, that firms have had an effective and efficient means of knowledge collection and dissemination.[56] For businesses that have developed knowledge management systems, the top knowledge areas for which data are collected include business processes, sales and marketing, and customer relations, followed by employee relations and product development.[57] This knowledge is disseminated through relational databases, text search systems, groupware products, and database tools.[58]

Developing a knowledge management system can provide benefits to a firm by reducing the cost of information gathering, improving customer support, identifying new market opportunities, reducing cycle times, and retaining knowledge from workers who leave the organization.[59] A study evaluating firms that used knowledge management inside their organizations indicated that the average positive return-on-investment ratio was 12:1.[60] Andersen Consulting (http://www.andersenconsulting.com) built a worldwide intranet network allowing over 49,000 employees access to databases containing industry data, best-practices advice, research, business approaches, and partnership information. Expertise developed for one project can be adapted to new projects.[61] Digital Equipment Corporation, now part of Hewlett-Packard (http://www.hp.com/), allowed employees from around the world to access information from its intranet data warehouse. Digital's number one priority was to train employees to use organizational knowledge. Digital wanted its employees to turn the data into information, and the information into knowledge.[62] Levi Strauss (http://www.levistrauss.com) has developed an intranet-based knowledge management system that allows employees around the world to share information and learn about products and strategies. Ideas generated in Europe, for example, can easily be transferred back to the United States. Employees can gain access to fact sheets, executive biographies, press releases, and advertisements. Levi Strauss also allows its employees to use the intranet to learn about cash flows or other business functions.[63]

Developing a system to manage knowledge requires more than just building a database; it requires a change in the culture of the organization to allow for trust and learning.[64] The development of an organizational culture that allows a business to compete in a virtual marketing age will be further explored in Chapter 10.

Personal Privacy

The right to privacy has become a central issue in e-business. E-businesses see benefits in using information on individuals to enhance the marketing process. Individuals, on the other hand, want control over their private information. Polls by Forrester Research and *BusinessWeek*/Harris have indicated that as many as 78 percent of individuals would use the Web more if their privacy was protected, and close to 50 percent indicate that the government should pass laws protecting privacy.[65] A major concern for U.S. citizens is not the collection of data but what those data will be used for. U.S. consumers are willing to provide data for customizable services and other uses for which they see benefits.[66]

The ability to easily collect and track individual profile data and behavior with current technology is bringing consumer privacy to the forefront of ethical concerns. Access to personal information gives companies a powerful tool to target promotions and develop products. Laws vary from country to country on who controls personal information. In the United States, when an adult engages in a transaction with a business, in most cases that business is free to use the personal information, sell it, or pass it on to others. In other countries, data pertaining to an individual are owned by that individual and can be released only by consent. In 1998, the European Union stipulated that data on EU citizens could not be sent to countries that do not provide the protections given in EU member countries. U.S. privacy laws do not meet these criteria; therefore, data can be transferred only when an individual agrees to have the information sent or when an approved contract exists.[67]

Web sites collect data in two ways: voluntarily and involuntarily. When an individual voluntarily gives information to a site for a specific purpose, there may not be a privacy issue, but when that information is used for other purposes, privacy concerns are raised. Data can also be collected on an involuntary basis. For example, newsgroup or discussion group postings can be combed to find information. When individuals log on to sites, they may fill in forms providing personal and demographic data. Cookies on browsers can provide information on an individual's surfing behavior. In most cases, cookies identify only the computer, not the user, unless the individual has registered from that computer to a Web site.[68]

The Federal Trade Commission (FTC) has intervened in e-business by requiring online businesses that ask for data to post a privacy policy outlining how the information will be used. If the company then uses those data in ways other than indicated in the policy, it can be sued for damages. In the United States, the Children's Advertising Review Unit (CARU) and the Federal Trade Commission have made recommendations and implemented regulations to govern the collection and use of children's private information. CARU's Web site (http://www.caru.org/) offers extensive advice on children's privacy issues.

The Internet industry is aware that if it does not regulate itself, it may face regulation from the federal government. In a 1998 survey, the FTC found that close to 90 percent of 1,400 commercial Web sites collected personal information, but only 14 percent of these Web sites disclosed their privacy policies, and only 2 percent offered a comprehensive privacy policy.[69] IBM has threatened to withhold advertising from sites that do not post privacy policies.[70] Industry groups have organized to develop policies. One group, the Online Privacy Alliance (http://www.privacyalliance.com), has brought together businesses and associations to help businesses create an environment of trust by fostering the protection of individual privacy rights. The group's guidelines are summarized in Table 9.6.

Table 9.6   Recommendations for Developing Privacy Policies

Policy Recommendation	Description
Notice and Disclosure	Explain to the public the company's policy on personal information. For children's sites, this disclosure should be directed toward parents and should include the following: ▶ Information on who is collecting the data. ▶ A description of the data being collected. ▶ How this data will be disclosed to any third parties (for children's sites, a parents' permission must be obtained). ▶ How the user can control the use of that information. ▶ Whether there are links to other Web sites that do not comply with the FTC's or CARU's guidelines.
Choice and Consent	Ask permission to compile information: ▶ When the information will be used for other than the original purpose, individuals should be allowed to opt out. ▶ Consent should be obtained before sending the information to a third party. ▶ Ask permission before sending targeted e-mail.
Data Security	Organizations need to take measures to do the following: ▶ Assure that data are accurate. ▶ Prevent loss, misuse, or alteration of data. ▶ Be sure data are transferred to third parties who will also take appropriate precautions.
Data Quality and Access	Organizations should do the following: ▶ Ensure that data are accurate, complete, and timely. ▶ Set up procedures to allow data to be corrected.

Sources: For more information, see "Guidelines for Online Privacy Policies," in Online Privacy Alliance [online] (June 15, 2002), available from <http://www.privacyalliance.com/resources/ppguidelines.shtml>; Gregory Dalton, "Pressure for Better Privacy," *InformationWeek,* June 22, 1998, 36–38; Linda A. Goldstein, "Child Care," *CIO Web Business* June 1, 1998, 32–34; and Hanna Hurley, "Online Privacy Policies: Be Aware," *Network Magazine,* November 1998, 72–76.

Employee Privacy

The privacy rights an individual may enjoy in the public domain do not necessarily apply when that individual is on the job. The Electronic Communications Privacy Act gave U.S. employers the right to monitor and control what employees do with private property such as computers and telephones. An employee's Web surfing and e-mail can be monitored by a business. Businesses that engage in this practice should post their policy to avoid possible liability.

Employees have been known to use organizational resources for purposes other than business. Compaq dismissed twenty employees who logged on to sexually explicit Web sites more than one thousand times. Salomon Smith Barney dismissed two top executives who downloaded pornographic images and sent them to others in their office. Smut surfing not only uses the resources of a business for nonbusiness purposes but also puts the business in jeopardy of sexual harassment lawsuits.[71]

Companies have options other than just posting warnings. Monitoring and filtering software can be used to track and block Web users in a business. A business must balance its desire to conserve resources with its need to treat employees as adults and encourage them to learn to use the Internet as an information-gathering tool. While employees may be cyberloitering or surfing the Net without a specific business purpose, they may also be gathering information on competitors, site designs, or other topics of practical use to a business.[72]

Knowledge Integration

Terms and Concepts

Concepts and Questions for Review

1. Explain the relationship between data and information.
2. What is the role of a marketing information system?
3. Outline the flows for the sources and uses of data in a marketing information system.
4. Explain how databases are structured.
5. List the sources of data for marketing.
6. Describe how data is collected from customers.
7. How is Web analytic data conducted?
8. Contrast the advantages and disadvantages of traditional marketing research and online marketing research.
9. How is competitive intelligence conducted?
10. Explain how snooping can be done ethically.
11. How is knowledge discovery undertaken using databases?
12. Contrast OLAP database searches with data mining.
13. Explain the dangers of using data mining techniques.
14. What roles can databases play in controlling business systems?
15. Explain how a company can manage knowledge.
16. What are some of the concerns related to privacy and the Internet?

Active Learning

Exercise 9.1 Developing a Virtual Library

A virtual library can aid in the competitive intelligence-gathering process by developing a set of links to sources of information. This assignment requires you to develop a table (like the following example table) that contains links to sites that provide information on an industry of interest, such as links to trade publications, competitors' sites, government sites, and so forth. The table should have the address linked to the site, the name of the site, and a description of the content that can be found at the site. After the table is created, develop a dated summary of the competitive intelligence found.

Internet Marketing

Site	Company or Journal	Description
http://www.internetweek.com	*InternetWeek*	Articles related to technology trends and company practices.
http://www.iw.com	*Internet World*	News journal covering a wide variety of topics related to the Internet.

Exercise 9.2 Database Field Exercises

Before a database can be developed, the fields of information to be collected must be identified. For this exercise, pick an industry and list the fields that will help a business identify current customer behavior, project future customer behavior, or determine the value of its customers. Once those fields have been identified, determine the sources that would be used to gather that information.

Database Field Exercise

Fields	Sources of Field Data
Age	Application forms, credit records, third-party data
Purchases	Credit cards, check numbers, or shopping card link to register receipt
Etc.	Etc.

Competitive Exercise 9.3 Determining Your Strategic Value

Assume you have been asked to devise strategies using lifetime value information. Use yourself or your team profile as an example. As a customer, you have a strategic value to a business. This value could be high or low. Using the following table, determine your strategic value for a number of businesses by rating yourself on recency, frequency, and monetary value. Use a five-point scale and compare yourself to other customers of the store.

Determining Your Strategic Value

Business (Name and Type)	Recency	Frequency	Monetary	Incentives	Business Strategy
	High 1-2-3-4-5 Low				

Once you have identified your value, determine which types of incentives would be necessary to turn you into a high-value customer, if you are not one already. Indicate the business strategy that should be undertaken (e.g., whether you should be given any incentives or dropped as a customer).

Exercise 9.4 Privacy Policies

Visit a Web site with a privacy statement. Determine if the policy complies with the suggestions outlined in the table that follows (which is based on Table 9.6).

Privacy Policy Analysis

Policy	How Site Complies
• Provide information on who is collecting the data.	
• Describe what information is to be collected.	
• Tell if these data will be disclosed to any third parties (for children's sites, obtain a parent's permission).	
• Explain how the user can control the use of that information.	
• Warn if there are links to other Web sites that do not comply with the FTC's or CARU's guidelines.	
• Allow individuals to opt out if the information will be used for other than the original purpose.	
• Obtain consent before sending the information to a third party.	
• Ask permission before sending targeted e-mail.	
• Prevent loss, misuse, or alteration of data.	
• Be sure data is transferred to third parties who will also take appropriate precautions.	
• Ensure that the data are accurate, complete, and timely.	
• Set up procedures to allow data to be corrected.	

Web Search—Looking Online

| Search Term: | Competitive Intelligence | First 6 out of 538,000 |

CIO. Targets chief information officers by providing in-depth information on industry trends and practices.
http://www.cio.com

DM Review. Covers data warehousing and data mining, offering searchable databases of trade articles.
http://www.dmreview.com

EWeek. Provides information on Internets, intranets, and infrastructure.
http://www.eweek.com

InternetWeek. Offers articles related to technology trends and company practices.
http://www.internetweek.com

Internet World. Covers a wide variety of topics related to the Internet.
http://www.iw.com

The CI Resource Index. Links to multiple sources of competitive intelligence.
http://www.bidigital.com/ci/

| Search Term: | Online Libraries | First 4 out of 2,468,420 |

CEOExpress. Offers an online library with links to newspapers, trade magazines, news feeds, and topic searches.
http://www.ceoexpress.com

CorporateInformation. Provides information on public and private companies from around the world.
http://www.corporateinformation.com

Fuld & Company. Includes links to more than five hundred intelligence-related Internet sites.
http://www.fuld.com

Business 2.0. Organizes an online resource library.
http://www.business2.com

| Search Term: | Marketing Research | First 4 out of 2,500,000 |

Dragon Web Surveys. Allows companies to build surveys online by linking their home page to the Dragon Web Survey site.
http://www.isurveys.com/dragon.html

MarketTools. Offers online survey development, survey hosting, and panel services.
http://www.markettools.com

Perseus. Sells software for marketing research and market polling; also offers research design consulting.
http://www.perseus.com

Speedback. Provides both qualitative and quantitative results for inquiries.
http://www.speedback.com

Search Term:	Database Management	First 3 out of 2,900,000

ACM SIGKDD. Organizes an Association for Computing Machinery special interest group on knowledge discovery in data and data mining.
http://www.acm.org/sigkdd

SPSS Business Intelligence Division. Outlines database techniques and how data mining can be used.
http://www.spss.com/spssbi/

StatSoft. Offers an online statistics textbook with a section on data mining.
http://www.statsoft.com/textbook/stathome.html

Search Term:	Knowledge Management	First 2 out of 95,270

Hyperion. Helps users improve efficiency, gain knowledge, and achieve wisdom through the process of turning information into success.
http://www.hyperion.com

KDnuggets. Lists information on knowledge management hardware and software.
http://www.kdnuggets.com/index.html

Search Term:	Privacy	First 3 out of 95,270

TRUSTe. Organizes a protection seal program designed to alleviate users' concerns about online privacy and build users' confidence in the Internet industry.
http://www.truste.org

Electronic Privacy Information Center (EPIC). Accesses an online privacy resource center.
http://www.epic.org

Federal Trade Commission Privacy Initiatives. Provides policies and procedures related to privacy issues.
http://www.ftc.gov/privacy/

References

[1] Meridith Levinson, "Slices of Lives," *CIO,* August 15, 2000, 126–136; Rick Whiting, "Mega Data Warehouse," *InformationWeek,* April 19, 1999, 31; Peter Fabris, "Advanced Navigation," *CIO,* May 15, 1998, 50–55.

[2] Linda McHugh, "Who's Doing What With Data Mining?" *Teradata Review,* Summer 1999, 23–31.

[3] Adapted from Sun Tzu, *The Art of War,* trans. Samuel B. Griffith (Oxford: Oxford University Press, 1971) 138.

[4] John Fontana, "Businesses Gear Up for Web Expansion," *InternetWeek,* September 14, 1998, 16–19.

[5] John Pallatto, "Business Tools Get Smart," *Internet World,* February 2002, 22–38.

[6] For more on the theory behind information as a competitive advantage, see Rashi Glazer, "Marketing in an Information-Intensive Environment: Strategic Implications of Knowledge as an Asset," *Journal of Marketing,* October 1991, 1–19.

[7] Megan Barnett, "Count On It," *The Industry Standard,* March 26, 2001, 68–73; Kim Ann Zimmerman, "Gathering Knowledge about Customers," *Knowledge Management World,* October 2001, 18–19.

[8] Heather Green, "The Information Gold Mine," *BusinessWeek E.Biz,* July 26, 1999, 16–30; Tom Davenport, "From Data to Knowledge," *CIO,* April 1, 1999, 26–28.

[9] Jonathan Berry, John Verity, Kathleen Kerwin, and Gail DeGeorge, "Database Marketing," *BusinessWeek,* September 5, 1994, 56–62.

[10] Rick Whiting, "Tower of Power," *InformationWeek,* February 11, 2002, 40–50; John Foley, "Towering Terabytes," *InformationWeek,* September 30, 1996, 48.

[11] Robert Shaw and Merlin Stone, *Database Marketing Strategy & Implementation,* (New York: John Wiley, 1990). 88.

[12] Marianne Kolbasuk McGee, "IT Renaissance?" *InformationWeek,* August 17, 1998, 36–41.

[13] B. G. Yovovich, "Scanners Reshape Grocery Business," *Marketing News,* February 16, 1998, 1, 11.

[14] "Is Customer Loyalty in the Cards?" *1to1 Magazine,* October 2001, 18–22.

[15] Steve Jarvis, "Follow the Money," *Marketing News,* October 8, 2001, 1, 10; Jesus Mena, "Mining E-Customer Behavior," *DB2 Magazine,* Winter 1999, 27–35.

[16] Edward Cone, "Taking No Chances," *InformationWeek,* December 12, 1994, 30–40.

[17] Meridith Levinson, "Harrah's Knows What You Did Last Night," *Darwin Magazine,* May 2001, 60–68.

[18] Mike Fillon, "Ritz-Carlton Gets Personnel," *Sales & Field Force Automation,* May 1998, 16.

[19] John W. Virity, "The Gold Mine of Data in Customer Service," *BusinessWeek,* March 21, 1994, 113–14.

[20] Christopher T. Huen, "Procter & Gamble Readies Online Market-Research Push," *InformationWeek,* October 15, 2001, 26; Leslie Marable, "Online Market Research Begins to Catch On," *Web Week,* March 31, 1997, 16–18; Roy Furchgott, "If You Like the Suit, Click Here," *BusinessWeek,* November 17, 1998, 8.

[21] Maricris G. Briones, "Cheaper Desktops Will Help Net Researchers Corral Clients," *Marketing News,* November 9, 1998, 1, 17.

[22] For a review of four survey software packages, see Esther Schindler, "Ask Anything," *Smart Reseller,* July 20, 1998, 88–91.

[23] "Online Focus Groups," in !Research [online] (November 10, 1998), available from <http://www.iresearch.com/pages/focus.html>.

24 Steve Jarvis and Deborah Szynal, "Show and Tell," *Marketing News,* November 19, 2001, 1, 13; Ruth Stevens, "Hold Your Next Focus Group Online," *iMarketing News,* January 24, 2000, 18; Aileen Crowley, "Looking for Data in All the Right Places," *PCWeek,* October 21, 1996, 51, 56.

25 J. D. Mosley-Matchett, "Leverage the Web's Research Capabilities," *Marketing News,* April 13, 1998, 6; Rudy Nadilo, "On-Line Research Taps Consumers Who Spend," *Marketing News,* June 8, 1998, 12.

26 "What Is CI?" in Society for Competitive Intelligence Professionals [online], (November 9, 1999), available from <http://www.scip.org/ci>.

27 Fontana, "Businesses Gear Up for Web Expansion," 16–17.

28 Chris Nerney, "The Competitive Intelligence Edge," *Network World,* November 9, 1998, 42; Ann Harrison, "Why IS Must Go Spying," *Software Magazine,* May 1998, 30–44.

29 Deborah Radcliff, "Guarding the Gates," *Computerworld,* April 1, 2002, 26–27; Louis Lavelle, "The Case of the Corporate Spy," November 26, 2001, 56–58; Alison Bass, "Defense against the Dark Arts," *Darwin Magazine,* June 2001, 66–77.

30 "SCIP Frequently Asked Questions," in Society of Competitive Intelligence Professionals [online] (October 26, 1998), available from <http://www.scip.org/ci/faq.asp>; Jennifer Bresnahan, "Legal Esp," *CIO Enterprise,* July 15, 1998, 56–63.

31 For more information on this topic, see Leonard M. Fuld, *The New Competitor Intelligence* (New York: John Wiley, 1994); Anne Stuart, "Click and Dagger," *WebMaster,* July/August 1996, 38–43; "SCIP Code of Ethics for CI Professionals," in Society of Competitive Intelligence Professionals [online] (October 26, 1998), available from <http://www.scip.org/ci/ethics.asp>.

32 Leonard M. Fuld, "Spyer Beware," *CIO Web Business,* August 1, 1998, 26–28.

33 John Hagel and Jeffrey Rayport, "The Coming Battle for Customer Information," *Harvard Business Review* (January/February 1997): 53–61; Scott Kirsner, "To Know Me Is to Pay Me," *WebMaster,* May 1997, 52–56.

34 Nick Wreden, "Get to Know Your Customer," *InformationWeek Solution Series Insert,* July 13, 1998, 8SS–12SS.

35 Aileen Crowley, "Delivering a Healthy Dose of Sales Data," *PCWeek,* November 24, 1997, 53.

36 Don Peppers and Martha Rogers, "Customer Strategic Value," *DM Review,* November 1998, 20; Paul C. Judge, "What've You Done for Us Lately?" *BusinessWeek,* September 14, 1998, 140–144; Mel Duvall, "Winery Juices Up Database Link," *Interactive Week,* November 2, 1998, 43; Dennis A. Pitta, "Marketing One-to-One and Its Dependence on Knowledge Discovery in Databases," *Journal of Consumer Marketing* 15, no. 5, (1998): 468–80.

37 For more information on this topic, see Peppers and Rogers, "Customer Strategic Value"; Don Peppers and Martha Rogers, *The One to One Future* (New York: Doubleday, 1996).

38 Rick Whiting and Jeff Sweat, "Profitable Customers," *InformationWeek,* March 29, 1999, 44–56.

39 Erin Kinikin, "How Valuable Are Your Customers," *E-Business Advisor,* September 2001, 32–36.

40 For more on RFM measurement, see Ron Kahan, "Using Database Marketing Techniques to Enhance Your One-to-One Marketing Initiatives," *Journal of Consumer Marketing,* 15, no. 5 (1998): 491–93.

41 Jim Laiderman, "Developing Retention, Acquisition, and Loyalty Programs," *Business Geographics,* November 1998, 24–27.

42 Steve Alexander, "Users Find Tangible Rewards Digging into Data Mines," *InfoWorld,* July 7, 1997, 61–62; Robert D. Small, "Debunking Data-Mining Myths," *InformationWeek,*

January 20, 1997, 55–60; Martin Marshall, "Data Mining: Rich Vein for Marketers," *CommunicationsWeek,* January 13, 1997, 1, 69.

43 Kimberlee Roth, "REI Builds Model Customers," *1to1 Magazine,* July/August 2001, 22.

44 Mike McNamee, "Isn't There More to Life than Plastic?" *BusinessWeek,* November 22, 1999, 173–76.

45 Information for this section is in part drawn from Jonathan Berry, John Verity, Kathleen Kerwin, and Gail DeGeorge, "Database Marketing," *BusinessWeek,* September 5, 1994, 56–62; Herman Holtz, *Databased Marketing* (New York: John Wiley, 1992); Robert Shaw and Merlin Stone, *Database Marketing & Strategy Implementation* (New York: John Wiley, 1990).

46 Nick Wreden, "The Mother Load," *CommunicationsWeek,* February 17, 1997, 43–47.

47 For more information, see Gary McWilliams, "Small Fry Go Online," *BusinessWeek,* November 20, 1995, 158–62.

48 Foley, "Towering Terabytes," 34–48; John W. Verity, "Coaxing Meaning Out of Raw Data," *BusinessWeek,* February 3, 1997, 134–38.

49 Srikumar S. Rao, "Birth of a Legend," *Forbes,* April 6, 1998, 128.

50 Peter Coy, "He Who Mines Data May Strike Fool's Gold," *BusinessWeek,* June 16, 1997, 40.

51 Christopher Elliott, "Give Your Data a Workout," *InternetWeek,* June 1, 1998, 32–34.

52 Rich Bohn, "Aurum Customer Enterprise," *Sales & Field Force Automation,* August 1998, 92–94; Sean Dugan, "Mining the Benefits of SFA," *InfoWorld,* October 5, 1998, 74; Shep Parke, "Gotcha! Avoiding the Unseen Perils of Sales Technology," *Sales & Field Force Automation,* November 1998, 30–38.

53 Ronald B. Lieber, "Here Comes SAP," *Fortune,* October 2, 1995, 122–24.

54 Bob Francis, "Open Door Policy," *PCWeek,* May, 1998, 87–88, 103.

55 Christopher Koch, "The Most Important Team in History," *CIO,* October 15, 1999, 41–52.

56 For more on this topic, see Justin Hibbard, "Knowing What We Know," *InformationWeek,* October 20, 1997, 46–64; or visit the *KMWorld Magazine* Web site, available from <http://www.kmworld.com/>, for online access to knowledge management topics.

57 Connie Moore, "KM Meets BP," *CIO,* November 15, 1998, 64–68.

58 Beth Davis and Brian Riggs, "Knowledge Management Get Smart," *InformationWeek,* April 5, 1999, 40–50.

59 Paul Penny, "Knowledge Management, Maximizing the Return on Your Intellectual Assets," *DM Review,* November 1998, 36–39, 64.

60 Gary Abramson, "Measuring Up," *CIO Enterprise,* May 15, 1998, 28–32.

61 Mary Ryan Garcia, "Knowledge Central," *InformationWeek,* September 22, 1997, 252–56.

62 Erin Callaway, "Digital Spins Training Web," *PCWeek,* November 24, 1997, 62, 70.

63 Lauren Gibbons Paul, "Eureka! Levi Finds Gold Mine of Data," *PCWeek,* May 13, 1996, 53–56.

64 Tom Davenport, "Knowledge Management, Round Two," *CIO Enterprise,* November 1, 1999, 30–33; Wendi R. Bukowitz and Ruth L. Williams, "Looking through the Knowledge Glass," *CIO Enterprise,* October 15, 1999, 76–85; Susan S. Hanley, "A Culture Built on Sharing," *InformationWeek,* April 26, 1999, 16ER–17ER.

65 "Forrester Technographics® Finds Online Consumers Fearful of Privacy Violations," in Forrester [online] (October 27, 1999), available from <http://www.forrester.com/ER/Press/Release/0,1769,177,FF.html>; Heather Green, Catherine Yang, and Paul C. Judge, "A Little Privacy Please," *BusinessWeek,* March 16, 1998, 98–102.

66 Brett Mendel, "Online i.d.entity Crisis," *InfoWorld,* October 18, 1999, 36–37; Kenneth Neil Cukier, "Is There a Privacy Time Bomb?" *Red Herring,* September 1999, 90–98; Edward C. Baig, Marcia Stepanek, and Neil Gross, "Privacy," *BusinessWeek,* April 5, 1999, 84–90; Nate Zelnick, "Is IT Privacy That Users Want, or Does Everyone Have a Price?" *Internet World,* March 15, 1999, 1, 45.

67 Daintry Duffy, "Continental Divide," *CIO,* April 15, 2002, 92–96; Gregory Dalton, "Privacy Law Worries U.S. Businesses," *InformationWeek,* October 26, 1998, 26; Peter Swire, "The Great Wall of Europe," *CIO Enterprise,* February 15, 1998, 26–30.

68 Bill Mann, "Stopping You Watching Me," *Internet World,* April 1997, 42–46.

69 Jim Kerstetter, "'Fessing Up to Data Deeds," *PCWeek,* July 13, 1998, 1, 14.

70 Nelson Wang, "IBM to Spurn Sites That Lack Privacy Policies," *Internet World,* 17, 25.

71 Tom Field, "Web Cops," *CIO,* November 15, 1997, 51–58; Art Jahnke, "Unsafe Sex," *CIO Web Business,* June 1, 1998, 18.

72 Kathryn F. Munro, "Hands Off," *Small Business Computing & Communication,* June 1999, 82–84; Peter Cassidy, "Beaching Surfers," *CIO Web Business,* February 1, 1999; Charles Waltner, "Web Watchers," *InformationWeek,* April 27, 1998, 121–26.

chapter 10
E-Business Management

Twenty-first century corporations are different than twentieth-century corporations in a number of ways: their organizational structure is Web-based or networked instead of pyramidal; the corporate focus is external instead of internal; management styles are flexible instead of structured; strength comes from the ability to change rather than from stability; and resources are counted in bits rather than physical assets.[1] Both brick-and-mortar-based and pure-play e-businesses are finding competitive advantages in this new corporate environment by developing the innovative management systems necessary to implement e-business strategies. An e-business needs to facilitate entrepreneurial leadership and innovation to be able to adapt to its rapidly changing environment. Intranets, extranets, and the Internet are being used as the technology base, speeding and improving communication flows inside the organization and acting as the hub for organizational knowledge. E-businesses are focusing on their core values and restructuring their businesses to gain competitive advantages and efficiencies. Marketing managers must be able to lead, to structure organizations, and to work collaboratively with different constituencies within a firm.

1. List the pillars of success for innovative businesses.
2. Explain how management systems can create value for a business.
3. Discuss the interplay between the management components of the e-business value chain.
4. Describe the roles that leadership and organizational culture play in giving an e-business its unique advantages.
5. Outline the role of organizational learning in giving an e-business a definite advantage.
6. Discuss how e-businesses are organizing themselves to compete.
7. Recommend the steps a business should take to restructure in order to be competitive in an e-business environment.
8. Identify the new management positions and duties used to meet e-business needs.

learning objectives

AT&T

vignette

"This elephant is beginning to dance."

C. Michael Armstrong
CEO of AT&T[2]

In 1907, AT&T was taken over by a group of New York bankers led by J. P. Morgan. AT&T then engaged in monopolistic practices by locking out smaller phone companies until they almost failed and then buying them at discounted prices. In 1913, strong public feeling about monopolies led the Justice Department to form an agreement with AT&T, giving it a near monopoly in telephone services in exchange for operating under government oversight. AT&T held this monopoly until January 1, 1984, when (after antitrust action) AT&T broke up its telecommunications monopoly in the United States.[3] This did not immediately change AT&T's monopolistic corporate culture.

Lack of leadership, vision, and innovation allowed AT&T to miss the Internet boom because it failed to capitalize on its advantages. In 1997, C. Michael Armstrong took over as CEO. Armstrong has attempted to speed decision making by changing AT&T's culture. He put in place an aggressive management team, collapsed the management structure, encouraged innovation, bought out 18,000 employees, sold off business units, and formed relationships with Internet and cable companies.[4] To aid in this transformation, AT&T uses an intranet to disseminate knowledge about the company. AT&T's 135,000 employees use the intranet to obtain stock data, audio and video clips of executive presentations, human resource information, e-mail addresses, and other items of interest.[5]

In the early 1900s, independent phone companies such as McConnell Telephone Exchange, Co. disappeared as the phone industry consolidated.

Armstrong's vision is for AT&T to be a one-source company for all telecommunications needs, including telephone, cellular, Internet, and content. To reach this goal, AT&T has formed alliances with Time Warner and has purchased a number of cable companies. AT&T has positioned itself to offer telephone, cable television, and broadband Internet access to about 40 percent of customers in the United States. In 2000, AT&T announced a restructuring plan to create a family of four businesses. Each was to be publicly traded, including AT&T Wireless, which was split off as an independent company. These moves may once again give AT&T a strong advantage in its competition against ISPs, Internet portals, and other phone service companies.[6]

▶ Thinking Strategically

Why do you think AT&T was a late mover into the Internet industry? List the types of skills AT&T's management and employees will need to be competitive in the online marketplace. Is AT&T too large to respond quickly to market changes? Explain the importance of a transformational leader in an organization like AT&T.

"The digital economy is revolutionizing how we think about the traditional corporate value chain, and it's also redefining relationships between manufacturers, suppliers, distributors, and consumers. The value chain is in fact a value network, or web, in which companies engage in multiple two-way relationships to bring increasingly complex products and services to market."

Doug Aldrich
Vice president and managing director of strategic information technology practice at A.T. Kearney[7]

Businesses are gaining distinct advantages by developing new e-business models to deliver goods and services and to enhance relationships with customers. One of the keys to achieving these advantages is the ability to develop management systems that are flexible enough to respond to a rapidly changing environment. Brick-and-mortar businesses are restructuring to adopt e-business models and gain efficiencies. These businesses face a challenge because they must be willing to break old value chains and develop e-business value chains to maintain competitiveness. Pure-play e-businesses may have had advantages in the 1990s because they constructed value chains that fit the demands of new technological environments, but large brick-and-mortar competitors have tooled up to compete.

Over time, businesses develop systems of operation, form a culture that fits their operational system, adopt strategic plans that reduce risk, and set financial targets for divisions. In an e-business environment, businesses are forced to be innovative in business models, products, business processes, and management practices. They must be able to overcome past **momentum** and find ways to compete. **Restructuring** businesses and adopting e-business techniques may require changes in business processes, moves into risky new venture areas, and uncertain returns.[8] Pursuing new business models requires an innovative orientation. Modesto Maidique and Robert Hayes have outlined six pillars of success for innovative businesses. Even though their study interviewed managers involved in high-technology companies and firms that engaged in research and development, these six pillars are important for all organizations looking to structure themselves for innovative and highly competitive environments. Table 10.1 lists these pillars of success and their implications for developing e-business value chains.

Momentum *refers to the general tendency of businesses to keep moving in the same direction. Like a big ship, the larger the business, the longer it takes to change direction.*

Table 10.1   Pillars of Success for Innovative Businesses

Pillar of Success	Description	Value Chain Implication
Business Focus	A business should stay within a highly focused product line to focus on its mission.	A business should determine what it is best at and focus on those priorities. It may want to outsource nonessential business functions.
Hands-on Management	Top management must become involved in the innovation process. Managers must support new ideas and processes and gain an understanding of the relevant technology.	Managers must develop cultures that allow for innovation and flexibility. They should also become technologically savvy to understand the issues related to organizing e-business.
Entrepreneurial Culture	Internal change agents must be fostered. Risk taking should be encouraged, and failure should be tolerated.	An innovative culture must be promoted in the firm. Innovative employees should be allowed to introduce new practices and to fail.
Adaptability	A business must be able to undertake major and rapid change when needed.	Firms must develop cultures that allow for flexibility and adaptability. Intranets can foster the free flow of communication, speeding change.
Organizational Cohesion (Sense of Community)	The organization must have everyone working toward the organizational goal. Ideas should flow freely and quickly.	Less attention should be paid to rank and seniority. Idea sharing and teamwork are important. Collecting and using organizational knowledge become a priority. Intranets can facilitate this process.
Sense of Integrity	A business must establish long-term relationships with all of its constituencies.	Employees must feel empowered to make decisions at lower levels in the organization. E-business corporation techniques can link e-business partners.

Source: Modesto A. Maidique and Robert H. Hayes, "The Art of High-Technology Management," in *Readings in the Management of Innovation*, ed. Michael L. Tushman and William L. Moore (Cambridge, Mass.: Ballinger, 1988).

Management and the Value Chain

Intranets, extranets, and the Internet are now becoming standard tools that businesses use to provide value to their customers. To seize market opportunities and gain competitive advantages in an e-business environment, businesses must evaluate the strengths and weaknesses of their current value chain and then devise business systems that are flexible and innovative.[9] Figure 10.1 outlines the management components of the e-business value chain currently being used to gain advantages. The interaction of these components helps set the direction and tone for the culture of a business.[10]

Figure 10.1   Management Components of the E-Business Value Chain

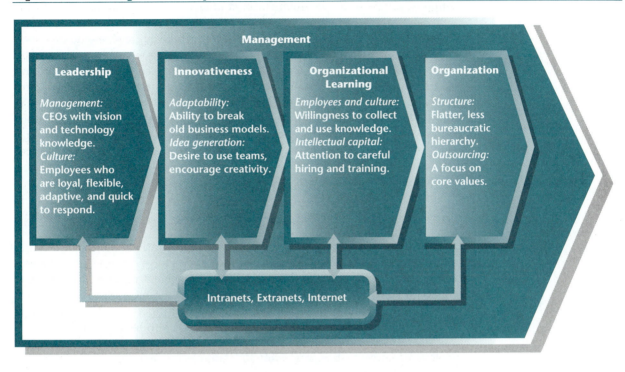

Information technology is used as a tool to enhance the e-business value chain and is aiding in the development of closer relationships with customers by speeding up the ordering and delivery of products, improving customer service, and lowering costs.[11] The impact of intranets, extranets, and the Internet is intertwined with the larger organizational changes outlined in this chapter.

Leadership

"Top management no longer runs the company. It's the young people who run the company; top management runs relationships."

Peter Drucker[12]

Twenty-three percent of Fortune 1,000 senior executives can explain what a modem does. Ninety-three percent of sixth graders can.[13]

Traditionally, the top management of an organization sets the vision for the company, oversees the development of strategy, and is in charge of delegating responsibility to be sure that plans and strategies are carried out. With the advent of new competitive paradigms, many top-level executives are changing their view of the management process, but not all executives are willing to embrace new business practices. There are a number of reasons some leaders of businesses have been slow to adopt e-business techniques. Top managers understand that changing business procedures and business models has a disruptive effect. Some e-business techniques have unproven returns, and executives believe that they may go the way of other failed fads. In addition, changes in technology and management practices can cause managers to feel disconnected from the processes they control.[14] New technology requires a relearning process, and new business practices can mean a shift in leadership power.

Forward-looking CEOs are learning to love the Net. A survey of 303 IT managers indicated that 61.7 percent saw their CEOs as advocates of Internet-based technologies, 36 percent saw them as neutral, and only 2.3 percent felt their CEOs were technology blockers.[15] Leaders of organizations have realized that information technology is a means of gaining competitive advantages. CEOs now see the use of information technology, the management of data, the impact of new technology, and the need for reengineering as the most important business issues they are facing. One of the main motivating factors for CEOs is the fear of losing their competitive edge if they do not keep up with technological change.[16] CEOs have used a number of techniques to motivate management teams and employees to accept e-business. Table 10.2 outlines four examples.

Table 10.2   Techniques to Motivate Management Teams

Company	Problem	Approach
Charles Schwab	Top management team was slow to accept that Schwab had to become a full-fledged net brokerage.	CEO David Pottruck had one hundred senior managers walk across the Golden Gate Bridge wearing jackets emblazoned with *Crossing the Chasm*.
Sega	Top management resisted movement to remake the company for e-business.	Chairman Isao Okawa defied Japanese consensus management techniques and threatened those who resisted change with being fired. Resistance disappeared overnight.
GE Aircraft Engines	A highly bureaucratic division needed to transform into an e-business.	CEO James McNerney converted an old warehouse into an idea laboratory with foosball tables and open work pods. Change agents were appointed.
Oracle	Sales executives were afraid that customers would not trust a Web-only strategy.	CEO Larry Ellison promised to keep older products after producing the Web-only products. He lied.

Source: Marcia Stepanek, "How to Jump-Start Your E-Strategy," *BusinessWeek E.Biz,* June 5, 2000, 96–100.

To manage these newly evolving organizations, top executives in successful firms are learning to enable their employees to help run the business. These leaders are creating innovative cultures, fostering organizational learning, promoting teamwork, and creating a new generation of leaders, thereby encouraging loyalty to the organization.[17] Each of the following sections will explain how successful leaders are building competitive organizations.

Organizational Culture

An organization's **culture** includes the shared values, beliefs, behaviors, and norms generally accepted and practiced by group members. The founder of the organization often sets the tone for an organization's culture. As the organization develops over time, the organizational culture must adapt to its competitive situation. Cultures can become self-selective and self-reinforcing. Organizations with cultures that fit a competitive environment may look to hire only individuals who fit the current culture. Individuals who rise through organizational ranks may be very good at operating within that culture; they, in turn, reinforce the culture. This can be problematic when a changing competitive environment threatens the organization. In this case, there may be a bad fit between the organization and its culture.[18] Businesses that develop cultures resulting in satisfied and engaged employees can substantially reduce turnover, preserve intellectual capital, and lower hiring and retraining costs.[19] This dynamic is illustrated in Figure 10.2.

A variety of cultural typologies have been developed, the full scope of which is beyond this text. But one cultural form, organic, has been recommended for environments that are highly uncertain and that do not hold for traditional marketing systems.[20] Organic cultures provide greater flexibility and responsiveness to environmental change. **Innovative organizations** often have organic forms of culture.[21] Organic organizations encourage change agents, discussed in Chapter 8. For these change agents to work effectively, there must be a culture of innovation in which new ideas can be developed, brought forward, nurtured, and implemented without fear of failure.

Some brick-and-mortar businesses have more bureaucratic cultures. These cultures may not fit a quickly changing and highly flexible environment. Such businesses are forced to find ways to change their culture or develop a strategy that allows them to compete. E-businesses are preparing their management systems for an environment of continuous change. Innovative enterprises are pushing responsibility toward the bottom of the organization, placing an additional burden on the organization to develop the conditions in which employees can act for the good of the

Strategic nSite

Culture

Organic cultures have decentralized control and informal relationships. Their organizational structures are often somewhat flat, and more responsibility is given to individuals at the bottom of the organizational hierarchy. The opposite of an organic culture is a **bureaucratic culture**. Hierarchies, rules and regulations, and strong management oversight characterize bureaucracies.

Figure 10.2   Environmental Fit

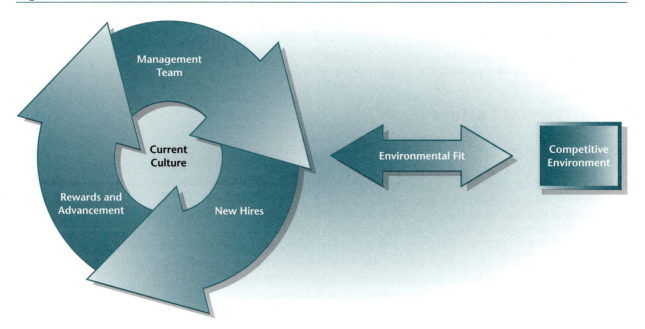

business. Leaders of innovative e-businesses are using the following strategies to develop responsive management systems:[22]

☐ **Encourage organizational learning.** E-businesses are developing learning organizations, where employees can learn from their environment and experiences.

☐ **Hire versatile talent.** E-businesses are attempting to hire employees who will fit flexible work situations.

☐ **Promote cross-functional teams.** Teamwork facilitates input from multiple constituencies within an organization.

☐ **Develop a sense of community.** Individuals must feel loyal to an organization and its organizational goals.

☐ **Establish intranets.** Intranets can link all internal constituencies within a business.

Strategic nSite

Innovative Organizations

Many Internet-based start-ups begin as highly organic companies. As they grow, they often look for "grown-ups," or individuals with greater levels of corporate and business experience, to aid in growth. These new leaders must then develop organizations that are efficient yet flexible enough to compete.

Organizational Learning

Organizational learning implies that a business system is able to develop insights, knowledge, and associations between the actions taken and the effectiveness of those actions. This ability should allow the organization to adapt by making incremental adjustments to the environment. Learning occurs at the individual level, but a business can help to spread knowledge throughout the organization. Once a widely accepted view of the world is developed, it can become part of the organization's culture. This can have advantages but also strong disadvantages if the culture does not change. A learning organization must renew itself.[23]

Although the importance of organizational knowledge is well known, the creation of learning organizations is just getting under way. A study indicated that of 431 European and American companies, 94 percent thought they could do a better job of leveraging their business knowledge. The top three reasons that companies implement knowledge management systems are to transfer best-practices information (89 percent of company responses), increase employee capabilities (83 percent), and provide customer and market information (77 percent).[24] Effective knowledge management can result in increased revenue by fostering best practices across frontline employees, improving team collaboration, and leveraging expertise.[25] Organizations are turning to online learning to offer training and education opportunities to employees and to save costs. General Motors has set up online learning for its 88,000 executives. The U.S. federal government is using online learning for more than 400,000 employees in a number of departments and agencies.[26] Figure 10.3 shows the growing amount of money being spent worldwide for online learning.

Creating a learning organization requires devising a knowledge culture where individuals have a shared belief in the importance of knowledge and its uses. The following suggestions can help lay the foundation of a learning organization:

☐ **Create a knowledge culture.** Lack of a knowledge culture is seen as the number one obstacle to knowledge creation in firms. It is important to make acquiring data part of almost every job description. Copying ideas from other firms can be a way to bring knowledge into a company. BP gives a Thief of the Year award to employees who bring in the best ideas in

Figure 10.3 Estimated E-Learning Market Spending

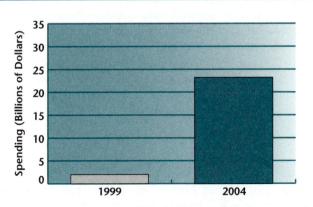

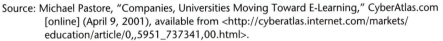
Source: Michael Pastore, "Companies, Universities Moving Toward E-Learning," CyberAtlas.com [online] (April 9, 2001), available from <http://cyberatlas.internet.com/markets/education/article/0,,5951_737341,00.html>.

applications development. Texas Instruments has a Not Invented Here, But I Did It Anyway award for those who borrow ideas. Employees and management need to talk about the knowledge creation process.

☐ **Set a value on the knowledge created.** Organizations and individuals are more likely to set priorities to collect and use knowledge if they can see returns from their efforts.

☐ **Democratize knowledge.** A firm must allow individuals in the organization to collect and use the acquired knowledge.

☐ **Use knowledge tools.** Tools such as organizational portals, e-mail, intranets, databases, guides, templates, and questionnaires can be used to obtain knowledge. Knowledge management tools such as Lotus Notes provide search engines for data repositories, organize and categorize data, allow collaboration, and provide links to other data topics.[27]

☐ **Understand what the organization knows and does not know.** Organizations should undertake knowledge audits to assess how knowledge can be better collected and used.

☐ **Act on the knowledge.** Access to organizational knowledge should be easy and encouraged. Intranets can facilitate this process.

☐ **Train workers.** Workers need to be able to access and use the knowledge created.[28]

Intranets can act as a hub for collecting and structuring organizational learning. Companies are using their intranets to allow employees to enter best-practices information into databases. When other employees have questions, they can query the database for examples of how to handle a problem. This process collects, stores, and disseminates knowledge. Maritz (http://www.maritz.com), a sales incentive company, uses its intranet to organize sales pitches. Background on different product categories is provided along with customers' FAQs (frequently asked questions) and recommended sales presentations.[29] Bay Networks, a computer network hardware and software firm, uses its intranet to structure organizational knowledge. Obtaining needed knowledge faster has resulted in a $10 million savings for the company.[30]

Intranets are evolving into **corporate portals.** These sites can offer employees access to information such as benefits, company news, employee directories, and education and training.[31] It is important that organizational knowledge is categorized so that employees can use the information efficiently to serve the organization and its customers. Employees are becoming overwhelmed by the amount of messages sent and received every day. Some workers can send or receive up to two hundred messages a day via telephone, e-mail, voice mail, postal mail, interoffice mail, fax, and other media.[32] Intranets and corporate portals should be designed to meet the information needs of employees and the company. There should be an indexing and categorization structure that allows easy access to information.[33]

Corporate portals *are internal Web sites that offer both internal company information and links to external sites such as suppliers or customers. Portals can be enhanced with search, learning, communication, and knowledge management functions.*

Human capital *is the skill that individuals gain through education, training, and experience.*

A **knowledge economy** *gains wealth based on what individuals can create from knowledge rather than what they can create from physical labor alone.*

Talent

E-businesses have recognized that **human capital,** or **talent,** is a key area of competitive advantage; in a **knowledge economy,** employees must have the capacity to learn and relearn tasks. Employees who have technical skills and the ability to work with others to achieve organizational goals are highly sought after in the e-business industry.[34]

Internet start-ups and high-technology companies have been pulling employees from traditional businesses.[35] The demand for technology workers in the United States has been so high that, in 1999, between 400,000 and 500,000 technical jobs went unfilled; in 2000, there was a shortage of more than 500,000 technical workers. U.S. companies that have not been able to meet their employee needs in the United States have sought to hire from overseas.[36] The technical skill shortage in Europe is expected to be even higher; in 2000, there were about 1.3 million more technical jobs than trained employees. IBM Germany paid employees up to $4,200 for finding qualified candidates for the company to hire.[37]

The gap in technical skills between older generations and the Net Generation is large. The **Net Generation (N-Gen)** refers to individuals born after 1977. This is the largest generation ever. These individuals often understand and have grown up with digital technology. The Internet has already played a role in their lives. They are comfortable with technology, and the youngest segment of this generation will not have known a world without the Internet.

E-Business Professionals

David and Michelle Chamberlain
Partners in .Com Land

Michelle received her BA in sociology. In 1992, she landed a job as a receptionist for someone she had never heard of before, Bill Gates. By 1994, she was a project manager at Microsoft, managing groups of copywriters, programmers, and marketers. The most typical problem she saw was that these different groups spoke different languages. To address

David and Michelle
Chamberlain

this, Michelle is pursuing her master's degree in organizational behavior to add a systems perspective to her strategic planning abilities.

David received his BA in finance in 1987. His entrepreneurial orientation led him to start programming and selling computers. While working as a financial analyst, he became a local area network expert. His experience led to a number of positions with companies where he helped change processes by freeing up information inside firms. In 1991, he moved to Seattle, where he worked for Corbis (http://www.corbis.com) when it had only fourteen employees. Currently, David works as chief information officer (CIO) for a large Seattle-based philanthropic organization.

David and Michelle recommend that college students learn strong communication skills. This includes the ability to listen and be a good team member. Students need to see how all parts of a business work together, and they must develop the ability to interact with individuals of different backgrounds and motivate individuals they do not have power over in order to help an organization reach its goals.

These individuals prefer collaboration to working alone and do not like the idea of having a traditional boss. Technologically savvy N-Gens have the ability to shift easily between jobs; when they invest their intellectual capital in organizations, they expect to be compensated for it.[38] The N-Gen attitude has become a point of contention between older managers and younger employees. In 1998, the forty-six-year-old chairwoman of iVillage, Candice Carpenter, saw her younger employees leaving to obtain higher pay. She saw this as a danger to her company. Whereas she and her senior managers had learned how to run companies over relatively long periods of time, her younger employees were simply pursuing paychecks. Many of the younger employees lacked the ability to work with others, and their judgment was not mature. Carpenter restructured the company. She replaced younger employees with older executives and implemented a radical mentoring program in which employees were pushed to develop as executives faster than they would have normally. This has helped to develop loyal culture where younger employees see rewards in staying for the long term.[39]

Organization

Developing e-business applications cuts across a large number of functional areas within organizations. Electronic communication enhances the ability of organizations to link marketing, production, accounting, and management to pursue strategic goals. These projects are often worked on in teams and require managers who have both technology and business backgrounds. Collaboration between functional groups can help change the culture of organizations and make them more customer focused.[40]

Community versus Hierarchy

The use of corporate intranets is allowing businesses to form **teams**, communities of workers who work on problems rather than rely on typical organizational hierarchies. Technology permits communities to include participants from around the world. Xerox uses a community approach to projects, allowing individuals from different departments to share ideas, best practices, and other types of information. Developing a culture of collaboration is not without problems, however. Individuals who are leaders or experts may be unwilling to share what they know because it is their source of power within the organization.[41]

Communities of workers represent social networks as opposed to organizational **hierarchies**. **Social networks** map how people in organizations actually communicate. This structure includes individuals, hubs, and communication flows.[42] Figure 10.4 illustrates the differences between traditional hierarchies and social networks.

Figure 10.4 shows the social network **hubs** of highly connected individuals within functional areas who carry on high levels of face-to-face communication. These hubs may be connected through **gatekeepers**, such as individual A in the marketing hub. This can increase the power of the gatekeeper, who controls the flow of information. All employees should be encouraged to engage in communication to lessen gatekeepers' power and to speed communication.

Business-based electronic communities can permit individuals inside organizations to tap knowledge resources through local intranet home pages.[43] E-mail allows each member of a hub to contact all other members; collaboration software permits individuals from around the world to work together on projects. General Electric Capital used an intranet to link 52,000 people in twenty-seven business units in more than fifty-seven countries. These different groups were not immediately willing to share all their knowledge, so the intranet was designed to allow divisions to hide data behind firewalls. To overcome the fear of information

A gatekeeper is an individual who controls the flow of information in a communication system.

Figure 10.4   Hierarchies and Social Networks

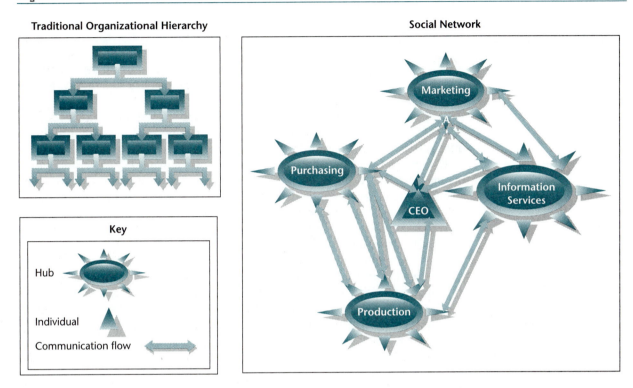

Traditional Organizational Hierarchy   Social Network

Key

Hub

Individual

Communication flow

sharing, GE Capital devised a promotion system based on how well employees shared their knowledge.[44]

Combining intranets and extranets allows individuals outside the organization, such as suppliers and customers, to interact with the organization. This communication system facilitates the growth of teams and virtual corporations, and it allows for distance workers. Each of these topics will be discussed in the following sections.

Teams

Developing successful e-business systems that focus on the needs of customers requires blending talent from different constituencies within a business. Marketers must work together with technology specialists, designers, and other individuals with specialized skills to create Web sites and e-commerce applications and to use databases and other technology-based tools.[45] Bringing together individuals from the marketing core and the technology core does not always work smoothly. These two groups often have different views of the world and how business should be conducted. Marketers sometimes see the technical core as lacking a customer

The traditional role of the **marketing core** (those directly involved in the marketing process) is to stay close to customers and act as an interface between the company and its customers.

orientation. The technical core sees marketers as reacting too quickly to short-term market demands. When these two groups act as a team—sharing their individual skills, perspectives, and alternative approaches to new product development—they are more likely to come up with solutions that result in competitive advantages.[46]

A five-year study of executives from more than eight hundred businesses in fifteen different industries found that the most important factors for aligning information technology with business practices were senior executive support for IT, IT management's involvement in strategy development, IT's understanding of the business, and a partnership between the business core and the IT core. The biggest inhibitor was the inability of individuals to develop relationships.[47] Just as information technology specialists are learning that they must understand business practices, so too must marketers understand that they must learn and embrace the technologies that will help them perform their jobs.

Technology-based tools are becoming more widely available to marketers. Marketing automation software is being designed to help with campaign management, sales lead management, database mining, and business-to-business relationships.[48] A lack of understanding of what technology can and cannot do may limit the marketer's ability to make sound design decisions as to how to use technology to meet the market's needs. The marketing core is beginning to realize that its goal of developing strong relationships with customers requires the support of information technology specialists. For example, marketers want to use database marketing techniques, but they need technologists to set up and maintain databases. The ultimate goal of one-to-one marketing requires that marketers and information technologists work together to develop strategic approaches and enable technological solutions.[49]

Collaboration software, or groupware, permits individuals to communicate via e-mail and message lists, share files, and open file archives. The goal is to have individuals collaborating on projects.

Collaboration software allows team members to work together across distances. The collaboration process has been enhanced through the development of intranets. The rapid development of e-business teams in distant locations allows team members to work together on projects, solve customers' problems, and then move on to other projects. The biggest problem in using collaboration software is creating a culture where individuals work well in teams and work well online.[50]

Virtual Corporations

Virtual corporations evolved throughout the 1990s. A **virtual corporation** business model allows a business to focus on its core competency while developing a temporary network of value chain components brought together to take advantage of market opportunities. For example, a business may see the possibility of a new product in the market. The company can hire a design firm, license with a separate manufacturer, contract independent agents to help sell, and use an ISP to develop and maintain a Web site for marketing and support. These temporary partnerships may last only as long as the market opportunity, or the business may wish to continue the relationships for the long term. The advantage of using a virtual corporation is that it brings together the best components in developing a value chain.[51] Virtual companies can create new ideas for products and services, position them in the marketplace, and develop a team of partners who can successfully get the product to market.[52]

The movement toward virtual corporations is being accelerated by the standardized interfaces used in extranets, intranets, and the Internet. Standardization allows all the components of the virtual corporation to use simplified linkages.[53] Not all companies have the human and mechanical or technical resources for developing and maintaining networked communication. Skills such as coding and scripting, site design, and systems management often need to be brought in from outside an organization.[54] To meet these needs, companies are outsourcing information technology services to countries as diverse as India and Ireland.[55] This saves on costs, enhances the technology that can be accessed, and facilitates market agility. The e-business channel system outlined in Chapter 4 typifies this partnership process. Marketing services are also being outsourced, allowing small specialty companies to emerge. The market value for outsourcing Web development services, which include marketing experts, ad agencies, Web developers, consultants, and systems integrators, is expected to reach close to $16 billion by the year 2002.[56]

Distance Workers

Telecommuting allows **distance workers** to connect with their job and work groups online from their homes. This trend is accelerating. In 1998, an estimated 52.1 million workers did all or part of their job by telecommuting from home. The number of teleworkers in Europe is expected to increase to over 28.8 million by 2005.[57] Some companies, such as AT&T and Cisco Systems, allow more than 50 percent of their workforce to telecommute. The average age of telecommuters is about forty-one years; 48 percent are knowledge workers. One study indicated that more than 60 percent of these employees saw telecommuting as having a positive effect on their careers. Telecommuters save companies money by lowering office space requirements. Many employees can occupy the same office or cubicle by **hoteling** in the office. Distance workers proclaim higher levels of work satisfaction, but they express concerns about being out of the office's political loop. Distance workers have less ability to form relationships with other employees and are less likely to be seen by managers who can aid in their advancement and promotion.[58]

Hoteling *is the sharing of a physical office space, such as a desk, cubicle, or entire office.*

To successfully implement telecommuting, businesses should do the following:[59]

☐ **Carefully select employees who telecommute.** Not all jobs or employees are likely to fit a telecommuting model. Employees who do not work well at a business are not likely to work well at home.

☐ **Provide training.** It may take distance workers up to eighteen months to adjust to working at home. Managers also need to be trained on how to feel comfortable supervising employees they cannot see.

☐ **Support telecommuters with technology.** Distance workers need equipment that is as good as or better than what can be found in the office. They also need support from a technology staff.

☐ **Facilitate face-to-face contact.** Contact between employees and supervisors must be encouraged to develop relationships. Distance workers may feel alienated from the organizational culture.

☐ **Ensure management support.** Most resistance comes from midlevel managers, so organizations must be sure that telecommuters receive top management support.

One of the ways that e-businesses are controlling information flows for team collaboration, distance workers, and virtual corporations is through restructuring intranets into corporate portals. Corporate portals, like public access portals, are centralized intranet Web sites that businesses use to permit access to e-mail, databases, document management, news services, and other Web sites. Portal sites are being used to manage knowledge for businesses, provide competitive intelligence, and support sales forces in the field.[60]

case 10.1

Buying into BuyPower

In May 1997, GM gave Ann Pattyn, director of the company's Consumer Marketing Initiative, ninety days to develop a way to sell cars over the Internet. With 21 percent of car buyers using the Internet for information and with the emergence of new online car sellers such as Autobytel and Microsoft, GM realized it had a problem. Pattyn's solution was the GM BuyPower site, which rolled out in a four-state area. Shoppers were able to configure a desired car, compare it to the competition, and conduct a search of dealer inventory to find the model. Buyers could then contact the dealers, who were required to respond within twenty-four hours with their best price. To obtain buy-in, a salesperson at each dealership was trained on how to make e-mail contacts. Despite these efforts, only 60 percent of the dealer networks signed up for the program. Providing more information online creates a problem for the traditional car sales business model. Dealers like to be able to switch customers between products to reduce their inventory.

To develop this program, Pattyn put together a six-person team and outsourced hosting and design to other firms. Rather than spend a lot of time researching, the goal was to get to market as fast as possible and learn from the market's interaction with the site. GM has thus made a vigorous effort to sell online, but Autobytel is projected to sell up to ten times as many GM cars as GM does from its site.[61]

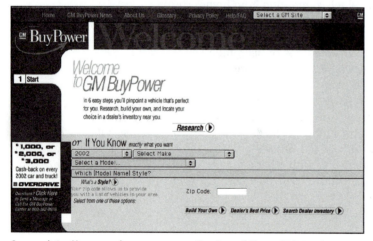

Source: http://www.gmbuypower.com. Courtesy of General Motors Inc.

▶ Thinking Strategically: Case 10.1

Determine who could be hurt in the new business model proposed by GM. List the key people who need to buy into the new selling process. What are the incentives and disincentives that salespeople have in adopting this model? Speculate on GM's top management support for this new business model. What key areas could be leveraged to speed adoption of this new business model?

Restructuring

"Destroy-your-business.com"

General Electric CEO Jack Welch's name for General Electric's Internet business unit.[62]

Becoming competitive in an e-business environment requires restructuring the value chain.[63] In 1994, the number one priority for senior information system executives (up from number eleven in 1989) was reengineering business processes through information technology.[64] By 1999, 86 percent of 399 businesses surveyed by *InformationWeek* saw IT as contributing to or leading in business and marketing transformation. The primary technology used in this transformation is the Internet, due to its ability to rapidly transfer information.[65]

Changing from one business model to another is a difficult process for any business. It may take five or more years for an organization to change cultural practices. In a highly turbulent environment, organizations do not have the luxury of evolutionary change; revolutionary change is more often the norm.[66] Businesses can take a number of approaches to become successful players in an e-business environment. It is possible for some organizations to implement change from the top leadership down. Organizations that are highly flexible and organic may respond well to change, and individual employees who are flexible may be able to break old patterns and retrain themselves. To avoid cultural conflict between existing, entrenched cultures and the innovative workers necessary to operate e-businesses, some firms opt to spin off new e-business divisions. These can act as separate units able to develop their own unique cultures, hire new talent, and operate without the bureaucracy of a larger organization.

A May 1993 *Fortune* magazine article designated IBM and General Motors as corporate dinosaurs. The reason cited for their decline was their inability to adapt to new market conditions due to fixed, bureaucratic cultures.[67] In 1993, new CEO Lou Gerstner helped IBM reorient itself toward the Internet by empowering a number of change agents. John Patrick, a senior strategy executive, wrote a white paper on how IBM should get connected. A group of individuals from around the world discussed the idea via Internet discussion groups. This allowed interested individuals to coalesce around the idea of developing Internet strategies. IBM also formed new divisions such as alphaWorks (http://www.alphaworks.ibm.com), an online laboratory designed to develop new ideas on how to commercialize products and collaborate with customers. New employees were hired to staff this division. Part of their job was to shake up the status quo and make IBM a cool place to work for the N Generation.[68]

Case 10.2

An Old Player in a New Gamble

Procter & Gamble has implemented a change program called Organization 2005 that will incorporate collaborative technology, business-to-consumer e-commerce, extranet-based supply chains, and database management systems. Top executives of P&G realize that they have a business with a 160-year history and an entrenched culture. One of the new ventures that P&G is pursuing is a Web-based direct-selling site that markets cosmetics and hair products customized to individual buyers. The new venture is called Reflect.com and was spun off from P&G's Cincinnati corporate headquarters; it is located in San Francisco. The employees who left P&G for Reflect.com were forced to resign so they could dedicate themselves to the online venture. P&G has maintained some contact with the new venture, however; P&G's lawyers review contracts for Reflect.com, and 50 percent of the board of directors are from P&G.[70]

▶ Thinking Strategically: Case 10.2

Speculate on the reasons why P&G would want to start a Web-based venture. Why P&G spin off this venture rather than have it in-house? Why was the venture located in San Francisco? List the advantages and disadvantages of having a corporate board tied to P&G. Visit the Reflect.com Web site (http://www.reflect.com). Evaluate Reflect.com against other customizable cosmetic sites. Speculate on the future of Reflect.com and P&G's ability to compete online with this current strategy.

GM has used the Internet to maintain market share, increase revenue, and reduce costs. GM implemented a program called eGM to improve customer relationships and drive sales. The company developed a business model and identified a number of challengers, including portals, information providers, transactional companies, dealers, manufacturers, and service companies. GM then determined if it needed to concede roles to challengers, collaborate with them, or compete against them. Part of the strategy was to form alliances with America Online and Kelley Blue Book to aid in obtaining sales.[69]

Business Process Reengineering

Changing from one business process to another requires a reengineering of procedures, processes, and standards, which is called **business process reengineering (BPR).** BPR does not have a high success rate. It is estimated that up to 70 percent of BPR projects fail. To increase the odds, the following five BPR steps are recommended:[71]

1) **Require top management commitment.** Top management must support the change process, and a clear leader of the change team must be designated.

2) **Understand the current business model.** Change leaders should model how the current business operates. To be sure current processes are understood, the new business model may be required to work with only small sections of large, complicated businesses.

3) **Identify key players in the organization.** Organizational knowledge is most likely held by key individuals in the firm. These individuals must be allowed to become part of the change process.

4) **Develop a communication plan.** Constant communication permits individuals to become part of the change process.

5) **Design an implementation plan.** It is important to decide how change will be undertaken. The following steps can aid in implementing a reengineering process:

   a) **Analyze leverage points.** A business needs to look for critical areas where change can be made.

   b) **Identify process breakthroughs.** Areas of possible business success need to be identified, and goals must be set. These areas are where change will have a positive impact on the organization.

   c) **Design business processes.**

   d) **Implement the business processes.** If the new processes result in positive change, further reprocessing is more likely to be accepted.

   e) **Institutionalize continuous improvement.** This facilitates continuous reengineering and change in an organization.

Intranets can act as leverage points for change. As employees become comfortable with Web browsing, additional layers of functionality can be added. Intranets also facilitate the rapid deployment of information and the collaboration necessary to achieve mission-critical goals.

Spin-Offs

Pure-play Internet companies are able to develop new e-business models, hire technologically savvy employees, move quickly to serve new markets, and set strategic goals that fit their competitive environment. Traditional businesses have attempted to achieve these objectives by spinning off divisions.

E-business **spin-offs** from larger companies gain the freedom to act as entrepreneurial ventures. A number of firms have recognized that e-business management requires a different set of skills than those needed to manage a brick-and-mortar business. Retailers such as Macy's, Office Depot, Barnes & Noble, and Toys "R" Us have spun off e-commerce divisions. AltaVista and Snap were spun off from Compaq and General Electric. These spin-offs have not performed as well as their pure-play Internet rivals, possibly because the spin-offs were late movers or because they have not fully broken off from their parent divisions.[72]

A spin-off is formed when a parent company creates an independent division. This could involve distribution of shares of stock in the new division to owners of the parent company.

Knowledge Integration

Terms and Concepts

Bureaucratic culture *299*
Business process reengi-
    neering (BPR) *310*
Collaboration
    software *306*
Community *304*
Corporate portal *302*
Culture *299*
Distance worker *307*
Gatekeeper *304*
Hierarchy *304*

Hoteling *307*
Hub *304*
Human capital *302*
Innovative
    organization *299*
Knowledge economy *302*
Marketing core *306*
Momentum *295*
Net Generation
    (N-Gen) *303*
Organic culture *299*

Organizational
    learning *300*
Restructuring *295*
Spin-off *311*
Social network *304*
Talent *302*
Team *304*
Telecommuting *307*
Virtual corporation *306*

Concepts and Questions for Review

1. List the pillars of success for innovative companies.
2. Explain the components of the management value chain.
3. Describe the technologies used to help provide value in the e-business management value chain.
4. What role does leadership play in the e-business management value chain?
5. Explain the role that organizational culture plays in an organization.
6. List some of the advantages of having an organic culture.
7. How can an organic culture be developed in an organization?
8. What is the role of organizational learning in adding value to an e-business?
9. Recommend how to develop a learning organization.
10. How does employee talent add value to an organization?
11. List ways in which N-Gen employees are different from older employees.
12. Explain the role that teams play in adding value to an organization.
13. How do the marketing core's beliefs compare to the technical core's beliefs?
14. What role does collaboration play in the team process?
15. Compare and contrast communities and hierarchies.
16. Explain how communities play a role in adding value to an e-business.
17. How do virtual companies differ from traditional ones?
18. Explain the role of distance workers and how they fit in an organizational community.
19. List some steps that can be taken to improve the chances for success in business process reengineering.

Active Learning

Exercise 10.1 Identifying Components of the Management Value Chain

Using the following figure, outline the management value chain for a business with which you are familiar. Indicate areas that can be improved by applying any e-business techniques outlined in this text.

Management

Leadership

Management:

Culture:

Innovativeness

Adaptability:

Idea generation:

Organizational Learning

Employees and culture:

Intellectual capital:

Organization

Structure:

Outsourcing:

Intranets, Extranets, Internet

Exercise 10.2 Message Count

Develop a log to keep track of the number of messages you receive in one day. Place the messages into categories that include phone calls, e-mails, voice mail messages, postal letters, interoffice mail, faxes, Post-it Notes, message slips, and any other sources. Rate the messages in terms of immediate action, information to remember for future action, organizational knowledge, and social information. Compare and contrast your list with others. Is it possible to remember all the messages received? Recommend a Web-based strategy that would help you receive, organize, and use the information you must work with every day.

Exercise 10.3 Mapping Social Networks

Develop a map of your social networks. This could include networks in business, at school, or with friends. Draw out any communication flows between individuals that link these networks together. Determine the role you play in each of the hubs.

Exercise 10.4 Design a Corporate Portal

Put yourself in the role of a chief information officer. Design a corporate portal for a business. Set up links to the types of information needed by each constituency inside the business. How could the Web site foster social networks? List the types of information that should be used to increase organizational knowledge. Justify the design of the Web site for the business's culture.

Competitive Exercise 10.5 Business Process Reengineering

Choose a business that you believe needs restructuring to compete in an e-business environment. Answer the following five questions relating to the reengineering process for this business:

1) How does the business model need to change?

2) How can top management's commitment be secured?

3) Which key players in the organization need to back the change?

4) What are some key leverage points that can be addressed?

5) What process breakthrough can be achieved?

Present your ideas and compare them with those of other individuals or teams.

Web Search—Looking Online

| Search Term: | Innovation | First 3 out of 4,225,520 |

Bill & Melinda Gates Foundation. Provides information on how to increase innovations in education, technology, and global health.
http://www.gatesfoundation.org

The Cap Gemini Ernst & Young Center for Business Innovation. Offers a source of new knowledge, insights, and frameworks for management.
http://www.businessinnovation.ey.com

SBIR/STTR. Gives information on two National Science Foundation programs offering opportunities and incentives for small businesses: the Small Business Innovation Research program and the Small Business Technology Transfer program.
http://www.eng.nsf.gov/sbir/about_sbir.htm

Business Process Reengineering and Business Innovation. Offers links to topics related to business process reengineering and innovation.
http://www.brint.com/BPR.htm

The Conference Board. Provides a place where visitors can gain cross-industry knowledge and share experiences and best practices with executives from more than three thousand organizations in sixty-seven countries.
http://www.conference-board.org

Hatch Organizational Consulting. Outlines culture change strategies.
http://www.hocinc.com

Healthyculture.com. Seeks to empower people to create cultures that support health and productivity at home, at work, and in the community.
http://www.healthyculture.com

Knowledge Management, Organizational Learning, and Learning Organizations. Organizes links to topics related to knowledge management and organizational learning.
http://www.brint.com/OrgLrng.htm

Workshop Report: Methodological Advances and the Human Capital Initiative. Reports on a National Science Foundation workshop on methodological advances in measuring human capital.
http://www.nsf.gov/pubs/1997/nsf9797/nsf9797.htm

Virtual Corporations, Virtual Communities, and Outsourcing. Provides links to topics related to virtual corporations and outsourcing.
http://www.brint.com/EmergOrg.htm

References

1   John A. Byrne, "Management by Web," *BusinessWeek,* August 28, 2000, 84–96.
2   Louis Trager, "AT&T Corp.'s Armstrong Righting a Sinking Ship—Year 1," *Interactive Week,* November 2, 1998, 62.
3   Steve Lubar, *Info Culture,* (New York: Houghton Mifflin, 1994).
4   Jared Sandberg, "She's Baaack!" *Newsweek,* February 15, 1999, 44–46; Trager, "AT&T Corp.'s Armstrong Righting a Sinking Ship—Year 1," 62–63.
5   Debby Young, "AT&T's Intranet Reaches Out to Touch Everyone," *CIO Web Business,* October 1, 1997, 78.
6   Allan Sloan, "AT&T's Golden Boy," *Newsweek,* May 10, 1999, 69–71; Nate Zelnick, "ISPs Fear AT&T Will Corner Market," *Internet World,* February 8, 1999, 1, 7.
7   Doug Aldrich, "The New Value Chain," *InformationWeek,* September 14, 1998, 280.
8   Mel Duvall, "To Spin Off or Not to Spin Off?" *Interactive Week,* October 28, 1999, 28–29.

9 Aldrich, "The New Value Chain," 278–280.

10 For more on this topic, see Richard J. Gascoyne and Koray Ozcubukcu, *Corporate Internet Planning Guide: Aligning Internet Strategy With Business Goals* (New York: John Wiley, 1997); Richard J. Gascoyne, "Adapt to the Internet," *InformationWeek*, May 5, 1997, 89–100.

11 Bruce Caldwell, "Time and Money Pay Off," *InformationWeek*, February 8, 1999, 16ER; Ralph Szygenda, "Information's Competitive Edge," *InformationWeek*, February 8, 1999, 4ER–10ER.

12 "Quote of the Week," *InformationWeek*, February 13, 1998, 14.

13 "Clueless in the Suites," *Newsweek*, April 20, 1997, 8.

14 Joel Maloff, "Do Execs Get the Net?" *Internet World*, November 1996, 64–68.

15 Tim Wilson, "Cautiously, CEOs Lead the Way," *InternetWeek*, September 14, 1998, 11–12.

16 Bruce Caldwell, Marianne Kolbasuk McGee, and Clinton Wilder, "CEOs Turn to IT," *InformationWeek*, June 22, 1998, 18–20.

17 Don Tapscott, "Leadership for the Internetworked Business," *InformationWeek*, November 13, 1995, 65–72; Thomas A. Stewart, "Managing in a Wired World," *Fortune*, July 11, 1994, 44–56.

18 For more on the development of organizational cultures and strategic fit, see Henry Mintzberg, "Organizational Design: Fashion or Fit?" *Harvard Business Review* (January/February 1981): 103–16; Rohit Deshpande and Frederick E. Webster Jr., "Organizing Culture and Marketing: Defining the Research Agenda," *Journal of Marketing*, 53 (January 1989): 3–15; Danny Miller, "Environmental Fit versus Internal Fit," *Organizational Science* 3, no. 2 (May 1992): 159–78; Rohit Deshpande, John U. Farley, and Frederick E. Webster Jr., "Corporate Culture, Customer Orientation, and Innovativeness in Japanese Firms: A Quadrad Analysis," *Journal of Marketing* 57 (January 1993): 23–27.

19 Daintry Duffy, "Cultural Evolution," *CIO Enterprise*, January 15, 1999, 44–50.

20 Barb Cole-Gomolski, "Unwary CIOs Can Walk into Business Disasters," *Computerworld*, April 19, 1999, 24; Larry English, "DQ Point 13: Education and Self-Improvement," *DM Review*, March 1999, 32–33.

21 Robert W. Ruekert, Orville C. Walker Jr., and Kenneth J. Roering, "The Organization of Marketing Activities: A Contingency Theory of Structure and Performance," *Journal of Marketing* 49 (Winter 1985): 13–25.

22 Megan Santosus, "The Organic Root System," *CIO*, December 15, 1998–January 1, 1999, 38–45; Megan Santosus, "Pop Quiz," *CIO*, December 15, 1998–January 1, 1999, 48–55; Justin Hibbard, "Cultural Breakthrough," *InformationWeek*, September 21, 1998, 44–55.

23 Daniel H. Kim, "The Link between Individual and Organizational Learning," *Sloan Management Review* (Fall 1993): 37–50; Mark Dodgson, "Organizational Learning: A Review of Some Literatures," *Organizational Studies* 14, no. 3 (1993): 375–94; C. Marline Fiol and Marjorie A. Lyles, "Organizational Learning," *Academy of Management Review* 10, no. 4 (1985): 803–13.

24 Julekha Dash, "Knowledge Power," *Software Magazine*, January 1998, 46–56.

25 Carol Hindebrand, "Making KM Pay Off," *CIO Enterprise*, February 15, 1999, 64–66.

26 Elisabeth Goodridge, "Feds Turn to E-Learning to Cut Costs," *InformationWeek*, June 4, 2001, 85; Elisabeth Goodridge, "GM Drives E-Learning," *InformationWeek*, May 16, 2001, 84.

27 Judy DeMocker, "Knowledge-Management Tools Billed as Key to Accessing Data on Intranets," *Internet World*, April 6, 1998, 18.

28 This section compiled from Perry Glasser, "The Knowledge Factor," *CIO*, December 15, 1998–January 1, 1999, 108–18; Tom Davenport and Larry Prusak, "Know What You

Know," *CIO,* February 15, 1998, 59–63; Michele S. Darling, "Building the Knowledge Organization," *Business Quarterly,* Winter 1996, 61–67; Jim Bair, "Knowledge Management: The Era of Shared Ideas," *Forbes,* September 22, 1997, 28.

29 Cheryl Dahle, "Fast Pitch," *Webmaster,* August 1997, 50–51.

30 Peter Fabris, "You Think Tomaytoes, I Think Tomahtoes," *CIO Web Business,* April 1, 1999, 46–52.

31 Pimm Fox, "Plugging into Portal Returns," *Computerworld,* April 8, 2002, 38.

32 "Message Overload," *Knowledge Management,* November 1999, 34; Tom Davenport, "Overload Redux," *CIO,* October 1, 1999, 32–34.

33 Claude Vogel, "Six Steps for Managing Portal Content," *Communication News,* September 2001, 82; Daintry Duffy, "Why Do Intranets Fail?" *Darwin Magazine,* November 2001, 56–62.

34 Daintry Duffy, "A Capital Idea," *CIO Enterprise,* November 15, 1999, 54–62; Mark Swanson, "Net Employees in the Driver's Seat," *NewMedia,* August 1999, 22; Mindy Blodgett, "Fast Forward," *CIO,* August 15, 1999, 46–58; J. Neil Weintraut and Jeffrey Davis, "The Startup Economy," *Business 2.0,* July 1999, 61–68; Don Tapscott, "Minds over Matter," *Business 2.0,* January 1999, 89–97.

35 Louis Trager, Randy Barrett, Kathleen Cholewka, Connie Guglielmo, and Steven Vonder Haar, "Nothing but Net: The Scarcity Syndrome," *Interactive Week,* June 7, 1999, 70–71; Barb Cole-Gomolski, "IT Labor Issues Add to Retailers' Woes," *Computerworld,* March 15, 1999, 4.

36 Charles Babcock, "Webnations: Filling the High-Tech Void," *Interactive Week,* November 22, 1999, 68–69.

37 Jack Ewing and Heidi Dawley, "The Missing Worker," *BusinessWeek,* December 27, 1999, 70–71.

38 Don Tapscott, "Growing Up Digital," *InformationWeek,* November 3, 1997, 64–73; Don Tapscott, "Minds over Matter," *Business 2.0,* January 1999, 89–97.

39 Pamela Kruger and Katharine Mieszkowski, "Stop the Fight," *Fast Company,* September 1998, 93–111.

40 Gregory Dalton, "Web-Organized," *InformationWeek,* January 25, 1999, 71–76; Tom Stein and Jeff Sweat, "Customer Culture," *InformationWeek,* January 25, 1999, 49–55; Lauren Gibbons Paul, "Over the Line," *CIO Web Business,* March 1, 1998, 54–59.

41 Noah Shachtman, "Group Think," *InformationWeek,* June 1, 1998, 77–84.

42 Dawne Shand, "Making Community," *Knowledge Management,* June 1999, 64–70; Carol Hildebrand, "Mapping the Invisible Workspace" *CIO Enterprise,* July 15, 1998, 18–20.

43 Mary Johnston Turner, "Electronic Communities Will Lead the Way for Corporations," *CommunicationsWeek,* May 26, 1997, 37.

44 Jennifer Bresnahan, "Capital Gains," *Webmaster,* August 1997, 36–40.

45 Ellis Booker, "Marketing Seizes Big E-Business Role," *InternetWeek,* September 6, 1999, 12; Martin LaMonica, "Learning to Play Nice," *InfoWorld,* June 28, 1999, 69; Jim Sterne, "Building Bridges," *CIO Web Business,* June 1, 1998, 58–60.

46 For more background on marketing interactions in teams, see Richard T. Hise, Larry O'Neal, A. Parasuraman, and James U. McNeal, "Marketing/R&D Interaction in New Product Development: Implications for New Product Success Rates," *Journal of Product Innovation Management* 7 (June 1990): 142–55; Robert W. Reukert and Orville C. Walker Jr., "Interactions between Marketing and R&D Departments in Implementing Different Business Strategies," *Strategic Management Journal* 8 (1987): 233–48; Robert W. Reukert and Orville C. Walker Jr., "Marketing's Interaction with Other Functional Units: A Conceptual Framework and Empirical Evidence," *Journal of Marketing* 51 (January 1987):

1–19; Ashok K. Gupta and Everett M. Rogers, "Internal Marketing: Integrating R&D and Marketing within the Organization," *Journal of Services Marketing* 5 (Spring 1991): 55–68.

[47] Jerry Luftman, "Enablers & Inhibitors," *InformationWeek,* September 14, 1998, 283–86.

[48] John Moore, "Untapped Market," *Smart Reseller,* January 25, 1999, 44–46.

[49] Jennifer Bresnahan, "Improving the Odds," *CIO,* November 15, 1998, 36–48; Jason Busch, "How to Get the Most Out of Your Web Marketing Efforts," *InternetWeek,* July 13, 1998, 29.

[50] For more on collaboration software use, see Richard Adhikari, "Groupware to the Next Level," *InformationWeek,* May 4, 1998, 106–11; Justin Hibbard, "Virtual Teams Improve Customer Service," *InformationWeek,* October 5, 1998, 30; Fred Hapgood, "Tools for Teamwork," *CIO Web Business,* November 1, 1998, 68–74.

[51] For more on this topic, see John A. Byrne, Richard Brandt, and Otis Port, "The Virtual Corporation," *BusinessWeek,* February 8, 1993, 98–103; Shawn Tully, "The Modular Corporation," *Fortune,* February 8, 1993, 106–13; William H. Davidow and Michael S. Malone, *The Virtual Corporation* (New York: HarperBusiness, 1993).

[52] Joyce Chutchian-Ferranti, "Virtual Corporation," *Computerworld,* September 13, 1999, 64; Steven Bell, "Ready, Set, Go Virtual," *CIO,* October 15, 1998, 86–90; David Joachim, "The Virtual Corporation: It's Closer Than You Think," *InternetWeek,* April 6, 1998, S3.

[53] Joachim, "The Virtual Corporation: It's Closer Than You Think"; Linda Musthaler, "Virtual Corporations," *LAN Times,* August 18, 1997, 90.

[54] Sari Kalin, "Good Help Is Hard to Find," *CIO Web Business,* June 1, 1998, 38–43.

[55] Mark Clifford and Manjeet Kripalani, "Different Countries Adjoining Cubicles," *BusinessWeek,* August 28, 2000, 182–84.

[56] Maryann Jones Thompson, "Market Spotlight: Internet Professional Services," *Industry Standard,* November 16, 1998, 42.

[57] "IDC Research: Teleworking on the Increase in Europe," in NUA [online] (October 26, 2001), available from <http://www.nua.com/surveys/index.cgi?f=VS&art_id=905357340&rel=true>.

[58] Kathleen Murphy, "Web Fosters Telecommuting Boom, and Many in the Industry Take Part," *Internet World,* February 9, 1998, 38; Anne Tergesen, "Making Stay-at-Homes Feel Welcome," *BusinessWeek,* October 12, 1998, 155–56; Edward C. Baig, "Saying Adios to the Office," *BusinessWeek,* October 12, 1998, 152–53; Melanie Warner, "Working at Home—The Right Way to Be a Star in Your Bunny Slippers," *Fortune,* March 3, 1997, 165–66.

[59] Bruce Caldwell and Jill Gambon, "The Virtual Office Gets Real," *InformationWeek,* January 22, 1996, 32–40; Jennifer Bresnahan, "Why Telework?" *CIO Enterprise,* January 15, 1998, 28–34; Todd Spangler, "Serving the 30-Second Commuter," *Interactive Week,* December 14, 1998, 30.

[60] For more on corporate portals, see Sarah L. Roberts-Witt, "Making Sense of Portal Pandemonium," *Knowledge Management,* July 1999, 37–48; Emily Fitzloff, "Portal Patrol," *InfoWorld,* May 17, 1999, 1, 32–33; Rick Overton, "Take the Vertical Challenge," *Business 2.0,* May 1999, 128; Beth Bacheldor, "Portals Make Business Sense," *InformationWeek,* October 18, 1999, 81–90; Jason Meserve, "Preparing Your Firm for Corporate Portals," *Network World,* October 4, 1999, 49; David Orenstein, "Corporate Portals," *Computerworld,* June 28, 1999, 73.

[61] David Diamond, "Can General Motors Learn to Love the Net?" *Business 2.0,* September 1998, 46–54.

[62] Jerry Useem, "Internet Defense Strategy: Cannibalize Yourself," *Fortune,* September 6, 1999, 121–34.

63 Paula Klein, "E-Business: No Quick Fix," *InformationWeek,* June 21, 1999, 5SS; Teri Robinson, "Reinventing the Business Wheel," *InformationWeek,* June 21, 1999, 6SS–10SS.

64 Ira Sager, "The Great Equalizer," *Business Week/The Information Revolution,* 1994, 100–107.

65 Clinton Wilder, "E-Transformation," *InformationWeek,* September 13, 1999, 44–62.

66 Charles Fishman, "Change," *Fast Company,* April–May 1997, 64–75.

67 Carol J. Loomis, "Dinosaurs?" *Fortune,* May 3, 1993, 36–42.

68 Luc Hatlestad, "New Shades of Blue," *Red Herring,* November 1999, 118–28; Eric Ransdell, "IBM's Grassroots Revival," *Fast Company,* October–November 1997, 182–99.

69 Marianne Kolbasuk McGee, "Wake-Up Call," *InformationWeek,* September 18, 2000, 55–65.

70 Marianne Kolbasuk McGee, "P&G Jump-Starts Corporate Change," *Internet Week,* November 1, 1999, 30–31; Marianne Kolbasuk McGee, "Lessons from a Cultural Revolution," *InformationWeek,* October 25, 1999, 46–62; Linda Himelstein and Peter Galuszka, "P&G Gives Birth to a Web Baby," *BusinessWeek,* September 27, 1999, 87–88.

71 Burnes P. Hollyman and Robert L. Howie Jr., "Mastering Change: Information Technology Integration in Successful Enterprises," *BusinessWeek,* December 19, 1994 (special advertising section); John H. Mayer, "Avoiding a Fool's Mission," *Software Magazine,* February 1998, 43–48.

72 Julia King, "Web Start-Ups Need to Leave to Succeed," *Computerworld,* May 24, 1999, 41; Brian E. Taptich, "Spin-off.com," *Red Herring,* April 1999, 40–46.

chapter 10 appendix
E-Business Careers

Marketing students can pursue a number of positions in the e-business environment. Throughout this text, the E-Business Professionals features have outlined the career paths and suggestions of individuals who have worked in e-businesses. This appendix will list a number of positions that can be found in such organizations. It also outlines the skills needed for these positions and how marketing students can develop an electronic profile of their skills.

1. List and describe the major career opportunities in the e-business field.
2. Identify sources of jobs for individuals looking for a career in e-business.
3. Understand how to construct a digital portfolio.

learning objectives

Organizational Positions

The importance of using information to aid in the development of business value is well recognized. Organizations request information from many sources, which then provide knowledge for others to share. Someone must be in charge of organizing and controlling the dissemination of this information coming from hundreds or thousands of different sources. This need has led to the rise of new organizational positions, which are outlined in the following sections.[1]

Chief Information Officer

Chief information officers (CIOs) are senior executives who are in charge of a company's information technology and systems and who help direct the use of this technology to support a company's goals. A CIO needs to understand both technological and business processes and should have a cross-functional perspective. CIOs often take a leadership role in reengineering business processes to utilize IT. CIOs are also taking leadership roles in implementing knowledge management systems. They help in the development of an organization's intranet and Web site.[2] CIOs do not necessarily have the skills required to become CEOs. A cross-cultural study of CIOs indicated that they were seen as lacking adequate business and functional experience as well as revenue-generating and marketing skills. They were also seen as too technical in their orientation.[3] Another position, vice president of e-commerce, can lead more directly to a CEO job.

Vice President of Electronic Commerce

A number of organizations have offered a new position responsible for the creation and execution of e-commerce business practices; the title being used is **vice president of electronic commerce.** The background required includes an MBA degree, technical training through an undergraduate degree, and a number of years of business and electronic commerce experience.[4]

Chief Knowledge Officer

Chief knowledge officers (CKOs) work with CIOs to oversee organizational knowledge management; they must act as knowledge champions to encourage individuals to add to the organization's knowledge and to use that knowledge.[5] CKOs need a unique combination of skills. They must have a strong comprehension of business practices to understand what types of knowledge are useful to the organization. They also need to know how to use technology to collect and disseminate that information. In addition, they need an entrepreneurial spirit to be champions and to get involved in restructuring how a business operates.[6]

Chief Privacy Officer

New international privacy regulations have motivated many firms to create the position of **chief privacy officer (CPO)**. A CPO must understand how a business operates and uses consumer information. This may require both business and legal skills.[7]

Webmaster

The position of **Webmaster** has recently evolved in organizations. Webmasters are often involved in designing Web pages and graphics, coding and maintaining pages, answering users' questions, aiding in Web strategic planning, compiling statistics, and making purchasing decisions. Webmasters must often be cross-functional experts, able to understand the marketing and media aspects of a company and the technological requirements of developing and maintaining Web sites. Intranets have more specialized requirements because they are involved in the management of an organization. Individuals who oversee intranets often come from marketing and management fields. Most Web sites are maintained by small cross-functional teams that often outsource specialized tasks such as design and coding.[8]

Historical nSite

Webmasters have gone by many other names, including the following:

- Digital communications specialist
- Electronic marketing specialist
- Manager, new media
- Cyber commander
- Web god/goddess
- Web wizard
- Spiderman/woman

Sources of Jobs

Using online job sites is just part of an overall job search strategy. In the year 2000, only 15 percent of the $7.6 billion spent on recruitment went to online job sites. Job sites most often allow individuals to post résumés for free; they make their money by charging employers for access to the information on

Table A10.1   Popular Online Job Sites

Name	Site	Description
Monster	http://www.monster.com	Online résumé site that serves over 93,000 companies.
6FigureJobs	http://www.6figures.com	Web site that offers executives and experienced professionals access to exclusive high-level jobs, executive recruiters, and career management tools.
Hotjobs	http://www.hotjobs.com	Leading career domain (a subsidiary of Yahoo!) that provides employers with progressive recruiting solutions.
Careerbuilder	http://www.careerbuilder.com	Online source for recruitment dollars and job searches.
DirectEmployers	http://www.directemployers.com	Employment search engine owned and managed by a non-profit employer association, the E-Recruiting Association.
ComputerJobs	http://www.computerjobs.com	IT employment Web site that provides visitors computer-related job opportunities and career-related content organized into eighteen vertical skill sets and more than nineteen major metropolitan markets.

potential employees. As with any job-posting system, the chance of securing an interview after posting a résumé is low. Many companies post job openings at their own corporate sites, allowing individuals to apply for specific positions.[9] Table A10.1 lists some popular online job sites.

Using online job sites should not replace the normal job search process of identifying networked individuals, using those individuals to obtain leads, targeting résumés and cover letters to job openings, and contacting key decision makers to let them know of your interest and your qualifications. To aid in this process, individuals who enter the job market with college experience may wish to develop a marketing portfolio to enhance their job search chances.

Portfolios

Students in many fields are required to develop **portfolios** of their work to apply for jobs in their field. Artists, design students, architects, writers, and others all keep track of their work knowing that the projects they complete can be used to demonstrate the knowledge and skills necessary to obtain a quality job.

Portfolios need not be an additional burden to students; students simply need to keep track of the work they do. Marketing majors should present a portfolio of their work to their advisor when they engage in a graduation check or before they start the interviewing process. Advisors can work with students to get the portfolio in shape to show to potential employers. Each section of the portfolio should indicate examples of a student's work related to the competencies outlined in the next section.

Competencies

The following is a list of competencies that students should have when they finish a marketing program:[10]

1) **Teamwork Ability**
   a) Ability to function effectively in team environments
   b) Interpersonal skills for successful execution of joint projects with others
   c) Conflict resolution skills

2) **Leadership Ability**
   a) Idea-selling skills
   b) Relationship development skills
   c) Ability to negotiate, communicate, and persuade
   d) Skills to muster and control resources to accomplish complex tasks

3) **Personal Drive and Organization Skills**
   a) Skills to accomplish tasks without supervision
   b) Ability to organize
   c) Prioritization ability
   d) Time management appreciation
   e) Ability to initiate and maintain projects
   f) Good judgment and decision making expertise
   g) Self-discipline and ability to function despite distractions
   h) Desire to seek out additional work until the job is complete

4) **Analytical and Writing Skills**
   a) Ability to read, write, understand, and use terminology.
   b) Qualitative and descriptive skills
   c) Business literacy in verbal and written applications
   d) Ability to follow complex written ideas.
   e) Skills to write and express complex ideas
   f) Ability to read help resources to master tasks

5) **Technology Mastery**
   a) Ability to use relevant hardware and software
   b) Skills to work comfortably with evolving technologies
   c) Information system design and function skills
   d) Web and multimedia abilities
   e) Basic programming understanding

f) Skills to develop Web pages

g) Ability to understand the issues involved in the implementation of technology in a firm

6) **Strategic Planning Skills**

   a) Innovation and entrepreneurship skills

   b) Ability to handle new and unique tasks

   c) Desire to engage in complex problem solving

   d) Ability to exercise creativity in unstructured tasks

   e) Logical reasoning skills

   f) Desire to think outside the box

   g) Ability to develop cohesive and cogent strategic plans

7) **Ability to Learn**

   a) Strong academic performance

   b) Non-major course knowledge

   c) Fundamental knowledge of business areas outside major

   d) Ability to function in culturally diverse environments

8) **Personal Skills**

   a) Balanced approach to personal, social, and professional development and maintenance

   b) Ability to function in social settings

   c) Listening, speaking, synthesis, and integration skills

9) **Selling and Product Management Background**

   a) Account management

   b) Buyer behavior

   c) Business-to-business selling

   d) Product management

   e) Marketing services

   f) Purchasing

   g) Sales territory management

   h) Ethics

10) **Market Research Background**

   a) Statistics

   b) Questionnaire design

   c) Marketing math

   d) Qualitative research

   e) Research report writing

11) **Promotion and Consumer Marketing Background**

   a) Direct marketing

   b) Media planning

   c) Communication design

   d) Consumer selling

   e) Marketing planning

12) **Marketing and Sales Analysis Background**
   a) Sales forecasting
   b) Sales territory management
   c) Pricing
   d) Marketing math
   e) Competitive analysis

13) **Retailing Background**
   a) Merchandising
   b) Media planning
   c) Consumer selling
   d) Pricing
   e) Purchasing

Developing an Electronic Portfolio

Figure A10.1 outlines the process of developing an electronic portfolio using IP protocols such as HTML and hyperlinks. An electronic portfolio can be hosted on an ISP or placed on a CD-ROM and sent to a potential employer. Portfolios can be used by potential employers to evaluate student skills. For further examples of marketing portfolios, use the search term *marketing portfolio and résumé* in your favorite search engine.

Knowledge Integration

Terms and Concepts

Chief information officer (CIO) *321*
Chief knowledge officer (CKO) *322*
Chief privacy officer (CPO) *322*
Portfolio *323*
Vice president of electronic commerce *321*
Webmaster *322*

Figure A10.1 Outlines for an Electronic Portfolio

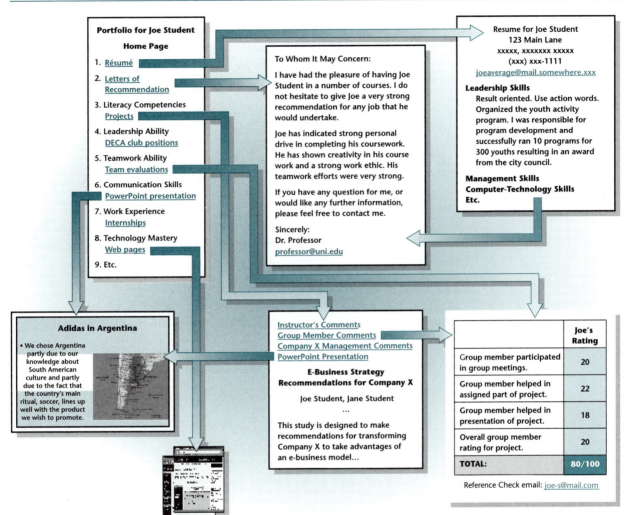

Portfolio for Joe Student
Home Page

1. Résumé
2. Letters of
   Recommendation
3. Literacy Competencies
   Projects
4. Leadership Ability
   DECA club positions
5. Teamwork Ability
   Team evaluations
6. Communication Skills
   PowerPoint presentation
7. Work Experience
   Internships
8. Technology Mastery
   Web pages
9. Etc.

To Whom It May Concern:

I have had the pleasure of having Joe Student in a number of courses. I do not hesitate to give Joe a very strong recommendation for any job that he would undertake.

Joe has indicated strong personal drive in completing his coursework. He has shown creativity in his course work and a strong work ethic. His teamwork efforts were very strong.

If you have any question for me, or would like any further information, please feel free to contact me.

Sincerely:
Dr. Professor
professor@uni.edu

Resume for Joe Student
123 Main Lane
XXXXX, XXXXXXX XXXXX
(xxx) xxx-1111
joeaverage@mail.somewhere.xxx

Leadership Skills
Result oriented. Use action words. Organized the youth activity program. I was responsible for program development and successfully ran 10 programs for 300 youths resulting in an award from the city council.

Management Skills
Computer-Technology Skills
Etc.

Adidas in Argentina

- We chose Argentina partly due to our knowledge about South American culture and partly due to the fact that the country's main ritual, soccer, lines up well with the product we wish to promote.

Instructor's Comments
Group Member Comments
Company X Management Comments
PowerPoint Presentation

E-Business Strategy
Recommendations for Company X

Joe Student, Jane Student
...

This study is designed to make recommendations for transforming Company X to take advantages of an e-business model...

	Joe's Rating
Group member participated in group meetings.	20
Group member helped in assigned part of project.	22
Group member helped in presentation of project.	18
Overall group member rating for project.	20
TOTAL:	**80/100**

Reference Check email: joe-s@mail.com

Concepts and Questions for Review

1. Explain the role of a chief information officer in a firm.
2. What is the role of a vice president of electronic commerce?
3. Descibe the role of a chief knowledge officer in a firm.
4. Why has the role of a chief privacy officer been created in some firms?
5. Explain what a Webmaster does.
6. How can an electronic portfolio be useful for individuals pursuing jobs?

Active Learning

Exercise A10.1 Career Path

Use the Internet to identify open positions for the careers outlined in this appendix. Develop a list of the specific skills required. Outline a career path that could lead to any of the positions you find.

Exercise A10.2 Electronic Portfolio

Develop an electronic portfolio from content you already have. Specify how this portfolio can be organized to show your skills to potential employers.

References

[1] Christopher Koch, "Authors, Authors Everywhere," *Webmaster,* January 1997, 36–40.

[2] "What is a CIO?" The CIO Executive Research Center [online] (December 17, 1998), available from <http://www.cio.com/forums/executive/description.html>.

[3] Mindy Blodgett, "The CIO Starter Kit," *CIO,* May 15, 1999, 38–50; David Pearson, "National Insecurities," *CIO,* February 1, 1999, 24.

[4] Robert Preston, "New Breed of Internet Exec Is Born," *InternetWeek,* October 25, 1999, 54–55; Sari Kalin, "Title Search," *CIO Web Business,* February 1, 1999, 42–47.

[5] Justin Hibbard, "Knowledge and Learning Officers Find Big Paydays," *InformationWeek,* June 15, 1998, 170; Julekha Dash, "Turning Technology into TechKnowledgey," *Software Magazine,* February 2, 1998, 64–73; J. Michael Pemberton, "Chief Knowledge Officer: The Climax to Your Career?" *Records Management Quarterly,* April 1997, 66–70.

[6] Michael M. Earl and Ian A. Scott, "What Is a Chief Knowledge Officer?" *Sloan Management Review,* Winter 1999, 29–38; Daintry Duffy, "Knowledge Champions," *CIO Enterprise,* November 15, 1998, 66–71; Barb Cole-Gomolski, "Knowledge Managers Need Business Savvy," *Computerworld,* January 25, 1999, 40.

[7] Fred Mogul, "Rise of the CPO," November 1, 2000, *InternetWorld,* 35–38; Shrei McGregor, "The CPO: Your Chief Profit Officer," *Profit,* August 2001, 63–66.

[8] Andrew Marlatt, "Running a Big Site? Better Be Good at Juggling," *Internet World,* March 29, 1999, 30; James C. Luh, "Intranet Webmasters Must Do It All," *Internet World,* December 7, 1998, 40; Elizabeth Gardner, "More Work—But More Money," *Internet World,* October 5, 1998, 8–10; and Elizabeth Gardner, "Backlash against Title of Webmaster," *Internet World,* September 15, 1997, 1, 38–39.

[9] Ann Harrington, "Can Anyone Build a Better Monster," *Fortune,* May 13, 2002, 189–92; Joan Raymond, "The Jaws of Victory," *Newsweek,* March 18, 2002, 38P.

[10] Norm A. Borin and Harry Watkins, "Critical Skills for Today's Marketing Undergraduates: An Employer Evaluation," *AMA Winter Educator's Conference Proceedings* 9, (1998), 238–45; Norm A. Borin and Harry Watkins, "Employers Evaluate Critical Skills of Today's Marketing Undergraduates," *Marketing Educator* 17, no. 3 (1998): 1–6.

chapter 11
E-Business Strategy

This chapter explores the dynamics of developing strategies in an e-business environment. A number of environmental drivers are forcing businesses to develop effective strategies. In the late 1990s, e-businesses attempted to react quickly and fill market niches before competitive firms could mobilize. In the new millennium, many businesses are learning to reassess their business model and implement e-business strategies by developing brand names, differentiating themselves from competitors, and strengthening their customer relationships. This chapter will explore the use of e-business techniques for gaining competitive advantages along with the process of evaluating a business model. E-business students and managers must be able to use the concepts and techniques outlined in this text to compete in today's dynamic environment.

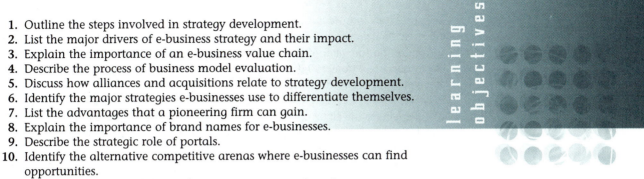

1. Outline the steps involved in strategy development.
2. List the major drivers of e-business strategy and their impact.
3. Explain the importance of an e-business value chain.
4. Describe the process of business model evaluation.
5. Discuss how alliances and acquisitions relate to strategy development.
6. Identify the major strategies e-businesses use to differentiate themselves.
7. List the advantages that a pioneering firm can gain.
8. Explain the importance of brand names for e-businesses.
9. Describe the strategic role of portals.
10. Identify the alternative competitive arenas where e-businesses can find opportunities.
11. Describe the measures that businesses can use to judge e-business success.

....

"Microsoft already owns America's offices, now it wants America's living rooms."

Jonathan Schwartz
Sun Microsystem's Chief Strategist[1]

....

Microsoft versus the World

In the early 1990s, Microsoft had near monopoly power in a number of software areas including operating systems, spreadsheets, and word processing. Microsoft was a powerful supplier of software to computer manufacturers, able to dictate prices and products on the Windows desktop. Microsoft's dominance in the market made it difficult for buyers to switch to new products. Corporate buyers felt safe purchasing Microsoft's industry-standard products. Few companies attempted to compete against Microsoft. If Microsoft announced that it would produce a product, software companies would stay away from that product category. Microsoft seemed to be safe and in control of the microcomputer industry.

Then came the rise of the Internet and the growth of the Web through the use of graphical browsers. In 1994, Microsoft's chairman, Bill Gates, realized Microsoft was not the first to move into this new Internet industry and had to play catch-up. Gates mustered his forces to have Microsoft's software retooled for the Internet. Microsoft may have been heading in the wrong direction, but within eight months it was able to change direction and become a dominant Internet player. Internet software or services that Microsoft could not produce itself it purchased, licensed, or obtained through alliance.[2]

Microsoft began to take market share away from Netscape by reverse engineering Netscape to develop Internet Explorer. By 2002, Netscape's share of the browser market had shrunk to about 15 percent. Many other companies have fallen to Microsoft's assaults, including Lotus, Borland, and WordPerfect. Some companies have managed to survive and compete against Microsoft. Companies such as Intuit and Palm have maintained competitiveness by being fast to market and constantly innovating.[3]

Meanwhile, Linux entered the market. Linus Torvalds, a Finnish graduate student, developed an alternative operating system and released the source code on the Internet. Programmers from around the world were free to add to, improve, and customize the software. After a slow start, Linux gained support. The installed base of Linux users grew from 100,000 in 1993 to an estimated 12 million by 1998. Linux has received support from companies such as IBM, Dell Computer, Intel, Netscape, Hewlett-Packard, Compaq, and Corel. Corel developed a free downloadable version of WordPerfect for the Linux operating system.[4] Microsoft sees Linux as a strong potential threat and reported to the Justice Department that freeware programs such as Linux prove that Microsoft does not have a monopoly in the marketplace.

Back at the Redmond ranch, Microsoft has been positioning itself for a much wider competitive environment. Microsoft has been moving to develop an Internet media- and commerce-based business. WebTV, MSNBC, and alliances with cable companies give Microsoft access to the television market. Expedia allows customers to purchase travel services, and CarPoint offers car sales; the Microsoft Network (MSN) is the second most popular online portal.[5]

Microsoft is evolving from a company that supplies software to a company that plans to link customers to goods and services. Microsoft's electronic commerce mission is *Making the Internet indispensable and relevant to every person and every business, every day.* To achieve this mission, Microsoft has determined that its main core competency is recruitment of the best high-technology workers. Microsoft attempts to hire the very smart and constantly reorganize to become more efficient.[6]

All that Microsoft touches does not turn to gold. Microsoft spent $3.5 on European cable companies to push Web-based TV into Europe. By 2002, Microsoft's investments had shrunk and the total number of cable TV Internet users was small. Part of the reason that this initiative failed was that Microsoft's software was too expensive and too complicated.[7]

Source: <http://www.msn.com/>. © Microsoft Corporation.

▶ Thinking Strategically

Determine the environmental factors influencing Microsoft. What are Microsoft's strengths and weaknesses? Decide which of Microsoft's strengths allow it to gain an advantage over its competitors. List environmental threats that Microsoft currently faces or could encounter in the future. What steps could Microsoft take to address those threats? Speculate on the future opportunities that Microsoft may have. List the different competitive arenas in which Microsoft is competing. What steps would Microsoft need to take to pursue those opportunities? Recommend a strategy that a company could use to compete in the same markets as Microsoft.

The vignette illustrates a number of issues addressed in this chapter. Businesses must develop strategies that allow them to compete if they are to survive. The full process of strategy development and implementation is beyond the scope of this text. Instead, this chapter will look at the broad process of strategy development for e-businesses by considering the current drivers of strategy and the major strategies undertaken in the e-business marketplace.

E-Business Professionals

Monica Rockwell
Windows.NET Server Marketing
http://www.microsoft.com

Monica Rockwell

Monica Rockwell graduated with a bachelor's degree in technical writing from the school of engineering at the University of Washington. She started working for Microsoft in 1989. Currently Monica works in Windows marketing, content management, and communications.

Part of her job is to develop business case studies of the successful use of Microsoft products. These case studies show how Windows.NET enhances connectivity within a company and between companies and suppliers. Microsoft's .NET strategy is designed to have Microsoft's products act as a standard platform for a secure extranet and intranet communication system. Microsoft built the .NET platform using IP standards, to help companies more easily take advantage of the Internet. This system allows all developers to use XML as a platform.

Monica states, "I believe in the company [Microsoft]. I believe that the company has changed the world and will change the world in a positive way. I am proud to work there."

Monica has seen Microsoft hire a large number of people during the Internet boom years. Now those employees need to prove their worth to keep their jobs.

For college students to work in a high-technology marketing area, they need to refine their writing and communication skills. It is important to be a powerful communicator, or your ideas carry no weight. Students must be able to both gather customer feedback and understand finances in order to help a company gain competitive advantages. The typical weaknesses that Monica sees in a marketing person are the inability to write and to otherwise communicate with others inside a firm.

What Is Strategy?

A **strategy** consists of a pattern of decisions that set the goals and objectives leading to long-run competitive advantages for a firm.[8] E-businesses must develop strategies to survive in their competitive environments. The tools and techniques outlined in this text are being used by e-businesses to gain competitive advantages. These businesses include not only pure-play Internet companies but also brick-and-mortar-based e-businesses. Competitive advantages come from gaining efficiencies in logistics and production, meeting customers' needs better than the competition, devising an effective business model, and being able to respond to a changing environment. A rapidly evolving and highly competitive environment is forcing businesses to reassess current strategies and develop new strategies to ensure long-term survival. The essence of strategy development for businesses involves four basic steps:

1) **Undertake a SWOT (strengths, weaknesses, opportunities, threats) analysis.** A **SWOT analysis** requires investigating the strengths and weaknesses of the business and analyzing new opportunities as well as threats from competitors and the environment.

2) **Determine distinctive competencies.** After performing a SWOT analysis, a business must determine where it has advantages over competitors or how it can achieve **distinctive competencies.** This process requires an analysis of a business's value chain to identify internal strengths and weaknesses that can help determine how a business can compete. Determining distinctive competencies and maintaining these over a long time period can be very difficult for a business.

3) **Determine the competitive arena.** Performing a SWOT analysis and identifying distinctive competencies allow a business to determine its **competitive arena.** This step helps establish the mission for the business by indicating the windows of opportunity to be pursued and the nature of the competitive environment in which a business can and wants to compete. Gaining an advantage often requires finding a fit between a firm's distinctive competencies and the nature of the competitive environment.

4) **Develop a plan to reach the business goals.** The strategic planning process outlines the actions and tactics a business must use to move from where and how it currently competes to where and how it needs to compete given its distinctive competencies. The planning process sets targets, maintains feedback, and implements control to aid in reaching strategic goals.

This strategy process is illustrated in Figure 11.1. In this figure, environmental **strategic drivers** force a business to evaluate and strengthen its **value chain** to undertake strategic actions both to pursue opportunities and to avoid or limit competitive threats.

Distinctive competencies *are unique areas of advantage in which a firm can differentiate itself from competitors.*

The competitive area *is the competitive environment in which a business operates.*

A value chain *is a way of envisioning the collection of activities that a business undertakes to design, produce, market, deliver, and support products or services.*

Drivers of Strategy

Businesses need to be able to respond to changes in turbulent environments. **Environmental turbulence** means that the environment is changing rapidly and unpredictably and is often characterized by rapid change in competitors' products and in customers' needs.[9] Environmental turbulence forces change in business strategies and in the distinctive competencies needed to compete. Some of the drivers leading to environmental turbulence are described in Table 11.1.

Figure 11.1   A Model of Strategy

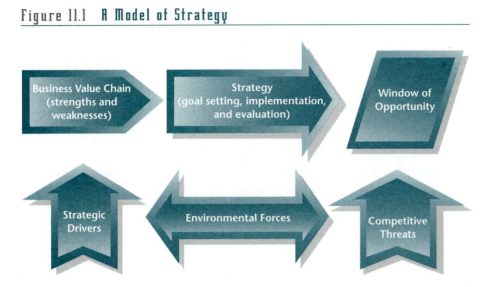

Table 11.1   Drivers of Environmental Turbulence

Environmental Drivers	Description
Technological Change	**Moore's law,** which states that the density of transistors on microprocessors doubles every two years while costs decrease, seems to be holding. This is allowing technology to be applied across a broader spectrum of products and uses.
Changing Customers	Customers around the globe are rapidly accepting Internet use and online purchasing. Most individuals are facing time compression in that there is not enough time for them to do everything they would like to do; technology is being used as an enabler, allowing individuals to accomplish more. Customers have more power due to an increase in access to information and negotiating power.
Shorter Product Life Cycles	Product life cycles are getting shorter due to the rapid development of new technology, aggressive marketing, and buyers' willingness to try new products.
Number of Competitors	Distance between competitors is vanishing. Online competition allows sellers from many different locations to sell anywhere. This is causing an increase in the intensity of competition and allowing international competitors to enter new markets.
Need for Speed	Time is collapsing across business applications. Instant connectivity is becoming the norm in business-to-business applications as well as in the way consumers shop.

Sources: Eric Chabrow, "Seeking the Deeper Path to E-Success," *InformationWeek,* March 6, 2000, 49–76; "10 Driving Principles of the New Economy," *Business 2.0,* premier issue; William Qualls, Richard W. Olshavsky, and Ronald E. Michaels, "Shortening of the PLC—An Empirical Test," *Journal of Marketing* (Fall 1981): 76–80; Milton D. Rosenau Jr., *Faster New Product Development* (New York: AMACOM, 1990).

These drivers can present both opportunities and threats to an e-business. E-businesses that understand these drivers and can leverage the technology necessary to serve customers have the opportunity to capture market share. Those that do not respond to these drivers will face competitive threats from faster, more nimble competitors. E-businesses are responding to this turbulence by leveraging assets and deploying technology. Businesses must be willing to take **proactive** steps to maintain current and future competitiveness. This includes evaluating current and new business models and determining if change is needed.

Before a business commits to a strategy, it should first undertake a SWOT analysis to help determine internal strengths and weaknesses and assess external opportunities and threats. An analysis of the e-business value chain can help a business identify its strengths and weaknesses. When taken into consideration along with opportunities and competitive threats, this analysis can help a business identify areas of distinctive competencies and the competitive arenas in which to operate.

*Being **proactive** implies acting in anticipation of future problems or opportunities, rather than being **reactive**— waiting and reacting to the environment.*

The E-Business Value Chain

Identifying the individual activities that a business undertakes to design, produce, market, deliver, and support products or services is the first step in determining how to deliver value to customers. A value chain considers the inbound logistical process (obtaining raw materials, logistical procedures, and production) and the outbound logistical process (outbound logistical procedures, marketing, sales, and support). To gain a distinctive competency, a business must be able to perform some function in its value chain better than its competitors can. This could mean providing a function at a lower cost or in a unique way. Businesses that compete in similar industries serving similar markets may have value chains that differ from those in other industries.[10] With the growth of e-business tools and techniques, a new perspective has been added to the value chain. The **e-business value chain** views information technology as part of a business's overall value chain, adding to the competitive advantages of a business.[11] A survey of more than four hundred information technology managers indicated that 96 percent believe that electronic sales and purchasing applications were very (61 percent) or somewhat (35 percent) important to their businesses.[12] According to the trade journal *InformationWeek*, the number one priority for businesses in the *InformationWeek* 500 (a list of the most innovative users of technology) is implementing e-business strategies and, specifically, improving supply chains and electronic data interchange.[13] This text has outlined a number of techniques that an e-business can use to gain advantages throughout its value chain. Figure 11.2 illustrates how these technologies impact the components of an e-business value chain.

As shown in Figure 11.2, a firm can gain cost advantages through the use of extranets, enterprise resource planning (ERP) software, and e-commerce. Although a

Figure 11.2   The E-Business Value Chain

Inbound Distribution Logistics

Extranets: Lower costs, increase speed.

Value Production

ERP software: Provides differential advantages, customization, dynamic pricing.

Marketing/ Sales

E-commerce: Lowers costs, eases new market entry, provides e-business promotion.

Customer Targeting and Support

Databases: Enable better CRM.

Internet: Lowers costs, speeds service.

Management

IT leadership: Encourages innovativeness, speed, flexibility, new product ideas.

Intranets: Lower costs, provide better communication.

Competitive Advantage through Stronger Customer Relationships

Supported by **E-Business Communication Platforms** and
E-Business Technological Infrastructure

survey of chief executive officers indicated that 78 percent viewed information technology as a source of competitive advantage, cost advantages may give firms industry parity or short-term advantages only, not long-term differential advantages. Chief financial officers have indicated that the most important criterion for evaluating technology investments is whether or not IT helps reduce operating expenses (71 percent of respondents). The next four most important criteria were related to gaining distinctive advantages: technology could enable the business to stay ahead of competition (62 percent), provide an opportunity to enhance operating revenue (44 percent), position the company to increase market share (40 percent), and help reduce lead times (39 percent).[14] Improvement of any component in the value chain can result in an overall improvement in customer satisfaction.

A key to implementing e-business technology is having a management team and employees who are willing and able to restructure an organization. This is part of the reason that Microsoft has stated that its distinctive competence is rooted in its hiring policy. Management and employees must be able to capitalize on the advantages that can be found in customer databases, online access to information between buyers and sellers, rapid responses to environmental change, and proactive innovation.[15] Not all the components of the e-business value chain must come from within the organization itself; many e-businesses outsource key components, form alliances with other businesses, or even acquire another firm.

Identification of a Distinctive Advantage

A **distinctive advantage** must come from some area in which a business can gain a long-term advantage over competitors. Technology by itself may not impart a competitive advantage; it must be leveraged to be responsive to the needs of the company and its customers. By lowering costs, improving responsiveness to customers, and improving businesses' ability to respond to environmental change, technology is already having an impact on the logistical and supply-chain processes across a large number of industries. Brick-and-mortar companies and pure-play e-businesses are learning how to use technology to increase sales and customer support. As these processes become more widely accepted in both business-to-business and business-to-consumer markets, however, they may not impart long-term advantages. Instead, they may be only the basis for competition in a market. For example, if a business is not able to leverage a technology such as e-mail, it may not be able to compete because it would not be able to respond rapidly enough to external customers and internal communication needs.[16]

Coca-Cola has linked together its production with eleven Anchor Bottling partners in an attempt to stay ahead of its global competitors and a changing market. This effort has connected 43 percent of Coke's production. Databases are used to provide information on store sales and customer use around the world. Coke bottlers in Australia and New Zealand have vending machines linked through cellular systems; they can report on the sales in each machine. Coca-Cola is hoping that this technology implementation will allow it to become a more efficient operation around the world. Figure 11.3 illustrates the e-business value chain being developed for Coca-Cola.[17]

Figure 11.3   Coca-Cola E-Business Value Chain

Inbound Distribution Logistics

Extranets: Link Coke with bottling partners and suppliers.

Value Production

ERP software: Links Coke with its bottling partners; provides interconnected management system.

Marketing/ Sales

E-commerce: Links vending machines via cellular.

Databases: Used with decision support systems to determine the effectiveness of marketing efforts.

Customer Targeting and Support

Internet: Provides more timely delivery to trade

Management

IT leadership: Willing to change and sell innovative, new approach in the soft-drink industry.

Intranets: Improve worldwide communication.

Competitive Advantage through Stronger Customer Relationships

The Coca-Cola example illustrates that Coke is increasing the efficiency of its operations, but it still needs to be able to maintain its brand name and product quality to keep its competitive position. Implementing an e-business value chain often requires a business to evaluate and reassess its business model.

Business Models

Once a business has identified its strengths and weaknesses along its value chain, it should assess if its business model should be restructured to gain additional efficiencies or to become more competitive. A **business model**, or **commerce model**, is the basic process flow indicating how a business operates. It indicates how business functions are linked together. Successful businesses have always modified their business models in response to changes in competitive environments. With the growth of the Internet and the World Wide Web and the introduction of e-business tools and techniques, businesses are either taking advantage of new business models or are forced to change to compete. A systematic approach to viewing organizations and the complex relationships required to make a business operate is called **business process modeling.** This approach requires analyzing how a business system operates. Four different perspectives can be used to model business processes:

- ☐ **The functional perspective** identifies the functions within a business and how they interact.
- ☐ **The behavioral perspective** identifies when and how functions are performed in a business.
- ☐ **The organizational perspective** identifies where and by whom functions are undertaken.
- ☐ **The informational perspective** identifies what types of information are used and how they flow.[18]

The identification of all of these processes and procedures can be complicated. Specialized software packages have been developed to help model flows. Throughout this text, information flows have been modeled for such processes as Internet communication and e-mail marketing campaigns. This section will concentrate on identifying functional flows.

Chapter 1 discussed generic business systems and e-business systems. These can be seen as representing a generic business model and an e-business model. Figure 11.4 offers a generic business model. This model shows the flow of products (or services) from suppliers to the producing company and then through warehousing and retailers to customers. Promotion is conducted through traditional media and sales efforts. Payment and information flows go from the customer to the company.

Figure 11.5 illustrates a generic e-business model. In this model, suppliers are linked electronically to the manufacturer. Customized products can be delivered through independent shippers directly to the customer. Web sites can both provide and collect information between the company and the customer. Payment flows are facilitated online by credit card companies or online billing and invoicing

Figure 11.4   A Generic Business Model

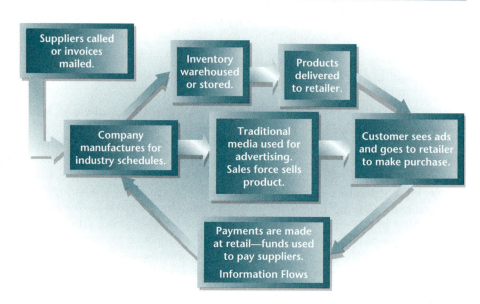

Figure 11.5   A Generic E-Business Model

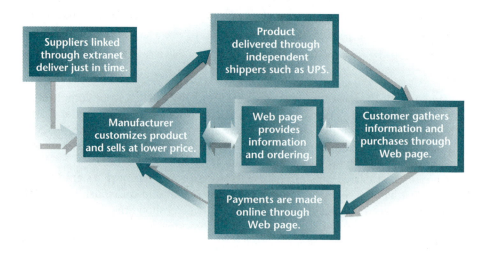

systems. It is not enough, however, to simply illustrate flows in a business model and implement technological change. These changes must be undertaken in a way that will allow for companies to leverage competitive advantages in the marketplace. The use of a value chain analysis, discussed earlier, can help in this process.

Developing e-business models requires identifying the functional process flows of a business and then modeling how the application of e-business procedures can result in competitive advantage. This is a six-step process:

1) Identify the functional areas and major players.

2) Indicate how these areas are linked and the directions of the flow.

3) Determine what e-business tools and techniques can be applied to the business model.

4) Develop a new e-business model flow.

5) Evaluate the competitive advantages of the model by using a value chain analysis.

6) Determine the likelihood of acceptance of the new model.

Higher education has not been spared from the business model changes challenging other industries and can serve as an example of a changing model. The use of the Internet for higher education is impacting three areas. The first is the student's use of the Internet as a communication and research tool. The second is the use of the Internet as a supplementary delivery system for class content and interaction. The third is the use of the Internet as a stand-alone distance-learning vehicle. The number of colleges and universities offering distance courses is expected to increase from 1,500 in the year 2000 to over 3,300 by 2004.[19]

Figure 11.6 illustrates the traditional higher education model. In this model, the professor is the major focus of content delivery. This delivery system is traditionally time and place dependent (usually in a classroom setting). The professor delivers information through lectures, facilitates discussions, and supervises testing and evaluation. For the most part, the student can take a passive role in the process by digesting the course material and responding through tests, papers, group discussions, and so forth.

Figure 11.6 The Traditional Higher Education Model

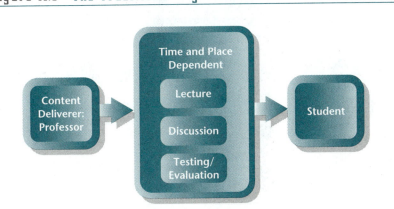

Figure 11.7 illustrates the e-learning higher education model. In this model, the professor takes on a new role as the developer and maintainer of a learning environment. This learning environment is time and place independent (usually in an interactive learning environment such as Blackboard or WebCT). The professor must develop a learning environment by supplying lectures, links, voice and video files, or other teaching materials and by structuring student discussions. The professor becomes the content specialist and the facilitator of the education process. Students interact online through discussion groups (time independent) or chat rooms (time dependent). Evaluation is enhanced because students can obtain immediate feedback on tests, and instructors can monitor students' actual behavior, such as how long students take to perform tasks or how often they view content and what content they view.

Business Model Analysis

Education facilitators (i.e., professors) are finding that the target market they serve is very willing to operate under an e-learning model. In this model, the education facilitator is losing control of information flows because of the amount of content available online or from publishing companies. In addition, the facilitator is operating in a richer communication environment. Students are able to direct themselves to content they feel they need additional time with. They are able to form learning communities and gain access to information on a 24/7 basis. The facilitators of these learning environments are able to track individual behavior and have the opportunity to offer individualized care to students.

The value chain components of the production of course content, communication, and support can give an e-learning business an advantage. A human inter-

Figure 11.7   The E-Learning Higher Education Model

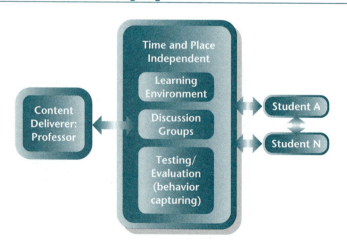

face is still desired for these complex learning environments, but the traditional lecture system may be less effective. Traditional higher education systems are adjusting their business models as private and public higher education institutions find themselves competing against for-profit education providers (such as Phoenix University and publishing companies). These changes to the higher education environment are impacting other learning environments as well. The corporate e-learning market in Europe alone could reach $4 billion from 2001 through 2004.[20]

It is important that a business realize it needs to use technology to underpin effective business models that will be accepted by both customers and employees and will provide for a long-term competitive advantage. Many pure-play e-businesses found that advertising-only models were not effective in providing the needed return. Others have evaluated e-business models and have rejected some applications. IKEA, for example, is a worldwide furniture and housewares retail company. It sells many products through catalogs and serves a younger urban market. IKEA, however, decided that an e-commerce model would not help the company maintain its competitive advantage. IKEA has set up its stores to make shopping a form of entertainment. When individuals enter the store, they walk through floors of products set up in display rooms. This experience cannot be duplicated on the Web. Instead, IKEA uses the Web (http://www.ikea.com) as a brochure site to enhance the brand.[21]

Another example of a changing business model occurred in the PC sales industry. Prior to 1998, the functional business model for selling computers could be illustrated in Figure 11.8. This model relied on traditional manufacturing, shipping, and retail sales methods.

Figure 11.8   Pre-1998 Computer Sales Functional Business Model

Inventory levels ordered based on sales projections.

Increases inventory costs as inventory waits in storage.

Product delivered through shippers to retail outlet.

Decreases product value as product sits in retail outlet waiting to be sold.

Manufacturer produces product to fit retail orders.

Personal sales backed by national and local advertising.
Increases sales costs.

Customer has immediate possession of product and can possibly return product and receive support.

Payments are made through cash, check, credit card, or invoice.

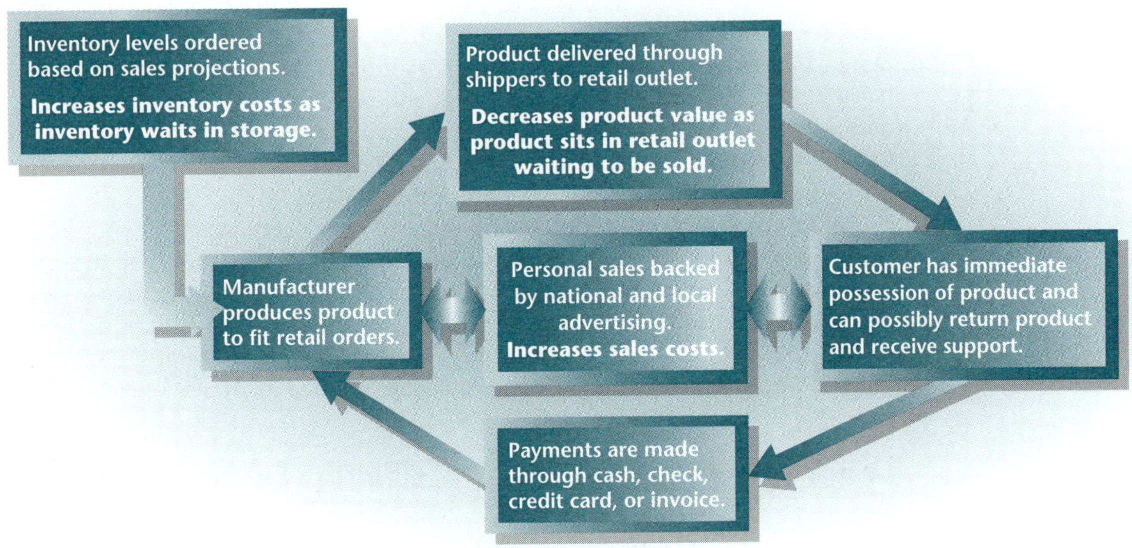

Dell Computer is just one of the pioneers using information technology to change industries. Dell's business model consists of more than just selling over the Internet. It gains efficiency by developing links to suppliers. It collects information on customers to increase knowledge on market trends. By moving this highly efficient model around the world, Dell is forcing its competitors to change their business practices. Nations are reacting by developing the infrastructure necessary to allow their businesses to compete on the same global scale.[22]

Most computer buyers search for information before they buy. Dell's Web site allows those buyers to immediately move to areas that interest them. In 1997, Dell received one Web visit for every phone inquiry; by 1998, there were three and a half Web visits for every phone inquiry. Potential buyers visit the Web site five to ten times to obtain information, have their questions answered, and determine prices before they buy. Because the Web visit is considerably less expensive, the cost savings are given back to the buyer.[23] Dell's business model is shown in Figure 6.6, page 181.

E-Business Strategies

Firms have traditionally taken two paths to gain distinctive advantages. The first is to attempt to be the low-cost (and therefore low-price) competitor. The second is to attempt a **differentiation strategy** by finding a unique market position against competitors. Information technology is allowing businesses to become more efficient through decreased costs in sales and marketing. In addition, improvement in internal and external communication is speeding manufacturing, research and development, and purchasing, resulting in cost savings.[24] Being the low-cost producer may not be enough to gain a long-term advantage because competitors can gain the same efficiencies. E-business technology can be both a blessing and a curse for businesses. A **frictionless market** implies that customers have almost perfect information and can compare prices around the world, and using intelligence agents to search out the best prices enhances this process. This forces businesses selling over the Internet, and those that compete against Internet sales, to lower prices or differentiate.[25] Table 11.2 outlines a number of strategies e-businesses are currently using to differentiate themselves.

For online sellers, speed and flexibility allow quick response to environmental change, size permits economies of scale, brand names give assurance to the buyer, and close customer relationships entice customers to return to a site. These strategies do not guarantee long-term advantages. Severe price competition may hurt all but the most efficient businesses or those with a differentiated niche. The following sections will expand on the strategies outlined in Table 11.2.

Leveraging Speed and First-Mover Advantages

Time-based competition implies that businesses are flexible enough to respond quickly to the environment, allowing advantages to be gained over slower busi-

Table 11.2   Methods of Differentiation

Differentiation Strategy	Advantages	Disadvantages
Leverage Speed and First-Mover Advantages	Provides lower costs, meets consumer needs, lowers risk perception, and raises prices.	Increases risks and may require large amounts of capital to maintain advantages; firms need to be flexible to be fast.
Build Brand Name	Gives buyers assurance when interacting with a site. Allows for easy name recognition.	Requires a large amount of capital to obtain and maintain a brand name.
Develop Portal and Marketplace	Allows for economies of scale and builds barriers to entry.	Needs a large amount of capital, pushing off profitability.
Pursue Niche Strategies	Lets a business focus and become an expert in one competitive arena; good strategy for smaller or weaker businesses.	Can be risky if the firm is dependent on one type of customer.
Enhance Customer Relationships	Allows businesses to build barriers to entry; by staying close to customers, business can meet their needs better.	Could result in a loss of power by the business supplying the product or service.

nesses. This has been especially true for **first movers** or **pioneering firms** and for firms that must innovate to compete against strong rivals such as Microsoft. When a firm innovates, it has, by definition, differentiated itself from the competition because it is the first to enter a competitive arena or is able to help define the competitive arena, giving it a first-mover advantage. Pioneering with new business models also allows for first-mover advantages, even for small businesses. Speed has become a major method of competing in a turbulent environment, and businesses are attempting to act as quickly as possible.[26]

Being fast has a number of advantages. These include lower costs, the ability to meet current needs, lower consumer risk perceptions, and higher prices. Being first to market can also increase risk if a firm tries to lead a market that is unwilling to follow. Some firms act as second movers or fast followers, relying on size or some other distinctive advantage to gain market share. Each of these first-mover advantages is discussed in the following sections.[27]

Lower Costs

Shortening the development time for new products or business processes may reduce costs. Being fast or a pioneer can increase the business's or product's time in a life cycle, spreading development costs over time and among the number of products produced. In addition, an early-entry firm can gain cost advantages through experience curves; when greater market shares are obtained, they obtain greater economies of scale. Firms that follow have less time in the life cycle to recover all costs.[28]

Ability to Meet Current Needs

A fast firm can gain distinctive advantages by meeting current market needs. The faster a business can respond to the market, the more likely that information from areas such as marketing research will be valid, resulting in actions that could lead to higher market share. Intuit, for example, uses its consumer information to innovate faster than its major rival, Microsoft. Fast movers typically have a substantially higher market share than later entrants. A product that is six months late to market may miss out on one-third of the potential profit over the product's lifetime.[29] Market share is an important consideration because of its impact on reducing per-transaction costs.

Lower Consumer Risk Perceptions

In circumstances in which the consumer lacks knowledge about a product (or product category) but also realizes that the product can offer benefits, the consumer may lower the risk involved in purchasing by choosing a product with an established image or brand name. This gives a strong advantage to the fast mover, as it may become the **comparison standard** for all rival products by setting the standard for performance. The fast mover also is likely to be the product that consumer innovators and early adopters try first; therefore, the product is likely to be recommended through word of mouth in the diffusion process.

Advertising and publicity for new products can aid consumer searches, but given the lack of alternative products in many innovative markets, advertising may have the effect of setting the relevant product attributes the consumer uses in the evaluation process. The first mover becomes the industry standard by which all entrants will be compared. Advertising can help hold customers to the first mover's products, allowing a higher price to be charged.[30]

The first mover gains advantages in **switching costs** by having firms invest in its technology. For customers, there are additional information advantages gained through brand name familiarity and the risk involved in switching between products. In the software industry, companies have used strategic tactics such as announcing new product variations to preempt competitors' market entry with new products.

Higher Prices

The first mover has an advantage in the price it can charge to the consumer and in the maintenance of that price when new competitors enter the market. Consumers will try a new product when the price charged is justified given the benefits of the product and the perceived risks in purchasing the product. The first

A switching cost is the additional cost involved in learning something new. For example, for a business, the costs involved in adopting a new software package include the software expense, support expense, training costs, and decreased productivity costs. The largest of these expenses are usually training, support, and decreased productivity.

mover can set a higher introductory price for an innovative buyer, who is often more risk tolerant and who may have higher income. Upon trying the product, the consumer gains additional information on the product benefits. With greater amounts of information available to the later-adopting consumer, backed by possible word of mouth about benefits, a higher price can be maintained. Because consumers lack information on their products, later-entering firms are forced to charge lower prices. In addition, the only remaining customers may be those who were more risk averse and do not want to purchase from the first mover, thus driving the later entrants' price even lower.

Second Movers

Amazon.com was not the first bookstore on the Internet. BookStacks was started in 1992 as a dial-up bulletin board service on the Internet.[31] Obviously, it is not enough for a firm to be the first entrant into the market, because this does not guarantee a long-term competitive advantage. A firm must have the expertise, resources, and creativity necessary to exploit first-mover opportunities. Pioneers must also find ways to forestall or neutralize the efforts of later entrants, or they will not gain the distinctive advantages outlined earlier.[32] The forestalling or neutralizing of later entrants can be even more important if there is easy entry into an industry because this can decrease the lead time needed by followers. **Second movers** (also called fast followers) can mitigate the advantages of first movers and help build barriers to any other firms that lag behind; second movers must close the distance between themselves and the first mover to limit the first mover's advantage and to obtain as many of the benefits as possible. The entry order of products has a direct effect on the expected market share, with later entrants gaining smaller market shares and diminished profits. Staples (http://www.staples.com), the office supply store, did not start selling online until 1998, long after its rivals. Staples waited until it could gain competitive advantages in serving its customers. In part, it does this through a group buying system.[33]

It is sometimes dangerous for firms to be pioneers. The Web has seen a large number of businesses develop and fade over the past few years. Some companies decide to wait on the sidelines until they see business models that look successful. Brick-and-mortar businesses with established brand names often do not need to rush to the Net; instead, they can rely on their advantages in brand names, delivery systems, and customer knowledge to allow them to enter the market. They also have much to lose if they fail to meet customer expectations through their Web site. Pioneers often use a great many resources educating the market to get it ready to buy; once the market is developed, firms may follow and take advantage of a more educated market. Firms that wait can also gain advantages by observing the competitive mistakes of pioneers. This may work for firms with established brand names, but for smaller start-up firms, entering late can increase costs considerably. These firms will have to spend heavily on advertising, finding new niches, and gaining distinctive advantages.[34]

Entry Barriers

The advantages held by pioneering firms can be built into barriers to entry for later followers or potential new entrants. A firm can build barriers by limiting entry into an industry through economies of scale, cost advantages, or high switching costs. These have already been outlined as advantages gained by fast firms and first movers. The Internet does offer relatively low barriers to entry. The technology is widely available and low in cost. In the virtual marketplace, gaining economic power from a large resource base can be a means of obtaining these advantages and limiting the number of substitutes available.[35]

Developing loyalty through brand names or strong customer relationships also acts as a barrier. The more the supplier can lock a user into a relationship, the larger the barrier to entry and the lower the power of the buyer. For consumers, a strong relationship could be due to assurance in a brand name; for industrial customers, it could include links to supply, just-in-time (JIT) inventory systems, or strong dependency on a customer.[36] Buyers, on the other hand, do not want to be locked into a single supplier. With the information advantages offered through the Internet, a larger number of suppliers and substitutes may be available.

Building Brand Name

A **brand** is a sign, symbol, design, term, name, or combination of these that allows for easy recognition of a product or company. Products with well-recognized brand names often give assurance to purchasers, because purchasers believe that the risk of using a brand name product is lower. The second most important reason that companies have Web sites is to help build brand and create corporate awareness.[37] As brick-and-mortar businesses have moved toward an online environment, they have had to be concerned with both protecting their brands and building an online brand presence.

As has already been discussed in this text, companies often attempt to protect their URL by obtaining similar, confusing, or abusive URLs. Some also actively search for the use of their trademarked brand online to prevent abuse. Companies can find it much harder to protect their brand when the Internet is used as a free speech venue. While some companies strongly prevent use of trademarked words and symbols, others foster independent sites. George Lucas, for example, allows sites such as TheForce.Net (http://www.theforce.net) to help build the fan base for the *Star Wars* movies. TheForce.net is run by volunteers who have amassed more than six thousand pages and serve more than fifty thousand fans per day. Companies that allow independent sites to work with brand content take the chance of losing control over their brand image.[38]

At the beginning of 2002, the top Internet brand names (based on the number of unique users) for selected categories include the following:

- [ ] **Search engines:** Yahoo!, MSN, Google
- [ ] **Automotive:** Kelley Blue Book, eBay Motors
- [ ] **Finance:** Yahoo! Finance, Quicken.com
- [ ] **Commerce:** Amazon.com, Yahoo! Shopping[39]

Building online brand names requires more than simply placing a name in front of the public. The ease of navigation and the user's overall experience influence the individual's attitude toward the Internet brand. Brands and businesses that exist offline can create brand image through the consumer's interaction with packaging, stores, salespeople, and advertising. Online branding comes from advertising and the individual's experience with the Web site.

Web sites such as AOL, Yahoo!, Netscape, and Amazon.com not only had first-mover advantages but also developed interfaces that were easy to use and provided services that were beneficial to the user. Without providing substantial benefits to consumers, brand name recognition will not result in loyal customer use.[40]

▶ Thinking Strategically: Case 11.1

Speculate on the reasons for AOL's portal success. Why was AOL able to grow to dominate Internet access? List some advantages that AOL's size gives it in the competitive portal arena. Compare and contrast AOL (http://www.aol.com) with other portal sites such as Yahoo! (http://www.yahoo.com), GO.com (http://www.go.com), or Excite (http://www.excite.com). How differentiated are these sites from each other? Justify AOL's use of strategic alliances to maintain its advantages.

case 11.1

Who's Laughing Now?

AOL has made a number of purchases to establish itself as the preeminent online portal site. In 1995, AOL formed an alliance with Microsoft to place the AOL icon on the Windows desktop, while AOL adopted Microsoft's Internet Explorer. In 1998, AOL purchased its competitor CompuServe and formed an alliance with China Internet (an Internet service in Hong Kong).[41] This was followed by America Online's $4.2 billion purchase of Netscape in an alliance with Sun Microsystems. AOL was able to increase the total number of users it services on the Internet by controlling two of the largest portals, AOL and NetCenter. It also took control of the Netscape browser and gained programming expertise from Sun. In 1999, AOL made an $800 million purchase of Gateway stock, allowing AOL to become the default portal for Gateway computers. AOL has formed an alliance with Wal-Mart; Wal-Mart stores promote AOL services, and AOL drives traffic to Wal-Mart's e-commerce site.[42] AOL has also formed an alliance with DIRECTV (http://www.directv.com) to allow AOL to be the access point for satellite-television–based browsing.[43] Finally, in the world's largest merger, AOL and Time Warner

continued on next page

AOL has used free software to allow individuals to sign up for services.

joined in a $110 billion merger. This merger gives Time Warner access to AOL's 26 million subscribers to offer broadband access and content.[44]

AOL has the size and will to take on Microsoft's MSN portal site. These two large portals have put pressure on smaller portal sites. The alliance between AOL and Microsoft could not last when both companies were trying to capture customers. AOL felt it was large enough to not need Microsoft's desktop and decided to continue to send out free disks.[45] Many analysts have questioned the merger between AOL and Time Warner. By May of 2002, the combined company had lost 60 percent of its value (over $117 billion). The reasons given were that the original value was too high and that the company was not reaching the goals of the merger, such as providing broadband content to users.[46]

Developing a Portal and Marketplace

As has been stated earlier in the text, a **portal** is an entrance point to online content. The portal concept has evolved across a number of markets and applications. **Customer portals** focus on the individual consumer and offer one-stop Internet access. By providing a number of services, such as searches, shopping, e-mail, and games, portals allow individuals to avoid browsing the Web but instead to rely on one Web site. Since this site drives eyeballs, it also drives advertising revenue and

*A **portal** is an entranceway onto the Internet. It is often the preferred starting point for searches, entertainment, information, e-mail, or other Internet-based products.*

alliances. The concept of a single public port to content is used as a means of pulling in a large number of users. AOL is a portal site to general Web content, specialized content created by AOL, and content from Time Warner. Other portals focus more on business markets.

Web sites that are able to generate high levels of traffic can gain advantages. As with any medium that sells advertising, the higher the number of viewers of a Web site, the higher the price the site can charge for an ad placement. In addition, an e-business's ability to gain sponsorships and alliances can depend on the number and quality of its users. AOL, Microsoft Network, and Yahoo! have become major general portals to the Internet. A portal can be more than just the first site that individuals see when they go online; it is often the site that users depend on to access other Internet services. Some portals, such as AOL, combine ISP service and portal content. The online service billing process gives companies a more loyal set of viewers and a larger database of information on those viewers, allowing for more targeted advertising.[47] MSN also acts as both an ISP and as a portal. MSN is the first site seen by millions of individuals who use Microsoft's Internet Explorer.

As less technologically savvy Internet users go online, they may look for portal brand names with perceived easy access to a confusing technology. Portals are attempting to offer an easy-to-use, all-in-one starting point for Web access. From homes, the most popular online service is AOL; the most popular home portal is Yahoo!. For businesses, the most popular portal is Yahoo!, followed by Netscape (purchased by AOL). Figure 11.9 shows the top domains as measured by the percentage of users who visit the sites (a single individual can visit more than one site).

Large general-use portals are good at obtaining a great number of visitors, but these visits have not necessarily resulted in increased sales for advertisers. To capture higher-quality audiences, some advertisers are using traditional media or more specialized portals.[48]

Figure 11.9 Top Domains

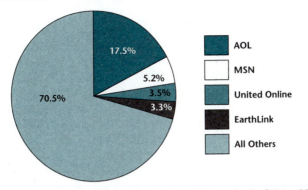

Source: Patricia Fusco, "Top U.S. ISPs by Subscriber: Q1 2002" in ISP-Planet [online] (May 29, 2002) available from <http://www.isp-planet.com/research/rankings/usa.html>.

Niche portals target narrow consumer markets. The number one sports site on the Web is ESPN (http://www.espn.com). This site is targeted toward males from ages eighteen to thirty-four. iVillage (http://www.iVillage.com) is a site targeted toward women. E*Trade (http://www.etrade.com) targets individuals interested in receiving financial information.

International portals target international markets. Web sites that are dominant in the United States are often the top Web sites for other countries. Yahoo!, AOL, and Microsoft Network are all among the top domains around the world. Portal sites such as Yahoo! have services for European, Asian, and other country-specific markets. Yahoo! en Español is designed for the Hispanic market. These general-service portals may not meet the market's needs as well as narrowly targeted portals. StarMedia (http://www.starmedia.com) is a portal site specifically designed to serve the Spanish-speaking markets of Central and South America as well as those in the United States.[49]

Business Portals provide a number of benefits for business markets, including improved customer satisfaction, better decision making, and improved productivity. Portals target business markets in a number of ways:

☐ **Commerce portals** target business professionals by offering forums related to products, product information, buying opportunities, order tracking, and other services.

☐ **Vertical portals** serve narrow niches within specific narrow industries. These portals can provide users a one-stop site for all information and commerce needs, allowing businesses to access industry or trade information and to buy and sell online. Such portals often include industry articles, job listings, e-commerce, and a variety of e-business communication systems.

☐ **Customer portals** provide company-specific information for customers, such as product information, inventory and order tracking, help desk applications, and other services.

☐   **Corporate portals** are often a firm's intranet applications. Internets provide information needed by employees, such as internal newsletters, human resource data, industry news, and other applications.[50]

Business portals are used in the transportation industry. FedEx (http://www.fedex.com) offers a customer portal site that allows customers to place and track orders and contact the company. FedEx also saw an opportunity to develop relationships with a rapidly growing customer segment by developing a vertical portal to serve small business markets (http://www.fedex.com/us/ebusiness/smallbusiness). This site offers articles, how-to guides, management libraries, and government information.[51] Yellow freight designed a customer portal site (http://www.myyellow.com) to offer the same types of services. The Yellow site provides a personalized set of services allowing customers to calculate rates, arrange pickups, monitor shipping, collect bills of lading, and communicate through the use of wireless Internet access, instant messaging, and voice over IP networks.[52]

Vertical portals can act as e-marketplaces. An **e-marketplace** is a hub where multiple buyers and sellers can display catalogs and other content, engage in commerce, coordinate workflows, develop communities, and connect to other sources of information. E-marketplaces have had a mixed success rate. Open e-marketplaces have had the problem of attempting to force business-to-business markets to change their business practices, including opening up transaction information and engaging in price competition. Many businesses have decided to develop private e-marketplaces that serve as customer portals.[53] Asay Publishing (discussed in Chapter 1) (http://www.asaypub.com) leveraged its trade magazines into a portal site supporting the print-on-paper office equipment aftermarket. The site provides information to sellers, buyers, and service repair personnel.

Pursuing Niche Strategies and Enhancing Customer Relationships

Although all businesses need to develop and maintain strong relationships with their customers, businesses that have not gained first-mover advantages and that lack the economic resources to develop strong online brand names or become Internet portals must be able to closely focus on customers and search for niche strategies. **Small- and medium-sized enterprises (SMEs)** differ from large corporations in that they do not have the capital and human resources of larger corporations. To compete, SMEs have traditionally used niche strategies to gain distinctive advantages over their larger competitors. A **niche strategy** requires that the SME find a competitive arena in which larger businesses, with their greater resources, are not competing. SMEs are currently using information technology to gain distinctive advantages. Companies with 500 or fewer employees spent over $200 billion on technology products and services in 1998, more than five times as many dollars as larger companies spent.[54]

Small businesses are using Web sites, intranets, and e-mail at close to the same percentages as larger businesses.[55] E-commerce applications have been accepted more slowly; this could be due to the relatively high cost of setting up and maintaining e-commerce applications. Outsourcing e-commerce to other e-business companies can lower these costs.[56]

Table 11.3 outlines the results of a survey of more than four hundred information technology managers worldwide and shows the main strategies that SMEs should use to compete in a global arena. In addition to using these competitive strategies, smaller businesses can take on larger competitors by being more innovative, faster to respond to environmental demands, and willing to change business models to gain distinctive advantages.

The recommendations given to SMEs are centered on their ability to focus on the customer. SMEs do have an opportunity to hold their current customers if they can leverage e-business tools and techniques before their larger competitors enter their market.

Table 11.3   SME E-Business Strategy Guide

Strategy	Percentage of Respondents	Advantages
Improve Customer Service Online	Over 80 percent	Allows channel members and consumers online access to product and inventory information.
Engage in Electronic Commerce	Over 60 percent	Gives SMEs access to larger markets without the cost of setting up new distribution systems and allows them to target narrow markets faster than larger competitors; lower overhead costs can be carried over to lower prices to customers.
Use Customer-Relationship Management Applications	Over 50 percent	Increases the speed of response to customers and allows for close to instant communication.
Increase Business-to-Business Connections through Extranets	Over 40 percent	Allows SMEs to act as virtual partners with other businesses and as e-business intermediaries linking larger businesses with very small suppliers; online access to inventory and supplies helps control costs.

Source: Natalie Engler, "Small but Nimble," *InformationWeek,* January 18, 1999, 57–62.

Engaging in Alliances and Acquisitions

Alliances are formal or informal relationships between independent companies that work together for a common purpose.

An acquisition exists when one corporation purchases all or a controlling part of another company.

The creation of an e-business value chain may come from the formation of **alliances** or through the **acquisition** of other firms. Online-only firms have a number of advantages over brick-and-mortar businesses, including established online brand names and a mastering of the technology needed to contact customers at low cost. They may also have weaknesses in the ability to provide service and in the logistical delivery components of the value chain. Without a physical location for customers to touch, feel, and return products, sales of some product categories may be limited. E-businesses without warehouses have encountered problems with controlling the delivery of products, resulting in untimely delivery to customers. Brick-and-mortar stores that are able to leverage the Internet as an alternative selling channel can obtain advantages over online-only sellers. For example, Charles Schwab (http://www.schwab.com) leveraged its online system with its brick-and-mortar and service support system to become the number one online brokerage business.[57]

Alliances allow partnering companies to pool expertise, enter new markets, share financial risks, and get products and services to markets faster. Alliances have been growing worldwide and have increased in the United States by 25 percent each year since 1987.[58] A number of companies are positioning themselves to be competitive in the e-business arena. For example, communication companies such as AT&T are purchasing cable TV companies. Television and media companies have developed a number of alliances with Internet companies, in part because homes with Internet access watch up to 15 percent less television than do non-Internet homes. Alliances are being used to build Internet portals because they allow content, expertise, and money to be pooled to develop sites that attract viewers. In the high-tech industry, **co-opetition** is developing as a new competitive model in which businesses that are competitors in some areas cooperate with each other in noncompetitive areas. The Java software platform is an example of co-opetition. When Sun Microsystems introduced the programming language in 1995, it sought out partners to ensure the language would be accepted by the industry. Sun even partnered with companies it competes with in other software or hardware areas.[59]

Choosing An Arena

To be successful, businesses must find a competitive arena in which they will have an advantage. A business must first define its mission—how it will serve a specific market with a specific product. Table 11.4 is a matrix of competitive arenas in which e-businesses can compete. One axis is based on the amount of resources a business can apply toward pursuing its opportunity; for example, businesses that are resource-rich are much more likely to gain brand name recognition if they do

Table 11.4   E-Business Strategy Matrix

	Low Differentiation	High Differentiation
High Resource	**Characteristics:** High brand name recognition. Large portals and general e-commerce sites. **Keys to success:** Heavy brand name advertising. **Examples:** Yahoo!, Amazon.com, Disney, Wal-Mart, Charles Schwab.	**Characteristics:** High brand name recognition within niche market. **Keys to success:** Developing vertical portals; serving niche community. **Examples:** iVillage, VerticalNet, ESPN.
Low Resource	**Characteristics:** Low brand name recognition. **Keys to success:** First-mover advantages; enhanced customer relationships. **Examples:** CDnow, eToys, SMEs with Web site support.	**Characteristics:** Low brand name recognition outside of niche market. **Keys to success:** First-mover advantages; serving niche market; enhanced customer relationships. **Examples:** Asay Publishing.

not already have it. Businesses can also differentiate themselves from larger competitors by pursuing niche markets or developing closer relationships with customers. Once a business chooses its competitive arena, it must develop a strategic plan to reach its goals.

Strategy Evaluation

The Internet stock market at the turn of the millennium was based on a bubble. Investors bid the price of Internet stocks to extremely high levels, only to see those investments come crashing back to earth. For example, while many traditional companies have valuations set at 7 to 20 times their earnings, in 1998 eBay had a valuation of 773 times its expected 1999 earnings.[60]

Many reasons have been given for this investment frenzy. At one time, Amazon.com achieved a **market capitalization** larger than its two major brick-and-mortar competitors, Barnes & Noble and Borders. The view was that Barnes & Noble's business model was outdated; the brick-and-mortar bookseller was required to carry $2 billion in leases, pay for inventory, move inventory to all of its stores, stack it on shelves, and staff more than one thousand locations. Amazon.com had one Internet-based location, owned its own warehouses, and collected money from its customers before it paid for merchandise. In addition, Amazon.com was expanding its business model into other product lines. Advertising-based business models such as

Market capitalization is the value of a company on the stock market. It is the number of shares outstanding times the value of those shares.

Historical nSite

Bubble Economies

The tulip craze of the seventeenth century was an **investment bubble.** A bubble occurs when the price of a commodity or product is bid beyond any rational level. Growers, dealers, and speculators traded tulip options, causing prices to skyrocket. In 1636, the bubble burst and almost brought down the entire Dutch economy.

case 11.2

The Sound of One Bubble Popping

Blue Mountain Arts was one of the first movers into the online greeting card business. This type of site allowed individuals to send rich-media-based cards at no cost. The original business model was advertising based. This model evolved into an alliance with commerce businesses and finally to a subscription-based model. In 1999, Excite purchased Blue Mountain for $780 million. Excite used an acquisition strategy to build its broadband portal site (http://www.excite.com), purchasing a number of sites and accumulating over $1 billion in debt.

American Greetings was a late mover into the online business. In 2001, its wholly owned AmericanGreetings.com purchased Blue Mountain for $35 million. AmericanGreetings.com's sites now include Blue Mountain (http://www.bluemountain.com), Egreetings (http://www.egreetings.com), and Beatgreets (http://www.beatgreets.com). These acquisitions place AmericanGreetings.com's sites in the top ten trafficked sites, with over 100 million unique users annually. AmericanGreetings.com has begun charging for the use of its sites. Hallmark (http://www.hallmark.com) does not charge but attempts to direct users to its stores to purchase gifts. Yahoo! Greetings (http://greetings.yahoo.com) offers free cards.[61]

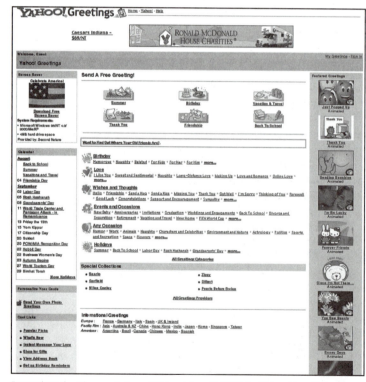

Reproduced with permission of Yahoo! Inc. © 2000 by Yahoo! Inc. Yahoo! and the Yahoo! logo are trademarks of Yahoo! Inc.

Yahoo! incurred little additional cost to obtain additional revenue; the addition of banners, positioning fees, and revenue sharing provided revenue streams with few additional costs. Nevertheless, most pure-play Internet firms were not able to provide the required return on investment to maintain high valuations.

▶ Thinking Strategically: Case 11.2

Speculate on the reasons that Excite would pay such a high price for Blue Mountain. How could the price then be so low for American-Greetings.com? Evaluate the strategy used by online greeting card companies. Determine if these business models have long-term viability. How can a company make a profit offering this service?

Figure 11.10 Greeting Card Traffic. Valentine's Week 2002 (21 Million Users)

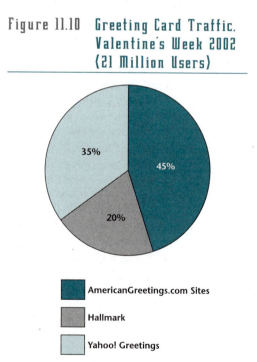

- AmericanGreetings.com Sites
- Hallmark
- Yahoo! Greetings

Return on Investment (ROI) Measures

Evaluating business models requires strong sets of measurements. Establishing these sets can be a problem for many e-business investors because the impact of changes in technology, business models, and business processes can cross over many functional areas. IT cost-benefit analysis typically looks for benefits in the following areas:

- ☐ **Operational efficiencies.** Includes lowering costs across a number of functional areas.
- ☐ **Productivity gains.** Measures increased productivity in areas such as time on task, error rates, training costs, and so forth.
- ☐ **Revenue.** Uses sales and revenue figures.
- ☐ **Customer satisfaction.** Quantifies softer measures such as increases in repeat purchase rates, influence on another's purchases, or other lifetime value measures.[62]

Return on investment (ROI) measures typically used to assess e-business investments include the following:

- ☐ **ROI.** Looks at net revenue over costs.
- ☐ **Payback analysis.** Determines the length of time it will take to recover the cost of the project.
- ☐ **Net present value analysis.** Determines the current value of a stream of future returns against current investment.
- ☐ **Economic value added.** Considers the operating profit minus the capital and debt used to generate the profit.[63]

Economic Welfare

Is society better off with an interconnected world? This is an economic welfare question, but also a strategy evaluation question. Although some may argue that there are problems with the Internet's ability to foster fraud, theft, pornography, invasion of privacy, or other ills, there are also social benefits. Such benefits to both businesses and individuals have been outlined throughout this text. In addition, businesses have the opportunity to gain considerable efficiencies in their business models and operations.

Perhaps the greatest social benefit is the Internet's ability to shift power to the individual through access to information and the individual's ability to use the Internet as a free speech venue. The Internet has opened the world to many around the globe. E-business tools such as the Internet are still in the early stages of their impact on society.

Knowledge Integration

Terms and Concepts

Acquisition *354*
Alliance *354*
Behavioral
    perspective *339*
Brand *348*
Business model *339*
Business portal *351*
Business process
    modeling *339*
Commerce model *339*
Comparison
    standard *346*
Competitive
    arena *334*
Co-opetition *354*
Customer portals *350*
Differentiation
    strategy *344*
Distinctive
    advantage *338*
Distinctive
    competency *334*

E-business value
    chain *336*
E-marketplace *352*
Environmental
    turbulence *334*
First mover *345*
Frictionless market *344*
Functional
    perspective *339*
Informational
    perspective *339*
International portal *351*
Investment bubble *355*
Market capitalization
    355
Moore's law *335*
Niche portal *351*
Niche strategy *352*
Organizational
    perspective *339*
Pioneering firm *345*
Portal *350*

Proactive *336*
Reactive *336*
Return on investment
    (ROI) measures *357*
Second mover *347*
Small- and medium-
    sized enterprises
    (SMEs) *352*
Strategic driver *334*
Strategy *333*
Switching cost *346*
SWOT (Strengths,
    weaknesses,
    opportunities,
    threats)
    analysis *334*
Time-based
    competition *344*
Value chain *334*
Vertical portal *352*

Concepts and Questions for Review

1. Describe the steps included in the process of strategy development.
2. Explain the importance of undertaking a SWOT analysis.
3. List the current drivers of strategy.
4. How can a value chain analysis help a business develop strategies?
5. Explain and demonstrate how a business can evaluate and redesign a business model.
6. List the strategic alternatives e-businesses are using.
7. What advantages can pioneering firms gain?
8. How can an e-business build barriers to other businesses?
9. List some of the advantages of having a brand name.
10. What are the advantages of having large amounts of resources for competing on the Internet?

11. Describe the different types of Internet portals and whom they target.
12. How can firms use alliances and acquisitions to gain advantages?
13. Recommend how small- and medium-sized enterprises can compete.

Active Learning

Exercise 11.1 Evaluating an E-Business Value Chain

Develop a value chain model for an industry or business. Using a model like the one shown in the following figure, identify the key e-business technologies needed to compete in the chosen industry. Identify which of the value chain components would give a business in that industry a distinctive advantage. Determine if it is possible to hold that advantage over time.

Model of E-Business Value Chain

Inbound Distribution Logistics	Value Production	Marketing/ Sales	Customer Targeting and Support	Management	Competitive Advantage through Stronger Customer Relationships
Extranets:	ERP software:	E-commerce:	Databases: Internet:	IT leadership: Intranets:	

Exercise 11.2 SWOT Box

Use the following matrix to undertake a SWOT analysis by identifying the strengths, weaknesses, opportunities, and threats faced by a business or industry.

Strengths:	Opportunities:
Weaknesses:	Threats:

Given this SWOT analysis, propose an e-business strategy that could be pursued to respond to an opportunity and limit future threats.

Exercise 11.3 Evaluating Differential Advantages

Use the following table to indicate the types of services offered by portal sites. America Online is given as an example. Each check represents an available service. After investigating all these sites, determine what allows each one to differentiate itself from the others. If you cannot find any differences, determine what that means for the long-term survival of some of these portal sites.

Portal Site Content

Major Portal Sites	Search	Free E-Mail	News	Sports	Games	Chat	Shopping	Personalization	Weather	Finance	Free Home Pages	Other
AOL	✓	✓	✓	✓	✓	✓	✓	✓	✓	✓	✓	
Yahoo!												
Netscape												
Excite												
Go Network												
Yahoo! GeoCities												
Microsoft Network												

Exercise 11.4 Strategy Analysis Matrix

Use the Internet to identify strategic positions for a number of e-businesses. Try to find at least one business for each cell in the following matrix. Identify which strategies these businesses are pursuing and what the keys to their long-term success will be.

E-Business Strategy Analysis Matrix

	Low Differentiation	High Differentiation
High Resource	Characteristics: Keys to success:	Characteristics: Keys to success:
Low Resource	Characteristics: Keys to success:	Characteristics: Keys to success:

Competitive Exercise 11.5 Evaluating an E-Business Model

Choose an industry. Develop a business model for how that industry currently operates and then develop an e-business-based model. Compare your model against those of other individuals or groups. Identify how this new model can gain a competitive advantage over other models in the industry.

Web Search—Looking Online

Search Term:	E-Business Strategy Support	First 3 out of 420,000

Business 2.0. Provides information and articles on cutting-edge business strategy.
http://www.business2.com

CIO Web Business. Targets chief information officers, offering in-depth information on industry trends and practices.
http://webbusiness.cio.com

IBM. Gives information on major e-business strategies, with case studies.
http://www.ibm.com/e-business

Search Term:	E-Business Models	First 2 out of 2,690,000

Ghost Sites' Museum of E-Failure. Shows sites that have failed or are likely to fail.
http://www.disobey.com/ghostsites/

Business Process Management Initiative. Supports the process of business process modeling.
http://www.bpmi.org

Search Term:	Internet Portals	First 2 out of 1,260,000

Europe Online. Provides a portal to Western Europe, with links to different countries and topics related to Europe.
http://www.europeonline.com

Search Engine Guide. Lists over 2,500 search engines and portal sites by category.
http://www.searchengineguide.com

Search Term:	SMEs Online	First 3 out of 4,880,000

SCORE. Offers information from the Service Core of Retired Executives on how to obtain free consulting.
http://www.score.org

Small Business Classroom. Provides training for small businesses, sponsored by the Small Business Administration.
http://classroom.sba.gov

Small Biz. Gives advice for small businesses in areas related to technology.
http://www.techweb.com/smallbiz

References

[1] Erick Schonfeld and Ian Mount, "Beating Bill," *Business 2.0,* June 2002, 36–46.

[2] Cheryl J. Myers, "M&A Insight," *Red Herring,* August 1999, 156; Brent Schlender, "Whose Internet Is It, Anyway?" *Fortune,* December 11, 1995, 120–42; Michael Neubarth, "Microsoft Declares War," *Internet World,* March 1996, 36–42; Kathy Rebello, "Inside Microsoft," *BusinessWeek,* July 15, 1996, 56–67; Brent Schlender, "Software Hardball,"*Fortune,* September 30, 1996, 107–116.

[3] Schonfeld and Mount, "Beating Bill."

[4] David Orenstein, "Corel to Give Out Free Linux WordPerfect," *Computerworld,* November 2, 1998, 105; Sandy Reed, "Linux Is Making the Transition from Bit Player to Overnight Sensation," *InfoWorld,* January 11, 1999, 69; Steven Levy, "Code Warriors," *Newsweek,* January 18, 1999, 60–62; Steve Hamm, Ira Sager, and Peter Burrows, "It Might Not Break Windows, But . . ." *BusinessWeek,* February 1, 1999, 36.

[5] Steve Hamm, Amy Cortese, and Susan B. Garland, "Microsoft's Future," *BusinessWeek,* January 19, 1998, 58–68; and Steven Vonder Haar, "Microsoft Rethinks the Online Road Ahead," *Interactive Week,* January 4, 1999, 38–40.

[6] Sandy Reed, "From .com Fever to New Technospeak, Microsoft Is a Company in Evolution," *InfoWorld,* June 28, 1999, 59.

[7] Mark Halper, "Europe Turns Off Pay Television,"*Fortune,* June 24, 2002, 20.

[8] For more on strategy and strategy definitions, see Paul F. Anderson, "Marketing, Strategic Planning and the Theory of the Firm," *Journal of Marketing* 46 (Spring 1982): 15–26; Yoram Wind and Thomas S. Robertson, "Marketing Strategy: New Directions for Theory and Research," *Journal of Marketing* 47 (Spring 1983): 12–25; Henry Mintzberg and James A. Waters, "Of Strategies, Deliberate and Emergent," *Strategic Management Journal* 6 (1985): 257–72.

[9] Danny Miller and Peter H. Friesen, "Innovation in Conservative and Entrepreneurial Firms: Two Models of Strategic Momentum," *Strategic Management Journal* 3 (1982): 1–25.

[10] For more on value chains, see Michael E. Porter, *Competitive Advantage* (New York: Free Press, 1980).

[11] David F. Carr, "Forging 21st-Century Value Chains," *Internet World,* June 15, 2001, 26–32; Peter Fingar and Ronald Aronica, "Empower Your Customers—The Driving Forces of the Real New Economy," *Internet World,* June 15, 2001, 33–35; Jeffrey F. Rayport and John J. Sviokla, "Exploiting the Virtual Value Chain," *Harvard Business Review,* November–December 1995, 75–85.

[12] Rusty Weston, "Value Chains Go Global," *InformationWeek,* January 18, 1999, 125–26.

[13] Rusty Weston, "What's Driving the E-Frenzy?" *InformationWeek,* September 27, 1999, 482.

[14] Carol Hildebrand, "IT and the Bottom Line," *CIO Enterprise,* June 15, 1998, 70–76.

15 For more on this, see Derek Slater, "The Corporate Skeleton," *CIO,* December 15, 1998–January 1, 1999, 100–106; Larry Downes and Chunka Mui, *Unleashing the Killer App: Digital Strategies for Market Dominance* (Boston: Harvard Business School Press, 1998).

16 For more on the relationship between IT and distinctive competencies, see Don Tapscott, David Ticoll, and Alex Lowy, "The Rise of the Business Web," *Business 2.0,* November 1999, 198–208; Howard A. Rubin, "The Millennium IT Manifesto," *InformationWeek,* September 27, 1999, 310–13; Bob Violino, "Customer at the Core," *InformationWeek,* September 27, 1999, 302–8; Gary H. Anthes, "Drucker: IT Hasn't Done Job," *Computerworld,* April 26, 1999, 51; Adrian Slywotzky, "How Digital Is Your Company?" *Fast Company,* February–March 1999, 94–112; Jeanne W. Ross, Cynthia Mathis Beath, and Dale L. Coodhue, "Develop Long-Term Competitiveness through IT Assets," *Sloan Management Review,* Fall 1996, 31–41.

17 Bob Violino, "Extended Enterprise," *InformationWeek,* March 22, 1999, 46–63.

18 Ray J. Paul, George M. Gaiglis, and Vlatke Hlupic, "Simulation of Business Process," *American Behavioral Scientist,* August 1999, 15–51.

19 "International Data Corporation: Schools to Double Spending on Elearning," in NUA [online] (December 20, 2000), available from <http://www.nua.ie/surveys/index.cgi?f=VS&art_id=905356263&rel=true>.

20 NUA, "IDC Research: Lucrative Prospects for Elearning in Europe," January 09, 2001, <http://www.nua.ie/surveys/index.cgi?f=VS&art_id=905356320&rel=true>.

21 Kayte VanScoy, "We Don't Need the Net," *Smart Business,* November 2001, 80–84.

22 Gary McWilliams, "Whirlwind on the Web," *BusinessWeek,* April 7, 1997, 132–36; Saroja Girishankar, "Dell's Site Has Business in Crosshairs," *InternetWeek,* April 13, 1998, 1, 59; Andy Serwer, "Michael Dell Rocks," *Fortune,* May 11, 1998, 58–70; Lisa Dicarlo, "Dell Raises Bar on E-Commerce," *PC Week,* June 15, 1998, 1, 16.

23 Lisa Chadderdon, "How Dell Sells on the Web," *Fast Company,* September 1998, 78–88.

24 Amy K. Larson, "Manufacturing Retools," *InternetWeek,* September 14, 1998, 44; Chuck Moozakis, "Survey Tracks IT Strides," *InternetWeek,* September 14, 1998, 13.

25 For more on this topic, see Robert Kuttner, "The Net: A Market Too Perfect for Profits," *BusinessWeek,* May 11, 1998, 20.

26 Clinton Wilder and Jeff Angus, "Faster Than the Speed of Data," *InformationWeek,* July 21, 1997, 36–54.

27 Brad Kleindl, "Accelerating New Product Development Speed," *Southern Business & Economic Review* 14, no. 4 (Winter 1994): 12–15.

28 Milton D. Rosenau Jr., *Faster New Product Development* (New York: AMACOM, 1990).

29 William T. Robinson, "Sources of Market Pioneer Advantages: The Case of Industrial Goods Industries," *Journal of Marketing Research* 25 (February 1988): 87–94; William T. Robinson and Claes Fornell, "Sources of Market Pioneer Advantages in Consumer Goods Industries," *Journal of Marketing Research* 22 (August 1988): 305–17; Joseph T. Vesey, "The New Competitors Think in Terms of 'Speed-to-Market,'" *SAM Advanced Management Journal* 56 (Autumn 1991): 26–33.

30 F. M. Scherer and David Ross, *Industrial Market Structure and Economic Performance* (Boston: Houghton Mifflin, 1992).

31 Elizabeth Gardner, "Early Adopters," *Internet World,* March 9, 1998, 76–78.

32 Roger A. Kerin, Rajan Varadarajan, and Robert A. Peterson, "First-Mover Advantage: A Synthesis, Conceptual Framework, and Research Propositions," *Journal of Marketing* 56 (October 1992): 33–52.

[33] Kevin Hogan, "Staples: At Last, On Top of the Game," *Business 2.0,* March 2001, 95.

[34] Sharon Machlis, "E-Commerce: Late Is Relative," *Computerworld,* May 18, 1998, 1, 16; Cheryl Currid, "The Perils of Pioneering," *InformationWeek,* August 11, 1997, 138.

[35] Fahri Karakaya and Michael J. Stahl, "Barriers to Entry and Market Entry Decisions in Consumer and Industrial Goods Markets," *Journal of Marketing* 53 (April 1989): 80–91; Michael Porter, *Competitive Strategy,* (New York: Free Press, 1980).

[36] Carl Shapiro and Hal R. Varian, "Lock 'em Up!" *CIO,* October 15, 1998, 72–76.

[37] Valerie Rice, "Leave Your Mark," *Smart Partner,* June 5, 2000, 36–42.

[38] Michael Mendung, "Not Forcing the Issue," *Business 2.0,* May 15, 2001, 36–39.

[39] "Top Ranking Brands and Channels for February 2002," in CyberAtlas [online] (April 4, 2002), available from <http://cyberatlas.internet.com/big_picture/traffic_patterns/article/0,,5931_1004191,00.html>.

[40] Michael Grebb, "Spend It or Lose It," *Business 2.0,* November 1999, 113–14; Evan I. Schwartz, "Brands Aren't Everything," in The Standard [online] (April 30, 1999), available from <http://www.thestandard.com/article/display/0,1151,4421,00.html>; Scott Kirsner, "Branding Tall," in *CIO Web Business* [online] (December 1, 1998), available from <http://www.cio.com/archive/webbusiness/120198_main.html>; Jeffrey Davis, "A New Way of Branding," *Business 2.0,* November 1998, 76–86.

[41] Elizabeth Gardner, "AOL Ups Rates, Cuts Staff as It Absorbs CompuServe," *InternetWeek,* February 16, 1998, 9.

[42] Steven Vonder Haar, "AOL, Wal-Mart Work on Mass Marketing Pact," *Interactive Week,* December 6, 1999, 9; Steven Vonder Haar, "Gateway May Open Doors for AOL," *Interactive Week,* October 25, 1999, 10.

[43] Catherine Yang, Richard Siklos, Steve Brull, and Larry Armstrong, "America Online—And on the Air," *BusinessWeek,* May 24, 1999, 33.

[44] Johnnie L. Roberts, "All for One, One for AOL," *Newsweek,* December 25, 2000/January 1, 2001, 63–65.

[45] Amy Borrus, "AOL's Point Man in the Web War," *BusinessWeek,* July 2, 2001, 56–57.

[46] Narc Gunther and Stephanie N. Mehta, "Can Steve Case Make Sense of This Beast?" *Fortune,* May 13, 2002, 75–80.

[47] Steven Vonder Haar, "Disney, Infoseek Make a Go of Online Service," *Interactive Week,* October 5, 1998, 9.

[48] Mark Halper, "Portal Pretense," *Business 2.0,* September 1999, 43–49; Heather Green and Linda Himelstein, "Portals Are Mortal After All," *BusinessWeek,* June 21, 1999, 144; Connie Guglielmo, "Thumbs Down on Portal-Play Deals," *Interactive Week,* May 3, 1999, 40.

[49] For more information, see Nelson Wang, "Planting a Flag in Latin America," *Internet World,* December 14, 1998, 54; Lee M. Tablewski, "Rising Star," *Business 2.0,* February 1999, 22–24.

[50] Peter Ruber, "Portals on a Mission," *Knowledge Management,* April 2000, 34–44.

[51] Emma Warrillow, "FedEx Courts Small Businesses with Tailored-Content Site," *1 to 1 Magazine,* April 2001, 44.

[52] Tim Wilson, "Portal, Exchange Deliver Goods for Freight Carrier," *Internet Week,* June 11, 2001, 71–72.

[53] Eric Young, "Web Marketplaces That Really Work," *Fortune/CNET Tech Review,* Winter 2002, 78–86; Kristina Blachere, "The Best-Kept Secret of B2B," *Smart Business Magazine,* April 2001, 116–120; Boris Lublinsky, Building a World Class E-Market," *EAI Journal,* August 2001, 20–26.

[54] Bruce Caldwell and Candee Wilde, "Emerging Enterprises," *InformationWeek,* June 29, 1998, 53–60; Candee Wilde, "Internet Levels the Field," *InformationWeek,* June 29, 1998, 64–66.

[55] Clinton Wilder, "E-Business Work Status," *InformationWeek,* January 4, 1999, 53–54.

[56] Richard De Soto, "Creating an Active Internet Presence: A New Alternative," *Telecommunication Magazine,* December 1998, 73–75.

[57] Luc Hatslestad, "Brick-and-Mortar and Online Retailers Come Together," *Red Herring,* December 1999, 127–30; Geoffrey James, "Clicks and Mortar," *Upside,* November 1999, 209–14; Bill Roberts, "Why Click Is Marrying Mortar," *Internet World,* November 15, 1999, 32–48.

[58] Peter Fabris, "Getting Together," *CIO,* December 15, 1998–January 1, 1999, 92–98.

[59] For more information on this topic, see Alex Frankel, "Mutual Aid," *CIO Web Business,* February 1, 1998, 48–52; Adam M. Bradenburger and Barry J. Nalebuff, *Co-Opetition: A Revolutionary Mindset That Combines Competition and Cooperation* (New York: Doubleday, 1996).

[60] Natalie Engler, "Small but Nimble," *InformationWeek,* January 18, 1999, 57–62.

[61] Andrea McKenna Findlay, "How Card Sites' New Approaches Reflect the Evolving Internet Medium," *Internet Retailer,* April 2002, 11; Mickey Alam Khan, "BlueMountain Quietly Goes for $35M," *iMarketing News,* October 1, 2001, 12.

[62] Alex Wright, "Designing for the Bottom Line," *Web Techniques,* December 2001, 27–30; "Research Results," *CIO Insight,* March 2002, 70.

[63] Ron Copeland, "ROI: The IT Department's Moving Target," *InformationWeek,* August 6, 2001, 45–47.

Cases

DoubleClick Inc.: Gathering Customer Intelligence[1]

INTRODUCTION

"This Monday, we revealed that the Federal Trade Commission (FTC) began a voluntary inquiry into our ad serving and data collection practices," explained Kevin Ryan, president of DoubleClick Inc. It was Thursday, February 17, 2000, in New York City and Ryan was preparing to answer media and investor questions.

"We are confident that our business policies are consistent with our privacy policy and beneficial to consumers and advertisers," he continued. "The FTC has begun a series of inquiries into some of the most well-known Web companies, including DoubleClick, and we support their efforts to keep the Internet safe for consumers."

Several Internet privacy activists had filed a formal complaint with the FTC after being informed by media sources that DoubleClick had the ability to determine a person's identity through the use of "cookies" and other databases. Here was an excerpt of an article in an early January 2000 edition of *USA Today*:

Activists charge DoubleClick double-cross

Web users have lost privacy with the drop of a cookie, they say

By Will Rodger, USATODAY.com

Say goodbye to anonymity on the Web.

DoubleClick Inc., the Internet's largest advertising company, has begun tracking Web users by name and address as they move from one Web site to the next, USATODAY.com has learned.

The practice, known as profiling, gives marketers the ability to know the household, and in many cases the precise identity, of the person visiting any one of the 11,500 sites that use DoubleClick's ad-tracking "cookies." What made such profiling possible was DoubleClick's purchase in June of Abacus Direct Corp., a direct-marketing services company that maintains a database of names, addresses and retail purchasing habits of 90 per cent of American households. With the help of its online partners, DoubleClick can now correlate the Abacus database of names with people's Internet activities.

DOUBLECLICK INC.

With global headquarters in New York City and over 30 offices around the world, DoubleClick was a leading provider of comprehensive Internet advertising solutions for marketers and Web publishers. It combined technology, media and data expertise to centralize planning, execution, control, tracking and reporting for online media companies. Along with its proprietary DART targeting technology, DoubleClick managed Abacus Direct, a database of consumer buying behavior used for marketing purposes over the Internet and through direct mail.

The privacy controversy over DoubleClick began in the summer of 1999, when DoubleClick announced it was merging with Abacus Direct in a deal valued at more than US$1 billion. Privacy experts had feared that DoubleClick would begin merging the two databases at some point. But they said they were unaware that DoubleClick had begun its profiling practice in late 1999. Before its Abacus purchase, DoubleClick had made its money by targeting banner advertisements in less direct ways. DoubleClick ad-serving computers, for instance, checked the Internet addresses of people who visited participating sites. Thus, people in their homes may see ads different from those seen by workers at General Motors, or a machine-tool company in Ohio.

Every time viewers saw or clicked on those banners, DoubleClick added that fact to individual dossiers it built on them with the help of the cookies it stored on users' hard drives. Those dossiers, in turn, helped DoubleClick target ads more precisely still, increasing their relevance to consumers and reducing unnecessary repetition.

The "owner" of those cookies remained anonymous to DoubleClick until it bought Abacus.[2]

Being tracked as they move around the Web "doesn't measure up to people's expectation on the Net," says Robert Smith, publisher of the newsletter *Privacy Journal*. "They don't think that their physical locations, their names will be combined with what they do on the Internet. If they (DoubleClick) want to do that they have to expose that plan to the public and have it discussed."[3]

A publicly-listed company, DoubleClick traded under the symbol DCLK on the NASDAQ exchange.[4]

DOUBLECLICK'S DART

Developed by DoubleClick and awarded U.S. Patent 5,948,061, DART was a Web-based, enterprise-class advertising management software package. It performed targeting, reporting and inventory management, allowing sites (or networks of sites) to manage all or some of their ad serving and reporting functions through DoubleClick's central servers. The benefit to advertising clients was the opportunity to build lifelong relationships with their customers (users) through personalization of advertising messages (see Figure 1). A client would begin by placing an advertising campaign with DoubleClick. With the use of DoubleClick's DART technology, advertising messages would be placed on sites most visited by the client's customers, and advertising results tracked. DoubleClick would then compile data gathered and present the results of the campaign to the client (see Figure 1).

Figure 1

CENTRAL CAMPAIGN MANAGEMENT

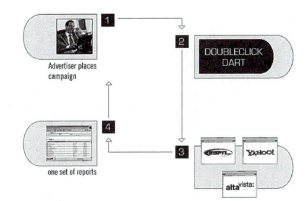

Web sites intending to sell banner advertisement could outsource the delivery of the site's online advertisement to DoubleClick. While serving the ads, DoubleClick would then utilize DART to collect, analyse and optimize online ads and their delivery.

BENEFITS OF DART[5]

Streamlined campaign management, pinpoint targeting and real-time, actionable reports all add up to one important metric — increased return on investment (ROI.) DART For Advertisers gives you the process and tracking refinement that empowers you to continuously optimize your campaigns and tie your marketing programs to real dollars generated. Here are a few of the benefits of using DART for Advertisers:

- **A Web-based Service Offering** — DART for Advertisers is available from anywhere based on permissions you control. And because it's a service, you get instant upgrades without application deployment or maintenance costs.

- **An Integrated Solution** — DART provides the industry's strongest ad management technology, built-in targeting and sophisticated reporting that, together, form the cornerstone of closed-loop marketing and enhanced ROI. Its constantly evolving feature set is based on the aggressive demands of leading-edge installed base.

- **Centralized Planning and Control** — No matter how extensive your media plan, DART for Advertisers provides a sophisticated media planning tool and enables you to buy and traffic ads across as many sites as you wish. So you can track requests for proposals (RFPs) and insertion orders, control creative changes and view standardized reports within and across campaigns like never before.

- **High-Level Targeting** — With built-in targeting capabilities, DART offers an unlimited array of targeting criteria to ensure you get the right message to the right person at the right time. DART's targeting capabilities are the best in the industry.

- **Consistent Reporting** — DART provides you a single set of real-time reports that span your entire campaign. Armed with detailed post-click, transaction and reach and frequency information, you can test different executions of selling messages, rich media and ad sizes — and then swap creative instantaneously to maximize campaign effectiveness.

- **Private Labeling** — With DART, agencies gain a competitive advantage by offering the leading online campaign management capabilities within their own suite of products and services.

DELIVERING DART

With an expansive team of engineers supporting DART's complex system, DoubleClick served up to 53 billion ads[6] to DART-enabled sites per month to companies in over 13 countries around the world. It accomplished this through the use of 23 global data centres, world-class hosting facilities like Frontier Global Center and Exodus Communications. It also possessed a network of nearly 800 media and ad servers (Microsoft NT Quad Processors) positioned around the world to assure reliability. The architecture it used was 100 per cent scalable, running Oracle databases hosted on Sun Solaris equipment. DART's frontend (user interface) was hypertext markup language (HTML) compliant and could be accessed from any browser and any platform.

DoubleClick had the ability to segregate ad serving from the site's back-end transaction processing, matching ads in under 15 milliseconds and serving ads at an average rate of one every 24 milliseconds.

DART IN OPERATION

DART's user profile database recognized unique users by their cookies and delivered a precisely targeted ad every time the user accessed Web pages that were using DART. First, by accessing the Web page, the user would trigger an ad "request" from DoubleClick. Next, if that user had previously visited DoubleClick sites, DoubleClick would recognize the user's cookie file and unique number, retrieving the IP address, country domain, company, browser and operating system. (If not, a cookie would be placed on the new user's computer at this time.) DART would match-up a targeted ad to the user-profile, then deliver a targeted ad to the user (see Figure 2).

Figure 2 — DoubleClick DART in Action

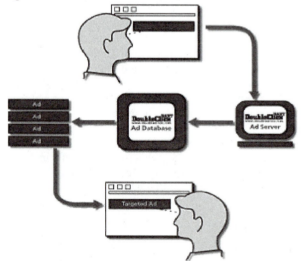

USING COOKIES AT DOUBLECLICK

Cookies were small text files stored on a user's hard drive and were employed by thousands of sites. Cookies enabled sites to "remember" users across site pages and across multiple visits to a site. Using cookies did not damage user files nor could they read information from a user's hard drive.

This feature enhanced e-commerce and Internet advertising in numerous ways, including allowing personalization features such as stock portfolio tracking and targeted news stories, and enabling shopping sessions and quick navigation across multiple zones of e-commerce sites. Cookies could remember user names and passwords for future visits, control ad frequency or the number of times a user saw a given ad, and could allow advertisers to target ads to a user's interest.

Ryan explained that DoubleClick did not employ cookies to exploit sensitive data.

> DoubleClick has never and will never use sensitive online data in our profiling. It is DoubleClick's policy to only merge personally identifiable information with personally identifiable information for profiling, after providing clear notice of a choice.

SELLING RESEARCH ON COLLECTED DATA

One of DoubleClick's business units collected traffic and usage data, and analysed the effectiveness of campaigns. From this research, the document produced for advertising clients was called Spotlight.

Spotlight allowed an advertiser to determine which media placement generated a specific type of post-click activity important to its media plan. Spotlight provided customizable metrics such as the number of registrations, number of sales, number of units purchased, types of services purchased, and actual sales revenue generated as a result of an advertiser's campaign.

Reports offered three levels of reporting including banner level, campaign level, and aggregate activity data at the advertiser level. Another feature offered conversion-to-activity rates by clicks, impressions and media costs. A third offered a counting methodology that credited activities to the last ad the user clicked on prior to performing the activity, for up to 90 days after the ad had stopped running (see Figure 3).

Abacus, the previously mentioned division of Double-Click, would, on behalf of Internet retailers and advertisers, use additional statistical modeling techniques to

Figure 3

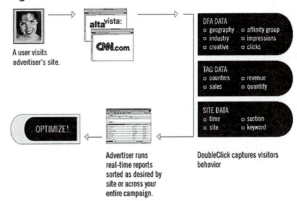

A user visits advertiser's site.

DFA DATA
- geography   □ affinity group
- industry   □ impressions
- creative   □ clicks

TAG DATA
- counters   □ revenue
- sales   □ quantity

SITE DATA
- time   □ section
- site   □ keyword

OPTIMIZE!

Advertiser runs real-time reports sorted as desired by site or across your entire campaign.

DoubleClick captures visitors behavior

identify those online consumers in the Abacus Online database who would most likely be interested in a particular product or service.

A COMPLAINT FILED WITH THE FTC

Jason Catlett of Junkbusters Inc. (an Internet privacy consultancy), David Banisar, deputy director of Privacy International, and the U.S. Electronic Privacy Information Center filed a complaint with the Federal Trade Commission charging that DoubleClick had deceived consumers by suggesting the company's technology let them remain anonymous. They expected to enlist a wide array of consumer groups to back their position.

More troubling to privacy advocates was DoubleClick's refusal to state which Internet sites were furnishing them the registration rolls that DoubleClick needed to link once-anonymous cookies to names, addresses, phone numbers and catalogue purchases. Catlett stated,

> The fact that DoubleClick is not disclosing the names of the companies who are feeding them consumers' names is a shameful hypocrisy. They are trying to protect the confidentiality of the violators of privacy.

Jonathan Shapiro, senior vice-president and Abacus unit chief bristled at Catlett's characterization, saying, "Any company that uses data from the Abacus database to target Internet ads must disclose it online." Moreover, he added, DoubleClick itself would hand over to privacy advocates the list of participating companies if it could. But as in many lines of business, partners frown when their relationships were disclosed without their permission. Shapiro concluded, "If they all bought a billboard and said they work with us, that would be great."

THE NEW PRIVACY POLICY

Ryan announced,

> Earlier in February, DoubleClick announced what we believe is the most aggressive Internet privacy policy ever and committed ourselves to a national campaign to educate consumers about online privacy. We also announced that we will only do business with online U.S. publishers that have privacy policies. We have engaged PriceWaterhouseCoopers to perform periodic privacy audits so that consumers remain confident that we are living up to our commitment to protect users' privacy. In addition, we have announced the creation of the DoubleClick Privacy Ad Board, and we are adding a new executive level position of Chief Privacy Officer.

DoubleClick explained in its privacy policy (see Exhibit 1) that it did not collect any personally-identifiable information about its users such as name, address, phone number or e-mail address. It did, however, collect non-personally identifiable information such as the server the user's computer was logged on to, his or her browser type, and whether the user responded to the ad delivered.

Non-personally identifiable information collected by DoubleClick was used for the purpose of targeting ads and measuring ad effectiveness on behalf of Double-Click's advertisers and Web publishers who specifically requested it. However, non-personally identifiable information collected by DoubleClick could be associated with a user's personally identifiable information if that user had agreed to receive personally-tailored ads.

In addition, with the delivery of ads via DART technology to one particular Web publisher's Web site, DoubleClick combined the non-personally identifiable data collected by DoubleClick from a user's computer with the log-in name and demographic data about users collected by the Web publisher and furnished to DoubleClick for the purpose of ad targeting on the Web publisher's Web site. DoubleClick had requested that this information be disclosed on the Web site's privacy statement.

There were also other cases when a user voluntarily provided personal information in response to an ad (a survey or purchase form, for example). "That person will receive notice that their personal information is being gathered," stated Shapiro. In those situations, Double-Click (or a third party engaged by DoubleClick) collected the information on behalf of the advertiser and/or Web site. This information was used by the advertiser, and/or Web site, to ensure that users received goods, services or information requested. Jennifer Blum, Media Relations, stated that only about a dozen of its affiliated sites had started to collect and use personal information. She acknowledged, however, that DoubleClick's goal was to gain agreement from all its partner sites to participate. Where indicated, DoubleClick could use the information in aggregate form to get a better general understanding of the type of individuals viewing ads or visiting the Web sites. Unless specifically disclosed, the personally-identifiable information collected by DoubleClick in these cases was not used to deliver personally-tailored ads to a user and was not linked by DoubleClick to any other information.

OPTING OUT OF BEING IDENTIFIED

DoubleClick did allow users the option of "opting-out" of being identified by DART. By logging on to Double-Click's site, the user could enter information to allow DoubleClick to recognize the particular user and assign him or her an "opt-out" cookie.

On subsequent visits by the user to DART-enabled sites, the opt-out cookie would disallow DART from assigning other cookies or from identifying the user's computer uniquely. DoubleClick discouraged this approach by stating in its privacy statement:

> DoubleClick believes that all users should have a positive Web experience. Because of this belief, we allow advertisers to control the frequency (the number of times) a Web user sees an ad banner. We also deliver advertising based on a user's interests if that user has chosen to receive targeted advertising. We believe that frequency control, and relevant content makes advertising on the Web less intrusive by ensuring that users are not bombarded with repeat and irrelevant ad messages. Opting-out removes our ability both to control frequency of exposure to individual users and to increase the level of relevant content.

The opt-out would be effective for the entire life of the user's browser or until the user deleted the cookie file on his or her hard drive. In each of these instances, the user would then appear as a new user to DoubleClick — unless the user denied the DoubleClick cookie again, a new cookie would be delivered to the user's browser.

DISCLOSURE AND SECURITY

DoubleClick made available all its information practices on its Web site, www.doubleclick.net, including in-depth descriptions of its targeting capabilities, privacy policy, and full disclosure on the use of cookies. DoubleClick was an active member of the Network Advertising Initiative, NetCoalition.com, Online Privacy Alliance, Internet Advertising Bureau, New York New Media Association, and the American Advertising Federation.

DOUBLECLICK CONFIDENT IN FACE OF INQUIRY

Ryan concluded,

> We renew our challenge to other Internet players to adopt similarly strong privacy policies. We are taking these steps because we believe they are good for consumers, good for our customers and sound business practices.

In spite of the FTC's inquiries, DoubleClick was confident that its internal practices were sound.

DoubleClick shares, trading at a high of US$131 during the beginning of January 2000, had dropped to the US$90 range since the charge was announced. Would the move to establish the new privacy policy aid in placating the fears of advertising clients afraid of a consumer backlash? Would the new privacy policy hold up to scrutiny? Was DoubleClick doing enough to satisfy the privacy concerns of Internet surfers? Last, were investors satisfied?

Exhibit 1

DoubleClick Privacy Policy

DoubleClick Privacy Statement

Internet user privacy is of paramount importance to DoubleClick, our advertisers and our Web publishers. The success of our business depends upon our ability to maintain the trust of our users. Below is information regarding DoubleClick's commitment to protect the privacy of users and to ensure the integrity of the Internet.

Information Collected in Ad Delivery

In the course of delivering an ad to you, DoubleClick does not collect any personally-identifiable information about you, such as your name, address, phone number or email address. DoubleClick does, however, collect non-personally identifiable information about you, such as the server your computer is logged onto, your browser type (for example, Netscape or Internet Explorer), and whether you responded to the ad delivered.

The non-personally identifiable information collected by DoubleClick is used for the purpose of targeting ads and measuring ad effectiveness on behalf of DoubleClick's advertisers and Web publishers who specifically request it. For additional information on the information that is collected by DoubleClick in the process of delivering an ad to you, please click here.

However, as described in "Abacus Alliance" and "Information Collected by DoubleClick's Web Sites" below, non-personally identifiable information collected by DoubleClick in the course of ad delivery *can be associated with a user's personally identifiable information* if that user has agreed to receive personally-tailored ads.

In addition, in connection solely with the delivery of ads via DoubleClick's DART technology to one particular Web publisher's Web site, DoubleClick combines the non-personally-identifiable data collected by DoubleClick from a user's computer with the log-in name and demographic data about users collected by the Web publisher and furnished to DoubleClick for the purpose of ad targeting on the Web publisher's Web site. DoubleClick has requested that this information be disclosed on the Web site's privacy statement.

There are also other cases when a user voluntarily provides personal information in response to an ad (a survey or purchase form, for example). In these situations, DoubleClick (or a third party engaged by DoubleClick) collects the information on behalf of the advertiser and/or Web site. This information is used by the advertiser and/or Web site so that you can receive the goods, services or information that you requested. Where indicated, DoubleClick may use this information in aggregate form to get a better general understanding of the type of individuals viewing ads or visiting the

Web sites. Unless specifically disclosed, the personally-identifiable information collected by DoubleClick in these cases is not used to deliver personally-tailored ads to a user and is not linked by DoubleClick to any other information.

Abacus Alliance

On November 23, 1999, DoubleClick Inc. completed its merger with Abacus Direct Corporation. Abacus, now a division of DoubleClick, will continue to operate Abacus Direct, the direct mail element of the Abacus Alliance. In addition, Abacus has begun building Abacus Online, the Internet element of the Abacus Alliance.

The Abacus Online portion of the Abacus Alliance will enable U.S. consumers on the Internet to receive advertising messages tailored to their individual interests. As with all DoubleClick products and services, Abacus Online is fully committed to offering online consumers *notice* about the collection and use of personal information about them, and the *choice* not to participate. Abacus Online will maintain a database consisting of personally-identifiable information about those Internet users who have received notice that their personal information will be used for online marketing purposes and associated with information about them available from other sources, and who have been offered the choice not to receive these tailored messages. The notice and opportunity to choose will appear on those Web sites that contribute user information to the Abacus Alliance, usually when the user is given the opportunity to provide personally identifiable information (e.g., on a user registration page, or on an order form).

Abacus, on behalf of Internet retailers and advertisers, will use statistical modeling techniques to identify those online consumers in the Abacus Online database who would most likely be interested in a particular product or service. All advertising messages delivered to online consumers identified by Abacus Online will be delivered by DoubleClick's patented DART technology.

Strict efforts will be made to ensure that all information in the Abacus Online database is collected in a manner that gives users clear notice and choice. *Personally-identifiable information in the Abacus Online database will not be sold or disclosed to any merchant, advertiser or Web publisher.*

Name and address information volunteered by a user on an Abacus Alliance Web site is associated by Abacus through the use of a match code and the DoubleClick cookie with other information about that individual. Information in the Abacus Online database includes the user's name, address, retail, catalog and online purchase history, and demographic data. The database also includes the user's non-personally-identifiable information collected by Web sites and other businesses with which DoubleClick does business. Unless specifically disclosed to the contrary in a Web site's privacy policy, most non-personally-identifiable information collected by DoubleClick from Web sites on the DoubleClick Network is included in the Abacus Online database. However, the Abacus Online database will not associate any personally-identifiable medical, financial, or sexual preference information with an individual. Neither will it associate information from children.

Sweepstakes

DoubleClick's Flashbase, Inc. subsidiary provides automation tools that allow our clients to provide online contests and sweepstakes ("DoubleClick sweepstakes").

All DoubleClick sweepstakes entry forms must provide a way for you to opt-out of any communication from the sweepstakes manager that is not related to awarding prizes for the sweepstakes. Entry forms must further provide consumers with a choice whether to receive email marketing materials from third parties. When you enter a DoubleClick sweepstakes, the information you provide is not be shared with DoubleClick or any third party, unless you agree by checking the opt-in box on the sweepstakes entry form. If you enter a sweepstakes, you agree that the sweepstakes sponsor may use your name in relation to announcing and promoting the winners of the sweepstakes. See the official rules of the sweepstakes you are entering for additional information.

DoubleClick does collect aggregate, anonymous information about the sweepstakes. That information is primarily used to help sweepstakes managers choose prizes and make other decisions regarding the organization of the sweepstakes. DoubleClick does not associate information provided through the sweepstakes with your other web browsing activities or clickstream data.

DoubleClick Research

DoubleClick Research is a subsidiary of DoubleClick, Inc. To review DoubleClick's privacy policy from the beginning, including information on opting out of the DoubleClick cookie, click here. DoubleClick Research provides surveys to users. All research survey responses are voluntary, and the information collected will only be used for research and reporting purposes, to help DoubleClick and our clients determine the effectiveness of our businesses, Web sites, or advertising campaigns.

If you participate in a survey, the information you provide will be used along with that of other study participants (for example, DoubleClick Research might report that 50% of a survey's respondents are women). DoubleClick may share anonymous individual and aggregate data with the company that requested the survey for research and analysis purposes.

The only individually identifiable information DoubleClick Research may use is the email address you provide, in order to contact sweepstakes prize winners. DoubleClick Research may also contact you through your e-mail address for other purposes if you tell DoubleClick Research that it may do so; for example, if you indicate in the survey that you wish to join a DoubleClick Research online research panel. When you submit your survey, your e-mail address and your response to the "future contact" question described above, are automatically stored in a database that is intentionally separated from your survey responses. Therefore, your e-mail address is not tied back to your survey responses. DoubleClick Research will not share the personally identifiable individual data you enter in response to survey questions with third parties.

For all other purposes, only aggregate data that has been stripped of all personally identifiable information will be used.

DoubleClick Research uses DART ad server technology to transmit the survey. In the course of providing this survey to you, a DoubleClick cookie may be placed on your browser. DoubleClick utilizes cookie technology for many purposes, including targeting ads to you on other web sites. In connection with DoubleClick Research Surveys, the cookie is used to control the research process, primarily to stop people from being asked to take the same survey twice. In addition, the types of advertising you have viewed on web sites during the course of your normal web surfing, such as whether you have viewed a particular ad or how many times you have viewed a particular ad, may be connected to your anonymous survey responses. This information is strictly for research purposes and is totally anonymous.

If your cookies are turned off or you have opted out, DoubleClick Research will be unable to recognize whether or not you have been offered a survey, and may inadvertently offer you the same survey in the future. To read more about DoubleClick's cookies, including information on how to opt-out of a DoubleClick cookie, click here.

Please contact DoubleClick Research at surveyhelp@doubleclick.net if you have questions or comments about DoubleClick Research or your participation in the survey or if you wish to later choose not to receive future email.

Email

DoubleClick uses DARTmail, a version of DART technology, to bring you emails that may include ads. Email is sent only to people who have consented to receive a particular email publication or mailing from a company. If at any time you would like to end your subscription to an email publication or mailing, follow either the directions posted at the end of the email publication or mailing, or the directions at the email newsletter company's Web site.

In order to bring you more relevant advertising, your email address may be joined with the information you provided at our client's website and may be augmented with other data sources. However, DoubleClick does not link your email address to your other Web browsing activities or clickstream data.

Information Collected by DoubleClick's Web Sites

The Web sites owned or controlled by DoubleClick, such as http://www.plazadirect.com/ and http://www.iaf.net/ may ask for and collect personally-identifiable information. DoubleClick is committed to providing meaningful notice and choice to users before any personally-identifiable information is submitted to us. Specifically, users will be informed about how DoubleClick may use such information, including whether it will be shared with marketing partners or combined with other information available to us. In most cases, the information provided by a user will be contributed to the Abacus Online database to enable personally-tailored ad delivery online. Users will always be offered the choice not to provide personally-identifiable information or to have it shared with others.

Access
DoubleClick offers users who have voluntarily provided personally-identifiable information to DoubleClick the opportunity to review the information provided and to correct any errors.

Cookies and Opt Out
DoubleClick, along with thousands of other Web sites, uses cookies to enhance your Web viewing experience. DoubleClick's cookies do not damage your system or files in any way.

Here's how it works. When you are first served an ad by DoubleClick, DoubleClick assigns you a unique number and records that number in the cookie file of your computer. Then, when you visit a Web site on which DoubleClick serves ads, DoubleClick reads this number to help target ads to you. The cookie can help ensure that you do not see the same ad over and over again. Cookies can also help advertisers measure how you utilize an advertiser's site. This information helps our advertisers cater their ads to your needs.

If you have chosen on any of the Web sites with which Abacus does business to receive ads tailored to you personally as part of Abacus Online's services, the cookie will allow DoubleClick and Abacus Online to recognize you online in order to deliver you a relevant message.

However, if you have not chosen to receive personally-targeted ads, then the DoubleClick cookie will *not* be associated with any personal information about you, and DoubleClick (including Abacus) will not be able to identify you personally online.

While we believe that cookies enhance your Web experience by limiting the repetitiveness of advertising and increasing the level of relevant content on the Web, they are not essential for us to continue our leadership position in Web advertising.

While some third parties offer programs to manually delete your cookies, DoubleClick goes one step further by offering you a "blank" or "opt-out cookie" to prevent any data from being associated with your browser or you individually. If you do not want the benefits of cookies, there is a simple procedure that allows you to deny or accept this feature. By denying

DoubleClick's cookies, ads delivered to you by DoubleClick can only be targeted based on the non-personally-identifiable information that is available from the Internet environment, including information about your browser type and Internet service provider. By denying the DoubleClick cookie, we are unable to recognize your browser from one visit to the next, and you may therefore notice that you receive the same ad multiple times.

If you have previously chosen to receive personally-tailored ads by being included in the Abacus Online database, you can later elect to stop receiving personally-tailored ads by denying DoubleClick cookies.

Your opt-out will be effective for the entire life of your browser or until you delete the cookie file on your hard drive. In each of these instances, you will appear as a new user to DoubleClick. Unless you deny the DoubleClick cookie again, DoubleClick's ad server will deliver a new cookie to your browser.

If you would like more information on how to opt-out, please click here.

Disclosure
DoubleClick makes available all of our information practices at www.doubleclick.net, including in-depth descriptions of our targeting capabilities, our privacy policy, and full disclosure on the use of cookies. In addition, we provide all users with the option to contact us at info@doubleclick.net with any further questions or concerns.

Security
DoubleClick will maintain the confidentiality of the information that it collects during the process of delivering an ad. DoubleClick maintains internal practices that help to protect the security and confidentiality of this information by limiting employee access to and use of this information.

Industry Efforts to Protect Consumer Privacy
DoubleClick is committed to protecting consumer privacy online. We are active members of the Network Advertising Initiative, NetCoalition.com, Online Privacy Alliance, Internet Advertising Bureau, New York New Media Association, and the American Advertising Federation.

For more information about protecting your privacy online, we recommend that you visit http://www.networkadvertising.org/, http://www

.netcoalition.com/, and http://www.privacyalliance .org/. If you have any additional questions, please contact us at info@doubleclick.net.

We also recommend that you review this Privacy Statement periodically, as DoubleClick may update it from time to time.

URL: corporate/privacy/default.asp
Copyright ©1996-2001 DoubleClick Inc.
DoubleClick's DART technology is protected by U.S. Pat. 5,948,061.
Source: www.doubleclick.com, February 2000.

ENDNOTES

[1]*This case has been written on the basis of published sources only. Consequently, the interpretation and perspectives presented in this case are not necessarily those of Doubleclick Inc. or any of its employees.*

[2]*These cookies were anonymous because although DoubleClick tracked the cookie (and subsequently, the user), it did not possess any means to identify the owner of the cookie. In effect, DoubleClick was cognizant of the user's surfing habits but not of the surfer's identity. With the additional database containing personally identifiable information, there existed a possibility that the information in the cookie could be matched with a surfer's profile, thus identifying the user.*

[3]*As reported in USA Today, Jan. 15, 2000.*

[4]*DoubleClick information and press releases were accessed from www.doubleclick.com.*

[5]*From www.doubleclick.com – Feb. 29, 2000.*

[6]*DoubleClick expected to serve over 53 billion ads per month by June, 2000.*

eLance.com: Preventing Disintermediation

Ken Mark and Professor Scott Schneberger prepared this case solely to provide material for class discussion. The authors do not intend to illustrate either effective or ineffective handling of a managerial situation. The authors may have disguised certain names and other identifying information to protect confidentiality.

INTRODUCTION

"What's the best way to prevent buyers and sellers from executing transactions outside of eLance's site?" wondered Beerud Sheth, co-founder and vice-president business development for Sunnyvale, California's eLance.com. It was July 21, 2000 and eLance was completing a beta test of its site, having facilitated over 30,000 transactions between project buyers and sellers since its August 30, 1999 site launch.

eLance was in the midst of closing its second round of venture financing which would allow it to execute its plan to become the premier online global services marketplace. In order to achieve this goal, it needed to prevent disintermediation — instances when eLance buyers and sellers, after being introduced on the eLance site, would decide to conduct future project-related transactions offline. Offline transactions would prevent eLance from mediating these transactions and gaining revenue from them.

To combat disintermediation, eLance had already put in place several onsite and offline features. As this was eLance's number one concern, Sheth wanted to know what more it could do.

OVERVIEW OF THE TRADITIONAL STAFFING INDUSTRY

In 1946, William Russell Kelly, anticipating a post-Second World War business and industrial boom, moved to Detroit and founded the Russell Kelly Office Service. The firm, a service bureau that sent its employees to fill in for vacationing or sick employees, set the standard for the newly created staffing industry, and coined the term

"Kelly Girls" to identify its staff, most of whom were female secretaries.[1]

The staffing industry was divided into two categories — temporary staffing agencies who hired workers and outsourced them to companies in return for a fee, and talent matchmakers who received a fee for matching freelance independent professionals with companies who required their specialized services.

There were basically two classifications of temporary workers whom the staffing industry counted on: agency-dependent contract employees and independent professionals. In the agency-dependent model, the agency located the assignment, recruited the contractor, negotiated with and billed the client. The agency also withheld applicable taxes from the contractor's regularly scheduled payroll cheque, with the difference between the client bill rate and the contractor pay rate (minus taxes) being the agency's revenue. Contractors were responsible for all of the above non-work related items. (See Exhibit 1: Traditional Staffing Industry.)

The independent professional phenomenon became a fundamental socio-economic shift in the American workforce. In 1999, there were an estimated 25 million independent workers in the United States, including 14 million self-employed, eight million independent contractors, and three million temps.[2] Within this group, an estimated eight million were highly skilled independent professionals. In addition, there were approximately four million untapped professionals — people actively thinking about freelancing — for example, moonlighters and work-at-home moms.

E-LANCING EMERGES

Freelancers weighed the freedom to be able to work on different, temporary projects against the absence of a fixed revenue stream. Professionals who chose this lifestyle most often relied on personal contacts or staffing agencies as a source for project work. These sources usually limited the freelancer to short-term contract work in his or her immediate geography and network. The emergence of the Internet in the early 1990s promised to remove this barrier of space and time.

Much was written about the opportunity to exchange employment information over this new medium. An excerpt from the article "The Dawn of the E-Lance Economy" by Thomas Malone and Robert Laubacher read:

The fundamental unit of such an economy is not the corporation but the individual. Tasks aren't assigned and controlled through a stable chain of management but rather are carried out autonomously by independent contractors. These electronically connected freelancers — e-lancers — join together into fluid and temporary networks to produce and sell goods and services. When the job is done — after a day, a month, a year — the network dissolves, and its members become independent agents again, circulating through the economy, seeking the next assignment.

FORMATION OF ELANCE.COM

Wall Street traders Beerud Sheth and Srini Anumolu founded eLance.com with a private placement in late 1998. On August 30, 1999, eLance.com launched the beta version of its global services marketplace from New York City. Its Web site proclaimed: "eLance is the premier global services marketplace. From business, computer and creative needs to family, financial and much more, eLance provides the resources for people to connect, communicate and complete their project." It continued: "Buyers can post a project description and receive bids from service providers or buy directly from thousands of fixed-price service listings. eLance support features include the Work Space for project development and remote delivery, service provider certifications, feedback ratings, and an international billing and payment system. Service providers find a global market at eLance, and can build their reputation through our feedback system."

THE ONLINE E-LANCING COMPETITION[3]

These new eLancing e-marketplaces were a way for independent professionals to increase their exposure to potential clients while limiting the amount of resources normally required for self-promotion and advertising and transaction costs. In some cases these sites also served as an effective and efficient way to access necessary services for business survival, including bill payment, insurance purchasing and tax report filing, in a convenient one-stop shopping location. A short list of some of eLance.com's online competition follows.

ANTS (FORMERLY JOB SWARM)

The personnel at JobSwarm.com had constructed a fully functioning site and its goals were to build traffic and membership. The opportunities posted on the site covered marketing, IT and writing. The site's main source of revenue seemed to be the five per cent finder's fee on all billable work completed by registered freelancers. Another possible source of revenue was the private label services it aimed to provide to partners like Startupbiz.com. The primary business model difference between Ants.com and eLance.com was that Ants recruited freelancers to offer the services that clients needed. The site had chosen to offer a program that promised to pay the individual referring another freelancer to the site royalties on the long-term work of that person.

GURU

Guru.com had focused on building a community that promoted freelancing as a lifestyle. By designing a visually appealing site, it sought to brand itself as the leading destination for freelancers. It also offered freelancer advice and support through numerous alliances with other content providers. It charged buyers to post projects that were staffing sites and a high percentage of its staffing was on location. Being a destination site for freelancers, it was expected to offer them additional services such as 401(k) plans, health benefits, and product advice. Guru.com was expected to focus on matching independent professionals (known as "gurus") with hirers.

FREEAGENT

FreeAgent.com offered many of the same services as its competition via a basic interface. It had been developed by Opus360, a company that placed IT contractors and provided benefits, including 401(k) plans and insurance for its contractors. Posting an opportunity on the site provided a client with project exposure to thousands of providers. As with the other services in this category, each provider was encouraged to provide an e-portfolio to help the client choose a potential partner. One of the key noticeable differences in its approach versus that of eLance.com's was the effort to promote repeat business to the site by charging clients for posting freelance opportunities on a sliding scale. This sliding scale offered the client, who might otherwise have been inclined to look elsewhere for talent, a clear option to reduce freelance recruiting costs for an ongoing business operation.

ELANCE.COM OVERALL SITE FEATURES

Since its launch date (late August 1999), eLance.com had the set of online tools shown in Table 1 available to

users. In addition, eLance.com planned to add billing and payment systems that allowed buyers and sellers in different countries to pay each other (with different currencies, if they so wished). Most improvements were done with the intention of eLance.com keeping buyers and sellers on its site throughout the transaction. To that end, it even offered both parties an online, virtual workspace for them to transfer their documents and files.

Table 1 — eLance.com Site Features, July 1999

Description	Platform upon which buyers and sellers post, review and bid on projects. Includes auction-style bids for projects, messaging, bid acceptance and notification.	File-sharing capability (50 MB space limit), messaging capability, and online scheduling. Can conduct online meetings.	Credit Card Billing and rating system allowing buyers and sellers to rate each other.
Primary Objective	Matching of buyers and sellers of project transactions.	To facilitate transfer of work between buyers and seller (especially international ones).	Develop the primary stream of revenue and put in place a self-managing rating system.

The development of additional functionality could aid the buyer, the seller, its partners or internal operations. Within these four groupings, the co-founders wondered what additional functionality would look like. Initial thoughts created the following list of possibilities:

- Launch regional sites. This would require eLance.com to facilitate personnel matching in various geographies and customize content to each particular geography.
- Provide robust independent professional profiles. This would allow buyers to research the sellers, reviewing their work experience and previous projects.
- Provide search engine. Using keywords, sellers and buyers could search for each other's project postings.
- Provide response management tool. Because of the number of project bids and postings that eLance.com was expected to attract, the response management tool would help buyers and sellers filter through the bids and posts.
- Provide quality control tool. The actual functionality of this product was not yet confirmed but the objective was to build a tool to aid buyers in assessing the

quality of a seller. At the time, a rating system had been rolled out by eLance.com.

- Content. One way to attract buyers and sellers was to create specific content relevant to each audience. This would involve in-house writing or syndication of content from other providers, posting articles on topics such as training, selection, workplace improvement or humor.

- Support different languages. eLance.com was considering launching foreign language sites including German and Spanish sites. This was still a new idea and eLance.com intended to explore it within a year.

REGISTERED USERS OF ELANCE.COM

eLance believed that any registered user could be both a buyer and a seller of services. Thus, there was no distinct demographic profile of eLance buyers. However, eLance noticed that buyers generally shared several common characteristics. The first two were time sensitivity and budget constraints — they wanted the electronic project completed and delivered on-time and on-budget. "These early adopters are often fast-growing tech-savvy start-ups, although many large corporations were using eLance as well," commented Sean Jacobsohn, business development manager. "In addition, buyers are users with limited time and financial resources, and limited employees. Seventy per cent of all buying requests originated in the United States, with an average amount of US$1,000 per transaction."

Projects ranged in price from US$5 to US$500,000. Sellers could design PowerPoint presentations, write a press release, help a small- or medium-sized business develop a Web site or do piecemeal software engineering. These independent professionals were part of the aforementioned 25 million independent workers in the United States. They ranged in profession from financial consultants, clerical staff and business writers, to graphic designers. Because of their independent status, they were constantly searching for new projects. With its growing number of buyers and its site functionality, eLance believed that its marketplace would draw many of these professionals in search of project work.

LEVERAGING THE POWER OF THE INTERNET

In creating eLance, Sheth and Anumolu sought to harness the power of the Internet. Here was a medium that allowed global, immediate access to buyers and sellers.

Not only were buyers able to find sellers for time-sensitive project work, they were able to choose between competing bids from anywhere in the world. Because each listed project was intended to be completed remotely, there was no need to limit bids to sellers within the vicinity of the buyer's physical office. In addition, the availability of eLance site tools allowed immediate, electronic delivery of projects via a shared Workspace.

There remained, however, several barriers to eLance's success. First, the notion of dividing a person's workload into several projects remained fairly new — eLance would have to ensure that its potential users were familiar and comfortable with posting and bidding for projects.

But more importantly, even if they were at ease with the concept of projects, eLance would have to present enough of a value proposition to buyers and sellers to dissuade disintermediation. There were several key features already incorporated into the eLance model.

PREVENTING DISINTERMEDIATION

Sheth explained:

Well, let me put it this way. You can never really prevent this disintermediation. You can just kind of mitigate the risk. Even an active large market place like eBay still grapples with a grey market as they call it. I think what we will do is make sure we give our users enough reasons that they don't need to go away, allowing them to stick around. We need for our users to arrive at that point where the easiest way to get the job done is through the site rather than off the site. In spite of the added cost, the user gains in terms of convenience, amount of time spent, effort exhausted, money spent — the cheapest way to transact is through our site.

So that's kind of the challenge that we as a company face and the way we address it is by providing a lot of value-added features. For example, our workspace component facilitates development and delivery, our billing and payment features make it easy to pay for the product once it's done, and both buyers and sellers leave feedback for each other. Leaving the feedback allows sellers to build a rating that will get them access to more work.

Sheth listed the onsite and offline features that eLance currently possessed to deter disintermediation.

ONSITE

Marketplace

The goal was to create a platform to support project transactions. Because it was open to anyone in the world with an Internet connection, eLance hoped that the marketplace dynamics (real-time, remote bidding, always the prospect of a "better deal") would continue to persuade buyers to post their projects onsite in the hope of getting the best bid.

Workspace

eLance provided the parties of each transaction in progress with 50 megabytes of workspace where projects could be shared and discussed.

Feedback Rating

Buyers and sellers were encouraged to rate each other on a scale of one to five (higher score denoting higher satisfaction with work completed). Because each subsequent project added to one's feedback rating, it was hoped that sellers would continue to bid for onsite projects to maintain their feedback rating and command higher prices.

Online Chat

This function allowed buyers and sellers to speak with each other — eLance.com's site dialled the phone number for both parties at the appointed time. Thus, no telephone numbers had to be exchanged.

Billing and Payment

eLance's site supported credit card payment by buyers — in essence, buyers could pay the seller's bill (generated and sent electronically via eLance) onsite. In addition, an icon appeared beside buyers pre-registered with credit cards, providing a higher level of assurance of payment.

Sample Templates

A collection of templates outlining typical bid requirements for various projects was available to both buyers and sellers to help them structure and manage their project transactions.

Online Arbitration

eLance provided online arbitration for disputed transactions via a third-party service, SquareTrade.com.

OFFLINE

Market Makers

eLance market makers facilitated transactions between buyers and sellers, intervening to prompt parties to clarify bids and replies.[4]

Account Managers

One idea was to focus on buyers involved in the majority of transactions. Using the 80:20 rule — 80 per cent of your volume comes from 20 per cent of your customers — eLance intended to provide these "power buyers" with an account manager to assist them in projects posting.

Electronic newsletter

eLance provided an electronic newsletter to its members filled with spotlights on recent projects, upcoming functionality and tips for buyers and sellers. It also sent an e-mail notifying sellers of projects postings which met their criteria.

CONCLUSION

In the following few weeks, eLance would be progressing to a live site from its beta version. It intended to start charging sellers 10 per cent of the cost of each project, but keep the service free for buyers. Because eLance felt that it was still in a testing phase for the next few months, it did not want to set any short-term goals for its live site.

Jacobsohn emphasized,

> We're very customer-focused. That's why it took us a year to start charging and see what value-added services we want on site — we will keep monitoring the customer experience so we have a high retention rate. Once we test it long enough, we will be able to set internal goals for these numbers.

Since an increasing number of projects would be transacted on the eLance site, senior management wanted to address the issue of disintermediation before it became an issue. Sheth concluded, "Once they develop a relationship with a buyer or seller, they will be tempted to take the relationship offline. What incentives (or disincentives) can we use to keep these people on our site?"

Exhibit 1

Traditional Staffing Industry

Overview

- 6% annual growth overall; 24 per cent growth in professional / technical markets
- 7,000 firms in industry with 17,000 locations
- Top 10 firms control 29% of US$72 billion industry

(Manpower Inc, Adecco Staffing Services, Interim Services, Norrell Corp, Kelly Services)
- 100 firms with revenues exceeding US$100 million
- 90% of firms offer training programs

Examples

Company	Type	Focus	Financial Performance	Other
Roth Staffing Company	Traditional temporary staffing service	75% of demand was for clerical or secretarial workers 25% of demand was for higher-skilled workers Company focused on driving volume of placements	Achieved US$74 million in 1998 20% revenue growth from 1994 to 1998 Expected to approach US$240 million in sales by 2003	Roth placed 5,000 temporary workers in 1999 65 offices in seven states
Robert Half International	Traditional temporary staffing service	Focused on high-priced financial and accounting talent	Achieved US$1.3 billion in 1997 43% CAGR from 1995 to 2000	Market capitalization US$5 billion
Aquent (formerly MacTemps)	Talent matchmaker	Focused on creative and technical talent	US$100 million in 1998, expected to top US$190 million in 2000.	Offices in nine countries 110% money-back guarantee Offers additional services such as training and factoring

Sources:
- US Bureau of Labor Statistics.
- Davidson, Linda; *Maximize the return on temp staff investments*; <u>Workforce</u>; Costa Mesa; November 1999; Volume 78, Issue 11.
- Welles, Edward O, <u>Number 1 company: The People Business Inc.</u>; Boston; Oct 19, 1999; Volume 21, Issue 15.
- www.aquent.com (December 2000).

ENDNOTES

[1]Laabs, Jennifer L; *Father Of The "Staffing Industry – William Russell Kelly – Dies"*; <u>Workforce;</u> Costa Mesa; March 1998; Volume 77, Issue 3.

[2]*US Bureau of Labor Statistics.*

[3]*The foundation of this section was outsourced on eLance.com on August 15, 2000.*

[4]*In the stock trading world, the market maker was the person who provided liquidity to the marketplace — a bank or trading firm might have a market maker to keep transactions flowing.*

NRG Investments: Choosing an Internet Startup for Venture Capital Financing

Ken Thomson prepared this case under the supervision of Professor Derrick J. Neufeld solely to provide material for class discussion. The authors do not intend to illustrate either effective or ineffective handling of a managerial situation. The authors may have disguised certain names and other identifying information to protect confidentiality.

INTRODUCTION

On a Friday afternoon in late August 2000, Margaret Taylor, director of NRG Investments, sat at her desk contemplating two very similar Internet business plans. Considering the mass of plans that NRG received — approximately 500 per month — it was not at all uncommon for her to see two or even three business plans at one time that were pitching the same idea. Good ideas were a dime a dozen, but successful startups were rare. Taylor had to determine the core critical success factors for this online business idea, and then use them to analyse the business plans before her. She had until Monday to decide which entrepreneur would receive the $500,000 equity infusion offered by NRG. Once her decision was made, Taylor would notify the entrepreneurs and prepare a presentation for NRG's board of directors indicating the reasons for her decision and the risks involved. The opportunity was attractive, but the choice was difficult. Which one of these businesses had the correct mix of "assets" to make it wildly successful and provide NRG with its desired returns? Taylor had three days.

THE NRG GROUP

The NRG Group was comprised of three operating units: NRG Solutions, NRG Factory and NRG Investments.

NRG Solutions[1] was the original operating unit of The NRG Group. This division specialized in youth-focused consulting and had completed projects for such well-known clients as Kraft, Ford, and Kellogg's. These clients were searching for ways to appeal to the 14-year-old to 24-year-old demographic, a part of the population that was notoriously difficult for marketers to understand.

NRG Factory[2] was the incubation division of The NRG Group. A business incubator makes it easier for start-up businesses to find, fund and implement ideas by drawing on a larger community of talent, knowledge and experience deployed for their use. This unit focused on businesses that have products or services that can be launched within 90 days of investment. The NRG Group provided management, strategy, formulation, personal coaching, accounting, technical infrastructure and/or office facilities to all of the companies within the NRG Factory.

NRG Investments, NRG's venture capital division, had a fund of approximately $15 million to invest in early-stage technology companies. NRG's *latest* area of investing interest was in "information personalization software" and "infrastructure software." Infrastructure software is the basic building blocks of connecting people with technology to enhance information flow, business delivery and personal fulfilment. This technology includes the physical foundations that support the flow and processing of information between end-users, and can also include:

- Electronic data transmission media and control devices (e.g., data and voice lines, satellite, antennas, routers, aggregators, repeaters, storage, etc.);
- Software used to send, receive and manage the signals that are transmitted; and
- Data manipulation and management tools.

NRG Investments' second area of investing, information personalization software, referred to tailored information processing software tools. This software was used to assist in the development of long-term customer, partner and personal relationships. Categories of personalization included:

- Artificial intelligence — (AI) based personalization — the use of AI systems to predict customer behavior.
- Interaction-based personalization — the building of interactive forms that directly ask customers what they like.
- Rule-based personalization — the creation of rules to manage customer interactions (e.g., if the customer does X, give the customer Y — useful for cross-selling and up-selling activities).

NRG Investments would invest between $500,000 and $3 million in companies that met its investment criteria (see Exhibit 1). Companies that are currently in NRG's investment portfolio are outlined:

- Starfire Technologies
  Develops and provides Internet-based advertising and marketing services to small- and medium-sized businesses. Starfire's services are currently being offered under the registered business name Star Pages™, Starfire's flagship Internet-based electronic advertising service, which was launched in April 1997. NRG Investment: $500,000

- Streetviews.com
  Facilitates exchange, understanding and timely discussion of in-depth information across the entire investment spectrum. Information and investment tools include news, quotes, charts, portfolio tracking, message boards and chat, in addition to the research product library. On-line in 2000. NRG Investment: $500,000

- MedComSoft
  Operates in the Canadian Internet and cellular-enabled healthcare information systems market. Consulting and implementation services facilitate the integration and adoption of information systems with medical care providers, payers, hospitals, and service providers, and result in simplified workflow, higher quality information and patient care, and decreased costs. Founded in 1994. NRG Investment: $1 million

- Charity.ca
  Links Canadian charities with donors, facilitates electronic transfer of donated funds, and automates issuance of CCRA e-tax receipts to donors. With annual charitable donations within Canada in excess of $4.5 billion, the potential demand for the Charity.ca service is enormous. Online in 2000. NRG Investment: $500,000

- ACEnetx
  Internet outsourcing vendor, provides Web hosting

services for interactive Web sites, Web-based applications, live and interactive Internet television, and integrated messaging services through proprietary patented technology. Client roster includes Nortel Networks, the Canadian Department of National Defense, Certicom Corporation, and Canadian Tire Acceptance. Established in 1995. NRG Investment: $500,000

Although NRG would not invest more than $3 million in any one deal, it was not opposed to investing as part of a syndicate — a group of venture capital organizations that invested co-operatively in a company to spread the investment risk across several firms, and to allow venture capitalists to achieve greater diversification with their limited pool of funds — on deals requiring in excess of $3 million. In return for its investment, NRG acquired a portion of the company's equity. NRG would not retain greater than 49 per cent of the equity of a company in which it invests, consistent with its philosophy that the management of target companies must have majority control of their businesses to ensure that they remain motivated, and that their focus was on adding value and growing their company.

Through its past investment decisions, NRG Investments had developed an iterative process to guide individuals through the decision-making process. A detailed diagram and description of this process is provided in Exhibit 2.

THE INVESTMENT DECISION

Taylor had two similar investments in front of her: ConciergeConnect Inc. (CCI) and Hotel Services Online (HSO). She had met with each of these entrepreneurs and conducted high-level research on the market (size, competition, etc.), evaluated strengths and weaknesses of the business concept, and concluded that each of these entrepreneurs would be a capable manager. Her decision would lie in the details.

Once Taylor had decided which company held the brightest prospects for future growth and return on NRG's investment, she had to face the issue of valuation. It was almost impossible to place a value on early-stage Internet companies because the Internet was an unproven medium for conducting business. There was no basis for establishing future earnings multiples, no comparable companies existed that would produce comparable company valuation ratios, and future cash flows were too uncertain

to develop a reliable discounted cash flow model. About the only certainty that Taylor could count on was that the value placed on a company by the entrepreneur would exceed the valuation offered by the venture capitalist!

Amidst the confusion surrounding valuation, venture capitalists typically calculate implied values based on a target ownership percentage and the intended investment amount. For example, if NRG'g target ownership percentage is 20 per cent, and their investment is $500,000, the implied value of the company is $2.5 million ($2,500,000 × 20% = $500,000).

THE ONLINE CONCIERGE SERVICES BUSINESS MODEL

The job of concierge within a high-traffic hotel, condominium or office complex was fast-paced, stressful and often frustrating. Requests from occupants might be as simple as making a dinner reservation or as complicated as renting a private luxury yacht on the evening of July 1st to observe the fireworks display over the Toronto Harbour. The concierge in a large, high-traffic property would be constantly inundated with requests from customers and, therefore, must be efficient and organized. Currently, the process undertaken by a concierge to fulfil such diverse requests can be arduous and time-consuming. By implementing the technology developed by CCI or HSO, a concierge could communicate via the Internet with third parties who can fulfil their guests' requests (see Exhibit 3).

Concierges would pay CCI or HSO a user fee to access and utilize the concierge software that was hosted on a CCI or HSO server. Using the CCI or HSO application, concierges would no longer spend time searching for contact information, making telephone calls, waiting for replies and confirmations, and performing bill settlement tasks. In essence, the systems promised to make concierge work more efficient and effective. It is important to note that neither CCI nor HSO would fulfil customer requests directly; rather, they would connect the concierges to the service providers. Thus, both CCI and HSO intended to be "application service providers" (ASPs). The ASP business model has recently become very popular, and The Gartner Group forecasts the total ASP market will be worth US$25 billion by 2004.

As outlined in the business proposals, both CCI and HSO systems would:

- make the process of fulfiling occupants' requests faster, easier and more organized, leading to improved guest satisfaction and retention;

- enable highly specialized requests to be archived, making their fulfillment much easier in the future; and
- improve concierge productivity, eliminating the need for a concierge assistant position in larger properties.

The online services that both CCI and HSO planned to offer were restaurant reservations, ticket purchases, travel arrangements, data storage, guest profile storage and contact management.

The concierge would have access to the reservation books of all restaurants that *choose* to subscribe to the system being developed by CCI and HSO. Both companies would offer restaurants an easily implemented online reservation system that would allow concierges to make reservation requests, and also allow restaurant managers to organize and track all of their reservations electronically. It would be in the best interest of restaurants to implement this software so that they could capitalize on the traffic that concierges channelled to their restaurants. Further, no automated reservation tracking system currently existed for restaurants, making the adoption argument even more compelling.

Both companies also planned to connect their concierge users with travel sites that could fulfil occupants' travel requests (e.g., bookings on airlines, trains, taxis, buses, boats, etc.). The process of making guest travel arrangements was especially difficult for concierges, and the Internet could ease much of the frustration surrounding this task by eliminating the need for numerous telephone calls between agent and concierge.

Both services also offered the concierges data storage and retrieval capabilities. First, the concierge would be allowed to archive all requests, for easy repeat bookings. The more challenging a request would be to fulfil, the more valuable the information storage feature would become. Second, the concierge would have the ability to build a profile on all those who used their services. A hotel concierge would be able to archive all past requests made for guests, such as their favorite restaurant, food or sporting event, their birthday or other special occasions, as well as any special requests. This would enable the concierge to proactively anticipate the requests of valued guests, offer unique suggestions to guests based on historic preferences, generate new ideas by comparing profiles of guests with similar interests, and observe valued guests' special occasions.

CCI's technology also included an artificial intelligence component that used information gathered on guests to generate a "profile" for that individual. Using this profile, the software would continuously search the Internet for restaurants, events or other items that might be of interest to that specific guest, and alert the concierge of its search results, and in this way build considerable loyalty and goodwill.

HSO's proposed product contained a unique piece of functionality called "Concierge Collaboration" which allowed concierges from different properties to communicate online, share archives of difficult requests, leverage the purchasing power of the concierge network to purchase various tickets, and collaborate on undocumented difficult requests.

KEY INVESTMENT CONSIDERATIONS

There were some areas in which the investment opportunities differed:

Management

The management of ConciergeConnection consisted of chief executive officer (CEO) Jorg Hansen, an experienced concierge who had worked with a luxury hotel chain for approximately 10 years, and chief technical officer (CTO) Jeffrey Windmeyer, an accomplished computer programmer who worked with Microsoft for 12 years. The two founders had hired two junior programmers, and had identified the need to hire individuals to fill roles in business development/strategic partnerships, and sales and marketing.

The management team of Hospitality Services Online was a complementary group of senior hospitality executives who had over 60 years of combined work experience in the hotel industry. John Rawlen, CEO, has held senior positions within such reputable hotel chains as Global Hotel Group and Premier Hotels. Matthew Charles was chief operating officer (COO) for a small private hotel chain that operated hotels in New York, Boston and Philadelphia. His contribution was integral to the growth of this hotel chain from two to 16 properties during his 18-year tenure. Charles also orchestrated the installation of a new information system within these hotels. George Silverman, director of sales and marketing, has held the position of general manager within two luxury hotel properties in New York City. With his intimate knowledge of the role of concierge, Silverman understood what functionality software should have that is targeted at these individuals.

Technology

Jeffrey Windmeyer of CCI developed a highly sophisticated piece of software, the code of which was protected under Canadian copyright laws. This software provided all of the functionality described above, and also included a customizable, easy-to-install interface for restaurants, ticket agencies, or for other third parties who would be interested in joining this network / marketplace.

HSO outsourced the development of their software to a mid-sized information technology company. The software would include the functionality described above, and would also include "Concierge Collaboration." An operating version of the software had yet to be completed, although the IT company has promised this by September 2000.

The technology infrastructure that was in place for both companies was sophisticated, and remarkably similar. Both companies were running Sun Microsystems Web servers that managed the flow of information between concierge clients, third-party service providers and CCI/HSO. CCI also implemented a payment server to manage per-use transactions (as described in their revenue model). This was also supplied by Sun.

The operating system employed by CCI was Linux-based. Reasons cited by management for this decision were low price, flexibility, lack of licensing restrictions, stability, performance, immunity to viruses, and encryption ability. HSO chose to implement a Windows NT operating system, stating the following benefits: product breadth, customization ability, upgradability and service.

To ensure the fastest and most reliable networking solutions, both CCI and HSO have installed optical networks capable of transmitting data at 10 gigabits per second.

Partnerships

ConciergeConnection has convinced 35 Toronto restaurants to utilize their software and join their concierge network. Windmeyer insisted that the sales process had not been difficult, that interest was high among restaurant owners, and that he expected at least 60 more restaurants to join in the next two months.

Hospitality Services Online had not yet established any partnerships with restaurants as their technology was not complete. They had, however, entered into preliminary discussions with Xpedia.com to provide all travel related services for their concierge customers. They had also discussed partnership possibilities with Ticketmaster.com to provide all sports and entertainment tickets.

Revenue Model

CCI intended to earn revenue on a "per transaction" basis. For example, if a concierge used the CCI system to book a reservation, they would be charged 25 cents. The hotel would not be charged an upfront installation fee or and annual user fee. All revenues would be transaction based. CCI expected that the average hotel would make 100 transactions per day. Further, restaurants that secured a reservation through this system would be charged $1; ticket sales agencies (travel or entertainment) would be charged one per cent on all sales generated through the concierge network.

HSO planned to charge hotels an upfront user fee of $10,000 to access their system and utilize their software. All other parties involved in the network (restaurants, ticket sales agencies) would not be charged for their participation.

CONCLUSION

Margaret Taylor had many points to consider in making this decision. Would this type of investment "fit" with the investing mandate of the Company, and with other investments made by NRG? Can NRG Investments add significant value to this company? Did the valuation seem reasonable, and could NRG retain enough equity without fear of dilution through successive rounds of financing? Which set of entrepreneurs could execute on the business plan presented? What were the most relevant criteria that Taylor should use to assess these investments? Was there any information that was lacking which would assist Taylor with her decision?

Taylor could ask herself an infinite number of questions, and probably not answer any of them completely. In the end, seed-level high-tech investments bear more risk than any other type. Their payoff, however, can be astronomical. To whom should Taylor address NRG's $500,000 cheque?

Exhibit 1

Investment Criteria[3]

1. **Ability of Management:** Does this management team have the skill and abilities to make this business successful?
2. **Business Concept / Revenue Model:** Is this business concept sound, and can it make money?
3. **Strategic Partnerships:** Are any strategic partnerships in place that will increase the probability of success of this venture?
4. **Scalability:** Can this business be expanded quickly without significant capital infusion?

5. **Competitive Advantage:** Has this business established any competitive barriers to entry?
6. **Market Size:** Is this market large enough to offer a significant return on investment?
7. **Ability to Add Value:** Does the NRG Group have any special ability to add value to this concept because of our relationships, skills or knowledge?
8. **"Fit" with Other Investments:** Are there any operating synergies between this investment and other companies in the NRG portfolio?
9. **Future Rounds of Financing:** Will future rounds of financing be required that will significantly dilute NRG's ownership position?
10. **Exit Strategy:** Is there a clear exit strategy for this company that will allow NRG to recognize liquidity in its investment?

Exhibit 2

Investment Process

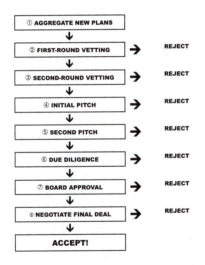

Step 1: Aggregate New Plans

Purpose: To aggregate new business plans submitted and to assign a review deadline.

Step 2: First-Round Vetting (PRELIMINARY)

Purpose: To conduct a *high-level* analysis of the business plan, and communicate results to the entrepreneur within five business days. No additional research is required at this stage. The following

"Initial Vetting Sheet" provides a guideline to determine whether the plan should progress to the next stage.

NRG Ventures Initial Vetting Document

Name of Analyst:_____

File Number:_____
Name of Business:_____
Name of Entrepreneur:_____

Size of Funding: $_____
Valuation: $_____

Objective: To determine whether we want to invest more time exploring this venture

☐ Yes   ☐ No

High-Level Analysis: Does this business plan have:
1. A clear problem statement?:_____
2. A clear vision statement?:_____
3. Synergy with NRG?:_____
4. A strong management team?:_____

More detailed analysis: Comment on the following aspects:
1. Leadership Team   6. Marketing Strategy
2. Strategy   7. Sales Strategy
3. Value Proposition   8. Unique Competitive Advantage
4. Business Model   9. Exit Strategy
5. Size of Market

Step 3: Second-Round Vetting (Detailed)

Purpose: To conduct a detailed review of the business plan. Some of these questions will be answered during a series of interviews / pitches.

The Idea / Market Condition / Opportunity / Business Plan

- Can we clearly visualize the venture's value propositions to the end user? NRG?
- Who are the venture's major competitors? What are their value propositions?
- Is the underlying technology of the product or service a disruptive technology or alternative technology?
- How does the customer make decisions about buying the product or services?
- How will the venture reach all the identified customer segments? What is necessary to overcome customer inertia and conservatism?
- Time-to-market factor. How quickly can the venture reach all the identified customer segments?
- How easy is it to retain a customer?

Management / Leadership Team Assessment

Arguably the most important part of The NRG Group ventures evaluation. Arthur Rock once said, "An entrepreneur without managerial savvy is just another promoter."[4] A good idea, unless it's executed, remains only a good idea. Good managers, on the other hand, can't lose. If their strategies don't work, they can develop another one. If a competitor comes along, they can turn to something else.

- What do they know? What skills, abilities, and knowledge do they have?
- Whom do they know? Where have they worked — and for whom?
- What is their track record? What have they accomplished — professionally and personally — in the past? What is their reputation within the business community? What experience do they have that is directly relevant to the opportunity they are pursuing?
- Whom do they plan to recruit, and how are they going to do it?

Step 4: Initial Pitch
Purpose: To gauge feasibility of the idea, and the capability of the entrepreneur and management team.

Step 5: Second Pitch
Purpose: To evaluate the management team and ask further questions. Management is the key determinant of a company's success. Therefore, a significant amount of time needs to be devoted to familiarizing ourselves with management.

Step 6: Due Diligence
Purpose: To determine if the business is clear of legal and financial liability, and whether the technology, management and business strategy are sound.

Step 7: Board Approval
Purpose: To inform the board of directors of the investment opportunity and seek approval.

Step 8: Negotiate Final Deal
Purpose: To structure a deal that is mutually beneficial to both parties and will allow for an ongoing, prosperous working relationship.

Exhibit 3
Business Model Diagram

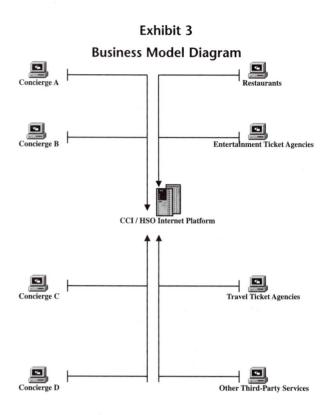

ENDNOTES

[1] NRG Solutions was spun off as a separate entity and became 100 per cent employee-owned shortly after this case was written.

[2] The NRG Factory concept was abandoned shortly after this case was written, leaving NRG Investments as the sole operating component of the NRG Group. (For further details, see: http://biz.yahoo.com/cnw/010122/ nrg_grp_ne_2.html, accessed 2-23-01).

[3] Note: It would be unreasonable to expect companies to meet all of these investment criteria. Some of these criteria are more important than others depending on the investment being considered. The job of the venture capitalist is to determine which criteria are most important for this business.

[4] One of America's leading venture capitalists who helped finance Fairchild Semiconductor, Teledyne, Apple and many other companies.

PacificLink iMedia: Designing an Internet Business

In July 2000, Alvin Lam and Andy Hui, co-founders of PacificLink iMedia (PacificLink), were evaluating their plans for expansion. PacificLink was a Web design and Internet marketing company that had been founded in 1998. The company had enjoyed good success in its 18 months of operations, growing from three to 19 employees. While looking out over Hong Kong's central business districts from the 20th floor window that housed half of PacificLinks' staff, Lam adjusted his tie and consid- ered PacificLink's vision for the future:

> We aim to provide one-stop solutions for our clients, helping them to jump start their Internet business with the minimal hassle. Within the next five years, we plan to branch out to other major cities in Asia.

EARLY PROJECTS

PacificLink iMedia (www.pacim.com) was the brainchild of Alvin Lam. After graduation from the Hong Kong University of Science and Technology's (HKUST) finance program, Lam worked for a small Web design company, also based in Hong Kong. However, he was not happy working with that company because it did not deliver good products, and the technology it used was not current. Lam explains:

> I was working for a Web design house and found many of our competitors were not even up-to- speed with what should have been the basic stan- dards of this new technological era. I thought I could do much better than they did. It didn't take much effort for me to talk Andy into the deal as he was already enthralled by the idea of running his own business. So that's how we got started.

Based on Lam's belief that he could do better than existing companies, he began to develop PacificLink in September 1998. During the first few months, PacificLink remained in a dormant stage while Lam was planning its future development. In November 1998, Lam left the small design house to work full time on PacificLink. At that time, two associates joined Lam: Andy Hui, a class- mate from HKUST's finance program, and Alex Lo, who had earned a degree in the United Kingdom in graphic communications.

The notion of starting a company was not new to Lam and Hui. While in university, Lam, who had possessed a passion for the Internet since his teenage years, had worked on several Internet-related projects. One of these was a financial Web portal called Financial Sources. Lam created this portal in the second year of his program, when he was 20 years old, as a way to assist his study. Lam explained more about the portal he developed.

> At that time, the concept of a portal was still very vague. I set up the Web site for the convenience of searching information for my own projects. It turned out that the site was frequented by many of my classmates.

Another of these projects was a Web page he designed as part of his student activities while at UST. Before founding PacificLink, Lam had tried his hand at developing a company called Hong Kong Innovation Technology (HKIT). This company was also a type of Web-based design house similar in scope to PacificLink. One important difference between HKIT and PacificLink was that HKIT was a SOHO type company. In Internet parlance, SOHO referred to a Small Office, Home Office. As a SOHO company, HKIT was typical of many start-ups in the Internet segment. Three other people worked with

Lam on developing HKIT, but the commitment of two of the three was lacking. As Lam put it,

> Only two out of the four partners worked a lot. The other two lacked initiative, passion and commitment. Without passion or commitment, people often do not see projects successfully through to their completion.

In the end, HKIT did not achieve the success expected for it. The company was eventually closed, and Lam moved on to other projects, such as his work at the small design house, and the founding of PacificLink.

THE INTERNET IN HONG KONG AND INTERNET MARKETING

The Hong Kong Internet industry had developed rapidly in 1999 and 2000. The growth was fueled in part by the creation of the enterprises section in the Hong Kong stock exchange. This new section was designed to facilitate the listing and financing of start-up companies. Another part of the growth came from the large number of young and talented entrepreneurs who had decided to take their chances working for their own companies, or as employees with start-up companies, rather than pursuing more traditional careers in Hong Kong's large companies like Hutchison Whampoa, or with multinationals in Hong Kong such as Goldman Sachs. The attraction for working with entrepreneurial Internet companies was augmented by the post-1997 slowdown in the traditional property and finance segments of Hong Kong's economy, and by the concurrent reduction in job prospects in traditional segments of the economy.

While Hong Kong's Internet segment had experienced considerable growth, it still lagged behind developments in the United States by at least one year. While a one-year lag was not long in old-style businesses, in the Internet segment, one year was a substantial lag. The listing trend, and the explosive growth of the NASDAQ, that had sparked the popularity of Internet-based businesses in the United States, was beginning to hit Hong Kong, as it had other countries in Asia such as South Korea and Japan. One of the strongest areas of growth, and one believed to hold much potential, was the Internet portal business. The success of the 1999 listing of China.com, reflected the potential for financial success among portal operators (see Appendix 1).

While PacificLink had three portals, its focus was to provide Web design and Internet marketing services to its client companies. An Internet marketing company provided a variety of services that helped client companies build an effective presence on the Internet. In 2000, building an effective presence on the Internet meant more than just presenting corporate demographic information on a Web page. It meant developing Internet-based advertising and marketing programs and providing promotional materials, customer support services and sales and database services.

To achieve this, an Internet marketing company had to be able to create interesting and interactive Web pages. An Internet marketing company faced the demand to provide a full range of services that enabled the implementation and creation of online sales strategies, while growing the popularity of client Web sites. When implemented effectively, an online presence could broaden the reach of the client company to a wider set of customers and businesses than would otherwise be possible.

PacificLink specialized in the Web design area. It functioned essentially as a service arm to clicks or bricks businesses. PacificLink could help a company develop a portal, a pure Internet play or a clicks business. Alternatively, it could help a bricks-type business, such as a hotel, develop an effective Internet presence. As an example of a service to a clicks business, PacificLink was engaged by Izzue.com to develop its Web site. The project, which was the largest that PacificLink had done in its first 18 months, involved creating 150 pages of content for Izzue.com.

PRODUCTS AND SERVICES OF PACIFICLINK

PacificLink provided a wide range of products and services to its clients, which included professional Web site design with interactive FLASH features, business Web hosting, portal site creations and e-commerce solutions. An objective of PacificLink was to provide a complete solution to businesses that wanted to gain the full range of benefits available from the successful deployment of the latest Internet-based technologies.

Professional Web Site Design

PacificLink's Web site design team tailor-made Web sites that created a distinctive image for their clients. The goal of the Web designers was to use leading-edge technology to provide a distinctive image through the client's Web site. In designing the Web site, the Web developers also worked with the client to decide on the content necessary to build up a unique but efficient site for the client. PacificLink had designed numerous Web sites for a variety of clients, including prominent Hong Kong companies such as Baleno and Regal Hotels (see Exhibit 1).

An important feature within the Web site designs of PacificLink was the use of 'FLASH Movie Openings.' FLASH (a registered trademark of Macromedia, Inc., an American company) was a leading-edge technology in Web site design that enabled developers to get away from the static Web graphics that typified the majority of Web pages in 2000. Traditional HTML coding did not permit developers to incorporate moving images and sounds into Web pages, as did the FLASH technology. PacificLink had created 'FLASH Movie Openings' for several clients including Jade Dynasty (www.kingcomics.com), a pre-launch movie for Izzue.com (www.izzue.com), and it had incorporated FLASH movies and FLASH games in the Jolly Shandy site (www.jollyshandy.com.hk).

Business Web Hosting

As part of its goal to provide a full range of e-business services, PacificLink offered Web site hosting to its clients. Web sites were hosted on PacificLink's secure business server which was dedicated to government, corporate and other private organizations. PacificLink did not permit personal clients to use its Web hosting services as a guard against illegal or illicit content appearing on its servers.

When a business or organization utilized PacificLink's Web hosting services, the company provided free advertising in the form of banner adds on PacificLink's own Web portals. These portals included HKED Search (www.hked.com), a portal devoted to listing guides to Hong Kong-based manufacturers, suppliers and other companies; Financial Sources Asia (http://fina.pacim .com), a complete financial Web site with easy to access features such as stock price quotes, trend analysis and listed company information; and MyTrendyMall (http://www.mytrendymall.com/), an electronic retailing site (see Exhibit 2).

One advantage of hosting on PacificLink's servers was the provision of banner advertising. PacificLink's Web portals received upwards of 200,000 page views per month, providing significant exposure to Web-hosted clients. As a further aid to the advertisement of hosted businesses, PacificLink helped clients register with the more than 2,000 search engines that existed, including leaders like Yahoo!, Infoseek and Altavista.

Portal Site Creations

Web portals provided content and specific services to browsers who accessed the portal's site (see Appendix

1). PacificLink helped clients develop portals that had a strong central theme, which was important to building a community of users. PacificLink's design for portals also included several other important features designed to attract and retain users. Some of these features were chat rooms, search engines, products search engines, voting systems, online games, mail list systems, screen savers, shopping carts, credit card payment gateways and Web mail.

In addition to product development, the integrated nature of PacificLink's services meant that PacificLink provided promotion for the newly-designed portal. PacificLink advised on marketing campaigns for the portal, and assisted with media advertising design and placement. Other promotional services were similar to those provided to companies that engaged PacificLink's Web hosting services; PacificLink's existing portals advertised the client portals, and the information in client's portals was directed to existing search engines.

PacificLink had designed several portals for a variety of clients. In addition to Izzue.com, PacificLink had created Chinese language portals for the health industry (www.healthcare2u.com/), for accountants (www .itaccountants.com), and for the Hong Kong textile industry (www.etextile.net).

E-commerce Solutions

A persistent concern in the adoption of e-commerce is one about the security of Web-based transactions. PacificLink utilized the latest SSL encryption technology to provide a means of secure transactions over the Internet. The SSL encryption technology used an SSL payment gateway to offer online shopping security at a level that met American online banking standards. Along with the technology, PacificLink advised customers on how to increase traffic to their Web site to increase the volume of sales made through the client's online shopping centre.

Other Services

PacificLink offered many other services, either as independent services to clients, or as part of a full e-solution to their clients' needs. Web site marketing was one of these services. Portals and businesses hosted on PacificLink's servers received this service, as did clients that wanted to achieve a stronger advertising effect for their Web site. This service included the optimization of 'Keyword Meta Tags,' to register among the first sites listed in lists output by search engines, as well as registration on at least 2,000 search engines. Clients for this service included Miramar Hotels (www.miramar-

group.com) and City Garden Hotel (www.citygarden
.com.hk), both in Hong Kong.

Apart from these key services, PacificLink facilitated a
company's entry into the Internet through its domain
name registration service. The company also offered
multimedia services such as the conversion of audio and
video files to any format, and the development of quick-
time videos (go to http://www.pacim.com/qtvr.htm for
a demonstration). Other ancillary services included
animated banner design, unique domain name e-mail
aliases, magazine advertisement design and interactive
CD production.

Growth of PacificLink

After its first 18 months of operations, PacificLink had
established a good presence in the Hong Kong Internet
business community, and had achieved a net profitable
position by its third month of operations. PacificLink was
among the top Web design companies in Hong Kong.
The company provided high-end service, with sophisticated leading-edge design and content, but it had a
lower price than its Hong Kong-based competitors.
Outside of Hong Kong, the company's reputation was
less well-established, although international companies
had contacted PacificLink about the provision of Web
site design services. Within Hong Kong, the company
had cemented its reputation with the design of its first
Web pages for IBM.

The project with IBM was a large one in which
PacificLink was part of a consortium of companies. The
objective of the project was to produce a demonstration
design of an Internet library, called DB2, for Hong Kong
Central Library. PacificLink's task was to develop a user-
friendly graphic interface. Lam secured this project by a
chance meeting with the IBM contact, during which the
IBM contact discovered that Lam was running a Web
design house. After conversations with Lam, the IBM
representative decided to give him an opportunity to
show what PacificLink could do. On a no-fee trial basis,
Lam and his colleagues joined the DB2 project. Their
work on the project was successful, and the participation
in the project with a large world-renowned company like
IBM provided PacificLink with its foot-in-the-door.

Once word got out about the quality of work Pacific-
Link had done on the DB2 project, other companies began
to consider PacificLink for their Web design projects. The
growth of PacificLink was rapid over the next 15 to 18
months. In December 1998, the company had operated
out of an office 300 square feet in size. By June 1999, this

floor space had doubled. By March 2000, the company
had relocated to a 1,600 square foot office on the 20th
floor of Knutsford Terrace in downtown Kowloon. In July
2000, the company was in the midst of another expansion,
that would double its floor space to 3,200 square feet.

In addition to its rapid change in size, PacificLink
operated in an industry segment that was developing
and changing rapidly, as were the technologies that
supported this business. As part of the underlying
changes in their industry, PacificLink, which was founded
as PacificLink Internet Marketing, changed its name to
PacificLink iMedia Ltd. This change was also made to
accommodate PacificLink's rapid expansion and to
reflect its broadening focus to a fuller range of Web
services, as captured in its mission statement:

> In the millennium, PacificLink's mission is to look
> for better ways to empower our clients' business
> so that they can realize their full potential on the
> Internet. We will continue to commit and dedicate
> to FLASH and Portal Web site development in
> order to bring more magical success to our
> coming clients.

In line with this mission statement, PacificLink specialized in professional corporate Web design. Consistent with
its goal of being a leading edge Web site designer, the
company took its first steps in specializing in FLASH Multimedia Presentation in early 1999. In the latter half of 1999,
the company began to concentrate on the development of
portals, as it continued to develop its FLASH Multimedia
Web design skills. The successful launch of Web sites for
several companies, such as FX Creations, Fonson, Funing
Property Management and ITAccountants.com, soon
followed (see Exhibit 1 for a list of major client companies).

FLASH presentations had become a defining element
for PacificLink by 2000. The unique capabilities of the
company in Web design were quickly recognized
through its achievement of the 2000 Platinum Award for
eTailing from the Hong Kong eAward, organized by the
Hong Kong Productivity Council, DigiHall and the Information Technology and Broadcasting Bureau. Hong
Kong eAward bestowed the Platinum award on Pacific-
Link for its design of the first fashion e-commerce portal
it developed for Izzue.com (http://www.izzue.com).

After receiving the eAward in April 2000, PacificLink
secured several new contracts. In May 2000, the Bank of
Communication and Carlsberg, Hong Kong, contracted
PacificLink's services for the development of their Web
sites. In June 2000, PacificLink entered into a contract

with ICP to develop a giant portal, with an anticipated release date of September 2000. A further contract for Web redesign was gained in the middle of June 2000.

RELATIONSHIPS IN PACIFICLINK

Business Partnerships

Business partnership formed an important part of Pacific-Link's business model. These partnerships were formal contractual agreements between PacificLink and its partners. The contracts did not have a specified duration, nor were they restrictive. By the terms of agreement in the business partnership contracts, PacificLink could seek other partners that provided similar services, or either partner could terminate the contract. While the contracts were not restrictive, Lam took these relationships seriously and did not form a business partnership idly.

One example of a PacificLink partner was a company called iAdvantage. iAdvantage provided facility management services. The business partnership with iAdvantage permitted PacificLink to advise a client to place its PacificLink-designed Web pages on PacificLink's server in iAdvantage. The advantage for PacificLink was that iAdvantage provided a reliable server-facility management service at a low cost to its client companies. PSINet was another business partnership with a Web hosting service; however, PSINet provided a more expensive hosting service for higher-end customers.

Among the other partnerships that PacificLink had formed was a link-up with Intel. This partnership provided a client referral system for PacificLink, and it was a conduit by which the latest technical information could flow to PacificLink. The partnership with Outblaze Ltd. connected PacificLink to a company that could provide Web mail services, while the partnerships with Global Solutions Network and Telewide Ltd. supplied account transactions and business registration services. Another partner, Jumbo Computer Supplies, was a vendor of computer hardware and peripherals.

Employee Relationships

In PacificLink's business partnerships, Lam placed a high value on the cultivation and maintenance of trust. The idea of trust also formed an important basis for employee relations within PacificLink. Lam's management philosophy meant charging employees with tasks and then letting the employee, or team of employees, follow through to completion of the task or project. This style typified many professional services firms in which employees had a high degree of flexibility and latitude in their jobs. Lam expected staff to manage their own behavior and projects, with little need for tight control or co-ordination from management. Most of the projects in PacificLink were conducted on a team basis, with a non-hierarchical management structure in place. Employees tended to spend 80 to 90 per cent of their time working on projects, with the other 10 to 20 per cent spent on exploring and learning how to use new technologies and new Web development tools.

Lam's management principles consisted of three key ideas: focus, dedication and motivation. Focus was required to become a leader within the niche where PacificLink operated. Lam's vision for PacificLink saw the company as a high-end graphic designer that achieved its leadership in the field through specialization and focus on Web design. Dedication was required to help solidify the company's reputation. Dedication meant that employees in the company saw all problems through to their resolution, and completed all projects as promised, regardless of the financial outcome. Motivation was particularly important in a start-up company, as financial rewards were not always clear. Lam saw his staff's intrinsic motivation to do a job well as a key component of the company's success to date.

NETALONE'S PARTIAL ACQUISITION OF PACIFICLINK

In March 2000, Netalone acquired 51 per cent of Pacific-Link's equity for a purchase price of HK$6.8 million (see Exhibit 3 for details of the acquisition). Netalone was a leading vertical e-commerce and applications services provider in Asia. Netalone's purchase of PacificLink strengthened Netalone's capabilities for the provision of interactive multimedia technologies such as FLASH. As well, Netalone's purchase of PacificLink was consistent with Netalone's strategy for growth. Netalone had used a mix of acquisitions and strategic business partnerships to rapidly build its presence in the e-commerce arena.

The acquisition of PacificLink represented a strengthening of the business relationship that had begun with the joint work done on the Izzue.com Web site. As well, it provided PacificLink with an injection of cash that was important to fund its continued strong growth, anticipated to continue at a similar rate through the remainder of 2000. While employees accounted for 60 to 70 per cent of the costs for PacificLink, its growth in fits and starts meant that it periodically encountered large expenses to fund the fixed costs of expansion.

Even though Netalone had acquired a 51 per cent stake in PacificLink, the management of the company stayed in the hands of Lam and Hui. As part of the acquisition, Netalone began to provide some back office services to PacificLink, such as accounting. This permitted PacificLink to retain its focus on the main aspects of its business. No accountants were employed at PacificLink, and all employees were full-time employees and involved in jobs that were directly related to the design of Web pages and the provision of Internet marketing services (see Exhibit 4). PacificLink did not employ the services of freelance staff.

FUTURE GROWTH

Lam perceived that PacificLink had opportunities to grow in several areas. These two areas could be broadly classified as product-line expansion and geographic expansion.

The main regions Lam was considering for geographic expansion were the Chinese Mainland, Singapore and Taiwan. An entry into the Chinese Mainland seemed to be the most obvious choice given its proximity to Hong Kong, and Netalone's recent acquisition of a mainland Chinese Internet company.

An entry into the Chinese Mainland would enable PacificLink to begin to capture the latent opportunities in the Chinese market. Unlike Hong Kong's Internet market position relative to the United States, where the developments in the Hong Kong Internet market lagged the U.S. by one year, the Hong Kong Internet market had a lead over the market in China by at least one year. This lead meant that HK-based firms had a competitive advantage in terms of design, ability to work with technology and maturity of business development.

While China had much potential in terms of business opportunity and market size (see Exhibit 5), capturing that potential would not busy easy. PacificLink was positioned as a high-quality, low-cost producer in Hong Kong. It could capture both the low-end and high-end segments of the Hong Kong market because of its unique positioning. Meanwhile, in China, servicing the low end of the market would be difficult because of competition from domestic producers that had lower price structures than PacificLink. If PacificLink entered China, Lam and Hui would have to decide if it could compete effectively, solely as a high end producer.

A second consideration related to staffing in the China operations. A major concern for PacificLink involved the maintenance of the quality and reputation of PacificLink's product. This could be a considerable challenge, given that high-quality managers were at a premium in China. Even large, multinational firms had difficulty attracting and retaining qualified managers. At a production personnel level, Lam was not confident that PacificLink could find local staff that could provide the same kind of creative and innovative solutions that had propelled PacificLink to its solid position in Hong Kong.

Aside from China, Lam was considering entry into Singapore and Taiwan. Like the Chinese mainland, neither of these countries was significantly culturally different from Hong Kong. Both Singapore and Taiwan were at a similar stage of Internet development as Hong Kong. While this meant that PacificLink would not enjoy the same kind of knowledge and experience-based advantage in Hong Kong that it would have in China, it did mean PacificLink could continue with its existing strategy of providing high-end services at a price lower than that of its competitors.

Singapore was also similar to Hong Kong in terms of its availability of potential staff, and if Lam located PacificLink in Taipei when entering Taiwan, there would be few problems in staffing PacificLink with high-quality individuals. Finally, the advanced state of the Internet industry in Taiwan and Singapore meant that, along with an existing set of competitors, the market potential was not latent, as in China; instead, it was there for the taking.

Aside from geographic expansion, Lam was considering expanding the range of services provided by PacificLink. In June 2000, the company focused its efforts on providing Web design and FLASH development services. It had ancillary products such as Web portals, but it was considering expanding its range of these as well. Some of these choices included moving further into the portal business, into B2C (business to customer), or even into WAP (wireless applications protocol) Web site design for cellular telephones. WAP was regarded to be a high growth area in coming years, particularly in Hong Kong where cellular telephone penetration was very high. The further development of B2B (business to business) services, to include additional ancillary services which were related to the maintenance of current customer Web sites, was another possibility.

While Lam regarded each of these as viable and attractive business opportunities, he was concerned about maintaining a focus on PacificLink's strengths. With PacificLink's anticipated doubling of size over the next six months, the main concern for the company was not with growth. Instead, as PacificLink realized the very real growth opportunities provided by the Internet, larger concerns centred around what types of growth opportunities to pursue and when to pursue them.

Exhibit 1

Clients and Web Sites Designed by PacificLink

Type of Organization	Client	URL
International	IBM	www.ibm.com
	Intergraph	www.intergraph.com
	USANA	www.usana.com
Retail Chain Stores	Monalisa Bridal	www.monalisabridal.com*
	Baleno Kingdom	www.baleno.com*
	FX Creations	www.fxcreations.com *
	Izzue.com	www.izzue.com*
	IT Ltd.	www.ithk.com*
	BB Minor	www.bbminor.com *
Internet Content Provider	ITAccountant.com	www.itaccountant.com*
(ICP) Partners	Etextile.net	www.etextile.net*
	Healthcare2u.com	www.healthcare2u.com*
	HK Cyber	www.hkcyberdaily.com
	Skynet Ltd.	
Corporate	Funing Property Management	www.funing.com.hk*
	Richard Tai Solicitors	www.richard-tai.com*
	M.POS	www.mpos.net/flash
Hotels	Regal Hotel	www.regalkowloon.cm*
Listed Companies	Starlight International Holdings	www.starlight.com.hk*
Manufacturing	Karson-Technology	www.karson-tech.com.hk*
	Tangs Art Design	www.tangaartdesign.hk
	Comstar Communication	

Source: http://www.pacim.com/main.htm. Accessed on June 30, 2000.

*Note: *Indicates Web site designed by PacificLink.*

Exhibit 2

PacificLink's Homepage and its Portals

PacificLink's Homepage

HKED Portal

Financial Sources Asia Portal

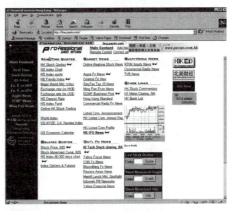

My Trendy Mall Portal

Source: http://www.pacim.com/main,htm. Accessed on June 27, 2000.

Exhibit 3

News Release for Netalone's Partial Acquisition of PacificLink

Netalone Invests in a Local Multimedia Design House

Hong Kong, March 23, 2000 – The Asian integrated Internet company netalone.com Limited, ("netalone"; stock code 336) announced today it has acquired a 51% stake in PacificLink iMedia Limited, ("PacificLink") for a cash consideration of HK$6.8 million.

PacificLink is a professional website design house with distinct expertise in utilizing FLASH multimedia skills in developing e-commerce portals. The partnership will further strengthen netalone's creative design resources in its Internet "skill factory". Netalone aims to become the most successful and sustainable vertical e-commerce enabler, venture catalyst and application services provider in Asia.

Dr. William Lo, Chairman and CEO of netalone, commented that, "we are excited at having the opportunity to expand our group's inventory of skills and expertise by investing in PacificLink. The acquisition is in line with our announced mission to build and expand our first class Internet skill factory, as PacificLink is a pioneer in Hong Kong in the area of interactive multimedia technology".

As netalone's multimedia creative arm, PacificLink will capitalize on the growing popularity of broadband Internet usage and expand its business to include broadband multimedia content development and web broadcasting. It will also act as a web image design consultant providing clients with multimedia and e-marketing solutions, said Mr. Alvin Lam, Director of PacificLink.

PacificLink's clients include multinationals, hotels, renowned retailers as well as Internet content providers. Major multimedia portals developed recently by PacificLink include baleno.com, FXcreations.com, Monalisabridal.com and Regalkowloon.com, all providing Internet platforms that enabled the retailers to enter into B2C and B2B e-business.

PacificLink was started in 1998 by Alvin Lam, Andy Hui and Alex Lo, all in their early or mid 20's. Dr. Lo said, "Their entrepreneurship and passion for Internet technology development strike a great impression on their customers. Netalone takes pride in taking them as close business partners."

Source: http://www.pacim.com/main.htm. Accessed on June 27, 2000.

Exhibit 4

PacificLink's Organizational Structure

Note: Employment stood at 16 people in June 2000. PacificLink planned to grow to 19 employees in July 2000, and 40 employees by December 2000.

Source: Company files.

Exhibit 5

Growth of Internet Use in Greater China

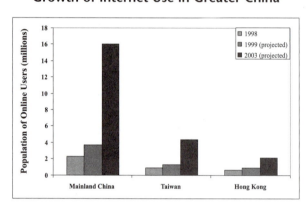

Source: Asian Wall Street Journal. Vol. XXIII, No. 214, July 5, 1999, p. 1.

Appendix 1

Internet Portals

Internet portals were sites that drew communities of users by offering diverse, yet comprehensive, forms of content and Internet connections. The content included news and access to free e-mail services. The portal's connections linked users to commonly accessed Web sites that presented timely news and information for the users of the Web page. The main objective of a portal operator was to draw a large group of repeat users. A portal wanted to develop a 'stickiness' in its user base, which meant that users automatically returned to the site because the content had a daily appeal to the user.

For portal developers in Asia, content and language were the main challenges to establishing a successful operation. Yahoo[1], which operated a highly successful portal for English speaking users, had had difficulty in capturing the Chinese speaking market because of its failure to adequately localize its offering. Government regulations and language differences also impeded entry into the Chinese speaking market by established companies.

The failure of existing portals to capture the Chinese speaking market created opportunities for new start-ups. One of these was China.com, a two-year old company in 1999, which was the first Chinese Internet company to go public. Before listing, China.com had looked to raise $60 million in its IPO on the basis of its large growth potential, not on its current earnings. In fact, China.com's initial listing exceeded expectations. Shares which were initially priced at $20, reached as high as $68, shortly after the initial offering.

The attraction of investors to China.com was two-fold: China and the Internet. China had a large and growing base of Internet users, to whom all companies wanted consistent and loyal access. However, China.com did not have a large amount of revenues in 1999, and it only averaged 100,000 hits per day, which was much less than the 2.1 million hits a day for Sina.com. China.com anticipated augmenting its revenues from the development of other businesses such as Web consulting and production. The revenues gained from its IPO would help support new business development, as well as provide funds for advertising of its existing site.

ENDNOTES

[1]*Far Eastern Economic Review. Riding the Wave, July 9, 1999, p. 78. The Wall Street Journal Interactive Edition; http://interactive.wsj.com/archive; July 1999.*

Glossary

© is the symbol used to indicate a registered copyright.

® is the symbol used to indicate a registered trademark; otherwise, notice is given as follows: Dr. Brad Kleindl(TM).

24/7/52 or 24/7 indicates that a business is open 24 hours a day, 7 days a week, 52 weeks a year.

A

Acquisition exists when one corporation purchases all or a controlling part of another company.

AIDA process indicates that the audience's attention must first be gained, interest created in the product or service, desire generated, and finally some action taken by the targeted audience.

Alliances are formal or informal relationships between independent companies that work together for a common purpose.

Analog signals are waves.

Application service provider (ASP) uses the Internet to provide, on a subscription basis, applications and services a business would normally provide for itself.

ASCII (American Standard Code for Information Interchange) is the built-in code used by most computers to represent the basic characters. For example, a computer stores the letter A in ASCII code as 1000001.

B

Bandwidth indicates the amount of digital information that can be carried over a line. The basic rule in developing multimedia (combined text, images, and sound) is that the richer the media, the larger the file, and therefore the higher the bandwidth needed to deliver the content in a given amount of time.

Banner ads are a common way to advertise on an Internet site.

Brick and mortar refers to tangible physical assets such as a factory, office building, or warehouse.

Brochure sites are designed to make visitors aware of and informed about a business's image or products.

Browser is the interface between the Web content and the user.

Business model (or commerce model) is the basic process flow indicating how a business operates. It shows how business functions are linked together.

C

Champion is an individual inside an organization who acts as an advocate for an innovation.

Channel conflict exists when a company sells products to the same market through more than one distribution system.

Chat involves a number of individuals who send messages over the Internet into a repository, or chat room, for viewing in real time. Chats can also be viewed at a later time.

Click-through occurs when an individual clicks on a banner to link to other sites.

Collaborative software (or groupware) permits individuals to communicate via e-mail and message lists, share files, and open file archives. The goal is to have individuals collaborating on projects.

Commerce service providers are companies that facilitate commerce for other businesses.

Company image is how a company is viewed by the public.

Comparison standard is a standard the customer uses to judge a product. For example, if a customer had first gained online search experience using Yahoo!, he or she will evaluate all other search engines against Yahoo!

Competitive arena is the competitive environment in which a business competes.

Competitive intelligence is gathered using a continuous process involving the legal and ethical collection of information and the monitoring of the competitive environment, giving managers the ability to make strategic decisions.

Computer network consists of a number of computers linked through a network server. The server controls the flow of information between the users.

Constituencies are those people involved with or served by an organization. Internet constituencies include governments, businesses, customers, ISPs, and schools.

Cookie is a small file left on the user's computer that is used to look up information on an e-business's database. This file retrieves information such as past actions, search interests, or past purchases, which can be used to personalize the site.

Corporate portals are internal Web sites that offer both internal company information and links to external sites such as suppliers or customers.

Customer relationship management (CRM) systems combine software and management practices to serve the customer from order through delivery and then after the sale.

Cybercafe is a small business that offers Internet access.

Cybermediaries are organizations that operate in electronic markets to facilitate the exchange process.

Cybersquatting is the practice of registering domain names, even trademarked names, with the intent to sell them at a later date.

D

Data are raw facts.

Data marts are small databases that serve a specific purpose in a firm. Data marts can be linked together in a network to share information.

Data mining is the process of using software to "drill" into a database to obtain meaningful information.

Database is a compilation of information.

Destination site is a Web site designed to entice the visitor to return over and over. This requires including extras, such as games, chats, contests, or new information, and any other content the targeted audience may desire.

Diffusion of innovations process is the process by which an innovation spreads over time through a series of adopters.

Digital convergence implies that multiple technologies will be used to access the Internet.

Digital signals are a series of ons and offs (110101001).

Disintermediation is the process of eliminating the middleman from the exchange process.

Distance workers complete all or part of their job by telecommuting from home.

Distinctive competencies are unique areas of advantage in which a firm can differentiate itself from competitors.

Domain name is the name used to access an Internet site.

Drop-ship means a manufacturer or wholesaler ships directly to the customer at the request of the seller (a retailer or broker).

Dutch auction works by having the seller lower the price continuously until a buyer decides to purchase at the stated price.

E

E-business value chain views information technology as part of a business's overall value chain and adds to the competitive advantages of a business.

E-business (or electronic business) is a system that uses a number of information-technology-based business practices to enhance relationships between a business and its customers.

E-cash (or electronic cash) allows individuals to purchase without paper dollars.

E-commerce is the practice of engaging in business transactions online.

Economic welfare is the net benefit an economic system provides to a society.

E-government is the delivery of government information and services online through the Internet or other digital means.

E-mail (or electronic mail) allows for the transfer of text-based content over the Internet.

Enduring involvement exists when an individual has a high-level interest in a topic over an extended time period.

Ethical dilemma exists when a proposed action benefits certain individuals, businesses, or societies, but at the same time has negative consequences for others.

Ethical snooping is fairness in the collection of data.

Extranets are Internet links between business suppliers and purchasers.

F

Filter is a software product that blocks unwanted material, such as pornography, from being downloaded from the Internet.

Firewalls are security measures designed to prevent hackers from gaining access through a server to a Web site.

Flaming is the process of sending angry e-mail messages, often characterized BY USING ALL CAPITAL LETTERS.

Fraud is an act of misrepresentation or deception.

Frequently asked questions (FAQ) are commonly asked question and related answers, often ordered by topic and posted on a Web site.

Fulfillment includes the activities necessary to deliver a product to a customer, including everything from ordering to delivery.

G

Gatekeeper is an individual who controls the flow of information in a communication system.

H

Hackers are individuals who attempt to break through online firewalls for pleasure or profit. They hack their way into computer networks.

High involvement exists when individuals consider a purchase or topic to be interesting or important, resulting in the individual attending more closely to information, attempting to comprehend complex messages, and being more willing to spend time with a Web site.

Home page is the main page (commonly the first page) that a visitor sees at a Web site. A home page is often linked to more pages.

Host is a server that is hooked up to the Internet.

Hoteling is the sharing of a physical office space, such as a desk, cubicle, or entire office.

Human capital is the skill that individuals gain through education, training, and experience.

Hyperbolic tree allows users to visually navigate hierarchies of hundreds or thousands of objects. Each level of the hierarchical structure is linked to other subcategories.

I

Infomediary is a firm that specializes in the capture, collection, or analysis of data. This service can be marketed to other businesses and can protect individual privacy.

Information is constructed from facts, gives meaning to phenomena, and allows managers to make decisions.

Infrastructure is the basic structure that allows a system to operate. For the Internet, this includes lines, browsers, computers, servers, and so forth.

Infrastructure attack occurs when an individual interferes with the operations of a computer system.

Innovation is a new idea, product, or process.

Integrated marketing communication uses a variety of communication technologies to reach organizational goals.

Interface links the user to the technology. An ideal interface does not require behavioral change on the part of the user.

Intermediaries are wholesalers and retailers that facilitate exchange between producers and consumers (both business and end users).

International portals are portals designed for international markets.

Internet is a global network of computer networks that use a common interface for communication.

Internet Service Provider (ISP) is the means of going online or linking to the Internet backbone that Internet users must have.

Intranet are Internet-based networks that operate inside a business.

IPO (initial public offering) occurs when a company first offers shares of its stock to the public.

K

Killer application (or killer app) is a software product that entices a user to adopt a larger technology.

Knowledge economy gains wealth based on what individuals can create from knowledge rather than what they can create from physical labor alone.

L

Last mile represents the narrowest access to the user, which is usually the link from an exchange to an individual's home or business.

Lifetime value of a customer (LVC) is the sum of expected lifetime earnings minus the lifetime costs (acquisition, operating, and customer service expenses) of a customer.

Linear communication follows a scripted flow.

Low-cost competitor is a strategy that can be used to gain a distinctive advantage.

M

Market capitalization is the value of a company on the stock market. It is the number of shares outstanding times the value of those shares.

Marketing decision support system (MDSS) provides information to aid in developing marketing strategies.

Mass customization is the process of producing individualized products at mass-production speeds and efficiencies.

Mental model is a set of relationships that a person keeps in mind to understand how the world, or a piece of it, operates.

Metaphors are language tools that allow a person to understand a new idea by relating it to previously understood concepts. "Surfing the net" is an example of a metaphor.

Metawarehouses are very large databases that centralize all data.

Micropayments are a means of paying for small Web transactions, often set up with digital wallets or charged to an individual's credit card.

Mirrored site is a Web site placed on more than one ISP, allowing less congestion and faster delivery of content.

Momentum refers to the general tendency of businesses to keep moving in the same direction.

Moore's law states that the density of transistors in microprocessors doubles every two years while costs decrease.

N

Net generation (N-Gen) refers to those individuals born after 1977.

Netiquette refers to proper etiquette over networks and includes the rules for common courtesy online and in cyberspace.

Niche sites are designed to target a market's psychographics by focusing on narrow activities and interests.

Nonlinear communication allows a free flow and exchange of information, as with conversations between individuals.

O

Online communities are groups of individuals who share common interests and use the Internet to foster their communities by accessing the same Web sites for information or support.

Open source code allows software to be improved through public collaboration by giving access to the inner workings of a software program.

Open standards are basic sets of instructions, such as programs or programming methods, that are not owned by a single company and are free for others to use.

Operating system is the program that controls a computer. Windows XP is an operating system, as are Linux, Mac OS, Windows NT, and DOS.

P

Panels allow researchers to pull respondents from a known pool.

Pareto principle (or 80/20 rule) dictates that 80 percent of profits come from 20 percent of a business's customers.

Penetration pricing sets prices lower in an attempt to capture market share for a product.

Permission-based marketing is when the customer opts in, or signs in, at a Web site and agrees to receive e-mail based on direct marketing.

Plug-ins allow rich content files, such as video, radio programs, and other multimedia content, to play through browsers.

Pornography exists online when material depicts erotic behavior intended to cause sexual excitement.

Portal is an entranceway onto the Internet. It is often the preferred starting point for searches, entertainment, information, e-mail, or any other Internet-based service.

Pricing strategies are used to set prices. There are two broad types of strategies: skimming pricing and penetration pricing.

Proactive implies acting in anticipation of future problems or opportunities rather than being reactive, or waiting and reacting to the environment.

Promotional mix includes the use of public relations and publicity, advertising, personal selling, sales promotions, and hypermedia such as Web sites.

Psychographics (lifestyle criteria) generally profile individuals based on their preferred activities, interests, and opinions.

R

Reactive implies waiting and reacting to the environment rather than being proactive.

Real-time chat groups allow several focus-group members to interact online at the same time and have real-time discussions.

Relationship marketing refers to the strategies a business must undertake to hold desirable customers over a long time period.

S

Sales auction sites allow individuals and businesses to sell products online and have potential customers bid on the price of the product.

Sales channels are the models that businesses use to sell to their customers. These include brick-and-mortar outlets, catalogs, direct marketing, or e-commerce.

Sales force automation (SFA) uses the information power of interactive media to enhance selling efforts.

Scams are acts of misrepresentation or deception.

Self-regulation occurs when an industry imposes its own voluntary standards on members.

Shill is an individual who takes the place of a real bidder by inflating the bids for an object, forcing other bidders to increase their offers.

Skimming pricing sets high initial prices to skim off payments from individuals.

Snail mail is mail delivered through a postal service.

Software wallet requires that a buyer set up an online account so that when a microtransaction is undertaken, the wallet is debited, or has money taken out. This system works much the same way as a smart card.

Source code is the original programming code on which a computer program is built.

Spam is the process of broadcasting unsolicited content to a large number of individuals over the Internet.

Spin-off occurs when a parent company creates an independent division. This could involve distribution of shares of stock in the new division to owners of the parent company.

Sponsorship (or co-branded ad) integrates a company's brand to the editorial content of the Web site.

Stickiness is the ability of a Web site to hold customers for a long period of time and get them to return to the site.

Streaming allows digital information to be sent in packets, or small units. These packets can be played as they stream in. This allows large multimedia files to play without downloading the entire file at once.

Stretch goals are goals that may seem impossible to reach. A stretch goal focuses a business on what it would like to achieve and motivates employees to be creative.

Supply chain is the network of suppliers and customers for goods, services, or information used from the point of origin to final consumption. It includes the suppliers, warehouses, shippers, distributors, and anyone else who may be involved in providing materials to a company.

Switching cost is the additional cost involved in learning something new. For example, for a business, the costs involved in adopting a new software package include the software expense, support expense, training costs, and slowed productivity costs.

Systems approach helps decision makers look at how all aspects of a strategic business unit (SBU) interact with each other. Systems are also seen as being organic in that they must change in response to their environment or face the possibility of becoming extinct.

T

Targeted e-mail is an effective means of directing users to an Internet site.

Threaded discussion lists allow individuals to add to an initial message with successive messages. For example, such lists allow a newsgroup user to add to a thread, or single conversation, by indicating a response to the prior message.

Top-level domains (TDLs) are the letters to the right of the dot in a domain name.

Transaction cost analysis is the process of assessing the overall cost of maintaining and finding new relationships. A firm will stay with a current partner if the cost of finding a new one is more than the cost of maintaining the current relationship.

U

Upstream traffic is communication from the browser to the provider. This usually requires small amounts of data to be sent back to the provider, which may then send large files downstream to the browser.

V

Value chain is a way of envisioning the collection of activities that a business undertakes to design, produce, market, deliver, and support products or services.

Vertical portals are designed to serve narrow niches within specific industries.

Viral marketing occurs when a customer promotes something through the use of a product or service, such as a Web site or e-mail.

Virtual private network can connect two businesses, such as a franchise and its headquarters, by using dedicated lines (communications lines that are not open to outside users) connected to ISPs. The ISPs then use the Internet for long-distance communication.

W

Web spiders (or bots) are software robots that "crawl" through the Internet looking at Web sites. They collect site information and send it back to the search engine database, allowing the information to be retrieved.

Webcast video allows for the streaming of video signals to an individual's Web-accessing device.

Webcasting allows users to have information delivered to their doorway, or browser, without requesting or searching for information.

World Wide Web (Web) uses graphically based Internet standards and has allowed easy access to information and communication around the world.

Company and URL Index

Note: Bold page numbers show URL for company.

Subject Index